Progress
in Neurotherapeutics and
Neuropsychopharmacology
2007

Published annually, volumes in this series provide readers with updates of recent clinical trial results, impacts of trials on guidelines and evidence-based practice, advances in trial methodologies, and the evolution of biomarkers in trials. The series focuses on trials in neurotherapeutics, including disease-modifying and symptomatic agents for neurological diseases, psychopharmacological management of neurological and psychiatric illnesses, and non-drug treatments. Each article is authored by a leader in the area of neurotherapeutics and clinical trials, and the series is guided by an Editor-in-Chief and Editorial Board with broad experience in drug development and neuropsychopharmacology. *Progress in Neurotherapeutics and Neuropsychopharmacology* is an essential update of recent trials in all aspects of the management of neurological and neuropsychiatric disorders, and will be an invaluable resource for practising neurologists as well as clinical and translational neuroscientists. Articles also available at http: www.cambridge. org/jid_PNN

Progress in Neurotherapeutics and Neuropsychopharmacology 2007

VOL. 2(1)   2007

Editor-in-Chief

Jeffrey L. Cummings, MD

Director, Deane F. Johnson Center for Neurotherapeutics at UCLA,

Director, UCLA Alzheimer Disease Center,

Department of Psychiatry and Biobehavioral Sciences,

David Geffen School of Medicine at UCLA,

Los Angeles, CA, USA

PUBLISHED BY THE PRESS SYNDICATE OF THE UNIVERSITY OF CAMBRIDGE
The Pitt Building, Trumpington Street, Cambridge, United Kingdom

CAMBRIDGE UNIVERSITY PRESS
The Edinburgh Building, Cambridge CB2 8RU, UK
40 West 20th Street, New York, NY 10011-4211, USA
477 Williamstown Road, Port Melbourne, VIC 3207, Australia
Ruiz de Alarcón 13, 28014 Madrid, Spain
Dock House, The Waterfront, Cape Town 8001, South Africa

http://www.cambridge.org

First published 2006

Printed in the United Kingdom at the University Press, Cambridge

A catalogue record for this book is available from the British Library

ISBN 9780521862547 (052186254X)
ISSN 17482321

Every effort has been made in preparing this book to provide accurate and
up-to-date information which is in accord with accepted standards and
practice at the time of publication. Nevertheless, the authors, editors
and publisher can make no warranties that the information contained
herein is totally free from error, not least because clinical standards are
constantly changing through research and regulation. The authors, editors
and publisher therefore disclaim all liability for direct or consequential
damages resulting from the use of material contained in this book. Readers
are strongly advised to pay careful attention to information provided by
the manufacturer of any drugs or equipment that they plan to use.

To Xue (Kate) Zhong
For adding so much to life

To Shi Zhen Li
For Xue

Contents

Progress in Neurotherapeutics and Neuropsychopharmacology, 2:1, ix–xii © 2007 Cambridge University Press
DOI: 10.1017/S1748232106000012   Printed in the United Kingdom

Contributors

Lauren E. Abrey
Department of Neurology
Memorial Sloan-Kettering Cancer
  Center
New York, NY, USA

R.F. Allegri
Department of Neuropsychiatry
CEMIC University
Buenos Aires, Argentina

P.M. Bagnati
Consultants Clinic
Mar del Plata, Argentina

John L. Beyer
Department of Psychiatry and Behavioral
  Sciences
Duke University School of Medicine
Durham, NC, USA

Alan Breier
Eli Lilly
Indianapolis, IN, USA

Joseph R. Calabrese
NIMH Bipolar Disorder Research
  Center
Mood Disorders Program
University Hospitals of Cleveland
Case Western Reserve University School
  of Medicine
Cleveland, OH, USA

Chih-Chia Huang
Department of Psychiatry
Taipei Veterans General Hospital
Institute of Clinical Medicine
National Yang-Ming University
Taipei, Taiwan

Jeffrey L. Cummings, MD
Departments of Neurology and
  Psychiatry and Biobehavioral Sciences
David Geffen School of Medicine at
  UCLA
Los Angeles, CA, USA
Deane F. Johnson Center for
  Neurotherapeutics at UCLA
UCLA Alzheimer Disease Center
Los Angeles, CA, USA
Augustus Rose Professor of
  Neurology
Professor of Psychiatry and
  Biobehavioral Sciences
David Geffen School of Medicine at
  UCLA
Los Angeles, CA, USA

Daniel Yen Lin
Lilly Research Laboratories
Indianapolis, IN, USA

Rob M.A. de Bie
Department of Neurology
Academic Medical Center
Amsterdam, The Netherlands

Rob J. de Haan
Department of Neurology
Academic Medical Center
Amsterdam, The Netherlands

Maurício Silva de Lima, MD, PhD
Medical Director
Eli Lilly Brazil
Federal University of Pelotas and
  Catholic University of Pelotas
Pelotas, Brazil

Charles DeBattista, MD
Department of Psychiatry and Behavioral
  Sciences
Stanford University School of Medicine
Stanford, CA, USA

Rianne A.J. Esselink, MD
Department of Neurology and
  Geriatrics
Radboud University Nijmegen Medical
  Centre
Nijmegen, The Netherlands

Prashant Gajwani
NIMH Bipolar Disorder Research
  Center
Mood Disorders Program
University Hospitals of Cleveland
Case Western Reserve University School
  of Medicine
Cleveland, OH, USA

Keming Gao
NIMH Bipolar Disorder Research
  Center
Mood Disorders Program
University Hospitals of Cleveland
Case Western Reserve University School
  of Medicine
Cleveland, OH, USA

Srihari Gopal, MD, MHS
Johnson & Johnson Pharmaceutical
  Research and Development
LLC, Titusville
NJ, USA

Michael F. Green
Department of Psychiatry and
  Biobehavioral Sciences
Geffen School of Medicine at UCLA
Department of Veterans Affairs VISN 22
  Mental Illness Research, Education,
  and Clinical Center
Los Angeles, CA, USA

David E. Kemp, MD
NIMH Bipolar Disorder Research Center
Mood Disorders Program
University Hospitals of Cleveland
Case Western Reserve University School
  of Medicine
Cleveland, OH, USA

Robert S. Kern, PhD
Department of Psychiatry and
  Biobehavioral Sciences
Geffen School of Medicine at UCLA
Department of Veterans Affairs VISN 22
  Mental Illness Research, Education, and
  Clinical Center,
Los Angeles, CA, USA

Michelle L. Kramer
Johnson & Johnson Pharmaceutical
  Research and Development
LLC, Titusville
NJ, USA

Anna Lembke, MD
Department of Psychiatry and Behavioral
  Sciences
Stanford University School of Medicine
Stanford, CA, USA

Tobey J. MacDonald, MD
Hematology-Oncology
Children's National Medical Center
NW Washington, DC, USA

Stephen R. Marder
Department of Psychiatry and
  Biobehavioral Sciences
Geffen School of Medicine at UCLA
Department of Veterans Affairs VISN 22
  Mental Illness Research, Education, and
  Clinical Center
Los Angeles, CA, USA

Jair de Jesus Mari
Department of Psychiatry
Federal University of São Paulo and
  Catholic University of Pelotas
RS, Brazil

Lisa A. Marsch, PhD
National Development and Research
  Institutes
Department of Psychiatry
St. Luke's-Roosevelt Hospital Center
New York, NY, USA

Kimford J. Meador, MD
Department of Neurology
McKnight Brain Institute
University of Florida
Gainesville, FL, USA

David J. Muzina
NIMH Bipolar Disorder Research Center
Mood Disorders Program
University Hospitals of Cleveland
Case Western Reserve University School
  of Medicine
Cleveland, OH, USA

Antonio M.P. Omuro, MD
Division de Neurologie Mazarin - Groupe
  Hospitalier Pitie-Salpetriere
Paris, France

Yuko Palesch
Medical University of South Carolina
Charleston, SC

Bernard Ravina, MD, MSCE
University of Rochester Medical Center
Rochester, NY, USA

Encarnita Raya-Ampil, MD
Department of Neurology and Psychiatry
University of Santo Tomas
Manila, Philippines

Zarife Sahenk, MD, PhD
Department of Neurology and
  Pediatrics
The Ohio State University
Columbus Children's Research
  Institute
Neuromuscular program
Columbus, OH, USA

P. Richard Schuurman
Department of Neurosurgery
Academic Medical Center
Amsterdam, The Netherlands

Johannes D. Speelman
Department of Neurology
Academic Medical Center
Amsterdam, The Netherlands

David C. Steffens
Department of Psychiatry and Behavioral
  Sciences
Duke University School of Medicine
Durham, NC, USA

F.E. Taragano, MD, PhD
Department of Neuropsychiatry
CEMIC University
Buenos Aires, Argentina

Nuestra Señora de las Nieves
Geriatric Institute
Buenos Aires, Argentina

Mauricio Tohen, MD, DrPH
Lilly Research Laboratories
Indianapolis, IN, USA

Department of Psychiatry
Harvard Medical School
McLean Hospital
Belmont
MA, USA

Tung-Ping Su, MB, MD
Faculty of Medicine
National Yang-Ming University
Taipei, Taiwan

Pepijn van den Munckhof
Department of Neurosurgery
Academic Medical Center
Amsterdam, The Netherlands

Joachim Yahalom
Department of Radiotherapy
Memorial Sloan-Kettering Cancer Center
New York, NY, USA

Progress in Neurotherapeutics and Neuropsychopharmacology, 2:1, 1–12 © 2007 Cambridge University Press
DOI: 10.1017/S1748232106000024   Printed in the United Kingdom

Progress in Neurotherapeutics and Neuropsychopharmacology 2007

Jeffrey L. Cummings

Deane F. Johnson Center for Neurotherapeutics at UCLA; UCLA Alzheimer Disease Center, Augustus Rose Professor of Neurology, Professor of Psychiatry and Biobehavioral Sciences, David Geffen School of Medicine at UCLA, Los Angeles, CA, USA; Email: jcummings@mednet.ucla.edu

ABSTRACT

There continues to be progress in neurotherapeutics and neuropsychopharmacology with each advancing year. Production of new molecular entities (NME's) remains small, but advances are being made in repurposing agents and extending their indications, obtaining more safety and tolerability data in long term and extension studies, introducing novel trial methodologies that provide insight into how to best to conduct trials and how best to treat diseases, and developing new formulations that improve adherence and decrease the barriers to patient compliance. Advances in how to test potential disease-modifying agents in patients with progressive neurological illnesses is advancing. Promising biomarkers have been identified in some neurological diseases.

Key words: Clinical trials, drug development, futility trials, Parkinson's disease, Amyotrophic Lateral Sclerosis, Schizophrenia

Progress in Neurotherapeutics and Neuropsychopharmacology 2006

Progress continues to be made in advancing our understanding of how best to treat neuropsychiatric illnesses and how best to conduct clinical trials to establish the worthiness of potential therapies. This introduction reviews major advances that have occurred in the past year emphasizing novel trial methodologies and approaches to establishing therapeutic efficacy.

The low level of discovery of new molecular entities (NME's) with therapeutic potential continues to be a notable observation despite increasing investment from the industry and NIH funding for clinical trials (Johnston, 2006). New drug discovery methodologies, including *in silico* drug discovery approaches, high throughput screening and constructing large molecular libraries have failed to produce a wave of new NME's that are making their way into advanced clinical trials and clinical

Correspondence should be addressed to: Jeffrey L. Cummings, MD, Alzheimer Disease Center, 10911 Weyburn Avenue, Suite 200, Los Angeles, CA 90095 7226, USA; Ph: +1 310 794 3665; Fax: +1 310 794 3148; Email: jcummings@mednet.ucla.edu

care. There continues to be optimism that these technologies will identify new therapeutic candidates that will succeed in preclinical assessments and enter advanced developmental phases.

The following chapter is organized by disease state to facilitate discussion of advances in treatment relevant to specific classes of patients. This organization is not meant to suggest that all therapeutic advances must be disease-specific; there is increasing evidence of cross-disease syndromic and phenotypic responses to therapeutic interventions independent of disease etiology.

Amyotrophic Lateral Sclerosis

The Northeast Amyotrophic Lateral Sclerosis (ALS) Consortium reported the results of a large trial of celecoxib, a cyclooxygenase-2 inhibitor, in the treatment of this progressive motor neuron disease (Cudkowicz *et al.*, 2006). Patients were randomized to receive either 800 mg of celecoxib per day or placebo for 12 months. This dosage of celecoxib had no evident beneficial effect on any measurable aspect of the disease. There was no effect on decline in muscle strength, vital capacity, motor unit number estimates, ALS functional rating scales/revised, or survival. Celecoxib was well tolerated without an elevated frequency of adverse events compared to placebo. The results of this study are a disappointment to ALS victims and to researchers alike. Investigators were striving to translate basic science observations of the presence of inflammatory changes in the central nervous system (CNS) of ALS on patients at autopsy into a potential for benefit from anti-inflammatory agents such as celecoxib.

This study demonstrates several aspects of the evolution of clinical trial methodologies to assess potentially disease-modifying agents in patients with neurodegenerative disorders. The design was a parallel group design with change in rate of decline of maximal voluntary isometric contraction strength as the primary outcome measure. Such parallel designs, emphasizing rate of change, have been adopted in studies of other neurodegenerative disorders, such as Alzheimer's disease (AD). Ninety of the 300 subjects had a lumbar puncture at baseline visit; 63 had a second lumbar puncture at month 2. No effect on prostaglandin levels were identified with treatment, but inclusion of this measure illustrates the desire to integrate biomarkers into clinical trials of neurodegenerative diseases. This trial had all of the three elements deemed necessary to establish disease-modifying effects of a candidate therapy: (1) evidence of efficacy in a validated animal model of ALS; (2) incorporation of a biomarker into the clinical trial, and (3) clinical trial design with measures relevant to disease progression (e.g. change in rate). Despite these well-motivated choices, the therapeutic intervention appears not to provide therapeutic benefit. One challenge with studies of this type, is the choice to study a single dose. At the end of the study, one is left with uncertainty regarding whether the lack of efficacy was related to choice of dose below the therapeutic level or due to the lack of a meaningful impact on the disease process regardless of dose. How best to conduct dose-finding in slowly progressing diseases where trial duration is likely to be 12–18 months is an unresolved challenge in the development of drugs for neurodegenerative diseases.

De Carvalho & Swash (2006) suggest one potential strategy for shortening the duration of preliminary testing for potential therapeutic agents in ALS. They showed that a subgroup of patients with rapid progression of ALS could be identified; clinical trials of such patients would require a shorter duration of time to demonstrate drug-placebo differences. This strategy might be particularly applicable in Phase II proof-of-concept and dosing studies. A repetition of the results in a more unselected representative population would then follow in Phase III.

Parkinson's Disease

Investigators and patients are eager to identify disease-modifying agents in Parkinson's disease (PD) as well as other neurodegenerative disorders. Palhagen *et al.* (2006) reported the results of a 7 year double blind placebo control trial of patients with new onset PD. There was an initial period of monotherapy with selegiline and a later phase of combination treatment with levodopa. Patients on selegiline had a better therapeutic outcome in both phases of the study. Selegiline may have symptomatic effects in PD that could explain some of these findings but the benefits seen in the long-duration portion of this study make it less likely that the benefits observed are strictly symptomatic in nature. This study was of unusually long duration (7 years); it used a straightforward drug-placebo comparison at end-point to determine therapeutic benefit of selegiline. No biomarker was incorporated into the study to help validate the disease-modifying effect.

There is enthusiasm for neurorestorative approaches in the treatment of PD with either fetal-nigral transplantation or use of nerve growth factor to maintain dopaminergic cell viability. A recently reported trial of cell line derived neurotrophic factor (GDNF) found no benefit after 6 months of therapy. There was a significant difference in favor in GDNF in $_{18}$F-dopa influx as measured on positron emission tomography (PET). This biological difference was not reflected in any clinical benefit (Lang *et al.*, 2006).

Two trials attempted to treat cognitive aspects of PD. Modafinil (Ondo *et al.*, 2006) was used in a double blind placebo controlled trial of daytime somnolence in PD, and the nicotinic agonist SIB-1508Y was tested for its possible cognitive-enhancing potential. Neither study identified a treatment benefit. A double blind placebo control trial of melatonin found only a 10-minute improvement in sleep time with 50 mg of melatonin, although there was an improvement in subjective sleep disturbance (Dowling *et al.*, 2005).

There has been progress in developing new formulations for the administration of dopaminergic therapy in PD. A transdermal delivery system has been developed for the dopamine receptor agonist rotigotine (Babic *et al.*, 2006). Transdermal delivery systems are becoming increasingly popular with emerging applications in AD and PD dementia, along with established indications in pain, hormonal therapy, smoking cessation, motion sickness, and delivery of cardiac agents.

A critical aspect of conducting randomized clinical trials is to understand better the patient population that is willing to engage in these critical experiments. Kim *et al.* (2006) studied patients with PD who either would or would not participate in a hypothetical Phase I gene transfer study. The investigators concluded that the decision to participate in this type of controlled trial would depend mostly on patient attitudes regarding risk, optimism about science, and action orientation rather than on functional, clinical or demographic characteristics. This study provides insight into patient motivations to participate in clinical trials.

Stroke

In the past year, advances in both the medical and surgical management of stroke have been reported (Lees *et al.*, 2006). As in other neurological disorders, there is a great desire to find neuroprotective compounds that would reduce permanent injury following ischemic stroke. In a large randomized double blind placebo control trial (1722 patients with acute stroke), intravenous NYX-059 produced significant benefit compared to placebo on the modified Rankin score of post-stroke disability. There was no concomitant improvement in the National Institutes of Health Stroke Scale. There was a lower incidence of hemorrhagic transformation and intracranial hemorrhage in patients receiving NXY-059. This was a promising beginning for a potential neuroprotective compound although further studies failed to establish a drug-placebo difference. Further studies of related agents are warranted.

In a large study of patients with greater than 50% carotid stenosis and symptoms of cerebrovascular disease, clopidogrel plus aspirin, was found to be significantly more effective than aspirin alone in reducing asymptomatic microemboli detected by transcranial doppler (Markus *et al.*, 2005). There were an insufficient number of cerebrovascular events to allow statistical analysis of this outcome. This trial is interesting in several ways. First, it is a trial of two active therapies without a placebo control group – a strategy that is necessary where placebo interventions might place patients at substantial risk. Second, transcranial doppler was used as a surrogate marker to evaluate anti-platelet therapy and provided preliminary evidence of differential benefit in patient populations too small to have enough clinical events to demonstrate therapeutic superiority of one intervention over the other.

Intracerebral hemorrhage has been the most treatment resistant of all forms of stroke. In a double blind placebo controlled trial of three doses of recombinant activated factor VII (40 μg/kl, 80 μg/kl or 160 mg/kl) administered within 1 hour of a baseline computed tomogram, all treatment groups had less growth of the hemo-toma compared to those receiving placebo. Reduced mortality and improved func-tional outcomes at 90 days were evident despite a small increase in the frequency of thromboembolic events (Mayer *et al.*, 2005). This study suggests that acute intervention in intracerebral hemorrhage can result in limiting the growth of the intracranial clot and limit mortality and morbidity. It is notable that only 12% of candidate patients with intracerebral hemorrhage (199 of 1636) were enrolled at the 38 study sites that collected complete screening data. These figures show the difficulty of conducting this type of research where acute intervention is required.

There have been relatively few studies comparing neurosurgical approaches to the treatment of neurological and neurovascular disorders. In one such study, 2143 patients with ruptured intracranial aneurysms were randomly assigned to neuro-surgical clipping or endovascular coiling. There was a greater likely hood of inde-pendent survival in year one, continuing for at least 7 years after endovascular coiling compared to neurosurgical clipping (Molyneux *et al.*, 2005). The risk of late re-bleeding was low but more common after coiling.

A problem that challenges investigators determined to find neuroprotective therapies for stroke patients is how best to identify the most promising therapeutic candidates given the large number of potential therapies that emerge from pre-clinical studies. Futility studies offer one potential mechanism for identifying such candidate therapies (Palesch *et al.*, 2005). In this approach, the proportion of positive outcomes in a single treated group is compared with a minimally worth-while success rate sufficient to warrant additional testing of the agent. Using this strategic design, agents can more quickly be tested and those likely to be futile eliminated from undergoing future trials. The purpose of futility trials is to iden-tify agents not likely to be of therapeutic benefic when tested in larger more con-ventional Phase II and Phase III clinical trials. Retrospective application of the methodology to agents which had progressed to Phase III showed a good fit between the predictive capacity of futility trials and actual Phase III results. Futility trials are being applied in other therapeutic situations including attempts to find treat-ments for PD (see Ravina, this volume).

Multiple Sclerosis

Multiple sclerosis (MS) is an active area of therapeutic research in neurological disorders. Magnetic resonance imaging (MRI) has been integrated into MS clin-ical trials. More successfully than into trials for treatment of other disease states. Use of this imaging approach provides insight into how biomarkers might be used in other clinical settings. Examining data from seventeen clinical trials, Barkhof *et al.* (2005) showed that T2 burden of disease added to the predictive value offered by clinical factors for gadolinium enhancement of MS lesions. Gadolinium enhancement is often used in trials to assist in the evaluation of efficacy of new drugs. This study imposes understanding of the predictors of gadolinium enhancement.

Massacesi *et al.* (2005) used measures of gadolinium enhancing brain lesions to show that azathioprine is effective in reducing new brain inflammatory lesions in MS.

Most immuno-modulatory agents currently available for treatment of MS involve subcutaneous or intramuscular injections that challenge compliance. A double blind placebo controlled trial of two doses of oral teriflunomide reduced gadolinium enhancing lesions on MRI, as well as T2 lesions per scan and new T2 lesions. There was a trend toward lower annualized relapse rates and lower relapsing rate in the treatment group. Significantly fewer patients receiving high dose of teriflunomide demonstrated an increase in disability. This Phase II trial represents a preliminary step in establishing an effective oral therapy for immuno-modulatory treatment of MS.

There have been few studies of the effect of ethnicity on therapeutic results. Cree *et al.* (2005) observed that African American subjects experience more exacerbations and are less likely to remain exacerbation free after initiation of treatment with interferon beta 1-a. It is not clear if this represents a difference in disease activity or therapeutic response, but the observation warrants further investigation. Ethnicity might be considered as an outcome- influencing variable in other studies.

Another oral therapy for MS that has undergone testing in a recent double blind placebo controlled trial is fingolimod (FTY72) (Kappos *et al.*, 2006). Two hundred fifty-five patients received either placebo or oral fingolimod at a dose of 1.25 mg or 5 mg daily. Those receiving fingolimod evidenced fewer gadolinium-enhancing lesions on MRI and a lower annualized relapse rate. Clinically asymptomatic elevations of alanine aminotransferase levels were more frequent in those receiving active therapy. One case of reversible encephalopathy occurred in the highdose fingolimod treatment group. This and related compounds deserve further investigation as potential oral therapy is for MS.

Alzheimer's Disease and Related Dementias

Current therapy for AD involves use of cholinesterase inhibitors and memantine. Cholinesterase inhibitors have traditionally been indicated for use of patients in mild to moderate AD – those who's Mini Mental State Examination (MMSE) scores are 10 and above. Recently, donepezil, was shown to be effective in patients with severe AD (Winblad *et al.*, 2006). The US Food and Drug Administration (FDA) reviewed this and additional documentation and has approved donepezil for treatment in severe AD as well as for patient with mild to moderate dementia with AD.

An investigation of the efficacy of rivastigmine in patients with PD dementia showed that this agent improved global function, cognition, activities of daily living, and behavior compared to placebo. Rivastigmine received FDA approval for treatment of PD dementia (Emre *et al.*, 2004).

Memantine was relatively recently introduced to the therapeutic armamentarium for AD. Reisberg *et al.* (2006) reported an open label extension of a 28-week randomized double blind, placebo controlled trial of memantine in patients with moderate to severe AD. Compared to their baseline, patients switched from placebo to active treatment evidenced functional, global and cognitive improvement relative to the decline had they experienced on placebo. The completion rate for the extension study was 78% with a favorable adverse event profile. This study suggests that patients delayed in treatment onset will experience improvement when treated with memantine and that patients on long-term therapy continue to benefit from treatment. The additional safety and tolerability safety information suggest that this agent has a benign safety and side-effect profile. The limitations of open label studies must be borne in mind when interpreting these results. Open label extensions involve patients who are tolerant of the agent and may include a disproportion number who have benefited from treatment. In addition, the open label nature of the study makes it difficult to draw efficacy conclusions (Cummings, 2006).

A treatment goal in dementia is to identify and concentrate on outcomes that are meaningful to individual patients. This individualization of therapeutic outcomes may be difficult to achieve but has been codified in the methodology known as "goal attainment scaling". Rockwood *et al.* (2006) applied this technique in a study of galantamine for the treatment of AD. In a randomized placebo controlled trial, clinician-rated goal attainment scaling significantly distinguished the treated from the placebo group. The patient-caregiver goal attainment scaling did not distinguish the two treatment groups. Traditional outcome measures, including the Alzheimer's Disease Assessment Scale Cognitive portion and the Clinician Interviewed-Based Impression of Change with caregiver input were significantly better in those receiving galantamine than in those receiving placebo at the end of the trial. This study presents an interesting new approach to attempting to expand the range of treatment outcomes relevant to dementia therapeutics.

Epilepsy

A clinical trial question that crosses many therapeutic interventions regards whether to use fixed or flexible dose approaches. In a unique trial, Elger *et al.* (2005), assigned patients to either placebo, fixed dose of pregabalin, or a flexible dose of pregabalin for twelve weeks. In the flexible dose arm, dosage could be adjusted based on tolerability. Both pregabalin regimens significantly reduced seizure frequency compared to placebo and the reduction was greatest in the fixed dose groups. Discontinuation rates also were higher in the fixed dose group. This suggests that there may be an efficacy–tolerability trade-off. Patients in the fixed dose arm received higher doses and achieved better seizure control, however they had significantly more side-effects and more discontinuations associated with adverse effects. These data may help structure future clinical trials particularly with agents where side-effects are common.

Searching for New Indications for Old Agents

An often effective strategy for developing new treatments is to use compounds approved for other therapeutic indications. This approach has advantages in that the tolerably and safety of the agent is established prior to clinical trials, and in many cases dosing decisions also can be based on existing information. Thus developing new indications for from existing therapies entails less risk and expense than developing novel therapeutic approaches. In the recent past, these have been several studies of existing agents in new therapeutic settings. Levetiracetam, an antiepileptic agent, was found in a short-term open label trial to reduce chorea in patients with Huntington's disease (de Tommaso *et al.*, 2005). Similarly, an open label trial of riluzole, an antiglutamatergic agent, used for the treatment of ALS, led to lower anxiety levels in patients with generalized anxiety (Mathew *et al.*, 2005). These preliminary open label studies warrant follow-up with double blind placebo controlled trials.

A blinded controlled trial of pregabalin for generalized anxiety disorder showed shat two doses of pregabalin (400 mg per day and 600 mg per day), as well as venlafaxine, produced significant improvement in Hamilton Anxiety Scale scores compared to placebo (Montgomery *et al.*, 2006). Patients on pregabalin 400 mg per day experienced significant improvement in all primary and secondary outcomes included in the trial. Discontinuation rates were lower in the placebo group and highest in the venlafaxine group.

A randomized placebo controlled trial of sertraline showed that this selective serotonin reuptake inhibitor typically used for the treatment of depression and anxiety was effective for reducing symptoms of night eating syndrome (O'Reardon *et al.*, 2006). Measures showing significant improvement included clinical global severity ratings, quality of life ratings, frequency of nocturnal eating and awakenings, and caloric intake after the evening meal.

Schizophrenia

Attrition rates have been a consistent challenge to data generalization in studies of antipsychotic drugs; discontinuation rates frequently approach 50% in placebo controlled trials. Kemmler *et al.* (2005), compared attritions in active control trials where the agent of interest is compared with an existing antipsychotic treatment to attrition in placebo-controlled trials. Discontinuation in placebo-controlled trials was significantly more common than in active controlled trials (48.1% versus 28.3%). The interaction between placebo control and attrition should be borne in mind when constructing antipsychotic drug trials.

The cognitive component of schizophrenia is an increasingly important object of study (see Kern chapter on MATRICS, this volume). Bender *et al.* (2006) examined the cognitive effects of olanzapine compared to clozapine in a randomized active controlled trial using executive function as the principal cognitive outcome measure. Improvements where seen in all measures of executive function, including the Stroop Color-Word Test, Tower of London, and Wisconsin Card Sorting Test. Improvement was independent of effects on positive symptoms and extrapyramidal side-effects. This suggests that atypical antipsychotics may benefit executive function.

The role of *N*-methyl-D-aspartate (NMDA) function in schizophrenia has been a source of consistent interest. Agents that enhance NMDA receptor function through the glycine modulatory site (e.g. D-serine) or through the glycine transporter (e.g. sarcosine) have been shown in previous studies to improve the symptoms of patients with chronic stable schizophrenia. In a randomized double blind placebo controlled trial of D-serine, sarcosine and placebo, Lanc *et al.* (2005) found that sarcosine produced greater reduction in the Positive and Negative Syndrome Scale (PANSS) than placebo or D-serine. Similar results were found for the Scale for the Assessment of Negative Symptoms (SANS). This study was unique in involving patients in an acute exacerbation of schizophrenia rather than patients with stable chronic disease. The findings suggest that sarcosine may be superior to D-scrine in patients with acute relapses. The study further supports the growing body of evidence suggesting a role for NMDA receptors in schizophrenia.

Obsessive–Compulsive Disorder

Simpson *et al.* (2006) studied clomipramine, exposure/ritual prevention plus clomipramine, and exposure/ritual prevention placebo and placebo in patients with obsessive-compulsive disorder. In this trial, exposure/ritual prevention led to a superior treatment outcome compared to clomipramine alone or placebo. An important aspect of this study is that the authors studied four separate definitions of response to treatment and three definitions of remission in the course of examining their treatment outcomes. They proposed a standard definition of response (at least 25% decrease on the Yale–Brown Obsessive–Compulsive Scale) and remission (a total score of ≤12 for at least 1 week on the Yale–Brown Obsessive–Compulsive Scale). Standardization of response and remission definitions will assist future studies of obsessive–compulsive disorder.

Summary

Advances in pharmacotherapy and clinical trial design promise to improve drug development strategies and therapeutic outcomes in patients with a variety of neurologic and psychiatric illnesses.

Acknowledgments

Dr. Cummings is supported by a National Institute on Aging, Alzheimer's Disease Research Center Grant (AG 16570) an Alzheimer Disease Research Center Grant of California, and the Sidell-Kagan Foundation.

Disclosure

Dr. Cummings has provided consultation to the following pharmaceutical companies: Acadia, Avanir, Cephalon, Eisai, EnVivo, Forest, Janssen, Lilly, Lundbeck, Merz, Novartis, Ono Pharma, Pfizer, and Sanofi-Aventis.

References

Babic, T., Boothmann, B., Polivka J., *et al.* (2006). Rotigotine transdermal patch enables rapid titration to effective doses in advanced-stage idiopathic Parkinson disease: subanalysis of a parallel group, open-label, dose-escalation study. *Clinical Neuropharmacology*, 29, 238–242.

Barkhof, F., Held, U., Simon, J.H., *et al.* (2005). Predicting gadolinium enhancement status in MS patients eligible for randomized clinical trials. *Neurology*, 65, 1447–1454.

Bender, S., Dittmann-Balcar, A., Schall, U., *et al.* (2006). Influence of atypical neuroleptics on executive functioning in patients with schizophrenia: a randomized, double-blind comparison of olanzapine vs. clozapine. *International Journal of Neuropsychopharmacol*, 9, 135–145.

Cree, B.A., Al-Sabbagh, A., Bennett, R., *et al.* (2005). Response to interferon beta-1a treatment in African American multiple sclerosis patients. *Archives of Neurology*, 62, 1681–1683.

Cudkowicz, M.E., Shefner, J.M., Schoenfeld, D.A., *et al.* (2006). Trial of celecoxib in amyotrophic lateral sclerosis. *Annals of Neurology*, 60, 22–31.

Cummings, J.L. (2006). What we can learn from open-label extensions of randomized clinical trials. *Archives of Neurology*, 63, 18–19.

Cummings, J.L. (2006). Challenges to demonstrating disease-modifying effects in Alzheimer's disease clinical trials. *Alzheimer's and Dementia*, 67, 726–727.

de Carvalho, M., & Swash, M. (2006). Can selection of rapidly progressing patients shorten clinical trials in amyotropic lateral sclerosis? *Archives of Neurology*, 63, 557–560.

de Tommaso, M., Di Fruscolo, O., Sciruicchio, V., *et al.* (2005). Efficacy of levetiracetam in Huntington disease. *Clinical Neuropharmacology*, 28, 280–284.

Dowling, G.A., Mastick, J., Colling, E., *et al.* (2005). Melatonin for sleep disturbances in Parkinson's disease. *Sleep Medicine*, 6, 459–466.

Elger, C.E., Brodie, M.J., Anhut, H., *et al.* (2005). Pregabalin add-on treatment in patients with partial seizures: a novel evaluation of flexible-dose and fixed-dose treatment in a double-blind, placebo-controlled study. *Epilepsia*, 46, 1926–1936.

Emre, M., Aarsland, D., Albanese, A., *et al.* (2004). Rivastigmine for dementia associated with Parkinson's disease. *New England Journal of Medicine*, 351, 2509–2518.

Johnston, S.C. (2006). Translation: case study in failure. *Annals of Neurology*, 59, 447–448.

Kappos, L., Antel, J., Comi, G., et al. (2006). Oral fingolimod (FTY720) for relapsing multiple sclerosis. *New England Journal of Medicine*, 355, 1124–1140.

Kemmler, G., Hummer, M., Widschwendter, C., et al. (2005). Dropout rates in placebo-controlled and active-control clinical trials of antipsychotic drugs: a meta-analysis. *Archives of General Psychiatry*, 62, 1305–1312.

Kim, S.Y., Holloway, R.G., Frank, S., et al. (2006). Volunteering for early phase gene transfer research in Parkinson disease. *Neurology*, 66, 1010–1015.

Lane, H.Y., Chang, Y.C., Liu, Y.C., et al. (2005). Sarcosine or D-serine add-on treatment for acute exacerbation of schizophrenia: a randomized, double-blind, placebo-controlled study. *Archives of General Psychiatry*, 62, 1196–1204.

Lang, A.E, Gill, S., Patel, N.K., et al. (2006). Randomized controlled trial of intraputamenal glial cell line-derived neurotrophic factor infusion in Parkinson disease. *Annals of Neurology*, 59, 459–466.

Lees, K.R., Zivin, J.A., Ashwood, T., et al. (2006). NXY-059 for acute ischemic stroke. *New England Journal of Medicine*, 354, 588–600.

Markus, H.S., Droste, D.W., Kaps, M., et al. (2005). Dual antiplatelet therapy with clopidogrel and aspirin in symptomatic carotid stenosis evaluated using doppler embolic signal detection: the Clopidogrel and Aspirin for Reduction of Emboli in Symptomatic Carotid Stenosis (CARESS) trial. *Circulation*, 111, 2233–2240.

Massacesi, L., Parigi, A., Barilaro, A., et al. (2005). Efficacy of azathioprine on multiple sclerosis new brain lesions evaluated using magnetic resonance imaging. *Archives of Neurology*, 62, 1843–1847.

Mathew, S.J., Amiel, J.M., Coplan, J.D., et al. (2005). Open-label trial of riluzole in generalized anxiety disorder. *American Journal of Psychiatry*, 162, 2379–2381.

Mayer, S.A., Brun, N.C., Begtrup, K., et al. (2005). Recombinant activated factor VII for acute intracerebral hemorrhage. *New England Journal of Medicine*, 352, 777–785.

Molyneux, A.J., Kerr, R.S., Yu, L.M., et al. (2005). International subarachnoid aneurysm trial (ISAT) of neurosurgical clipping versus endovascular coiling in 2143 patients with ruptured intracranial aneurysms: a randomised comparison of effects on survival, dependency, seizures, rebleeding, subgroups, and aneurysm occlusion. *Lancet*, 366, 809–817.

Montgomery, S.A., Tobias, K., Zornberg, G.L., et al. (2006). Efficacy and safety of pregabalin in the treatment of generalized anxiety disorder: a 6-week, multicenter, randomized, double-blind, placebo-controlled comparison of pregabalin and venlafaxine. *Journal of Clinical Psychiatry*, 67, 771–782.

Ondo, W.G., Fayle, R., Atassi, F., et al. (2005). Modafinil for daytime somnolence in Parkinson's disease: double blind, placebo controlled parallel trial. *Journal of Neurology Neurosurgery and Psychiatry*, 76, 1636–1639.

O'Reardon, J.P., Allison, K.C., Martino, N.S., et al. (2006). A randomized, placebo-controlled trial of sertraline in the treatment of night eating syndrome. *American Journal of Psychiatry*, 163, 893–898.

Palesch, Y.Y., Tilley, B.C., Sackett, D.L., et al. (2005). Applying a phase II futility study design to therapeutic stroke trials. *Stroke*, 36, 2410–2414.

Palhagen, S., Heinonen, E., Hagglund, J., et al. (2006). Selegiline slows the progression of the symptoms of Parkinson disease. *Neurology*, 66, 1200–1206.

Reisberg, B., Doody, R., Stoffler, A., et al. (2006). A 24-week open-label extension study of memantine in moderate to severe Alzheimer disease. *Archives of Neurology*, 63, 49–54.

Rockwood, K., Fay, S., Song, X., et al. (2006). Attainment of treatment goals by people with Alzheimer's disease receiving galantamine: a randomized controlled trial. *CMAJ*, 174, 1099–1105.

Simpson, H.B., Huppert, J.D., Petkova, E., et al. (2006). Response versus remission in obsessive–compulsive disorder. *Journal of Clinical Psychiatry*, 67, 269–276.

The Parkinson Study Group*** (2006). Randomized placebo-controlled study of the nicotinic agonist SIB-1508Y in Parkinson disease. *Neurology*, 66, 408–410.

Winblad, B., Kilander, L., Eriksson, S., *et al.* (2006). Donepezil in patients with severe Alzheimer's disease: double-blind, parallel-group, placebo-controlled study. *Lancet*, 367, 1057–1065.

Progress in Neurotherapeutics and Neuropsychopharmacology, 2:1, 13–26 © 2007 Cambridge University Press
DOI: 10.1017/S1748232106000036   Printed in the United Kingdom

A Randomized Trial Comparing Unilateral Pallidotomy with Bilateral Subthalamic Nucleus Stimulation in PD: Perspectives for Future Implication in Clinical Practice*

Rianne A.J. Esselink

Department of Neurology and Geriatrics, Radboud University Nijmegen Medical Centre, Nijmegen, The Netherlands;
E-mail: r.esselink@neuro.umcn.nl

Rob M.A. de Bie and Rob J. de Haan

Department of Neurology, Academic Medical Center, Amsterdam, The Netherlands;
E-mail: r.m.debie@amc.uva.nl; rob.dehaan@amc.uva.nl

P. Richard Schuurman and Pepijn van den Munckhof

Department of Neurosurgery, Academic Medical Center, Amsterdam, The Netherlands;
E-mail: p.r.schuurman@amc.uva.nl and p.munckhof@amc.uva.nl

Johannes D. Speelman

Department of Neurology, Academic Medical Center, Amsterdam, The Netherlands;
E-mail: j.d.speelman@amc.uva.nl

Key words: Parkinson's disease, pallidotomy, subthalamic nucleus stimulation.

Introduction and Overview

Parkinson's disease (PD) is one of the most prevalent progressive neurodegenerative disorders. Approximately 0.3% of the general population has PD and prevalence increases with age (de Lau & Breteler, 2006). Initially dopaminergic treatment is beneficial, but after 4–6 years of drug treatment response fluctuations and dyskinesias can arise (Ahlskog & Muenter, 2001). In the advanced stages of the disease patients often cycle between episodes with parkinsonism causing severe disability (off phase) and episodes with good mobility (on phase) complicated by dyskinesias.

Correspondence should be addressed to: Rianne AJ Esselink, MD, Departments of Neurology and Geriatrics, Radboud University, Nijmegen Medical Centre, P.O. Box No. 9101, 6500 HB Nijmegen, The Netherlands; Ph: +31 024 3618860; Fax: +31 024 3541122; E-mail: r.esselink@neuro.umcn.nl

*Conflicts of interest: J.D. Speelman acts as an independent consultant for Medtronic Ltd. (Minneapolis). An unrestricted research grant was received from Medtronic Ltd. (Minneapolis) for the workgroup Movement Disorders at the Academic Medical Center, University of Amsterdam. RAJE, RMAB, and JDS received travel grants from Medtronic Ltd. (Minneapolis) to participate in scientific meetings.

Unilateral pallidotomy is an effective surgical treatment for patients with advanced PD who have severe limitations in functioning despite optimal pharmacological treatment (de Bie *et al.*, 1999; Lang *et al.*, 1997; Laitinen *et al.*, 1992). In a randomized-controlled trial (RCT) comparing unilateral pallidotomy with optimal pharmacological treatment with a follow-up period of 6 months, including 37 patients (19 pallidotomy and 18 medication) off phase Unified Parkinson's Disease Rating Scale (UPDRS) motor part improved in 31% of the pallidotomy group versus mild worsening of scores in the medication groups (8%) (de Bie *et al.*, 1999). Additionally on phase dyskinesias improved in 50% of the pallidotomy group, but did not change in the medication group and functioning during activities of daily living (ADL) significantly improved in the pallidotomy group only. In 2003 the RCT performed by Vitek *et al.* (2003) demonstrated similar results. Bilateral pallidotomy further reduces parkinsonian symptoms and dyskinesias, however the effectiveness is limited due to a high-complication rate (de Bie *et al.*, 2002; Merello *et al.*, 2001; Ghika *et al.*, 1999).

In 1993 the Grenoble group introduced continuous electrical stimulation of the subthalamic nucleus (STN) for the treatment of advanced PD. Over the last decade cohort studies on bilateral STN stimulation revealed off phase motor UPDRS improvement in approximately 50% with amelioration of dyskinesias and substantial reduction of dopaminergic drugs (The Deep-Brain Stimulation For Parkinson's Disease Study Group, 2001; Houeto *et al.*, 2000; Moro *et al.*, 1999; Kumar *et al.*, 1998; Limousin *et al.*, 1998).

Purpose of the Trial

In patients with advanced PD, unilateral pallidotomy is more effective than optimal pharmacological treatment. Cohort studies on bilateral STN stimulation suggested even more improvement of motor symptoms and functioning in these patients. Therefore, we conducted a RCT comparing the effects and adverse effects of unilateral pallidotomy and bilateral STN stimulation in patients with advanced PD (Esselink *et al.*, 2004).

Clinical Trial

Subjects

Patients were recruited from all four Dutch hospitals experienced in pallidotomy and STN stimulation for PD between April 2000 and May 2001. Inclusion criteria were: 1. idiopathic PD (Gelb *et al.*, 1999), 2. unequivocal reduction in off phase symptoms on levodopa, 3. at least one of the following symptoms despite optimal pharmacological treatment: severe response fluctuations, dyskinesias, or bradykinesia. Exclusion criteria were: predominantly unilateral symptoms without severe response fluctuations, severe brain atrophy on computed tomography (CT) or magnetic resonance imaging (MRI) scans, Hoehn & Yahr (1967) stage 4 or 5 in the best on phase, Dementia Rating Scale (Mattis, 1976) score of less than 120, psychosis or depression at inclusion, previous stereotactic operation, and physical condition making stereotactic surgery hazardous.

All patients gave their written informed consent. The medical ethics committees of the participating hospitals approved the study.

Trial Methods

Patients were assessed at baseline and at 6 months after surgery by the same blinded assessor, who was specialized in movement disorders and not involved in the treatment of the patient.

Randomization was done by a computer program and included a minimization procedure according to: severity of PD (Hoehn and Yahr ⩽3 versus stage 4 or 5 in the off phase), and "treatment center".

Surgery

Stereotactic surgery was done under local anesthesia, as previously described using ventriculography, MRI, or CT scan to determine the position of the target structure (Esselink et al., 2004). In patients assigned to unilateral pallidotomy the most severely affected side was operated. Micro-electrode recordings were not routinely used. After macro-electrode test-stimulation either a radiofrequency thermo-lesion was made in the globus pallidus or a four contact electrode (model DBS-3389, Medtronic, Minneapolis) was implanted bilaterally in the STN. The electrodes were connected to the implantable pulse generator (Itrel II, Soletra, or Kinetra, Medtronic, Minneapolis) under general anesthesia.

Instruments/Measures

Baseline and outcome assessments were done in standardized off and on phases. Off phase was defined as the condition after 12 h overnight dopaminergic drug withdrawal. The on phase was the condition 1 h after suprathreshold levodopa dose. At post-operative assessments the stimulator was turned on.

Outcome measures included clinical rating scales, changes in drug treatment, and adverse effects. The clinical rating scales consisted of the motor UPDRS (Fahn & Elton, 1987) (parkinsonian symptoms in off and on phases), Clinical Dyskinesias Rating Scale (Hagell & Widner, 1999) (dyskinesias severity; on phase only), the UPDRS 4 items 32 and 33 (Fahn & Elton, 1987) (dyskinesias duration and severity in the past week), ADL UPDRS (Fahn & Elton, 1987) and the Schwab and England scale (Fahn & Elton, 1987) (functional scales in off and on phases), and the Parkinson's Disease Quality of Life questionnaire (PDQL) (de Boer *et al.*, 1996).

Changes in levodopa equivalent daily (LED) dose were calculated as previously described (Esselink *et al.*, 2004). Adverse effects were scored using a standardized checklist.

Primary Outcome Measure

The primary outcome measure was the change from baseline to 6 months on the off phase motor UPDRS.

Secondary Outcome Measures

Secondary outcome measures were changes from baseline to 6 months on the on phase motor UPDRS and dyskinesias scales, off and on phase functional scales, quality of life scale, levodopa equivalent dose, and adverse effects.

Analysis

Analysis was done according to the intention-to-treat principle. Most outcome scores were non-normally distributed therefore outcome measures were described in median scores, including interquartile range. The change scores of the pallidotomy and STN stimulation patients were compared using the Mann–Whitney U-test.

Results

Thirty-four patients were randomized: 14 were assigned to unilateral pallidotomy and 20 to bilateral STN stimulation. The baseline characteristics of the patients did not essentially differ between the treatment groups (Esselink *et al.*, 2004). One pallidotomy patient committed suicide 3 weeks after surgery. Data on 33 patients were therefore available for analysis. One STN patient was re-operated 3 months after the first operation because of electrode displacement. In two STN patients the assessor was unblinded.

The median off phase motor UPDRS score in the group of pallidotomy patients improved from 46.5 to 37 points (20%) and in the group of STN patients from 51.5 to 26.5 (49%). The difference in median change score between the two groups was 12-points in favor of the STN patients ($p = 0.002$; Figure 1).

The ADL UPDRS and the Schwab and England scale improved in both groups. For the Schwab and England scale the difference in improvement between the groups tended to be in favor of the STN patients.

For on phase assessment the median motor UPDRS score in the pallidotomy patients worsened from 15.5 to 19 points and improved in the STN patients from 21 to 13, with a difference in median change scores of six points between the groups ($p = 0.02$; Figure 1). The median duration of dyskinesias (UPDRS item

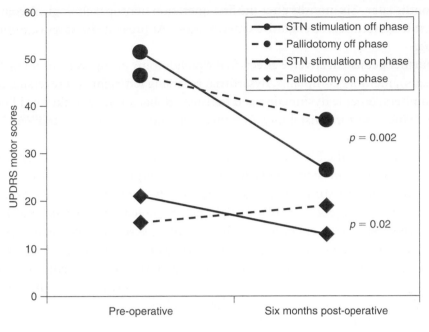

Fig. 1.
Effects of bilateral STN stimulation and unilateral pallidotomy on UPDRS motor scores.

32) did not improve in the pallidotomy patients and improved one point in the STN patients ($p = 0.004$). The severity of dyskinesias (UPDRS item 33 and Clinical Dyskinesias Rating Scale), the ADL UPDRS, the Schwab and England scale as well as the PDQL improved in both groups.

The median daily levodopa equivalent dose in the pallidotomy patients was reduced by 12% from 1260 to 1110 and in the STN patients by 33% from 935 to 625 ($p = 0.02$). The median voltage of stimulation was 2.3 V (range 1.4–3.5), pulse width 60 µs (range 60–90), and frequencies 145 Hz (range 100–185). After STN stimulation frequent follow-up visits were necessary before the optimal stimulation parameters were established.

Tolerability and Safety

Ten of the 14 pallidotomy patients and nine of the 20 STN patients had adverse effects (Esselink *et al.*, 2004). Adverse effects were persistent in nine pallidotomy patients, and in eight STN patients. Two adverse effects were severe. One pallidotomy patient committed suicide 3 weeks after a successful pallidotomy; preoperatively she already had symptoms of an anxiety disorder. One STN patient had severe fluctuating cognitive, behavioral, and mood disorders after the operation, not affected by switching off the stimulator. Brain CT did not show new lesions, but both electrodes appeared to be displaced and were therefore replaced

3 months later. Six months after the first operation neuropsychological examination still showed severe cognitive deterioration. At present she stays in a nursing home.

Further persistent adverse effects in the pallidotomy group were: drooling (four patients), memory complains, dysarthria, reversing left/right and reversing order of numbers, erectile dysfunction and transient global amnesia, mild word fluency disturbance, postural instability, freezing, and mild concentration problems, and mild eyelid apraxia.

Six patients in the STN group had emotional lability, which was transient in three. This was the most frequent adverse effect in this group and did not occur after pallidotomy in our study. Three STN patients had equipment-related adverse effects; one patient complained of a tight extension lead in the neck, and in one center the first two patients who got a Kinetra pulse generator the electrodes were displaced and needed repositioning. Since then a new technique fixating the electrode with a platinum platelet to the skull was introduced. Further persistent adverse effects in the STN group were: increased drooling (two patient), postural instability, mild dysphasia, dysarthria, and dysphagia.

Unique Aspects of the Trial

This is the only RCT comparing unilateral pallidotomy with bilateral STN stimulation and one of the few RCT's comparing STN stimulation with another type of stereotactic surgery for PD (Anderson *et al.*, 2005).

Conclusions

Bilateral STN stimulation is more effective than unilateral pallidotomy in reducing symptoms in patients with advanced PD.

Influence on the Field

Long-Term Follow-Up

At present four studies have been published describing the long-term outcome after bilateral STN stimulation (Schupbach *et al.*, 2005; Rodriguez-Oroz *et al.*, 2005, 2004; Krack *et al.*, 2003). From the study of Rodriguez-Oroz *et al.* (2004), part of the patient group was included also in the multi-center study by Rodriguez-Oroz *et al.* (2005), therefore the study from 2004 will not be discussed. Table 1 presents an overview of the results of these studies. Comparing off phase pre-operative data with off phase long-term follow-up data, total motor UPDRS scores, the patients' individual motor symptoms (except speech), and ADL functioning

Table 1. **Results of Bilateral STN Stimulation at 3–5 years Follow-up. Values Represent Percentages**

	KRACK (2003)	SCHUPBACH *ET AL.* (2005)	RODRIGUEZ–OROZ (2005)
Number of patients	Included 49 Data on 42	Included 37 Data on 30	Included 68 Data on 37
Baseline versus long-term	0 versus 5 year	0 versus 5 year	0 versus 3 to 4 year
UPDRS motor off/on	54*/−33*	49%/0	50*/11
Tremor off/on	75*/50		87*/80*
Rigidity off/on	71*/33		59*/36*
Bradykinesia off/on	49*/−91*		43*/9
Axial off/on		40*/−21	
Speech off/on	0/−125*		5/−45*
Gait off/on	52*/−100*		41*/−33
Balance off/on	44*/−30		31*/−8*
Dyskinesias on	71*/58*	59*	59*
UPDRS ADL off/on	49*/−92*	37*/−24	43*/−17
LED	−63*	−55*	−34*

All scores represent percentages of change of pre-operative scores compared with follow-up scores unless otherwise stated; Positive signs imply improvement, negative signs deterioration, except for LED (−means decrease in medication; UPDRS: Unified Parkinson's Disease Rating Scale; ADL: Activities of daily living; LED: Levodopa Equivalent daily Dose.)
*Significant difference compared to baseline assessment.
No symbol: $p \geqslant 0.05$ between baseline and follow-up.

remained improved. On phase total motor UPDRS scores and ADL scores remained stable or worsened between baseline and 5-year follow-up.

Between short-term and long-term post-operative follow-up total motor UPDRS scores in off and on phases remained stable in one study (Schupbach *et al.*, 2005) and became worse in two studies (Rodriguez-Oroz *et al.*, 2005; Krack *et al.*, 2003). Tremor, rigidity, and in one study (Rodriguez-Oroz *et al.*, 2005) also bradykinesia scores appeared stable whereas axial symptoms (speech, gait, and balance) and bradykinesia in the other studies deteriorated in off as well as in on phases. On phase dyskinesias improvement was stable for 5 years as was dopaminergic drugs reduction. Between short-term and long-term post-operative follow-up off and on phase ADL scores deteriorated in all studies. The finding that axial symptoms deteriorated more than limb symptoms (tremor, rigidity, and bradykinesia) between short and long-term follow-up probably was due with the natural course of the disease. During the natural disease course the severity of the axial symptoms increases while the levodopa responsiveness of these symptoms decreases (Bonnet *et al.*, 1987; Markham & Diamond, 1986). Levodopa responsiveness on individual symptoms is a good predictor of effect of STN stimulation (Welter *et al.*, 2002). The waning effectiveness of STN stimulation on axial symptoms during follow-up could therefore be a reflection of the decreased levodopa responsiveness of axial symptoms and/or the natural course of the disease.

Studies Comparing Globus Pallidus Internus Stimulation and STN Stimulation

One RCT has been published directly comparing the efficacy of bilateral globus pallidus internus (GPi) stimulation with bilateral STN stimulation (Anderson *et al.*, 2005). Part of the patients included in this study participated in an earlier "pilot" RCT of the same group (Burchiel *et al.*, 1999). Twenty of the originally 23 patients completed the 1-year follow-up, 10 patients had GPi stimulation, and 10 patients had STN stimulation. Off phase UPDRS motor scores improved after 1 year of both GPi and STN stimulation (39% versus 48%). Bradykinesia tended to improve more with STN than with GPi stimulation. Off phase ADL functioning improved equally in both treatment groups. No improvement in on phase UPDRS motor scores and ADL functioning was observed in either group. On phase dyskinesias were reduced by stimulation at both GPi and STN (89% versus 62%). Dopaminergic drugs were reduced by 38% in the STN-stimulated patients, compared to 3% in GPi patients. Cognitive and behavioral complications were observed only in combination with STN stimulation.

A multi-center prospective non-randomized cohort study by The Deep-Brain Stimulation for PD Study Group (2001) described the results of bilateral STN stimulation and bilateral GPi stimulation 6 months after surgery without direct comparison between both interventions. Three to four-year follow-up of a part of this cohort was described by Rodriguez-Oroz *et al.* (2005). At 6-month follow-up motor scores in off and on phase, off phase ADL functioning, and on phase dyskinesias improved in both treatment groups, although STN stimulation appears to be associated with a greater benefit than GPi stimulation for off phase motor function. Only STN stimulation permitted a reduction in the use of dopaminergic medication (The Deep-Brain Stimulation For Parkinson's Disease Study Group, 2001). Independent of the target the incidence of hemorrhage correlated with the number of micro-electrode passes (The Deep-Brain Stimulation For Parkinson's Disease Study Group, 2001). At 3–4-year follow-up off phase motor scores, off phase ADL functioning, and on phase dyskinesias were still improved compared to pre-operative scores in both treatment groups. Dopaminergic drugs were still significantly reduced only in the STN group. Adverse effects were less frequently encountered in patients treated with GPi stimulation (Rodriguez-Oroz *et al.*, 2005).

A prospective, non-randomized study by Krause *et al.*, including six patients after GPi stimulation and 12 after STN stimulation with a follow-up of 1 year, demonstrated an improvement of off phase UPDRS motor scores, tremor scores, and Schwab and England ADL functioning only after STN stimulation (Krause *et al.*, 2001). Dyskinesias were reduced in both groups, whereas dopaminergic drugs were reduced after STN stimulation and increased after GPi stimulation.

Two studies retrospectively compared the results of bilateral GPi stimulation and bilateral STN stimulation (Volkmann *et al.*, 2001; Krack *et al.*, 1998). The study of Volkmann *et al.* (2001) compared 1 year results in 11 patients after GPi stimulation and 16 patients after STN stimulation. Their results were comparable to those of Anderson *et al.* (2005), although the levodopa equivalent dose reduction in the STN group was larger. Furthermore, Volkmann *et al.* described that STN stimulation patients required significantly less electrical power of stimulation, but needed more intensive post-operative monitoring than the GPi patients.

Krack *et al.* (1998) retrospectively compared the result of GPi stimulation and STN stimulation in 13 consecutive patients with young onset PD (eight STN, five GPi). Off phase UPDRS motor score and bradykinesia improved more with STN stimulation. The improvement of on phase dyskinesias was comparable in both groups. Dopaminergic drugs were reduced 56% in the STN group and increased 28% in the GPi group.

The above mentioned studies have in common that surgery in both targets equally reduced on phase dyskinesias, dopaminergic drug reduction was substantial only after STN stimulation, and battery consumption was lower after STN stimulation than after GPi stimulation. The studies of Anderson *et al.* (2005), Rodriguez-Oroz *et al.* (2005), and Volkmann *et al.* (2001) described more adverse effects after STN stimulation. Not all results were consistent, Anderson *et al.* and Volkmann *et al.* found equal reduction of off phase motor scores in STN and GPi stimulation patients, whereas Krack *et al.* and Krause *et al.* found more improvement in the STN patients. Anderson and Krack found (tendency towards) more improvement of bradykinesia after STN stimulation.

While the study of Anderson *et al.* (2005) is the only RCT's up to now comparing bilateral GPi stimulation with bilateral STN stimulation, definite conclusions on superiority of one or the other target, cannot be drawn.

Subthalamotomy

Lesioning in the STN has generally been avoided for fear of inducing hemiballism (Lee & Marsden, 1994; Whittier & Mettler, 1949). Only four cohort studies are available on subthalamotomy and comparative studies are lacking. The results of three studies (Alvarez *et al.*, 2005; Patel *et al.*, 2003; Su *et al.*, 2003) will be discussed here, in a fourth study only a few clinical data were mentioned (Vilela *et al.*, 2001). Two studies concerned unilateral subthalamotomy (Patel *et al.*, 2003; Su *et al.*, 2003). The study of Su *et al.* (2003) demonstrated improvement on off and on phases UPDRS motor scores (both 30%), ADL functioning (30% and 38%), and on phase dyskinesias (80%). The study by Gill *et al.* demonstrated only improvement on off phase ADL functioning (Patel *et al.*, 2003). Alvarez *et al.* (2005) described their results in 18 patients after bilateral subthalamotomy with a follow-up period of 24 months. Off and on phase UPDRS motor part improved with, respectively, 50% and 35%, off and on phase ADL functioning both with

50%, and on phase dyskinesias ameliorated with 50%. Post-operative hemiballism did occur in up to one-third of the patients, but generally resolved spontaneously, and other side-effects seemed to be limited. The role of subthalamotomy in the treatment of PD will have to be determined by further studies.

New Targets

Recently low-frequency stimulation (10–25 Hz) of the pedunculopontine nucleus in two patients produced improvement of UPDRS motor scores including gait and postural instability (Plaha & Gill, 2005). This target needs to be further explored in humans (Jenkinson *et al.*, 2005; Mazzone *et al.*, 2005).

Bilateral STN stimulation is currently the most applied surgical treatment for advanced PD. In one RCT (Anderson *et al.*, 2005) comparing bilateral STN stimulation with bilateral GPi stimulation complications (specially on cognitive, affective, and behavioral domains) seem to occur more frequently after STN stimulation. This is in agreement with two cohort series including both types of surgery (Rodriguez-Oroz *et al.*, 2005; Volkmann *et al.*, 2001). Future research will have to determine if STN stimulation will remain the target of first choice for PD.

Unilateral pallidotomy is less effective than bilateral STN stimulation (Esselink *et al.*, 2004). Nevertheless we still consider unilateral pallidotomy as an optional treatment for PD patients in remote areas where the mandatory frequent follow-up for adjustment of stimulation parameters is impossible, or in well-informed patients who decide against stimulation.

Bilateral lesioning procedures in thalamus or internal pallidum are accompanied by higher-complication rates than unilateral procedures and should therefore be considered only in a small subgroup of patients in a staged procedure. In one RCT thalamic stimulation was as effective as thalamotomy for the treatment of tremor, but stimulation was associated with fewer complications than lesioning (Schuurman *et al.*, 2000). Currently the role of thalamic surgery in PD is limited as it mainly improves tremor.

The role of subthalamotomy in the treatment of PD will have to be determined by further studies.

Other areas for research include improvement of patient selection, further determination of outcome predictors, and improvement of the surgical procedures, in order to reduce adverse effects. Future research will lead to determining target choice based on individual needs and risk profile.

One of the controversies concerning the surgical procedure is the value of micro-electrode recording. With micro-electrode recording neuronal activity is registered and various brain nuclei can be identified on the basis of their specific firing pattern (Benazzouz *et al.*, 2002; Lozano & Hutchison, 2002). Proponents of this technique claim improved accuracy of lesion location or electrode placement, decrease of complications, and improvement of clinical results of surgery (Benazzouz *et al.*, 2002; Sterio *et al.*, 2002) compared to macro-stimulation techniques, where target identification during surgery is based on effects and adverse effects of test stimulation. Criticizers of micro-electrode recording suggest that the macro-stimulation techniques is safer than the use of the micro-electrode recording technique, especially concerning the incidence of intracerebral hemorrhage (Hariz & Fodstad, 1999).

Translation to Clinical Practice

Currently STN stimulation is the most applied surgical treatment for PD. Future research will have to determine whether the STN will remain the optimal surgical target for all PD patients.

Careful pre-operative patient evaluation and selection is one of the main determinants for success of surgery in PD.

Patients eligible for stereotactic surgery should have:

1. advanced idiopathic PD;
2. unequivocal reduction in off phase symptoms on levodopa (not necessary for tremor); and/or
3. severe response fluctuations, dyskinesias or parkinsonism despite optimal adjustment of antiparkinsonian medication; and/or
4. PD with dominating pharmacological treatment resistant tremor.

Contraindications for surgery are:

1. dementia;
2. major depression or psychosis at time of surgery;
3. history of severe psychosis and (hypo)mania that was not drug induced;
4. balance and/or speech as the most disabling symptom;
5. general health condition making stereotactic surgery hazardous (e.g. cardiopulmonary disease);
6. frail patients above 70 years of age;
7. still largely ADL dependent in the best on phase (in case of severe tremor still consider thalamic surgery);
8. severe brain atrophy or vascular encephalopathy on brain imaging (CT or MRI).

The Core Assessment Program for Neurosurgical Interventions and Transplantation in Parkinson's Disease (CAPSIT-PD) protocol is generally accepted as a guideline for pre-operative patient evaluation (Lang & Widner, 2002). Furthermore it is important that patients and their families have a realistic expectation of the intervention. It should be emphasized to the patient that in case of stimulation, a period of weeks or even months of programming and adjustment of drugs follows surgery before an optimal result is established.

Summary

The first choice for treatment of PD is pharmacological. Not until motor complications such as response fluctuations and dyskinesias arise should surgery be considered. Before deciding on surgical intervention, careful patient evaluation and selection should be done, based on the generally accepted criteria. Surgery should be offered only to these patients who are expected to have (rather) good results of surgery with a (rather) low-risk profile. At this time bilateral STN stimulation is the surgical treatment of first choice. The exact place of GPi stimulation needs to be determined by future research. In a small selection of patients uni- or bilateral pallidotomy or subthalamotomy can be considered. Indication for thalamic surgery in PD is limited because it mainly improves tremor.

References

Ahlskog, J.E., & Muenter, M.D. (2001). Frequency of levodopa-related dyskinesias and motor fluctuations as estimated from the cumulative literature. *Movement Disorders*, 16, 448–458.

Alvarez, L., Macias, R., Lopez, G., *et al.* (2005). Bilateral subthalamotomy in Parkinson's disease: initial and long-term response. *Brain*, 128, 570–583.

Anderson, V.C., Burchiel, K.J., Hogarth, P., Favre, J., & Hammerstad, J.P. (2005). Pallidal vs subthalamic nucleus deep brain stimulation in Parkinson disease. *Archives of Neurology*, 62, 554–560.

Benazzouz, A., Breit, S., Koudsie, A., Pollak, P., Krack, P., & Benabid, A.L. (2002). Intraoperative microrecordings of the subthalamic nucleus in Parkinson's disease. *Movement Disorders*, 17 (Suppl. 3), S145–S149.

Bonnet, A.M., Loria, Y., Saint-Hilaire, M.H., Lhermitte, F., & Agid, Y. (1987). Does long-term aggravation of Parkinson's disease result from nondopaminergic lesions? *Neurology*, 37, 1539–1542.

Burchiel, K.J., Anderson, V.C., Favre, J., & Hammerstad, J. (1999). Comparison of pallidal and subthalamic nucleus deep brain stimulation for advanced Parkinson's disease: results of a randomized, blinded pilot study. *Neurosurgery*, 45, 1375–1384.

de Bie, R.M.A., de Haan, R.J., Nijssen, P.C.G., *et al.* (1999). Unilateral pallidotomy in Parkinson's disease: a randomised, single-blind, multicentre trial. *Lancet*, 354, 1665–1669.

de Bie, R.M.A., Schuurman, P.R., Esselink, R.A.J., Bosch, D.A., & Speelman, J.D. (2002). Bilateral pallidotomy in Parkinson's disease: a retrospective study. *Movement Disorders*, 17, 533–538.

de Boer, A.G.E.M., Wijker, W., Speelman, J.D., & de Haes, J.C.J.M. (1996). Quality of life in patients with Parkinson's disease: development of a questionnaire. *Journal of Neurology Neurosurgery and Psychiatry*, 61, 70–74.

de Lau, L.M., & Breteler, M.M. (2006). Epidemiology of Parkinson's disease. *Lancet Neurology*, 5, 525–535.

Esselink, R.A.J., de Bie, R.M., de Haan, R.J., et al. (2004). Unilateral pallidotomy versus bilateral subthalamic nucleus stimulation in Parkinson's disease: a randomised, observer-blind, multi-centre trial. *Neurology*, 62, 201–207.

Fahn, S., Elton, R.L., & Members of the UPDRS Development Committee (1987). Unified Parkinson's disease rating scale. In: Fahn, S., Marsden, C.D., & Calne, D.B. (eds.), *Recent Developments in Parkinson's Disease*. Florham Park, NJ: Macmillan Healthcare Information, pp. 153–163.

Gelb, D.J., Oliver, E., & Gilman, S. (1999). Diagnostic criteria for Parkinson disease. *Archives of Neurology*, 56, 33–39.

Ghika, J., Ghika-Schmid, F., Fankhauser, H., et al. (1999). Bilateral contemporaneous posteroventral pallidotomy for the treatment of Parkinson's disease: neuropsychological and neurological side effects. Report of four cases and review of the literature. *Journal of Neurosurgery*, 91, 313–321.

Hagell, P., & Widner, H. (1999). Clinical rating of dyskinesias in Parkinson's disease: use and reliability of a new rating scale. *Movement Disorders*, 14, 448–455.

Hariz, M.I., & Fodstad, H. (1999). Do microelectrode techniques increase accuracy or decrease risks in pallidotomy and deep brain stimulation? A critical review of the literature. *Stereotactic and Functional Neurosurgery*, 72, 157–169.

Hoehn, M.M., & Yahr, M.D. (1967). Parkinsonism: onset, progression and mortality. *Neurology*, 17, 427–442.

Houeto, J.L., Damier, P., Bejjani, B.P., et al. (2000). Subthalamic stimulation in Parkinson's disease: a multidisciplinary approach. *Archives of Neurology*, 57, 461–465.

Jenkinson, N., Nandi, D., Aziz, T.Z., & Stein, J.F. (2005). Pedunculopontine nucleus: a new target for deep brain stimulation for akinesia. *Neuroreport*, 16, 1875–1876.

Krack, P., Pollak, P., Limousin, P., et al. (1998). Subthalamic nucleus or internal pallidal stimulation in young onset Parkinson's disease. *Brain*, 121, 451 457.

Krack, P., Batir, A., Van Blercom, N., et al. (2003). Five-year follow-up of bilateral stimulation of the subthalamic nucleus in advanced Parkinson's disease. *New England Journal of Medicine*, 349, 1925–1934.

Krause, M., Fogel, W., Heck, A., et al. (2001). Deep brain stimulation for the treatment of Parkinson's disease: subthalamic nucleus versus globus pallidus internus. *Journal of Neurology Neurosurgery and Psychiatry*, 70, 464–470.

Kumar, R., Lozano, A.M., Kim, Y.J., et al. (1998). Double-blind evaluation of subthalamic nucleus deep brain stimulation in advanced Parkinson's disease. *Neurology*, 51, 850–855.

Laitinen, L.V., Bergenheim, A.T., & Hariz, M.I. (1992). Leksell's posteroventral pallidotomy in the treatment of Parkinson's disease. *Journal of Neurosurgery*, 76, 53–61.

Lang, A.E., & Widner, H. (2002). Deep brain stimulation for Parkinson's disease: patient selection and evaluation. *Movement Disorders*, 17 (Suppl. 3), S94–S101.

Lang, A.E., Lozano, A.M., Montgomery, E.B., Duff, J., Tasker, R.R., & Hutchinson, W.D. (1997). Posteroventral medial pallidotomy in advanced Parkinson's disease, *New England Journal of Medicine*, 337, 1036–1042.

Lee, M.S., & Marsden, C.D. (1994). Movement disorders following lesions of the thalamus or subthalamic region. *Movement Disorders*, 9, 493–507.

Limousin, P., Krack, P., Pollak, P., et al. (1998). Electrical stimulation of the subthalamic nucleus in advanced Parkinson's disease. *New England Journal of Medicine*, 339, 1105–1111.

Lozano, A.M., & Hutchison, W.D. (2002). Microelectrode recordings in the pallidum. *Movement Disorders*, 17 (Suppl. 3), S150–S154.

Markham, C.H., & Diamond, S.G. (1986). Modification of Parkinson's disease by long-term levodopa treatment. *Archives of Neurology*, 43, 405–407.

Mattis, S. (1976). Mental status examination for organic mental syndrome in the elderly patient. In: Bellak, L., & Karasu, T.B. (eds.), *Geriatric Psychiatry: A Handbook for Psychiatrists and Primary Care Physicians*. New York: Grune & Stratton, pp. 77–121.

Mazzone, P., Lozano, A., Stanzione, P., *et al.* (2005). Implantation of human pedunculopontine nucleus: a safe and clinically relevant target in Parkinson's disease. *Neuroreport*, 16, 1877–1881.

Merello, M., Starkstein, S., Nouzeilles, M.I., Kuzis, G., & Leiguarda, R. (2001). Bilateral pallidotomy for treatment of Parkinson's disease induced corticobulbar syndrome and psychic akinesia avoidable by globus pallidus lesion combined with contralateral stimulation. *Journal of Neurology Neurosurgery and Psychiatry*, 71, 611–614.

Moro, E., Scerrati, M., Romito, L.M.A., Roselli, R., Tonali, P., & Albanese, A. (1999). Chronic subthalamic nucleus stimulation reduces medication requirements in Parkinson's disease. A multidisciplinary approach. *Neurology*, 53, 85–90.

Patel, N.K., Heywood, P., O'Sullivan, K., McCarter, R., Love, S., & Gill, S.S. (2003). Unilateral subthalamotomy in the treatment of Parkinson's disease. *Brain*, 126, 1136–1145.

Plaha, P., & Gill, S.S. (2005). Bilateral deep brain stimulation of the pedunculopontine nucleus for Parkinson's disease. *Neuroreport*, 16, 1883–1887.

Rodriguez-Oroz, M.C., Zamarbide, I., Guridi, J., Palmero, M.R., & Obeso, J.A. (2004). Efficacy of deep brain stimulation of the subthalamic nucleus in Parkinson's disease 4 years after surgery: double blind and open label evaluation. *Journal of Neurology Neurosurgery and Psychiatry*, 75, 1382–1385.

Rodriguez-Oroz, M.C., Obeso, J.A., Lang, A.E., *et al.* (2005). Bilateral deep brain stimulation in Parkinson's disease: a multicentre study with 4 years follow-up. *Brain*, 128, 2240–2249.

Schupbach, W.M., Chastan, N., Welter, M.L., *et al.* (2005). Stimulation of the subthalamic nucleus in Parkinson's disease: a 5 year follow up. *Journal of Neurology Neurosurgery and Psychiatry*, 76, 1640–1644.

Schuurman, P.R., Bosch, D.A., Bossuyt, P.M., *et al.* (2000). A comparison of continuous thalamic stimulation and thalamotomy for suppression of severe tremor. *New England Journal of Medicine*, 342, 461–468.

Sterio, D., Zonenshayn, M., Mogilner, A.Y., *et al.* (2002). Neurophysiological refinement of subthalamic nucleus targeting. *Neurosurgery*, 50, 58–67.

Su, P.C., Tseng, H.M., Liu, H.M., Yen, R.F., & Liou, H.H. (2003). Treatment of advanced Parkinson's disease by subthalamotomy: one-year results. *Movement Disorders*, 18, 531–538.

The Deep-Brain Stimulation for Parkinson's Disease Study Group (2001). Deep-brain stimulation of the subthalamic nucleus or the pars interna of the globus pallidus in Parkinson's disease. *New England Journal of Medicine*, 345, 956–963.

Vilela, F.O., Silva, D.J., Souza, H.A., *et al.* (2001). Stereotactic subthalamic nucleus lesioning for the treatment of Parkinson's disease. *Stereotactic and Functional Neurosurgery*, 77, 79–86.

Vitek, J.L., Bakay, R.A., Freeman, A., *et al.* (2003). Randomized trial of pallidotomy versus medical therapy for Parkinson's disease. *Annals of Neurology*, 53, 558–569.

Volkmann, J., Allert, N., Voges, J., Weiss, P.H., Freund, H-J., & Sturm, V. (2001). Safety and efficacy of pallidal or subthalamic nucleus stimulation in advanced PD. *Neurology*, 56, 548–551.

Welter, M.L., Houeto, J.L., Tezenas du, M.S., *et al.* (2002). Clinical predictive factors of subthalamic stimulation in Parkinson's disease. *Brain*, 125, 575–583.

Whittier, J.R., & Mettler, F.A. (1949). Studies on subthalamus of rhesus monkey: hyperkinesia and other physiologic effects of subthalamic lesions, with special reference to the subthalamic nucleus of Luys. *Journal of Comparative Neurology*, 90, 319–372.

Progress in Neurotherapeutics and Neuropsychopharmacology, 2:1, 27–38 © 2007 Cambridge University Press
DOI: 10.1017/S1748232106000048   Printed in the United Kingdom

The Phase II Futility Clinical Trial Design

Bernard Ravina
University of Rochester Medical Center, Rochester, NY; Email: Bernard.Ravina@ctcc.rochester.edu

Yuko Palesch
Medical University of South Carolina, Charleston, SC

Key words: Futility, clinical trials, Phase II, historical control.

Introduction

Experimental pharmacologic interventions are tested in a systematic series of studies (Food and Drug Administration, 1997). Phase I trials, involving healthy participants or patients, assess safety and determine the dosage range and schedule of administration that can be used in subsequent trials. Phase II trials further assess safety and evaluate the likelihood that patients will or will not benefit from the experimental intervention. The estimate of putative treatment effect obtained from Phase II trials, in combination with information on safety and feasibility, is used to determine if Phase III trials are warranted. In this way Phase II trials are used to prioritize agents for further clinical testing (Piantadosi, 1997). Phase III trials are the definitive steps in evaluating an experimental treatment. These clinical trials are designed and powered to determine clinical efficacy.

Phase III clinical trials generally have clear design parameters, including randomization, parallel placebo or active controls and double blinding, where feasible (Food and Drug Administration, 1997). The sample size and organizational complexity required for many Phase III trials often make them large, costly undertakings. Despite the promise of new agents, there has been a high failure rate of Phase III clinical trials in neurology. This is especially true in trials assessing neuroprotection. For example, Kidwell *et al.* examined 88 clinical trials of potentially neuroprotective agents in acute stroke conducted over more than 40 years. These trials tested thirty-seven different agents and enrolled more than 17 000 subjects, but none of the agents were eventually determined to be efficacious (Kidwell *et al.*, 2001). Similarly in Parkinson's disease (PD) and other related neurodegenerative diseases,

Correspondence should be addressed to: Bernard Ravina MD, MSCE, University of Rochester Medical Center, 1351 Mt. Hope Ave. Rochester, NY 14620; Email: Bernard.Ravina@ctcc.rochester.edu

no intervention has been shown to clearly offer neuroprotection or to slow disease progression (Ravina *et al.*, 2003). The low success rate of Phase III trials and the burgeoning number of potential interventions underscore the need for efficient Phase II trials that can prioritize drugs for Phase III trials.

Compared to Phase III trials there is broad variability in the aims and basic design of Phase II clinical trials. Ravina *et al.* reviewed the characteristics of 115 Phase I and II neurology clinical trials published in 2002 (Ravina *et al.*, 2004). Sixty percent of the trials assessing preliminary efficacy and safety (Phase II) had no control group, parallel or historical. Seventeen percent had a parallel placebo group, although the studies were not comparative efficacy trials according to the pre-specified aims. Only 20–25% of the Phase II trials documented power or sample size calculations. Given the importance of Phase II studies, methodological rigor is needed in this part of clinical development so that only meritorious agents are tested further.

Conceptual Basis of Futility Studies

The futility design is one type of Phase II clinical trial that is relatively new to neurology. Futility trials are conceived of as one-arm studies in which all participants receive the active agent, and their outcomes are compared to a pre-specified value. The goal is not to determine efficacy. The aim is to eliminate agents that show low potential for further development (Elm *et al.*, 2005; Herson, 1979). This is in contrast to the traditional two group (interventional and placebo control) Phase II design that often has the elements of a Phase III trial but less statistical power (Table 1). In the futility design, the active treatment group is generally compared to a pre-determined threshold value(s) based on clinical judgment or historical data. The threshold value may be derived from clinical trials, observational studies or clinical experience. The threshold value is chosen to represent a clinically important cut-off, such that drugs that fail to meet this threshold should be highly unlikely to have clinically important benefits.

Table 1. **Comparison of Hypotheses for Traditional Design and One-Arm Futility Trial**

COMPARISONS	NULL HYPOTHESIS	ALTERNATE HYPOTHESIS	REJECTION OF NULL MEANS
Traditional design Two groups: active, control	Intervention equal to control	Intervention better than control	Intervention effective
Futility design One active group compared to historically derived cut-off	Intervention better than or equal to cut-off	Intervention inferior to cut-off	Intervention ineffective, "Futile"

Conceptually, there are several appealing aspects to the futility design. First, all participants receive the active therapy, and therefore, there is potential to gain more experience with the experimental intervention than if half of the participants received placebo. Second, the design is logically consistent with the aims of Phase II or middle development trial, which is to weed out ineffective interventions so that promising ones may be moved forward. All of the same variables of interest can be studied in a futility design, but, by definition, a Phase II trial is not intended to definitively demonstrate efficacy (Piantadosi, 1997). Third, the futility design has the potential to have greater statistical power than conventional studies of the same sample size that compare active therapy to a concurrent placebo control group (Elm *et al.*, 2005; Green *et al.*, 1997; Herson, 1979). Last, because there is no concurrent placebo group, an unbiased estimate of treatment efficacy cannot be established and therefore no direct conclusion can be drawn about efficacy. This point is important in preserving clinical equipoise for Phase III trials.

Futility trials have been used successfully in cancer research for many years (Gehan, 1986; Herson, 1979), and are accepted as a standard Phase II trial design. The design can be adapted as a traditional design to accommodate multiple dosages and multiple agents. Even in randomized Phase II clinical trials testing multiple agents, less than 5% of oncology studies have concurrent placebo arms (Lee & Feng, 2005). Additionally, greater than 90% of these trials are open label. While the conceptual advantages of the futility design are appealing and there is a clear track record supporting their use in oncology, the question is whether or not the same statistical and design assumptions can be adapted to neurological diseases.

Statistical Framework and Design Considerations

A futility study compares the outcome in a single, treated arm against a pre-determined threshold value reflective of a clinically meaningful value observable over a relatively short period of time. For example, the observed outcome in a futility trial may be defined as the proportion of treated patients who fail treatment (p_{tx}). The definition of treatment failure depends on the disease. For example, for multiple sclerosis (MS) patients, treatment failures might be a new demyelinating event, or for PD patients, development of a complication like wearing off or dyskinesias. The proportion can also be stated as successes where the primary outcome is the proportion of subjects with good outcomes. For example, in stroke this might be defined as the proportion of patients with little or no functional impairment at 3 months after treatment. The proportion of patients expected to fail (or succeed) in the untreated group is defined as p^*. This p^* is often obtained from historical data, such as the placebo arm of previous clinical trials or observational studies. The reduction (increase) in failures (successes) considered clinically meaningful, defined as (Δ), is specified before the Phase II trial begins, and may be derived from the same sources as p^*. If the observed proportion of failures (successes) in the treatment group is statistically greater than the pre-specified threshold value $p^* - \Delta(p^* + \Delta)$, then it would be concluded that it would be futile to evaluate the treatment further for efficacy.

Both p^* and Δ are used to estimate sample size for Phase II. The approach used is similar to that used in developing sample size estimates for Phase III studies. For a continuous outcome such as change in Unified Parkinson's Disease Rating Scale (UPDRS), the threshold can be the hypothesized mean change in the historical control (p^*) group reduced (lower score is better) by a clinically meaningful treatment effect (Δ). Determination of the threshold value is important as too small a value of Δ for a given control value, p^*, might allow an ineffective treatment to be carried on to Phase III, whereas too large a value of Δ could exclude drugs that might demonstrate efficacy in Phase III.

The hypotheses being tested in a single-arm Phase II futility study with a binary outcome with proportion of failure represented by p are:

$$H_0: p_{tx} \leq p^* - \Delta \qquad \text{versus} \qquad H_A: p_{tx} > p^* - \Delta.$$

In case of proportion of success, the hypotheses are:

$$H_0: p_{tx} > p^* + \Delta \qquad \text{versus} \qquad H_A: p_{tx} < p^* + \Delta.$$

If we reject the null hypothesis, we conclude that the proportion of patients on treatment (p_{tx}) who fail (succeed) is greater (less) than the pre-specified threshold $p^* - \Delta(p^* + \Delta)$, and it is futile to proceed to a Phase III efficacy trial. Conversely, if we fail to reject the null hypothesis, we did not observe enough failures to conclude futility, and we would consider further testing of the treatment in a Phase III efficacy trial. Regardless of the results of the Phase II study, we have not demonstrated efficacy.

The futility hypotheses differs from hypotheses specified in traditional Phase III trials of efficacy (Table 1), and the Type I (α) and Type II (β) error probabilities are interpreted differently. Table 2 compares the interpretation of these error probabilities in Phase II futility study versus Phase III efficacy designs (Clark *et al.*, 1999).

Table 2. **Interpretation of α and β Under Phase II Futility and Phase III Efficacy Studies**

STUDY TYPE	TYPE I ERROR (α)	TYPE II ERROR (β)
Phase II futility study	Chance of calling an effective treatment *in*effective	Chance of failing to identify an *in*effective treatment
Traditional Phase III superiority trial	Chance of calling an *in*effective treatment effective	Chance of missing an effective treatment

Adapted from Palesch *et al.* (2005).

Just as in Phase III trials, for Phase II futility trials, α and β are selected relative to the questions under investigation. We do not want to miss an effective agent; consequently we are less concerned about failing to reject the null hypothesis when the alternative is true (falsely concluding an ineffective treatment is possibly effective). Additionally, because Phase II trials are intended to be relatively short, the sample size should be kept small. Thus, we set β (false positive) greater than α (false negative). We may choose α to be 0.10 and β to be 0.15 or 0.20. If we fail to reject the null hypothesis, we may proceed to a Phase III trial of efficacy, generally with smaller error probabilities (values of β and α) and larger sample sizes, and this Phase III trial will be more likely to detect a false positive. In the case of a binary outcome, the statistical test of the futility hypothesis is the one-sample test for comparing binomial proportions (normal approximation) (Ravina, 2006). For a continuous outcome, the test can be a one-sample t-test.

Selecting Historical Controls

The validity of the assumptions made in planning a futility trial depends on the appropriate choice of the historical control and threshold value. Ideally, the historical group used for selecting the threshold should be similar to the group to be enrolled in patient characteristics and assessment conditions. Otherwise the historical assumptions may not be valid. Pocock developed criteria for the use of acceptable historical controls that specify not only the similarity of the two groups but the similarity of the study organization and patient assessments (Pocock, 1976). We present a modified version of these criteria and suggest that historical controls and the target group to be enrolled should be the same or similar in terms of the following:

- distribution of important patient characteristics,
- standard(s) of care,
- eligibility requirements for the study,
- methods of treatment evaluation and participant assessment,
- performance of study evaluations by the same organization or investigators,
- training in study procedures/assessments.

Pocock also notes that investigators should insure the absence of other indicators suggesting a systematic difference in the historical group, such as dramatic differences in recruitment rates between the current study and the reference study. These conditions are stringent and are most likely to be met in the setting of collaborative research groups that perform multiple clinical studies over time.

Selecting the Threshold

As with any clinical trial, the study must be powered to distinguish a treatment effect of a certain magnitude and smaller differences will require larger sample sizes. The larger the Δ, the more likely potentially useful drugs may be discarded as futile. The smaller the Δ, the more likely investigators are to carry forward whatever may be ineffective drugs. The futility threshold should be regarded as a cut-off point such that performance below this cut-off would suggest that the drug is not of clinical interest. Determining this threshold is a matter of clinical judgment based on clinical relevance and the track record of previous agents, if available. It is important to recognize that there is a range around the threshold representing statistical uncertainty. The one-sample test described above essentially tests whether or not the active group could have been drawn from a population with a mean value of the futility threshold. An intervention may yield results slightly worse than the futility threshold, but would not be rejected as futile. This is because the result is close enough to the threshold that it cannot be rejected as coming from a different distribution.

Retrospective Applications of the Futility Design

The futility design has been applied retrospectively to Phase III clinical trials in PD and stroke. The main idea of these simulations is to determine if a smaller trial using the one-arm futility design would have accurately predicted the eventual Phase III trial outcome.

In one simulation, the authors re-evaluated the *Deprenyl And Tocopherol Antioxidative Therapy Of Parkinsonism* (DATATOP) trial (The Parkinson Study Group, 1989). DATATOP was a Phase III trial conducted by the Parkinson Study Group that enrolled patients with recent onset of PD, not requiring levodopa therapy. Eight hundred patients were randomized to tocopherol/placebo or deprenyl/placebo, in a 2×2 factorial design. Twenty-four months follow-up was planned but treatment codes were revealed after 14 months based on an interim analysis. Deprenyl was considered efficacious, although interpretation of these results remains controversial. The tocopherol arm was continued but eventually failed to show efficacy.

Tilley *et al.* used DATATOP data through 12 months of follow-up in order to make it consistent with the short-term nature of a Phase II trial (Tilley *et al.*, 2006). The simulation used the same outcome of time to need for levodopa therapy and the same assumptions about the outcome and the minimally clinically significant 10% absolute reduction in the rate of reaching the endpoint. Tilley *et al.* then constructed two single-arm Phase II futility studies and computed the needed sample size of 124 for each drug. The simulation was conducted using the first 124 patients enrolled in the tocopherol arm (placebo for deprenyl) and then the first

124 subjects enrolled in the deprenyl arm (placebo for tocopherol). The simulation showed that tocopherol would have been rejected as futile but deprenyl would not have been and would have been considered for a Phase III trial.

While the Phase II simulation sample size was large ($N = 124$), there is a reduction from the 400 needed to compare either tocopherol or deprenyl directly with concurrent placebo. In the Phase II design the tocopherol group would have been followed only 12 months at a decreased cost to the study. This example shows that the futility design would have correctly predicted the results of the Phase III trial and would have excluded tocopherol from further study, saving valuable resources and preventing exposure to drugs without the potential for further benefit.

Similar retrospective analyses have been done in ischemic stroke by Palesch *et al.* (2005). For each of six Phase III trials (Palesch *et al.*, 2005; Clark *et al.*, 1999; The Publications Committee (TOAST) Investigators, 1998; The RANTTAS Investigators, 1996), they calculated the sample size for the futility design based on the outcome and hypothesis parameters (p^* and Δ) of the original study, but with $\alpha = 0.10$ and $\beta = 0.15$. The resulting size was nearly an order of magnitude smaller than the original study, partly because of the higher α and, in some cases, β levels, but mainly because of the single-arm design. For example, for the ECASS-II (Hacke *et al.*, 1998) trial, which assessed intravenous (IV) thrombolysis with alteplase, the original study using $\alpha = 0.05$ and $\beta = 0.20$ planned to enroll 800 subjects, while the futility design would require 134. The simulations showed that three (Palesch *et al.*, 2005; Clark *et al.*, 1999; The RANTTAS Investigators, 1996) of the six treatments from the Phase III trials could have correctly been shown to be ineffective in futility studies much sooner because of the smaller sample sizes. The other three trials could not be rejected as futile. In the corresponding Phase III trials two (Hacke *et al.*, 1998; The Publications Committee (TOAST) Investigators, 1998) yielded non-significant treatment effects, but the third trial, the NINDS recombinant tissue plasminogen activator (rt-PA) trial, showed that the treatment was effective (The National Institute of Neurological Disorders and Stroke rt-PA Stroke Study Group, 1995).

Recent Experience with Futility Trials

There are few examples of the prospective use of futility trials in neurological disorders. One example highlights both the potential benefits and drawbacks of this study design. The National Institute of Neurological Disorders and Stroke (NINDS) funded Neuroprotection Exploratory Trials in PD (NET-PD) studied creatine and minocycline as potentially neuroprotective compounds (Ravina, 2006).

The pilot trial studied the 12-month impact of these drugs in parallel on the rate of progression on the UPDRS in otherwise early, untreated PD patients.

The rate of progression was based on the placebo arm of the DATATOP (The Parkinson Study Group, 1989) study conducted several years earlier and the similar rate seen in the smaller but more recent trial of coenzymeQ$_{10}$ (Shults *et al.*, 2002). The threshold value was defined as 30% less progression on the total UPDRS than the 10.65 unit change in DATATOP, or 7.46. A sample size of 65 per group was used for power greater than 85% to reject the null hypothesis of non-futility if in fact the true mean total UPDRS worsening was greater than the threshold of 7.46 at the design alternative of 10.65.

Because the DATATOP trial was conducted several years earlier a small concurrent placebo group was enrolled. This group was not intended to be directly compared to the active arms but to be used as a check on the historical assumptions. A direct comparison to placebo would require approximately a four-fold larger sample size or risk a high false negative rate.

Results of the NINDS trial showed that neither drug could be rejected as futile. However, the rate in the placebo arm was better (less progression) than expected based on DATATOP. The authors used the placebo data to update the DATATOP rate of progression and conducted a sensitivity analysis, essentially establishing a range of plausible values for the true range of progression given the historical and current data. Both drugs remained non-futile throughout the range of values tested.

Valuable information was gained in this study about the safety and tolerability of these drugs in PD and the studies tested the ability to recruit this patient population. It is not yet known whether or not this futility trial of creatine and minocycline will be predictive of future results in placebo-controlled Phase III clinical trials. The results highlight the risks of using historical data especially on outcomes that are operator dependant like the UPDRS. It is important to note, however, that the same historical assumptions would have been made in planning a direct placebo comparison study. This would have led to a much larger trial that would have been under powered for the slower rate of UPDRS progression. Thus, the futility trials may have identified an important variable before committing to a larger study.

In stroke, the recently completed interventional management of stroke (IMS) I trial adopted the single-arm futility design (The Interventional Management of Stroke Study, 2004). This multi-center trial evaluated the futility of an IV plus intra-arterial (IA) delivery approach of rt-PA for ischemic stroke. The values under the null and alternative hypotheses for the futility design were derived from the rt-PA group and the placebo group data, respectively, of the NINDS rt-PA Stroke Study (The National Institute of Neurological Disorders and Stroke rt-PA Stroke Study Group, 1995). The trial failed to show the futility of the IV+IA approach and provided valuable information about the safety and potential efficacy of the IV+IA approach. No calibration group was used here so the validity of the historical assumptions was not directly assessed.

Testing Historical Assumptions: The Use of Calibration Groups

The use of historical or other external controls has been a controversial issue, and historical controls have no place in randomized Phase III trials aimed at proving efficacy. The successful use of the futility design in cancer and the simulations in stroke and PD suggest the use of historical controls can be productive. However, even seemingly objective measurements like tumor size are subject to changing standards of care and cohort effects or sampling variability. Concerns about changing standard of care and sampling variability prompted the inclusion of a calibration placebo group in the NET-PD study and the results show that these concerns were well founded.

Some authors have advocated for control arms in futility studies as a check or calibration on the historical rate of response or progression (Herson & Carter, 1986). The calibration group is not a traditional control group in that no formal comparison of efficacy is made between the experimental and calibration control arms. Rather the calibration group is used to determine if the group of subjects recruited for the trial meets expectations in terms of their response or progression rate and has the capacity to respond to the experimental intervention. The use of a calibration group, in which patients may be on placebo or some standard of care, adds to the sample size and thereby reduces some of the efficiency of the futility design. However, Herson and Carter (1986) have shown that the inclusion of a calibration group becomes efficient when multiple agents are tested simultaneously.

The calibration group may show one of three results: (1) consistent with historical estimates, (2) more responsive than historical estimates or (3) less responsive than historical estimates. Table 3, adapted from Herson and Carter (1986), suggests ways to interpret the range of results that may be obtained with a calibration group. For example, if the calibration group does worse than expected and the experimental interventions appear futile, it may be that an unusually unresponsive patient group was recruited and that the results should not be accepted. In this case the trial may be repeated. In NET-PD, the calibration group performed

Table 3. **Interpretation of Calibration Group Results**

	INVESTIGATIONAL AGENT	
CALIBRATION GROUP	REJECTED AS FUTILE	CANNOT REJECT AS FUTILE
Greater than expected activity	Accept results	Question results consider trial repetition[*]
Expected level of activity	Accept results	Accept results
Less than expected level of activity	Question results consider trial repetition[*]	Accept results

[*]Consider sensitivity analyses. Adapted from Herson and Carter (1986).

better than expected and the drugs were non-futile. In this case it may be difficult to discern a treatment effect from a more responsive group of patients. In situations such as this, the size of the calibration group becomes important because the investigators must decide how much weight to place on the calibration group compared to the generally larger body of historical evidence.

Future Directions: The Value of Ongoing Databases

Given the expected rapid progress in therapeutics in neurology, treatment standards will likely change and this may make it difficult to conduct futility trials with historical controls. To keep pace with changing practice standards, we will need ongoing data repositories that can follow large numbers of subjects over time. Such efforts are already under way in PD and other areas. The PD-Data Organizing Center (PD-DOC) sponsored by NINDS/NIH has developed a core dataset covering motor and non-motor manifestations of PD. The intent of PD-DOC is to follow a large cohort of patients throughout the course of their PD (http://dev.pd-doc.org). Data will be made accessible to investigators and can be used for hypothesis generation or to develop historical controls. The advantage of such a large ongoing effort is that it will capture temporal changes in patient care, and smaller groups of patients with particular characteristics may be used as historical controls.

Conclusions

The futility design offers several theoretical advantages over the traditional, placebo-controlled Phase II design. These include reduced sample size and more appropriate false negative and false positive rates for Phase II trials. These theoretical advantages are supported by retrospective analyses of clinical trials in PD and stroke. Despite the success of this paradigm in oncology, however, it is not yet clear how useful it will be in neurology. The critical element required for an effective futility study is an appropriate historical reference standard. The NET-PD study highlights the problem of using historical controls in a rapidly evolving field. The development of objective biomarkers that are stable over time and the advent of large databases that capture the treated natural history will support the use of historical controls. This should enable the use of the futility design, leading to more rapid and efficient clinical development programs.

References

Clark, **W.M.** *et al.* (1999). Recombinant tissue-type plasminogen activator (Alteplase) for ischemic stroke 3 to 5 hours after symptom onset. The ATLANTIS Study: a randomized controlled trial. Alteplase Thrombolysis for Acute Noninterventional Therapy in Ischemic Stroke. *Journal of the American Medical Association*, 282, 2019–2026.

Elm, J.J., Goetz, C.G., Ravina, B., Shannon, K., Wooten, G.F., Tanner, C., *et al.* (2005). A responsive outcome for Parkinson's disease neuroprotection futility studies. *Annals of Neurology*, 57(2), 197–203.

Food and Drug Administration (1997). In *Federal Register*, Vol 24. (ed. HHS) 66113–66118.

Gehan, E.A. (1986). Update on planning of phase II clinical trials. *Drugs under Experimental and Clinical Research*, 12, 43–50.

Green, S., Benedetti, J., & Crowley, J. (1997). *Clinical Trials in Oncology*. London: Chapman & Hall.

Hacke, W. *et al.* (1998). Randomised double-blind placebo-controlled trial of thrombolytic therapy with intravenous alteplase in acute ischaemic stroke (ECASS II). Second European-Australasian Acute Stroke Study Investigators. *Lancet*, 352, 1245–1251.

Herson, J. (1979). Predictive probability early termination plans for phase II clinical trials. *Biometrics*, 35, 775–783.

Herson, J., & Carter, S.K. (1986). Calibrated phase II clinical trials in oncology. *Statistics in Medicine*, 5, 441–447.

Kidwell, C.S., Liebeskind, D.S., Starkman, S., & Saver, J.L. (2001). Trends in acute ischemic stroke trials through the 20th century. *Stroke*, 32, 1349–1359.

Lee, J.J., & Feng, L. (2005). Randomized phase II designs in cancer clinical trials: current status and future directions. *Journal of Clinical Oncology*, 23, 4450–4457.

Palesch, Y.Y., Tilley, B.C., Sackett, D.L., Johnston, K.C., & Woolson, R. (2005). Applying a phase II futility study design to therapeutic stroke trials. *Stroke*, 36, 2410–2414.

Piantadosi, S. (1997). *Clinical Trials: A Methodological Perspective*. New York: John Wiley & Sons Inc.

Pocock, S.J. (1976). The combination of randomized and historical controls in clinical trials. *Journal of Chronic Diseases*, 29, 175–188.

Ravina, B. (2006). NINDS Net PD Investigators; A randomized, double-blind, futility clinical trial of creatine and minocycline in early Parkinson disease. *Neurology*, Mar 14; 66(5): 664–671. Epub 2006 Feb 15.

Ravina, B.M., *et al.* (2003). Neuroprotective agents for clinical trials in Parkinson's disease: a systematic assessment. *Neurology*, 60, 1234–1240.

Ravina, B., Janis, S., Keleti, J., & Marler, J.M. (2004). Funding evidence: the National Institute of Neurological Disorders and Stroke Clinical Trials Program. *NeuroRx*, 1, 317–322.

Shults, C.W. *et al.* (2002). Effects of coenzyme Q10 in early Parkinson disease: evidence of slowing of the functional decline. *Archives of Neurology*, 59, 1541–1550.

The Interventional Management of Stroke Study (2004). Combined intravenous and intra-arterial recanalization for acute ischemic stroke. *Stroke*, 35, 904–911.

The National Institute of Neurological Disorders and Stroke rt-PA Stroke Study Group (1995). Tissue plasminogen activator for acute ischemic stroke. *New England Journal of Medicine*, 333, 1581–1587.

The Parkinson Study Group (1989). Effect of deprenyl on the progression of disability in early Parkinson's disease. *New England Journal of Medicine*, 321, 1364–1371.

The Publications Committee (TOAST) Investigators (1998). Low molecular weight heparinoid, ORG 10172 (danaparoid), and outcome after acute ischemic stroke: a randomized controlled trial. The Publications Committee for the Trial of ORG 10172 in Acute Stroke Treatment (TOAST) Investigators. *Journal of American Medical Association*, 279, 1265–1272.

The RANTTAS Investigators (1996). A randomized trial of tirilazad mesylate in patients with acute stroke (RANTTAS). *Stroke*, 27, 1453–1458.

Tilley, B.C., Palesch, Y.Y., Kieburtz, K., Ravina, B., *et al.* Optimizing the ongoing search for new treatments for Parkinson disease: Using futility designs. *Neurology*, 2006; 66(5): 628–633.

Progress in Neurotherapeutics and Neuropsychopharmacology, 2:1, 39–78 © 2007 Cambridge University Press
DOI: 10.1017/S174823210600005X   Printed in the United Kingdom

Clinical Trials in Dementia

Encarnita Raya-Ampil

Department of Neurology and Psychiatry, University of Santo Tomas, Manila, Philippines;
Email:kanlaon200@yahoo.com

Jeffrey L. Cummings

Departments of Neurology and Psychiatry and Biobehavioral Sciences, David Geffen School of Medicine at UCLA, Los Angeles, CA, USA; Email:jcummings@mednet.ucla.edu

ABSTRACT

Dementia, particularly Alzheimer's disease (AD), is increasing by patient population included in clinical trials. The methodology for trials of AD patients have been defined in terms of outcomes, standard measures and analytic techniques. Trial methodology is evolving with experience as new potential therapies become available. Screening criteria, instrumentation choices, duration of trials and analytic strategies may have a profound impact on the conclusions that can be derived from trials. The components of AD trials are reviewed in detail in this chapter.

Introduction

Dementia is a health problem affecting millions of people worldwide. Its prevalence increases with age and it is typically a disease of the elderly. The impact of this disorder lies not only in the loss of patient autonomy and caregiver burden that ensue as it progresses but also on its marked economic effects. With improving health care management in both affluent and developing countries, a rise in the aging population and subsequent rise in dementia cases is anticipated.

Alzheimer's disease (AD) is the leading cause of dementia. In the United States alone, AD was estimated to affect 4 million Americans in 1990 (Evans, 1990). This number is expected to rise to 8.5 million by the year 2030 (National Institute of Health, National Institute on Aging, 1999) and 14 million by the year 2050 (Evans, 1990). The overall prevalence rate of AD is 2–3% at the age of 65 years (Evans *et al.*, 1989). Prevalence rates double every 5 years after age 60 so that almost 50% of individuals of 85 years and older may be affected by this disorder

Correspondence should be addressed to: Jeffrey L. Cummings, MD, Departments of Neurology and Psychiatry and Biobehavioral Sciences, Reed Neurological Research Center, David Geffen School of Medicine at UCLA, 710 Westwood Plaza, Suite 2-238, P.O. Box No. 951769, Los Angeles, CA 90095-1769, USA; Tel: 310 206 5239; Fax: 310 206 5287; Email: jcummings@mednet.ucla.edu

(Evans *et al.*, 1989). The United States is spending 100 billion US dollars/year to care for individuals with AD (Institute on Aging, 1996; Ernst and Hay, 1994).

The large population affected by dementia and the unmet need for more efficacious treatment has led to randomized-controlled trials (RCTs) of promising treatments. The largest numbers of trials have been done with cholinesterase inhibitors (ChE-Is), the first class of agents approved by the Food and Drug Administration (FDA) for the treatment of AD. Recently, trials led to the approval of memantine, an *N*-methyl-D-aspartate (NMDA) antagonist as a treatment for patients with moderate to severe AD. These trials of approved agents are very influential in determining how future trials of antidementia agents will be conducted for AD, vascular dementia (VaD) and other entities such as mild cognitive impairment (MCI). Lessons learned from these trials will guide trial conduct not only for symptomatic agents with AD but also for compounds that may have disease-modifying effects. This chapter reviews published trials to derive guidelines on how future trials may be conducted. We concentrate on trials of AD and MCI only.

Defining AD, MCI and VaD

Precision in clinical diagnosis is essential to ensure valid outcomes in clinical trials. RCTs in AD and MCI have utilized various diagnostic criteria to guarantee subject homogeneity.

MCI has been a diagnostic dilemma from the time that the term was coined. Most regard it as a transition state between normal aging and early AD. More recently, new concepts of MCI emerged, making assessment and management more complex. Some regard MCI as early or incipient AD (Morris *et al.*, 2001) (Table 1).

Currently, MCI can be classified on the basis of the affected cognitive domain/s (Petersen *et al.*, 2001) – single memory domain, single nonmemory domain and multiple cognitive domain with or without involvement of memory. The amnestic type (single or multiple domain) is the most closely correlated with AD. Other MCI types may lead to either AD or other dementia syndromes, broadening the possibility of patient outcome. Currently, therapeutic trials have limited recruitment to the amnestic type of MCI (Petersen *et al.*, 2005; Salloway *et al.*, 2004) since this is

Table 1. **Criteria for Amnestic MCI**

1. Memory complaint, preferably corroborated by an informant
2. Impaired memory function for age and education
3. Preserved general cognitive function
4. Intact activities of daily living
5. Not demented

the most certain prelude to AD. A majority of studies have adopted delay to progression to AD using a survival type of outcome as the research design approach.

AD is a progressive degenerative disorder, which leads to cognitive decline that is severe enough to cause functional deterioration. Several criteria are available to clearly define this entity: Diagnostic and Statistical Manual of Mental Disorders, Fourth Edition (DSM-IV) (American Psychaitric Association, 1994); International Classification of Diseases, 10th revision (ICD-10) (World Health Organization, 1993) and the National Institute of Neurological and Communicative Disorders and Stroke and the Alzheimer's Disease and Related Disorders Association (NINCDS–ADRDA) (McKhann *et al.*, 1984) criteria. The level of diagnostic certainty is indicated in the NINCDS–ADRDA criteria. Neuroimaging has been included for the purpose of excluding other dementias in the differential diagnoses. Its postconsensus sensitivity and specificity for the diagnosis of AD range from 0.83–0.95 and 0.79 to 0.84 (Holmes *et al.*, 1999; Lopez *et al.*, 1999; Blacker *et al.*, 1994) while clinicopathological sensitivity and specificity are 0.64–0.86 to 0.89–0.91 (Blacker *et al.*, 1994; Tierney *et al.*, 1988). Interrater reliability is moderate (Blacker *et al.*, 1994). The NINCDS–ADRDA criteria for AD has been regularly used in trials due to their established validity (Tables 2 and 3).

Severity of Dementia

It is essential for dementia severity to be specified in clinical trials to ensure patient population homogeneity and gauge treatment response. The spectrum of dementia

Table 2. **DSM-IV Criteria for Diagnosis of AD (American Psychiatric Association, 1994)**

(A) AD is characterized by progressive decline and ultimately loss of multiple cognitive functions, including both:
   1. Memory impairment – impaired ability to learn new information or to recall previously learned information.
   2. And at least one of the following:
      (a) loss of word comprehension ability (aphasia);
      (b) loss of ability to perform complex tasks involving muscle coordination (apraxia);
      (c) loss of ability to recognize and use familiar objects (agnosia);
      (d) loss of ability to plan, organize and execute normal activities.
(B) The problems in "A" represent a substantial decline from previous abilities and cause significant problems in everyday functioning.
(C) The problems in "A" begin slowly and gradually become more severe.
(D) The problems in "A" are not due to:
   • Other conditions that cause progressive cognitive decline, among them: stroke, Parkinson's disease, Huntington's chorea, brain tumor, etc.
   • Other conditions that cause dementia, among them: hypothyroidism, HIV infection, syphilis and deficiencies in niacin, vitamin B12 and folic acid.
(E) The problems in "A" are not caused by episodes of delirium.
(F) The problems in "A" are not caused by another mental illness: depression, schizophrenia, etc.

Table 3. **NINCDS–ADRDA Criteria for Diagnosis of Probable AD (McKhann *et al.,* 1984)**

(I)	Dementia established by clinical examination, and documented by a standard test of cognitive function (e.g. MMSE, Blessed Dementia Scale, etc.), and confirmed by neuropsychological tests.
(II)	Significant deficiencies in two or more areas of cognition, for example, word comprehension and task-completion ability.
(III)	Progressive deterioration of memory and other cognitive functions.
(IV)	No loss of consciousness.
(V)	Onset from age 40 to 90, typically after 65.
(VI)	No other diseases or disorders that could account for the loss of memory and cognition.
(VII)	Diagnosis of probable AD is supported by:

(VII) continued:

1. Progressive deterioration of specific cognitive functions: language (aphasia), motor skills (apraxia) and perception (agnosia).
2. Impaired activities of daily living and altered patterns of behavior.
3. A family history of similar problems, particularly if confirmed by neurological testing.
4. The following laboratory results:
   • Normal cerebrospinal fluid (lumbar puncture test).
   • Normal electroencephalogram (EEG) test of brain activity.
   • Evidence of cerebral atrophy in a series of CT scans.

(VIII) Other features consistent with AD
1. Plateaus in the course of illness progression.
2. CT findings normal for the person's age.
3. Associated symptoms, including: depression, insomnia, incontinence, delusions, hallucinations, weight loss, sex problems and significant verbal, emotional and physical outbursts.
4. Other neurological abnormalities, especially in advanced disease, including: increased muscle tone and a shuffling gait.

(IX) Features that decrease the likelihood of AD
1. Sudden onset.
2. Such early symptoms as: seizures, gait problems, and loss of vision and coordination.

depends on its longitudinal course that is defined by three domains: cognition, behavior and function. Generally, dementia severity can be divided into three stages. In the early mild stage, the initial manifestations of minor memory impairment emerge with concomitant decline in complex activities. In the moderate stage, behavioral changes become more prominent, with involvement of cognitive domains other than memory – typically language and visuospatial skills. Behavioral changes become more apparent at this point and patients have more difficulty in coping with daily activities such as housework and hobbies. In the severe stage, patients are unable to live without assistance and they manifest more disturbing behavioral symptoms. Institutionalization is common in this stage of the illness.

The Global Deterioration Scale (GDS) (Riesberg *et al.*, 1982), Clinical Dementia Rating (CDR) (Hughes *et al.*, 1982) and Mini-Mental State Examination (MMSE) (Folstein *et al.*, 1975) are instruments that are frequently used for assessing dementia severity. Both the GDS and CDR are global assessment instruments which examine cognition, function and behavior. The MMSE, however, is limited to the measurement of cognition in terms of orientation, attention, memory, language and figure copying. It has been regularly used as an instrument for the staging of dementia since it examines the "core" manifestations of the disorder which are the main target of therapeutic trials.

The MMSE was formulated by Folstein and colleagues as a practical method of grading the cognitive state (Folstein *et al.*, 1975) of psychiatric inpatients. Advantages of this instrument are its brevity and ease of administration. It has an adequate sensitivity of 86% and a specificity of 92% when a cut-off score of 23–24/30 is used (O'Connor *et al.*, 1989). Its ceiling and floor effects, though, lessens its sensitivity in detecting mild and severe cognitive impairment, respectively. MMSE scores are influenced by age and education. The presence of within subject and between subject variability challenges the applicability of MMSE scores; they have wide standard errors of measurement. The natural variability of the disease also contributes to score fluctuations. Despite these caveats, the use of MMSE is widespread in the staging of dementia, and is commonly used to define a restricted range of dementia severity for patients included in clinical trials (Table 4). It is rarely used as an outcome measure.

The Ethical Conduct of Dementia Trials and Informed Consent

Research trials involve experimentation and, to protect human subjects, various guidelines have been implemented. As in all research studies involving human subjects, the principles of minimization of harm, beneficence and veracity are maintained in dementia trials. Conduct of dementia trials is complicated by inclusion of subjects with varying severity of cognitive impairment, a condition that makes them vulnerable to exploitation.

A multitude of "ethically approved" RCTs in dementia therapy has been conducted in the past years. From these studies, acetylcholinesterase inhibitors have been approved as a class of drugs that is effective and safe in AD patients. In 2001, the American Academy of Neurology issued guidelines in the management of AD and these described acetylcholinesterase inhibitors as a standard treatment for this disorder (Doody *et al.*, 2001). Thus, assignment of subjects to placebo in future clinical trials may be regarded by some as unethical since a standard drug is available.

Determination of the capacity to consent is a much discussed aspect of dementia trials. Differing levels of disease severity produce differing levels of incapacity and challenge the ability of the patient to participate in consent discussions. The presentation of the purpose, methodology and procedures, risks, benefits and alternatives must be very clear and simple for cognitively impaired subjects to comprehend. The extent of the subject's grasp of the details of the study and decision-making capacity should be evaluated. This involves examination of

Table 4. **MMSE Range of Subjects in AD and MCI RCTs**

DIAGNOSIS	AGENT	RCT	DURATION OF RCT (WEEKS)	MMSE/SMMSE RANGE
Alzheimer's disease Mild to moderate	Metrifonate	Cummings *et al.* (1998), Morris *et al.* (1998)	30 (12[a]), 36 (26[a])	10–26
	Tacrine	Davis *et al.* (1992), Farlow *et al.* (1992), Knapp *et al.* (1994)	6, 12, 30	10–26
	Donepezil	Rogers *et al.* (1998a); Rogers *et al.* (1998b), Winblad *et al.* (2001)	12, 24, 52	10–26
	Galantamine	Tariot, *et al.* (2000)	20	10–22
		Rockwood *et al.* (2001), Raskind *et al.* (2000)	12, 24	11–24
	Rivastigmine	CoreyBloom *et al.* (1998) and Rosler *et al.* (1999)	26, 26	10–26
	Diclofenac/Misoprostol	Scharf *et al.* (1999)	25	11–25
	Prednisone	Aisen *et al.* (2000)	52	13–26
	Estrogen	Mulnard *et al.* (2000)	52	14–28
	Rofecoxib or Naproxen	Aisen *et al.* (2003)	52	13–26
	Rofecoxib	Reines *et al.* (2004)	52	14–26
	Acetyl-L-carnitine	Thal *et al.* (1996)	52	13–26
Moderate to severe	Donepezil	Feldman *et al.* (2001)	24	5–17[b]
	Memantine	Reisberg *et al.* (2003)	28	3–14
MCI	Donepezil	Salloway *et al.* (2004), Petersen *et al.* (2005)	24, Survival design (time to reach endpoint)	≥24

MMSE: Mini-Mental State Examination.
SMMSE: Standardized Mini-Mental State Examination.
RCT: Randomized controlled trial.
[a] Duration of active treatment.

(1) understanding of the relevant facts of the trial disclosed to him, (2) appreciation of the research risks and potential benefits and (3) reasoning in terms of comparing options and drawing consequences from these options (Alzheimer Association, 2004).

If a subject is deemed incompetent to give informed consent, proxy consent is obtained from an individual who has the capacity and legal authority to give it. Typically, the caregiver is given this task since he/she is the one who addresses the daily needs of the subject and knows the latter's preferences. Competence and benevolence of the caregiver must be ensured in these circumstances.

In the mild to moderate stages of the disease process, the subject will still be able to contribute to research trial decisions. The investigator must ensure that the subject is still part of the choices made by the proxy. Later, the subject loses the ability to participate meaningfully and the caregiver becomes the sole decision-maker. It is at this point that assent (or dissent) should be obtained from the subject. This is judged behaviorally based on the cooperativeness of the subject with the study procedures (Alzheimer Association, 2004). Consistent resistance of the subject with study procedures may be taken as dissent, a probable basis for discontinuation from the study.

Generalizability of Clinical Trial Results

A drug's value is ultimately tested once it is marketed for the targeted population. The terms "efficacy" and "effectiveness" distinguish between how well the intervention/drug *can* work under ideal circumstances such as that in clinical trials and how the intervention/drug *does* work under "field conditions" such as that in the community (Koepsell & Weiss, 2003). The drug's applicability depends on the inherent characteristics (demographic and medical) of the cohort of subjects enrolled in the clinical trial and how representative they are of the population who will eventually use it. Subject selection by using inclusion and exclusion criteria potentially limit the generalizability of the results of the clinical trial. The National Institute of Mental Health Clinical Antipsychotic Trials of Intervention Effectiveness (NIMH–CATIE) is an example of an effectiveness study of psychotropic use in AD with a methodological design that assures applicability of the results in the community setting (Schneider *et al.*, 2001).

In RCTs of acetylcholinesterase inhibitors, recruitment bias was observed toward subjects who are healthier, better educated, younger and of higher socio-economic status (Schoenmaker & Van Gool, 2004; Cummings, 2003). This has the effect of excluding subjects who have complicated medical histories and are taking specific medications. Caregivers may be more aggressive in seeking medical help when their relatives are in the early stage of dementia biasing recruited populations to earlier more mild disease.

Another confounding factor on the generalizability of trials is the drug's eventual applicability in different ethnic populations. RCTs require major funding and for this reason, these are conducted in affluent countries. This fundamentally explains why Caucasians compose the greater part of the subjects in trials globally. However, there is a mixture of ethnic populations in the United States and Caucasians should not dominate disproportionately. Examination of the population recruited in acetylcholinesterase inhibitor trials which were conducted in the United States show that the samples were 91–99% White (Cummings, 2003). Problem may arise due to differences in the pharmacokinetics of the drug in various ethnic populations resulting in varied first pass metabolism and systemic bioavailability. Activity of the cytochrome P450 enzymes differ among various ethnic groups possibly leading to disparate side-effect profiles, dosaging and efficacy.

Highly specialized centers conduct clinical trials. Involved physicians have expertise in handling dementia cases and are highly motivated to recruit patients. Complete laboratory and neuroimaging work-up are also on hand. Subjects in these centers are diagnosed with precision and handled differently as compared to those in the community setting. There is stronger and more accessible patient support systems in trial centers. This may have great impact in the care of dementia patients since it would result in better compliance and fewer problem behaviors. This setting again distinguishes clinical trials from routine care.

Outcome Assessments in Dementia Trials

AD affects primarily the memory with subsequent involvement of other cognitive domains. This change causes concomitant deterioration in function and behavior. The efficacy of antidementia drugs therefore should be evaluated based on these domains: cognition, behavior and function.

The efficacy of an antidementia drug is measured through various outcome assessment scales and psychometric tests. As required by the US FDA, the cognitive improvement that results from drug administration should be supported by (1) positive change in a performance-based cognitive instrument and (2) clinically meaningful effect seen globally or functionally (Leber, 1990). These two factors comprise the primary outcome measures in dementia clinical trials. Secondary outcome measures are included to further document the effect of a drug on the other aspects of the subject's life. These secondary outcome measures do not need to be positive for the drug to be approved and marketed. Assessment scales examining the subject's quality of life, noncognitive behavioral symptoms and economic impact of the illness usually compose the secondary outcomes.

Outcome measures must possess certain properties before they can be employed in clinical trials. The instruments must be valid, reliable and sensitive. Validity confirms whether the tool measures what it is intended to measure.

Reliability (test/retest, interrater and/or intrarater) refers to the replicability of results so that the same value will be obtained under multiple circumstances. Sensitivity is the capacity to detect change over time especially with treatment. It is best if the instruments are effective in detecting changes even in the extremes of the spectrum of the illness, eliminating floor and ceiling effects. Other important properties are ease of use and short administration time, and availability of multiple equivalent forms to avoid practice effects with repeated use. Ideally, these should be independent of demographic and socioeconomic factors such as gender, education and cultural background.

Primary Outcome Measures

Performance-Based Cognitive Assessment

Cognition is composed of multiple domains, all of which are inevitably affected at the late stage of dementia. Consensus on cognitive domains that may be assessed include the following: memory, attention, processing speed, visuospatial function, praxis, language, executive function and abstraction (Ferris *et al.*, 1997). A combination of different psychometric tests can fully evaluate these domains. However, it is more appropriate for disease-specific instruments to be used in a chronically progressive illness so that it can appropriately reflect the outcome at study endpoint.

The Alzheimer's Disease Assessment Scale (ADAS) was designed to evaluate the severity of both cognitive and noncognitive manifestations of AD patients (Rosen *et al.*, 1984). Cognitive domains include memory, orientation, language and praxis while the noncognitive domains include mood state and behavioral changes. The cognitive portion has a maximum score of 70 with a higher score indicating more severe impairment. Its advantages include short administration time, ability to detect changes from the mild to severe stages and is appropriate for patients in different environments (Rosen *et al.*, 1984). There is excellent interrater and test/retest reliability of the ADAS-cog at 0.99 and 0.92, respectively. It is the most widely used objective cognitive assessment scales in dementia RCTs. The ADAS-cog is the prevailing primary outcome measure of efficacy that evaluates changes in the core manifestations of dementia. The ADAS-cog lacks tests examining executive function, a domain that is affected frequently. The Alzheimer's Disease Cooperative Study (ADCS) has extended the ADAS-cog by adding two executive tests, a cancellation and a maze task.

Global Measures

The overall clinical impact of an antidementia drug is evaluated using global assessment scales. These assess the multidimensional manifestations of the illness in terms of cognition, behavior and function. There are two categories of global measures: (1) global severity scales, which ascertain the absolute severity of the patient's condition, and (2) global change scales, which determine the overall improvement or deterioration of the subject. Global scales have less structure, thus partially avoiding the influence of subject characteristics and rating variance. The available global scales were specifically designed for use in AD or primary degenerative dementia so that results are specific to the illness. These are sensitive measures for long-term assessment of efficacy since changes can be quantified when other assessments are affected by floor effects.

Global assessment scales of change were developed to measure a "clinically meaningful" treatment effect that translates into practical usefulness. All of the measures are 7 point scales which are rated as follows: 1 = very much improved, 2 = much improved, 3 = minimally improved, 4 = no change, 5 = minimally worse, 6 = much worse, 7 = very much worse. These assess change from a specified baseline. Unlike the symptom scales, these are relatively unstructured, relying on an experienced clinician to conduct a thorough and accurate interview on which the rating is based. Even though reliability is compromised with this format, the sensitivity to measure meaningful change is retained so that it remains as one of the primary efficacy measures.

The first global assessment scale was the Clinician Global Impression (CGI), an unstructured instrument that was widely used in neuropsychopharmacological trials (Knopman *et al.*, 1994). The CGI was first utilized in a dementia RCT involving tacrine by Davis *et al.* (1992) with ADAS-cog as the other primary measure of efficacy. However, significant improvement was noted only in the ADAS-cog but not in the CGI which indicated the latter's lack of sensitivity to the treatment effect of tacrine. A guideline-based global assessment scale, the Clinical Interview Based Impression (CIBI), was then developed which was used in the 30-week tacrine trial by Knapp *et al.* (1994). Both ADAS-cog and CIBI yielded significantly positive results which led to the FDA approval of tacrine. Several global assessment scales emerged to further improve the instrument's reliability (Table 5). To date, Clinical Interview Based Impression of Change with caregives input (CIBIC-plus) is the most frequently used global assessment instrument in dementia RCTs.

Global severity or staging scales such as the CDR Scale (Hughes *et al.*, 1982) and the GDS (Reisberg *et al.*, 1982) are frequently used as entry criteria or as secondary outcome measures. The CDR is a worksheet-based semistructured interview that evaluates 6 domains: 3 cognitive (memory, orientation, judgment and problem solving) and 3 functional (community affairs, home and hobbies, and personal care). Rating is based on a 5 point scale in which 0 = none, 0.5 questionable dementia, 1 = mild impairment, 2 = moderate impairment and 3 = severe impairment. It can be scored in two ways: (1) as a sum of boxes (SB) by obtaining the sum of the ratings of each of the six CDR domains/boxes and (2) as a global rating based on a scoring system wherein the memory box/domain is the main consideration. Preference for this instrument is due to its clinically based assessment and high interrater reliability resulting in a level of agreement

Table 5. **Global Outcome Measures (Severity and Change Scales) Utilized in AD and MCI Trials as Either Primary or Secondary Measure of Efficacy**

GLOBAL OUTCOME MEASURES	RCT THAT USED OUTCOME AS PRIMARY MEASURE OF EFFICACY	RCT THAT USED OUTCOME AS SECONDARY MEASURE OF EFFICACY
Severity		
CDR (global and/or sum of boxes)	Thal *et al.* (1996)	Rogers *et al.* (1998a), Rogers *et al.* (1998b), Aisen *et al.* (2000), Petersen *et al.* (2005), Mohs *et al.* (2001), Aisen *et al.* (2003), Mulnard *et al.* (2000), Sano *et al.* (1997)
GDS	Scharf *et al.* (1999)	Reisberg *et al.* (2003), Morris *et al.* (1998), Winblad *et al.* (2001), Petersen *et al.* (2005), Knapp *et al.* (1994), Corey-Bloom *et al.* (1998)
Change		
CGI (Guy, 1976)	Davis *et al.* (1992), Farlow *et al.* (1992) Scharf *et al.* (1999), Le Bars *et al.* (1997)	Thal *et al.* (1996)
CIBI (Knopman *et al.*, 1994) CIBIC-plus (Knopman *et al.*, 1994)	Knapp *et al.* (1994) Tariot *et al.* (2000), Cummings *et al.* (1998), Rogers *et al.* (1998a), Rogers *et al.* (1998b), Reisberg *et al.* (2003), Rockwood *et al.* (2001), Morris *et al.* (1998), Raskind *et al.* (2000), Feldman *et al.* (2001), Reines *et al.* (2004), Rosler *et al.* (1999), Corey-Bloom *et al.* (1998)	
ADCS–CGIC (Schneider *et al.*, 1997)	Mulnard *et al.* (2000), Salloway *et al.* – MCI version (2004)	

CDR: Clinical Dementia Rating; GDS: Global Deterioration Scale; CGI: Clinical Global Impression; CIBI: Clinical Interview Based Impression; CIBIC-plus: Clinical Interview Based Impression of Change plus caregiver information; CGIC: Clinical Global Impression of Change.

of 80% (Burke *et al.*, 1988). The GDS is also a useful instrument in staging primary degenerative dementia. It is capable of accurately delineating stages of dementia throughout the course of AD (Reisberg *et al.*, 1982). It rates cognitive decline based on a 7 point scale with the following scoring system: 1 = none, 2 = very mild, 3 = mild, 4 = moderate, 5 = moderately severe, 6 = severe, 7 = very severe. Interrater and test/retest reliability are high, both at 0.92 (Reisberg *et al.*, 1994).

Secondary Outcome Measures

Mini-Mental State Examination

The MMSE may be included as an entry criterion or as a supplementary measure of cognition (Petersen *et al.*, 2005; Reines *et al.*, 2004; Reisberg *et al.*, 2003; Mohs *et al.*, 2001; Winblad *et al.*, 2001; Mulnard *et al.*, 2000; Scharf *et al.*, 1999; Corey-Bloom *et al.*, 1998; Cummings *et al.*, 1998; Rogers *et al.*, 1998a, b; Le Bars *et al.*, 1997; Sano *et al.*, 1997; Thal *et al.*, 1996; Knapp *et al.*, 1994; Davis *et al.*, 1992). Compared to the ADAS-cog, its result is better understood by non-AD specialists and can be easily translated into more practical terms. However, its limited sensitivity makes it a poor primary outcome measure.

Activities of Daily Living

Functional impairment is an essential component of the clinical syndrome of dementia. It is required for the clinical diagnosis of dementia and included in the NINCDS–ADRDA criteria (McKhann *et al.*, 1984) and the DSM-IV criteria (American Psychiatric Association, 1994). The resulting dependence affects not only the patient but also the quality of life of the caregiver and becomes an important factor that leads to institutionalization. Changes in activities of daily living (ADL) are frequently included as a secondary outcome measure. Functional deterioration is only moderately correlated with the cognitive status of patients with AD (Gelinas *et al.*, 1999) and seems to be an expression of other integrative abilities of the individual. This makes functional assessment all the more important in clinical trials since cognitive tests cannot fully gauge improvement in other aspects of the patient's life.

Drug effect in terms of reversibility, stabilization or slower deterioration of ADL can be monitored through the use of functional assessment scales (Gauthier *et al.*, 1997). Different instruments for this purpose have been developed for AD (Table 6), incorporating either basic or instrumental/complex ADLs or both. It is necessary for complex ADL to be incorporated in the examination since functional deterioration occurs in hierarchical order, initially affecting difficult tasks before simpler ones. Ideally, caregiver information should be obtained for data reliability since loss of insight as the disease progresses makes self-report impossible (Table 7).

Neuropsychiatric Symptoms

Neuropsychiatric manifestations are common in AD. They reflect the underlying neuropathological and neurotransmitter changes in the brain. Incidence increases with disease severity but symptoms are variable and differ among afflicted individuals. Assessment of these behavioral manifestations is essential since it can influence the individual's state, further aggravating the existing cognitive and functional impairment. Presence of disruptive behavior increases caregiver burden and is

Table 6. **Comparison of General Characteristics and Reliability of the Different Functional Assessment Scales Utilized in Dementia RCT**

DESCRIPTION OF INSTRUMENT	PSMS AND IADL (LAWTON & BRODY, 1969)	PDS (DEJONG ET AL., 1989)	DAD (GELINAS ET AL., 1999)	ADCS-ADL (GALASKO ET AL., 1997)	ADFACS (MOHS ET AL., 2001)
General characteristic	Caregiver questionnaire	Caregiver questionnaire developed as a measure of QOL changes; bipolar analog scale	Proxy respondent scale (completed either by caregiver as a questionnaire or as a structured interview)	Informant-based questionnaire	Informant-based questionnaire
Population/ Environment	AD/Community and residential care	AD/Not indicated	AD/Community dwelling	AD/Community dwelling	AD/Not indicated
Administration time	Not indicated	10–15 min	<15 min	30–45 min	Not indicated
Gender influence	IADL different for male and females (5 points male; 8 points female)	Not indicated	No influence (including age and education)	Gender biased items removed	No influence
ADL inclusion	Both BADL and IADL	Both BADL and IADL	Both BADL and IADL	Both BADL and IADL	Both BADL and IADL
Number of items (score range)	PSMS: 6 items IADL: 8 items	29 QOL factors (0–100)	40 items (0–100)	24 items (0–78)	16 items (0–54)
Correlation with dementia severity	Not indicated	Yes (GDS)	Yes (MMSE and GDS)	Yes (MMSE)	Not indicated
Reliability	Test/retest: reproducibility coefficient 0.96 Interrater 0.87–0.91 (Pearsonianr)	Test/retest: 0.898 (Pearson product–moment correlation)	Test/retest 0.96 (Intraclass correlation coefficient) Interrater: 0.95 (Intraclass correlation coefficient)	Test/retest: 0.4–0.75 (k statistics)	Not indicated
Special qualities			Evaluates aspects of the activities that are impaired (initiation, planning, organization, effective performance) Nonapplicable domain does not influence scoring since total score is converted into a percentage		

PSMS: Physical Self-Maintenance Scale; BADL: Basic Activities of Daily Living; IADL: Instrumental Activities of Daily Living; PDS: Progressive Deterioration Scale; DAD: Disability Assessment in Dementia; ADCS-ADL: Alzheimer's Disease Cooperative Study–Activities of Daily Living; ADFACS: Alzheimer's Disease Functional Assessment and Change Scale; QOL: Quality of Life.

Table 7. **Functional Assessment Scales Utilized in Different Dementia RCTs as Primary or Secondary Outcome Measures of Efficacy**

FUNCTIONAL ASSESSMENT SCALE	RCT THAT USED SCALE AS PRIMARY OUTCOME MEASURE	RCT THAT USED SCALE AS SECONDARY OUTCOME MEASURE
PSMS and IADL		Feldman *et al.* (2001), Cummings *et al.* (1998), Scharf *et al.* (1999), Thal *et al.* (1996), Davis *et al.* (1992), Knapp *et al.* (1994)
PDS	Corey-Bloom *et al.* (1998), Rosler *et al.* (1999)	Davis *et al.* (1992), Knapp *et al.* (1994), Winblad *et al.* (2001)
DAD		Feldman *et al.* (2001), Raskind *et al.* (2000), Morris *et al.* (1998), Rockwood (2001)
ADCS-ADL	Reisberg *et al.* – adapted to severe state (2003)	Aisen *et al.* (2003), Reines *et al.* (2004), Tariot *et al.* (2000), Petersen *et al.* – MCI version (2005)
ADFACS	Mohs *et al.* (2001)	

PSMS: Physical Self-Maintenance Scale; IADL: Instrumental Activities of Daily Living; PDS: Progressive Deterioration Scale; DAD: Disability Assessment in Dementia; ADCS-ADL: Alzheimer's Disease Cooperative Study–Activities of Daily Living; ADFACS: Alzheimer's Disease Functional Assessment and Change Scale

one of the determinants of eventual nursing home placement. These symptoms can also predate the onset of dementia and may be present in MCI.

Several instruments that measure behavioral symptoms are available and employed in dementia clinical trials. These are used as primary outcome measures when the target symptom is behavior (e.g. with psychotropic agents) and as secondary outcome measures when the target symptom is cognition (e.g. with cholinergic agents) and behavior is evaluated as an auxiliary effect. Characteristically, these can be categorized into broad-spectrum scales when they sample a comprehensive range of symptoms and focused scales when more items are dedicated into the subtleties of a particular behavioral domain (Patterson & Bolger, 1994). Some characterize the symptoms by their frequency and severity which is very helpful in gauging the disruptiveness of the behavior and becomes an indirect measure of caregiver burden. Frequently used assessment scales in dementia clinical trials are the following: Neuropsychiatric Inventory (NPI) (Cummings *et al.*, 1994), Behavioral Pathology in Alzheimer's Disease Rating Scale (BEHAVE-AD) (Reisberg *et al.*, 1996), CERAD Behavior Rating Scale for Dementia (CBRSD) (Tariot *et al.*, 1995), Cohen Mansfield Agitation Inventory (CMAI) (Cohen-Mansfield, 1985), Cornell Scale for Depression in Dementia (CSSD) (Alexopoulos, 1988), Brief Psychiatric Rating Scale (BPRS) (Overall & Gorhal, 1988; Overall & Gorham, 1962) and Positive and Negative Syndrome Scale (PANSS) (Kay *et al.*, 1989) (Table 8).

The NPI, BEHAVE-AD and CBRSD are examples of broad-spectrum scales, developed primarily for the evaluation of dementia patients (Table 8). These are

Table 8. **Comparison of the Characteristics of the NPI, BEHAVE-AD and CBRSD**

INSTRUMENT CHARACTERISTICS	BEHAVE-AD	CBRSD	NPI
Overview	Developed through retrospective review of 57 AD outpatient charts using information from nursing staff, physicians and family members	Items from literature review and expert panel. Some items dram from other scales. Items are homogeneously scaled, anchored. Emphasize frequency rather than severity	Assesses a wide range of behaviors with potential to differentiate between dementia syndromes. Items suggested by expert panel by "Delphi" method. The format used minimizes administration time and optimizes the capture of information
Population	AD outpatients with mild to severe cognitive loss	AD outpatients	Elderly dementia patients
Informant	Caregiver	Caregiver	Caregiver
Administration	Clinician in person or by phone or self-administered	Structured interview by technician	Clinician interview
Administration time	45 min	30 min	20 min
Time interval	2 weeks	1 month (behaviors occurring prior to 1 month but since dementia onset are also noted)	1 month
Items	25 plus 2 global ratings	48	10 items in 5 domains: mood changes (dysphoria, euphoria), agitation (aggression, aberrant motor behavior), personality alterations (apathy/indifference, irritability/lability, disinhibition), psychosis (delusions, hallucinations) and anxiety; sleep and appetite changes included later on
Frequency	No	0 = not since illness began 1 = 1–2 days/past month,	1 = <1 time/week, 2 = 1 time/week, 3 = several

(Continued)

Table 8. **(Continued)**

INSTRUMENT CHARACTERISTICS	BEHAVE-AD	CBRSD	NPI
Severity	Rating differs for each specific item. Includes severity estimates that indirectly consider caregiver impact: absent = 0, mild = 1, moderate = 2, severe = 3	2 = 3–8 days, 3 = 9–15 days, 4 = >16 days, 8 = since illness began, but not in past month	times/week but <1 time/day, 4 = ≥1/day 1 = mild, 2 = moderate, 3 = severe
Caregiver impact	Directly assessed by items 21 and 23 and part II	No	No
Reliability	– Interrater r = 0.90 (severity ratings for scale as a whole) – Reliability of symptom presence or absence = 0.62–1.0	Interrater k = 0.77–1.0 (n = 104)	Interrater r = 0.96–1.0 (frequency), 0.98–1.0 (severity) Test/retest r = 0.79 (frequency), 0.86 (severity) Overall (Cronbach A) r = 0.88
Validity	Has content and construct validity (derived from patient records)	Has construct and content validity; convergent validity with CMAI	Has construct and content validity; convergent validity with Hamilton Rating Scale for Depression (HAM-D) and BEHAVE-AD
Scoring	Total score or in seven domains (paranoid/delusional ideation, hallucinations, activity disturbances, aggressive behavior, sleep disturbance, affective symptoms, anxiety/phobic symptoms)	Initial study suggested eight factors: depressive symptoms, psychotic symptoms, poor self-regulation, irritability/agitation, vegetative features, apathy, aggression, affective lability	For each of the 10 items, total score = frequency × severity
Suggested use	Demonstration of behavioral disturbance and quantification of behavioral effects of antipsychotics or other interventions	Detailed elicitation/quantification of broad range of psychopathology in mild to moderate AD patients	Assessment and quantification of symptoms

Source: Data taken from *Weiner et al.* (1996).

valid and reliable instruments that can be used in clinical and research settings. The NPI is widely used in dementia clinical trials due to its comprehensive list of symptoms that commonly occur in individuals with dementia. It also has accompanying questions for every symptom so that appropriate probing can be done and includes a frequency and severity component for every symptom category. Major dementia RCTs (Aisen *et al.*, 2003; Reisberg *et al.*, 2003; Feldman *et al.*, 2001; Rockwood *et al.*, 2001; Winblad *et al.*, 2001; Tariot *et al.*, 2000; Morris *et al.*, 1998) have used the NPI as a standard gauge of behavior outcome. CBRSD was used in the trial by Sano *et al.* (1997) as a secondary outcome measure. The BEHAVE-AD was more frequently employed in trials involving psychotropic agents (Brodaty *et al.*, 2003; De Deyn *et al.*, 1999; Katz *et al.*, 1999).

The CMAI and CSDD are focused scales. These are useful when particular symptoms are targeted by the clinical trial. For example, the CMAI was used as a primary outcome measure to demonstrate the efficacy of risperidone in agitation and aggression in subjects with AD (Brodaty *et al.*, 2003). The CSDD was likewise the primary outcome measure in the sertraline RCT (Lyketsos *et al.*, 2000) that determined the drug's effect on depression in subjects with AD.

The BPRS and PANSS are broad-spectrum scales that were developed for use in psychiatry populations. These have been employed in several dementia trials involving psychotropic agents since it covers a variety of symptoms aside from psychosis. The BPRS was the primary measure of efficacy for the control of agitation and aggression in dementia in carbamazepine (Tariot *et al.*, 1988) and divalproex sodium RCTs (Porteinsson *et al.*, 2001). The PANSS has five symptomatic dimensions (negative, positive, excitation, cognitive and depression) and the quetiapine trial (Zhong *et al.*, 2004) used the excitation component (PANSS–EC) to evaluate the drug's efficacy in agitation that occurs in dementia.

Other Measures of Efficacy

Aside from treatment efficacy, pharmacoeconomics, caregiver burden and quality of life in dementia have been addressed in dementia RCTs. Although these are not required as outcome measures for drug approval, their usefulness is based on a more practical aspect of efficacy, one that can be seen and experienced in daily life. Caregiver burden scales determine the impact of dementia on the people who are considered direct healthcare providers. They experience stress and burden. One way of determining burden is by recording how much time is spent attending to the patient. This can be assessed using the Caregiver Activities Time Survey, the Caregiver Activity Survey (Davis *et al.*, 1997) or the Caregiver Time Questionnaire (Wimo *et al.*, 1998).

The economic impact of dementia is overwhelming since the burden extends to the national level. It is directly related to the number of people affected by the disorder and the duration of the disease (Whitehouse, 1997). Incurred costs include

(1) medical resources used to treat the illness (medication, cost of institutionalization, etc.), (2) nonmedical resources and (3) lost productivity caused by disability (both patient and caregiver) (Whitehouse, 1997). Since maintenance of patients with dementia eventually translates into cost of care, some RCTs include pharmacoeconomic measures. The AD2000 trial (AD2000 Collaborative Group, 2004) determined the healthcare cost of dementia from the societal perspective in terms of delaying institutionalization or requiring other health services and the cost-effectiveness of the drug (donepezil). Reisberg *et al.* (2003) similarly evaluated post-benefit by utilizing the Resource Utilization in Dementia (RUD) (Winblad *et al.*, 2000), which assesses the burden on the caregiver and provides AD-related health economics data, in a memantine trial.

Quality of life scales encompass the overall effect of the treatment on the patient in terms of social, psychological, cognitive and functional well being. Either the patient or caregiver's quality of life can be assessed. However, information will be derived mainly from the caregiver once the patient's communication and insight problems emerge.

Transcultural application of these instruments may alter their validity and reliability. Interpretation of results should therefore be done with caution when these are used outside the cultures in which they were developed.

Clinical Trial Designs

The US FDA requires that agents tested should be superior to placebo in terms of its cognitive and global effects. The standard format of antidementia drug RCTs is the parallel group design wherein there is direct comparison between the experimental and placebo group. In this comparison, the active drug and placebo are allocated to different subjects randomly. The 12-week tacrine study by Farlow *et al.* (1992) utilized this design, although randomization of subjects was stratified. AD drug trials (acetylcholinesterase inhibitors, NMDA antagonists, psychotopics, SSRIs, etc.) follow this standard format due to its straightforward approach. This design was also used in the MCI trial of Salloway *et al.* (2004), comparing donepezil with placebo. Between-patient variability can deleteriously affect the outcome of parallel group studies and cannot be eliminated with this format. The crossover design eradicates this confounding variable by applying the treatment sequentially to the same subject. Aside from reducing error variance, sample size is diminished since subjects can be used several times in the analysis while increasing the statistical power of the clinical trial. However, this strategy is rarely used primarily due to difficulty in re-obtaining baseline values during the treatment shift in patients with a progressive disorder. There is also uncertainty if the changes noted with the second treatment are due to the remaining or carry over effect of the first one. The required washout periods of the drugs are unknown and may be lengthy.

The current trend in antidementia drug development is toward disease modification. The above cited study designs are adequate for measuring symptomatic change (has no effect in the survival and function of degenerating neurons) and are less applicable to assessing disease modification. A variety of trial designs have been suggested to assist in establishing disease-modifying effects. Paul Leber (Leber, 1997) suggested the randomized-withdrawal and randomized-start designs to determine the disease-modifying effect of the antidementia drug (Figures 1 and 2). The randomized-withdrawal design (Figure 1) is based on the hypothesis that withdrawal of a disease-modifying drug will not produce loss of the incremental changes noted compared to the withdrawal of a symptomatic drug. The major drawback of this design is the uncertainty as to how long the subjects need to be observed to determine the outcome. Consequently, it will require a

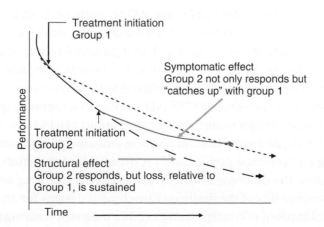

Fig. 1.
Randomized withdrawal design (adapted from Leber *et al*. (1997)).

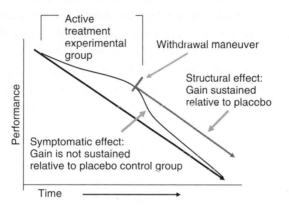

Fig. 2.
Randomized start design (adapted from Leber *et al*. (1997)).

considerable number of subjects since attrition is expected to be high secondary to the length of the trial and withdrawal of a treatment that may be beneficial to the subject. Blinding is also compromised since everyone becomes aware that all patients are taking placebo at the end of the trial. These potential limitations led to the formulation of the staggered start design (Figure 2) which has two phases: the first is similar to a placebo-controlled, randomized, parallel study while the second entails all subjects to be given the active treatment. A significant drug–placebo difference should be apparent after the first phase before the second phase can be started. If the active drug has a disease-modifying effect, the placebo group's performance cannot catch up with that of the treatment group in the second phase of the study.

Sano *et al.* (1996), utilized a time-oriented, valid-outcome measure to assess disease progression that includes the main domains affected in AD – cognition and function. The survival design examines the longitudinal course of dementia to measure the antidementia drug effect on disease progression. Endpoints are not based primarily on neuropsychological tests, unlike in other trial designs. Instead, readily observable, clinically meaningful endpoints that represent disease progression are utilized. The primary efficacy outcome measure is the time to reach specified endpoints. Similarly, Mohs *et al.* (2001) used a survival design to evaluate the length of time the function is preserved in AD patients with the use of donepezil.

Amnestic MCI lends itself to use of survival designs since longitudinal examination of patients can reveal either progression or nonprogression to AD. Most MCI clinical trials used this study design with progression to AD as the endpoint (Petersen *et al.*, 2005; http://www.alz.org/news/05q1/012405.asp). A limitation of this scheme is the difficulty in defining precisely progression to AD.

An enrichment design was utilized in the tacrine study of Davis *et al.* (1992). The first or enrichment phase consisted of finding the "best dose" response of each patient to tacrine as defined by the ADAS without producing intolerable side effects. Subjects who continued in the subsequent parallel group RCT were the "enriched population" or those who had a potential to respond to the treatment as seen in the first phase of the study. RCTs which include subjects who have a higher risk of acquiring AD such as those with positive family history, presence of ApoE4 alleles, presence of CSF AD biomarkers, hippocampal atrophy on magnetic resonance imaging/computed tomography (MRI/CT) scan or bilateral temporo-parietal hypometabolism on positron emission tomography (PET) scan are recruiting an "enriched population". A drawback of this study design is the potential to skew the outcome favorably toward the active drug and in the end, limit the generalizability of the findings. Enrichment designs for an antidementia drug are useful in proof of concept studies or as a means of entering the market by showing evidence of efficacy. However, it should be followed by a trial that employs less restrictive designs so as not to limit the generalizability of findings.

Special Clinical Trial Design Features

Long-term drug trials may incorporate special design features to improve accuracy of findings and to confirm additional hypotheses. Single blind run ins added before initiation of the double blind phase involve administration of placebo to both treatment groups for a specified period of time without the knowledge of subjects and caregivers. Its primary aim is to minimize the "placebo effect" to which the initial changes from baseline may be contributed. By doing this, both groups equally start at the same level. The galantamine efficacy and safety trials utilized this feature (Rockwood *et al.*, 2001; Raskind *et al.*, 2000; Tariot *et al.*, 2000).

Single blind washout periods are sometimes done at the end of the double blind treatment. This entails administration of placebo to both treatment groups in an effort to determine the withdrawal effect of the study drug. In the donepezil trials (Rogers *et al.*, 1998a, b), the washout periods showed the return of the performance of the donepezil group to baseline values – an indication that the observed improvement after drug administration was a symptomatic and not a disease-modifying effect. This is also useful for the assessment of untoward reactions secondary to drug removal and to gain information on how long the clinical response is sustained after drug discontinuation.

Open label extensions conducted after the double blind study is a method of determining safety of prolonged treatment. Limited efficacy data are collected in open label extensions.

Randomization

Randomization allocates subjects to treatment arms wherein each arm is exposed to a different condition. Usually only two arms are employed in phase III trials: experimental and control. In Phase II or when several treatment doses are being considered, additional treatment arms become necessary. For example, in the MCI trial by Petersen *et al.* (2005), three arms were utilized and subjects received either (1) 2000IU of Vitamin E daily, (2) 10 mg of donepezil daily or (3) placebo. Sano *et al.* (1997) likewise expanded the treatment allocation by means of a 2×2 factorial design to further examine treatment combinations. Four treatment arms were used: (1) selegiline and A-tocopherol, (2) placebo and A-tocopherol, (3) selegiline and placebo and (4) placebo only. Multiple treatment arms are used to compare response to different dosages of the drug (Rockwood *et al.*, 2001; Winblad *et al.*, 2001; Mulnard *et al.*, 2000; Raskind *et al.*, 2000; Tariot *et al.*, 2000; Corey-Bloom *et al.*, 1998; Rogers *et al.*, 1998a, b).

Length of Clinical Trials

Duration of the trial and number of recruited patients are very important factors that contribute to the validity of the outcomes of the RCT's. Duration of phases II and III should be long enough to ensure that the efficacy and safety of the drug are adequately explored. Efficacy of antidementia drugs cannot be seen before 3 months of drug exposure and may be evident only after 6 months. Although longer duration (>6 months) is ideal, the number of subjects completing the study and their compliance are concerns in longer studies.

Adequate clinical trial length is essential in demonstrating treatment effect in a progressively deteriorating disorder. Drug effect (symptomatic versus disease-modifying), target symptoms (cognitive versus noncognitive/behavioral) and outcome measures (biological versus assessment scales) are important factors that should be considered in determining the trial length. Trials with insufficient duration can yield inaccurate and potentially misleading results in view of the fact that small but important changes from baseline may remain undetected. Longer trials ($\geqslant 1$ year) are ideal considering the chronicity of the disorder being examined but ethical, attrition and compliance problems may be encountered which could compromise study interpretation. Winblad *et al.* (2001) conducted the first published long-term (1 year) efficacy and safety study of donepezil on AD while the AD2000 trial (AD2000 Collaborative Group, 2004) has extended the duration to 2 years. Most trials involving agents that may have a neuroprotective or disease-modifying effect are conducted for 12 to 18 months (Table 4) since time must be allotted for their structural effect to become apparent.

Neuropsychiatric symptoms are encountered throughout the spectrum of dementia and may even herald its onset. Numerous studies have been conducted involving psychotropics (typical and atypical), anticonvulsants (carbamazepine and valproate) and antidepressants (Selective Serotonin Reuptake Inhibitors, SSRI's) to determine which agent alleviates these symptoms. Patterns of analysis may either be (1) reduction in emergence of behavioral symptoms wherein asymptomatic patients are followed up longitudinally to determine which regimen has fewer symptoms at endpoint or (2) comparing which regimen produced more change/reduction in the behavioral symptoms from baseline to endpoint. The length of the trials is notably shorter than those addressing cognitive symptoms, ranging from 6 to 12 weeks, since acute symptomatic improvement is the goal.

Statistical Analyses

Subject noncompliance and dropouts complicate clinical trial interpretations. These subjects cannot be excluded from analysis since they may have demographic or disease characteristics that are different from those who completed the trial and adhered to the treatment randomly assigned to them. It is for this reason that most clinical trials use the intention-to-treat (ITT) principle which provides unbiased and reliable interpretation of treatment effect. Intention-to-treat analyses typically include all subjects who were randomized to treatment, received at least one study drug dose and provided a baseline assessment and at least one post-baseline assessment. It is a conservative method that makes it possible for the potential treatment benefit on patients to be evaluated regardless of whether or not they completed the study. With this, the random assignment of subjects to treatment groups is preserved during data analysis and potential bias is observed (Koepsell & Weiss, 2003). This differs from the fully evaluable (case; OC) population analysis wherein those who completed the entire study analyzed.

Analysis of longitudinal data can be problematic since missing data are evident. Different methods of statistical analysis have been adopted to treat these data sets. The most widely used technique that addresses missing data is the Last Observation Carried Forward (LOCF). LOCF is a method in which the subject's last available assessment is imputed for all remaining unobserved response measurements. It has the advantage of preserving the sample size but it presumes that the subjects' responses have been constant from the last observed value to the trial endpoint. This unwarranted assumption about the missing data may result in either under-estimating or overestimating the treatment effects. Type I errors can be generated from this so that a treatment difference can be falsely endorsed when in fact there is none. Despite these caveats, the method is frequently used due to its simplicity and ease of implementation and relatively conservative method of treating data. Newer regression models are being developed as alternatives to LOCF approaches.

OC analysis utilizes only the data of subjects remaining in the trial at a specified point in time. In this method, a direct relationship of the data used and the obtained results is observed. However, loss of power and subsequent validity of results may occur since data of the noncompleters are unexploited. Results that are statistically significant for both types of analysis clearly support their accuracy. Conversely, cautious interpretation of results should be done when results are significant only in the OC analysis.

All statistical analysis should be planned in detail prior to the initiation of the clinical trial since changes afterwards may introduce bias in the system. However, changes that are made prior to breaking of the blind still have limited implications for study interpretation. Analyses that are conducted afterwards (post hoc) are less compelling. This also applies for specification of subgroup analysis which is done on the basis of an expectation of a larger treatment effect in some subgroups than in others (Koepsell & Weiss, 2003).

Clinical trials with survival data require different statistical treatment since subjects have varying endpoints producing asymmetries in data distribution. If the data from the subjects who did not make it to the endpoint are excluded, bias may be introduced into the results. Studies using the survival design have three general objectives: to estimate the time-to-event, to compare the time-to-event between/among the groups and to determine the relationship of the co-variables to the time-to-event. The hazard ratio and survival time are two important functions that are examined to generate the answers to these questions (Everitt & Pickler, 2004). The Cox proportional-hazards regression and Kaplan Meier analysis were used to evaluate these, respectively, in the trials of Mohs *et al.* (2001), Sano *et al.* (1997) and Petersen *et al.* (2005). The Cox proportional-hazards model controls for any bias in the predetermined covariates among the treatment arms since these change over time. It is used to estimate the hazard ratio which is the risk of progression to an event over time in the treatment group versus the placebo group. The Kaplan–Meier method provides survival time estimates to clinically evident decline or to a chosen event (e.g. death, institutionalization or loss of the ability to perform basic ADL).

An adequate sample size ensures that treatment effect can be reliably derived from the clinical trial at a specified endpoint. For ethical reasons, the sample size should be well justified; samples too small or too large are not warranted. Factors that affect sample size determination are the power of the study to detect a drug–placebo difference and the chosen level of significance of the statistical tests. Confounders and attrition rate should be considered in sample size determination for which it should be adjusted appropriately.

The study should have enough "power" to accurately detect the smallest possible difference in the primary outcome measure that has clinical significance produced by the treatment. Power is usually set at 80% so that there is a 20% probability of missing the difference between the treatment and placebo group. Some clinical trials use a power of 90% to further reduce the chance of a false negative result. The level of significance or "p" value is the probability of incorrectly identifying a treatment difference between the treatment and placebo arm when actually there is none (false positive result). By convention, a value of ≤ 0.05 is frequently used. Sample size is inversely proportional to the chosen level of significance while it is directly proportional to the power of the study.

Sample size calculation is based on the primary outcome measure and how much change is required to produce a clinically meaningful effect. Previous phases II and III clinical trials and longitudinal studies establish these changes. For example, in the ADAS-cog a 4-point change is utilized for 6-month trials and 7-point change for 1-year trials for clinically significant change to be detected (Doraiswamy *et al.*, 2001). For the CIBIC-plus a 0.3–0.4 change is usually targeted (Feldman *et al.*, 2001; Rogers *et al.*, 1998a). In the 1-year study of Mohs *et al.* (2001) where preservation of function was determined as an effect of donepezil, power was calculated based on functional performance that is, the 1-year value for significant functional decline in the placebo and donepezil group based on a previous study. Most base the power of the study on one of the primary outcomes (either ADAS-cog or the global assessment) while some base it on dual outcomes (both ADAS-cog and global assessment) (Cummings *et al.*, 1998; Morris *et al.*, 1998).

Drug–Placebo Difference

The drug–placebo difference is the discrepancy between the deterioration of the placebo group and the improvement, stabilization or reduced deterioration in the treatment group (Cummings, 2003). It is derived by determining the difference between the mean change from baseline scores of the actively treated and placebo groups at a specified endpoint. The FDA requires proof of efficacy in terms of statistically significant improvement on specified outcome measures in the treatment group.

The effect size is the definitive basis of a drug's efficacy. It is determined by dividing the drug–placebo difference by the standard deviation using specific outcome measures.

A summary of the drug–placebo differences of the RCTs in MCI and AD based on outcome measures can be seen in Tables 9, 10 and 11. The drug–placebo difference varies among the studies and among the class of therapeutic agents. The range of treatment effect produced by acetylcholinesterase inhibitors in the ADAS-cog is 2–3.9 and 0.2–0.47 in the global assessment scales among subjects with mild to moderate AD. Among the other class of therapeutic agents, only Ginkgo biloba (Le Bars *et al.*, 1997) produced significant drug–placebo difference in the ADAS-cog but this was not supported by the global evaluation.

Table 9. **Drug–placebo differences on the ADAS-cog and Global Assessment Scales among the various therapeutic RCTs in mild cognitive impairment and Alzheimer's disease (intent-to-treat analyses – except Farlow *et al.*)**

AGENT/STUDY	ADAS-COG		GLOBAL ASSESSMENT SCALE (CGI, CGIC, CIBIC-PLUS)	
	D/P DIFFERENCE	SIGNIFICANCE (*P* VALUE)	D/P DIFFERENCE	SIGNIFICANCE (*P* VALUE)
MILD TO MODERATE ALZHEIMER'S DISEASE				
Tacrine				
Farlow *et al.*[a] (1992)				
20 mg	0.9	NS	0	NS
40 mg	1.4	NS	0.1	NS
80 mg	3.8	0.015	0.5	0.015
Davis *et al.* (1992)	2.4	<0.001	NR	NS
40 or 80 mg				
Knapp *et al.* (1994)				
80 mg	1.4	NS	0.1	NS
120 mg	2	0.008	0.2	0.04
160 mg	2.2	0.002	0.2	0.04
Donepezil				
Rogers *et al.* (1998b)				
5 mg	2.49	<0.0001	0.36	0.0047
10 mg	2.88	<0.0001	0.44	0.0001

(*Continued*)

Table 9. **(Continued)**

AGENT/STUDY	ADAS–COG		GLOBAL ASSESSMENT SCALE (CGI, CGIC, CIBIC–PLUS)	
	D/P DIFFERENCE	SIGNIFICANCE (*P* VALUE)	D/P DIFFERENCE	SIGNIFICANCE (*P* VALUE)
MILD TO MODERATE ALZHEIMER'S DISEASE				
Rogers *et al.* (1998a)				
5 mg	2.5	<0.001	0.3	0.003
10 mg	3.1	<0.001	0.4	0.008
Galantamine				
Tariot *et al.* (2000)				
16 mg	3.1	<0.001	0.41	<0.001
24 mg	3.1	<0.001	0.44	<0.001
Raskind *et al.* (2000)				
24 mg	3.9	<0.001	0.28	<0.01
32 mg	3.4	<0.001	0.29	<0.05
Rockwood *et al.* (2001) 24 or 32 mg	1.7	<0.01	NR	0.01
Rivastigmine				
Corey-Bloom *et al.* (1998)				
1–4 mg	1.73	NR	0.26	NR
6–12 mg	3.78	<0.001	0.29	<0.01
Rosler *et al.* (1999)				
1–4 mg	0.03	NS	0.14	NS
6–12 mg	1.6	NS	0.47	<0.001
Metrifonate				
Cummings *et al.* (1998)				
10–20 mg	1.5	0.02	0.04	NS
15–25 mg	1.3	NS	0.29	0.005
30–60 mg	2.94	0.0001	0.35	0.0007
Morris *et al.* (1998) 30–60 mg	2.86	0.0001	0.28	0.0071
Mulnard *et al.* (2000) Estrogen 0.625 or 1.25 mg/day		2	NS	0.1 NS
Le Bars *et al.* (1997) Ginkgo biloba 120 mg/day				
(a) AD and MID	1.4	0.04	0	NS
(b) AD only	1.7	0.02	0	NS
Reines *et al.* (2004) Rofecoxib 25 mg/day	0.6	NS	0.03	NS
Scharf *et al.* (1999) Diclofenac/Misoprostol	1.14	NS	0.24	NS

Note: Only studies with complete data are included.
ADAS-cog: Alzheimer's Disease Assessment Scale; Global Assessment Scales: CGI-Clinical Global Impression; CIBI-Clinical Interview Based Impression; CIBIC-plus: Clinical Interview Based Impression of Change plus caregiver information; CGIC: Clinical Global Impression of Change Sig: Significant; NS: Not significant; NR: Not reported
[a]Evaluable-Population Analysis.

Table 10. **Drug–Placebo Differences on the MMSE among Various Therapeutic RCTs in MCI and AD (Intent-to-Treat Analyses – Except Farlow *et al.*)**

AGENT/STUDY	MMSE	
	D/P DIFFERENCE	SIGNIFICANCE *P* VALUE
MILD TO MODERATE ALZHEIMER'S DISEASE		
Tacrine		
Farlow *et al.*[a] (1992)		
20 mg	0.1	NS
40 mg	0.4	NS
80 mg	0.7	NS
Davis *et al.* (1992)		
40 or 80 mg	0.7	NS
Knapp *et al.* (1994)		
80 mg	0.6	NS
120 mg	0.4	NS
160 mg	0.9	0.02
Donepezil		
Rogers *et al.* (1998b)		
5 mg	1.21	0.0007
10 mg	1.36	0.0002
Rogers *et al.* (1998a)		
5 mg	0.96	<0.004
10 mg	1.26	<0.001
Mohs *et al.* (2001)		
10 mg	NR	NS
Winblad *et al.* (2001)		
10 mg	NR	Sig
Rivastigmine		
Rosler *et al.* (1999)		
1–4 mg	0.15	NR
6–12 mg	0.68	<0.05
Metrifonate		
Cummings *et al.* (1998)		
10–20 mg	1.11	0.003
15–25 mg	0.63	NS
30–60 mg	1.37	0.003
Morris *et al.* (1998)		
30–60 mg	0.43	NS
Sano *et al.* (1997)		
Vitamin E, Selegiline or both	NR	NS
Mulnard *et al.* (2000)		
Estrogen 0.625 or 1.25 mg/day	0.4	NS
Thal *et al.* (1996)		
acetyl-L-carnitine 3g/day	0.4	NS
Reines *et al.* (2004)		
Rofecoxig 25 mg/day	0.44	NS
Scharf *et al.* (1999)		
Diclofenac/Misoprostol	1.37	NS
Donepezil Feldman *et al.* (2001)[b]		
10 mg	1.79	<0.0001

(Continued)

Table 10. **(Continued)**

AGENT/STUDY	MMSE	
	D/P DIFFERENCE	SIGNIFICANCE P VALUE
MILD TO MODERATE ALZHEIMER'S DISEASE		
Memantine Reisberg *et al.* (2003)		
20 mg	0.7	NS
Donepezil Petersen *et al.* (2005)		
10 mg	0.44	NS

Note: Only studies with complete data are included.
MMSE: Mini-Mental State Examination; Sig: Significant; NS: Not significant; NR: Not reported.
[a]Evaluable-Population Analysis.
[b]sMMSE: Standardized Mini-Mental State Examination.

Table 11. **Comparative Effects of Therapeutic Agents in AD Clinical Trials on the ADAS-cog and MMSE at 6 Months (Intent-to-Treat Analyses Except Farlow *et al.*)**

AGENT/RCT	TREATMENT DURATION (WEEKS)	ADAS–COG DRUG–PLACEBO DIFFERENCE	MMSE DRUG–PLACEBO DIFFERENCE
Metrifonate			
Morris *et al.* (1998)	26	2.86	
30–60 mg			
Tacrine			
Knapp *et al.* (1994)	30		
80 mg		2.2	0.8
120 mg		3.1	0.9
160 mg		4.2	2.5
Donepezil			
Winblad *et al.* (2001)	52		1.4
10 mg			
Rivastigmine			
Rosler *et al.* (1999)	26		
1–4 mg		0.03	0.15
6–12 mg		1.6	0.68
Corey-Bloom *et al.* (1998)	26		
Galantamine			
Raskind *et al.* (2000)	52		
24 mg		3.9	
32 mg		3.4	
Ginkgo biloba			
Le Bars *et al.* (1997)	52	1.33	
Estrogen			
Mulnard *et al.* (2000)	52	1.3	0.7

Note: Included trials have duration of ⩾6 months and either have data at 6 months or have graphs from which data can be extrapolated.

Placebo Responses

Use of a placebo arm in an RCT is a standard procedure as long as it is ethical and feasible. Comparison of drug–placebo outcomes determines the investigational

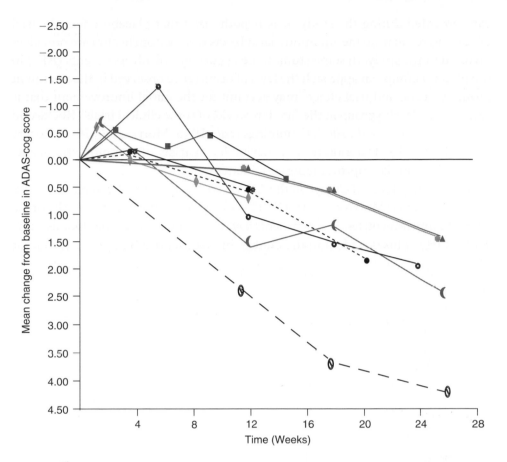

Fig. 3.

Mean change from baseline (intent-to-treat analyses) in the ADAS-cog scores of the placebo groups of different acetylcholinesterase inhibitor clinical trials with duration of 3–6 months in mild to moderate AD (mean change from baseline derived from available data while other values were extrapolated from the graphs).

▲ Raskind *et al.* (2000)	✤ Rosler *et al.* (1999)	◖ Morris *et al.* (1998)
▪▪▪● Tariot *et al.* (2000)	○ Rogers *et al.* (1998b)	◆ Cummings *et al.* (1998)
✻ Rockwood *et al.* (2001)	■ Rogers *et al.* (1998a)	◍ Rosler *et al.* (1998)

drug's efficacy. In AD, it is expected that an efficacious drug will produce improvement or stabilization in primary assessments while the placebo group continues its course of deterioration.

Irregularities in the placebo response are apparent in some clinical trials (Figure 3). Factors that contribute to this effect are fluctuation of the symptoms, methodological inconsistencies and the beneficial effects of improved medical care provided during the study. It is hypothesized that placebo effects or trial effects can result from the attention that subjects receive from healthcare providers involved in the study. In some studies, the occurrence of adverse events (AEs) in the placebo group can approach the level of occurrence observed in the treatment group. Placebo and trial effects may account for the initial improvement that is seen in the placebo group in the first few weeks of some clinical trials (Rockwood *et al.*, 2001; Tariot *et al.*, 2000; Cummings *et al.*, 1998; Morris *et al.*, 1998; Rogers *et al.*, 1998a, b). Deterioration is inevitable, in trials of symptomatic agents despite these initial improvements and fluctuations.

The expected rate of change in the ADAS-cog scores annually in patients with AD is 7–8 points (Morris *et al.*, 1993). This varies depending on the severity of the cognitive impairment; less severe patients have a slower rate of decline (Doraiswamy *et al.*, 2001). This is evident in the Ginkgo biloba trial (Le Bars *et al.*, 1997), for

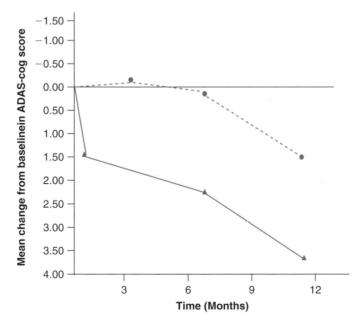

Fig. 4.

Mean change from baseline (intent-to-treat analyses) in the ADAS-cog scores of the placebo groups of two 1-year clinical trials involving estrogen replacement and Ginkgo biloba (mean change from baseline derived from available data while other values were extrapolated from the graphs). Patients in the estrogen clinical trial had an MMSE range of 14–28 while those in the Ginkgo biloba trial had an MMSE range of 9–26. (━▲━ Mulnard *et al.* (2000); ▪▪▪▪▪ Le Bars, *et al.* (1997)). (Other trials not included due to unavailable mean ADAS-cog scores of change from baseline along the course of the trial.)

example, which included subjects with a lower range of MMSE scores and higher magnitude of decline compared to those in the estrogen trial which included subjects with higher MMSE scores (Figure 4).

Attrition and Adverse Effects

Clinical trials suffer from subject dropout and the effects of attrition must be anticipated in trial design. Dropouts are AEs, due to refusal to follow up, lack of efficacy, violation of study protocol and presence of AEs.

Diminution of the subject pool is expected as the length of the trial is increased due to dropouts. Attrition is a potential problem because each dropout is equivalent to lost data which may eventually lead to inadequate sample or worse, skewing of the outcomes. Selective attrition can produce changes in the subject pool so that it inadvertently becomes unrepresentative of the subjects originally entered into the study. Results become unreliable in this setting.

AEs are another cause of subject dropout. AEs are defined as newly emergent events/symptoms occurring after the first dose of the study drug or clinically significant worsening of a pre-existing condition after the first dose of the study drug. Treatment emergent signs and symptoms (TESS) is another term that is frequently used to indicate AEs. A serious adverse event (SAE) pertains to any event that is considered life threatening or resulting in hospitalization, permanent disability or death. Occurrence of a serious AE that is deemed related to drug exposure may be grounds for withdrawal of a drug that is already released in the market. Clinical trials include tolerability and safety studies critical to determining any AEs that may occur with a drug.

Both the active treatment and placebo group experience AEs and all are reported whether these are deemed related or not related to the drug exposure. AEs range from incidental symptoms, part of the inherent deterioration of the disorder, secondary to existent medical disorder or related to drug exposure. Subject variability may account for the assortment of symptoms encountered as AEs and they can be observed among placebo groups as well as active intervention groups (Table 12).

Most AEs in acetylcholinesterase inhibitor trials are causally related to the drug's mechanism of action. Cholinergic manifestations are usually transient and mild, although some may be moderate in severity. These are dose related and studies which utilized a forced titration rate increased cholinergic AEs in subjects (Morris *et al.*, 1998; Rogers *et al.*, 1998a). In comparison, those that employed a longer dosage titration schedule had lower incidence of these AEs and better drug tolerability (Rogers *et al.*, 1998b).

Deaths occur during clinical trials. The probability of mortality is increased in a dementia trial due to an expected lower survival rate in this population and the age

Table 12. **Gastrointestinal and Selected Other Adverse Events in the Placebo Group (In Percent of Occurrence) of Acetylcholinesterase Inhibitors (donepezil, rivastigmine and galantamine) in Mild to Moderate Alzheimer's Disease Clinical Trials**

ADVERSE EVENTS	DONEPEZIL				RIVASTIGMINE	GALANTAMINE		
	ROGERS ET AL. (1998A)	ROGERS ET AL. (1998B)	WINBLAD ET AL. (2001)	MOHS ET AL. (2001)	ROSLER ET AL. (1999)	ROCKWOOD ET AL. (2001)	TARIOT ET AL. (2000)	RASKIND ET AL. (2000)
Anorexia		2		6	2	2.4	3.1	5.6
Nausea	8	4		9	10	11.2	4.5	13.1
Vomiting		2			6	4	1.4	7.5
Abdominal pain			5.6		3	1.6		4.2
Diarrhea	3	7	6.9	17	9		5.9	9.9
Constipation			6.3					
Dyspepsia				6				
Weight loss				6		0.8		4.7
Agitation				13			9.4	
Confusion			6.3					
Insomnia			6.9	8				
Somnolence						0.8		
Dizziness	8	4	4.2		7	4		11.3
Headache			6.3	9	8			
Fatigue		2			3			
Syncope			2.8					
Vertigo			2.1					
Anxiety			5.6					
Depression			7.6					
Asthenia			3.5	7				
Urinary tract infection	13		6.9	13				

Note: Included are AEs with rate of occurrence that differed by at least 5% between the treatment group and the placebo.

of the subjects included. Deaths have been rare in most trials and were judged to be unrelated to drug exposure.

Presenting Clinical Trial Results

The CONSORT statement was developed in 1996 (Begg *et al.*, 1996) with the purpose of improving the accuracy of conducting and reporting RCTs. This obligates investigators to provide transparency as to the details of the trial from recruitment of subjects to its results. By following the CONSORT criteria, investigators are more likely to conduct ethical trials and produce valid, unbiased results. CONSORT criteria make it easier for readers to evaluate and understand the RCTs and there is an assurance that the results can be relied upon. Inadequate reporting of RCTs has led to biased interpretation of results with overestimation or underestimation of treatment effects. Currently, a 22-item CONSORT checklist and a flow diagram are available for use and these are constantly updated and modified (Moher *et al.*, 2001).

Table 13 shows how CONSORT criteria can be applied to trials of AD and MCI.

Disease-Modifying Trials

Disease-modifying drugs have emerged as the focus of dementia drug development. The methodological strategies of clinical trials involving this class of therapeutic agent may differ from those involving symptomatic agents since the former target the neurodegenerative process of AD. Patients in the early stage of AD should ideally be included since they will receive the most benefit from disease intervention. Evidence of disease course alteration can be established in longer trials (i.e. $\geqslant 1$ year) since the natural progression of AD needs to be observed. This will also ensure that the treatment effect is not due to disease fluctuation that is present in AD. A larger sample population is necessary since attrition rate is expectedly higher in clinical trials with longer duration. Outcome measures other than neuropsychological tests such as biomarkers need to be employed to support the disease-modifying effect of the therapeutic agent. Use of biomarkers as surrogate endpoints can also reduce the required sample size and the duration of clinical trial, saving on time and resources. Pharmacoeconomic measures should be integrated to justify long-term societal benefits from the drug.

Acknowledgment

The authors wish to acknowledge Lynn Fairbanks, Ph.D., a Professor of the Department of Psychiatry and Biobehavioral Sciences, UCLA, for her special contribution in the statistical section of this manuscript.

Table 13. **Features of Current MCI and AD RCT As These are Adapted to the CONSORT Checklist**

PAPER SECTION AND TOPIC	ITEM	EXAMPLES OF FEATURES OF MCI AND DEMENTIA TRIALS
Title and abstract	1	Intervention stated (duration of the trial sometimes included) in randomized, double blind, placebo-controlled study
Introduction Background	2	Basis for the trial of intervention in human subjects. Examples: Cholinergic hypothesis for AchEIs/ Glutaminergic excitotoxicity via NMDA receptor for memantine/Oxidative damage and free radical generation for antioxidants/Inflammatory response for prednisone and NSAIDS/estrogen replacement
Methods Participants	3	Subjects of both sexes, any race, ≥50 years old (or other age range), no significant medical disorder, adequate hearing and vision for testing, recruited from community/ nursing home/other institutions, ambulant/or assisted Diagnosis of MCI, AD, VaD based on criteria (Petersen *et al.* for MCI; NINDS–AIREN for VaD; NINCDS–ADRDA for AD) Severity of dementia specified via MMSE range or through other measures (e.g. CDR) Acceptable concomitant medications Exclusion of those with contraindication to the administration of the intervention Thorough discussion of approval by ethical board, if ethical standards are met and how consent is taken Multicenter involving tertiary centers with adequate facilities and personnel trained to diagnose, treat and handle MCI and dementia cases
Interventions	4	Placebo and interventional drug compared via parallel-group trial; treatment arms specified Fixed dose/dose titration/titration sequence if it is a dose-finding study Pill distribution (both placebo and interventional drug) including time
Objectives	5	Efficacy and safety of intervention Time to reach an endpoint (cognitive and/or functional deterioration)
Outcomes	6	Primary and secondary outcome measures assessing cognitive, global, functional states and/or quality of life Intervals of assessment stated, including endpoint
Sample size	7	Derived through power analysis (usually power of 80% with a specified alpha value) Based on review of clinical studies of drugs of the same class and results of earlier phase II studies Determined using the primary efficacy variable to achieve a certain power; estimate based on clinically relevant change in the score of the said variable from baseline
Randomization (sequence allocation/ allocation concealment/ Implementation)	8–10	Sequence allocation by simple/blocked or stratified randomization Via computer-generated randomization list by the pharmaceutical company

Table 13. **(Continued)**

PAPER SECTION AND TOPIC	ITEM	EXAMPLES OF FEATURES OF MCI AND DEMENTIA TRIALS
Blinding (masking)	11	Double blind with occasional inclusion of single blind run-in or single blind wash-out
Statistical methods	12	*Efficacy*: Drug–placebo difference between baseline and endpoint in specified outcome measures using least squares (LS) mean Statistical analysis used specified for both categorical and continuous variables ITT or PP (LOCF and OC): population defined Fully evaluable population (EP): population defined Survival analysis *Safety*: Included data defined (e.g. All patients who received at least one dose of study medications and who provided any post baseline follow-up data) Incidence of AEs or TESS compared among the treatment arms
Results Participant flow	13	Diagram of the number of subjects in every stage of the trial (enrollment, intervention, allocation, follow-up and analysis)
Recruitment	14	Recruitment period specified
Baseline data	15	Demographic and clinical characteristics of the population allocated to placebo and intervention shown Comparison made between the groups to determine any significant difference in the characteristics that may contribute to biased outcome
Numbers analyzed	16	Number of subjects who were included in each analysis (dependent on type of analysis, e.g. ITT, LOCF and OC)
Outcomes and estimation	17	Effect size based on clinically meaningful change produced by the intervention Statistically significant D/P difference based on each of the primary and secondary efficacy variables (level of significance specified) For survival studies: statistically significant difference between placebo and intervention in delaying the time to reach an endpoint
Ancilllary analyses	18	Subgroup analysis based on certain features of the subjects where efficacy of the drug may be different (e.g. Early onset versus late onset)
Adverse events	19	Including serious AEs and any deaths Determination if occurrence is beyond acceptable limit and if there is association with exposure to intervention
Discussion Interpretation	20	Interpretation and explanation of positive and/or negative results
Generalizability	21	Limitations of the study that will limit its application to the targeted population in a community setting (e.g. differential recruitment in terms of race, highly specialized centers, etc.)
Overall evidence	22	Evidence-based conclusion regarding efficacy and safety of intervention in the subset of patients studied Recommendations in future studies

References

A Randomized Double-Blind, Placebo-Controlled Trial to Evaluate the Efficacy and Safety of Galantamine in Subjects with Mild Cognitive Impairment (MCI) Clinically at Risk for Development of Clinically Probably Alzheimer's Disease. Gal-INT-18 and Gal-INT-11. http://www.alz.org/news/05q1/012405.asp. Accessed on November 17, 2005.

AD2000 Collaborative Group (2004). Long term donepezil treatment in 565 patients with Alzheimer's disease (AD2000): randomized double-blind trial. *Lancet*, 353, 2105–2115.

Aisen, P., Davis, K., Berg, J., *et al.* (2000). A randomized controlled trial of prednisone in Alzheimer's disease. *Neurology*, 54, 588–593.

Aisen, P., Schafer, K., Grundman, M., *et al.* (2003). Effects of rofecoxib or naproxen vs. placebo on Alzheimer disease progression. *Journal of the American Medical Association*, 289, 2819–2826.

Alexopoulos, G., Abrams, R., Young, R., *et al.* (1988). Cornell Scale for depression in dementia. *Biological Psychiatry*, 23, 271–284.

Alzheimer Association (2004). Research consent for cognitively impaired adults: recommendations for institutional review boards and investigators. *Alzheimer Disease & Associated Disorders*, 18, 171–175.

American Psychiatric Association (1994). *Diagnostic and Statistical Manual of Mental Disorders, Fourth Edition (DSM-IV)*. Washington, DC: American Psychiatric Association, 143–147.

Begg, C., Cho, M., Eastwood, S., *et al.* (1996). Improving the quality of reporting of randomized controlled trials: the CONSORT statement. *Journal of the American Medical Association*, 276, 637–639.

Blacker, D., Albert, M., Bassett, S., *et al.* (1994). Reliability and validity of NINCDS–ADRDA criteria for Alzheimer's disease. The National Institute of Mental Health Genetics Initiative. *Archives of Neurology*, 51, 1198–1204.

Brodaty, H., Ames, D., Snowdon, J., *et al.* (2003). A randomized placebo-controlled trial of risperidone for the treatment of aggression, agitation and psychosis of dementia. *Journal of Clinical Psychiatry*, 64, 134–143.

Burke, W., Miller, O., Rubin, E., *et al.* (1988). Reliability of the Washington University Clinical Dementia Rating. *Archives of Neurology*, 45, 31–32.

Cohen-Mansfield, J. (1985). Agitated behaviors in the elderly ill. Preliminary results in the cognitively deteriorated. *Journal of the American Geriatrics Society*, 34, 722–727.

Corey-Bloom, J., Anand, R., Veach, J., *et al.* (1998). A randomized trial evaluating the efficacy and safety of ENA 73 (rivastigmine tartrate), a new acetylcholinesterase inhibitor, in patients with mild to moderately severe Alzheimer's disease. *International Journal of Geriatric Psychopharmacology*, 1, 55–65.

Cummings, J. (2003). Use of acetylcholinesterase inhibitors in clinical practice: evidence-based recommendations. *American Journal of Geriatric Psychiatry*, 11, 131–145.

Cummings, J., Mega, M., Gray, K., *et al.* (1994). The neuropsyciatric inventory: an efficient tool for comprehensively assessing psychopathology in dementia. *Neurology*, 44, 2308–2314.

Cummings, J., Cyrus, P., Bieber, F., *et al.* (1998). Metrifonate treatment of the cognitive deficits of Alzheimer's disease. *Neurology*, 50, 1214–1221.

Davis, K., Thal, L., Gamzu, E., *et al.* (1992). A double-blind, placebo-controlled multicenter study of tacrine for Alzheimer's disease. *New England Journal of Medicine*, 327, 1253–1259.

Davis, K., Marin, D., Kane, R., *et al.* (1997). The Caregiver Activity Survey (CAS): development and validation of a new measure for caregivers of persons with Alzheimer's disease. *International Journal of Geriatric Psychiatry*, 12, 978–988.

De Deyn, P., Rabheru, K., Rasmussen, A., *et al.* (1999). A randomized trial of risperidone, placebo, and haloperidol for behavioral symptoms of dementia. *Neurology*, 53, 946–955.

DeJong, R., Osterlund, O., & Roy, G. (1989). Measurement of quality-of-life changes in patients with Alzheimer's disease. *Clinical Therapeutics*, 11, 545–554.

Doody, R., Stevens, J., Beck, C., et al. (2001). Practice parameter: management of dementia (an evidence-based review): Report of the Quality Standards Subcommittee of the American Academy of Neurology. *Neurology*, 56, 1154–1166.

Doraiswamy, P., Kaiser, L., Bieber, F., et al. (2001). The Alzheimer's Disease Assessment Scale: evaluation of psychometric properties and patterns of cognitive decline in multicenter clinical trials of mild-to-moderate Alzheimer's disease. *Alzheimer Disease & Associated Disorders*, 15, 174–183.

Ernst, R.L. & Hay, J.W. (1994). The US economic and social costs of AD revisited. *American Journal of Public Health*, 84, 1261–1264.

Evans, D.A. (1990). Estimated prevalence of Alzheimer's disease in the United States. *Milbank Q* 68, 267–289.

Evans, D.A., Funkenstein, H.H., Albert, M.S., et al. (1989). Prevalence of Alzheimer's disease in a community population of older persons. Higher than previously reported. *Journal of the American Medical Association*, 26, 2551–2556.

Everitt, B. & Pickler, A. (2004). *Statistical Aspects of the Design and Analysis of Clinical Trials*. London: Imperial College Press, pp. 45–50, 203–204.

Farlow, M., Gracon, S., Hershey, L., et al. (1992). A controlled trial of tacrine in Alzheimer's disease. *Journal of the American Medical Association*, 268, 2523–2529.

Feldman, H., Gauthier, S., Hecker, J., et al. (2001). A 24-week, randomized, double-blind study of donepezil in moderate to severe Alzheimer's disease. *Neurology*, 57, 613–620.

Ferris, S., Lucca, U., Mohs, R., et al. (1997). Objective psychometric tests in clinical trials of dementia drugs. *Alzheimer Disease & Associated Disorders*, 11, 34–38.

Folstein, M., Folstein, S., & McHugh, P. (1975). Mini-mental state: a practical method for grading the cognitive state of patients for the clinician. *Journal of Psychiatric Research*, 12, 189–198.

Galasko, D., Bennett, D., Sano, M., et al. (1997). An inventory to assess activities of daily living for clinical trials in Alzheimer's disease. *Alzheimer Disease & Associated Disorders*, 11 (Suppl. 2), S33–S39.

Gauthier, S., Bodick, N., Erzigkeit, E., et al. (1997). Activities of daily living as an outcome measure in clinical trials of dementia drugs. *Alzheimer Disease & Associated Disorders*, 11 (Suppl. 3), 6–7.

Gelinas, I., Gauthier, L., McIntyre, M., et al. (1999). Development of a functional measure for persons with Alzheimer's disease: the disability assessment for dementia. *Americal Journal of Occupational Therapy*, 53, 471–481.

Guy, W. (ed.) (1976). Clinical Global Impression (CGI). ECDEU assessment manual for psychopharmacology. Rockville, MD: US Department of Health and Human Services, Public Health Service, Alcohol Drug Abuse and Mental Health Administration. NIMH Psychopharmacology Research Branch. pp. 218–222.

Holmes, C., Clairns, N., Lantos, P., et al. (1999). Validity of current clinical criteria for Alzheimer's disease, vascular dementia and dementia with Lewy bodies. *British Journal of Psychiatry*, 174, 45–50.

Hughes, C., Berg, L., Denziger, W., et al. (1982). A new clinical scale for the staging of dementia. *British Journal of Psychiatry*, 140, 566–572.

Institute on Aging (1996). *Progress Report on Alzheimer's Disease 1996*. Bethesda, Md: National Institute on Aging, NIH publication, pp. 96–4137.

Katz, I., Jeste, D., Mintzer, J., et al. (1999). Comparison of risperidone and placebo for psychosis and behavioral disturbances associated with dementia: a randomized, double-blind trial. *Journal of Clinical Psychiatry*, 60, 107–115.

Kay, S., Opler, L., Lindenmayer, J., et al. (1989). The positive and negative syndrome scale: a rationale and standardization. *British Journal of Psychiatry*, 155 (Suppl. 7), 59–65.

Knapp, M., Knopman, D., Solomon, P., et al. (1994). A 30-week randomized controlled trial of high-dose tacrine in patients with Alzheimer's disease. *Journal of the American Medical Association*, 271, 985–991.

Knopman, D., Knapp, M., Bracon, S., *et al.* (1994). The clinician interview-based impression (CIBI): a clinician's global change rating scale in Alzheimer's disease. *Neurology*, 44, 2315–2321.

Koepsell, T. & Weiss, N. (2003). *Epidemiologic Methods*. New York: Oxford University Press, pp. 64–67, 261, 327–329.

Lawton, M. & Brody, E. (1969). Assessment of older people: self-maintaining and instrumental activities of daily living. *Gerontologist*, 9, 179–186.

Le Bars, P., Katz, M., Berman, N., *et al.* (1997). A placebo-controlled, double-blind, randomized trial of an extract of Ginkgo Biloba for dementia. *Journal of the American Medical Association*, 278, 1327–1332.

Leber, P. (1990). *Guidelines for the Clinical Evaluation of Antidementia Drugs*, Food and Drug Administration, Washington, D.C.

Leber, P. (1997). Observations and suggestions on antidementia drug development. *Alzheimer Disease & Associated Disorders*, 10, S1, 31–35.

Lopez, O.L., Litvan, I., Catt, K.E., *et al.* (1999). Accuracy of four clinical diagnostic criteria for the diagnosis of neurodegenerative dementias. *Neurology*, 53, 1292–1299.

Lyketsos, C., Sheppard, J., Steele, C., *et al.* (2000). Randomized, placebo-controlled, double-blind clinical trial of sertraline in the treatment of depression complicating Alzheimer's disease: initial results from the depression in Alzheimer's disease study. *American Journal of Psychiatry*, 157, 1686–1689.

McKhann, G., Drachman, D., Folstein, M., *et al.* Clinical diagnosis of Alzheimer's disease: report of the NINCDS–ADRDA Work Group under the auspices of Department of Health and Human Services Task Force on Alzheimer's disease. *Neurology*, 34, 939–944.

Moher, D., Schulz, K., Altman, D., *et al.* (2001). The CONSORT statement: revised recommendations for improving the quality of reports of parallel-group randomized trials. *Journal of the American Medical Association*, 285, 1987–1991.

Mohs, R., Doody, R., Morris, J., *et al.* (2001). A 1-year, placebo-controlled preservation of function survival study of donepezil in AD patients. *Neurology*, 57, 481–488.

Morris, J., Edland, S., Clark, C., *et al.* (1993). The consortium to establish a registry for Alzheimer's disease (CERAD). Part IV. Rates of cognitive change in the longitudinal assessment of probable Alzheimer's disease. *Neurology*, 43, 2457–2465.

Morris, J., Cyrus, P., Orazem, J., *et al.* (1998). Metrifonate benefits cognitive, behavioral, and global function in patients with Alzheimer's disease. *Neurology*, 50, 1222–1230.

Morris, J.C., Storandt, M., Miller, P., *et al.* (2001). Mild cognitive impairment represents early-stage Alzheimer's disease. *Archives of Neurology*, 58, 397–405.

Mulnard, R., Cotman, C., Kawas, C., *et al.* (2000). Estrogen replacement therapy for treatment of mild to moderate Alzheimer disease. *Journal of the American Medical Association*, 283, 1007–1015.

National Institute of Health, National Institute on Aging (1999). *Progress Report on Alzheimer's Disease 1999 (NIH Pub. No. 99-4664)*. Bethesda, MD: US Department of Health and Human Services.

O'Connor, D.W., Pollitt, P., Hyde, J.B., *et al.* (1989). The reliability and validity of the mini-mental state in a British community survey. *Journal of Psychiatric Research* 23, 87–96.

Overall, J. & Gorham, D. (1962). The Brief Psychiatric Rating Scale. *Psychological Reports*, 10, 799–812.

Overall, J. & Gorhal, D. (1988). Introduction: the Brief Psychiatric Rating Scale (BPRS): recent developments in ascertainment and scaling. *Psychopharmacology Bulletin*, 24, 97–99.

Patterson, M. & Bolger, J. (1994). Assessment of behavioral symptoms in Alzheimer's disease. *Alzheimer Disease & Associated Disorders*, 8 (Suppl. 3), 4–20.

Petersen, R.C., Doody, R., Kurz, A., *et al.* (2001). Current concepts in mild cognitive impairment. *Archives of Neurology*, 58, 1985–1992.

Petersen, R.C., Thomas, R.G., Grundman, M., *et al.* (2005). Vitamin E and donepezil for the treatment of mild cognitive impairment. *New England Journal of Medicine*, 352, 2379–2388.

Porteinsson, A., Tariot, P., Erb, R., *et al.* (2001). Placebo-controlled study of divalproex sodium for agitation in dementia. *American Journal of Geriatric Psychiatry* 9, 58–66.

Raskind, M., Peskind, E., Wessel, T., *et al.* (2000). Galantamine in AD: a 6-month randomized, placebo-controlled trial with a 6-month extension. *Neurology*, 54, 2261–2268.

Reines, S., Block, G., Morris, J., *et al.* (2004). Rofecoxib: no effect on Alzheimer's disease in a 1-year, randomized, blinded, controlled study. *Neurology*, 62, 66–71.

Reisberg, B., Ferris, S., de Leon, M., *et al.* (1982). The Global Deterioration Scale for assessment of primary degenerative dementia. *American Journal of Psychiatry*, 138, 1136–1139.

Reisberg, B., Scaln, S., Franssen, E., *et al.* (1994). Dementia staging in chronic care populations. *Alzheimer Disease & Associated Disorders*, 8 (Suppl. 1), S188–S205.

Reisberg, B., Auer, S.R., Monteiro, I.M., *et al.* (1996). Behavioral pathology in Alzheimer's disease (BEHAVE-AD) rating scale. *International Psychogeriatrics*, 8 (Suppl. 3), 301–308.

Reisberg, B., Doody, R., Stoffler, A., *et al.* (2003). Memantine in moderate-to-severe Alzheimer's disease. *New England Journal of Medicine*, 348, 1333–1341.

Rockwood, K., Mintzer, J., Truyen, L., *et al.* (2001). Effects of a flexible galantamine dose in Alzheimer's disease: a randomized, controlled trial. *Journal of Neurology Neurosurgery and Psychiatry*, 71, 589–595.

Rogers, S., Doody, R., Mohs, R., *et al.* (1998a). Donepezil improves cognition and global function in Alzheimer's disease. *Archives of Internal Medicine*, 158, 1021–1031.

Rogers, S., Farlow, M., Doody, R., *et al.* (1998b). A 24-week, double-blind, placebo-controlled trial of donepezil in patients with Alzheimer's disease. *Neurology*, 50, 136–145.

Rosen, W., Mohs, R., Davis, K., *et al.* (1984). A new rating scale for Alzheimer's disease. *American Journal of Psychiatry*, 141, 1356–1364.

Rosler, M., Anand, R., Cicin-Sain, A., *et al.* (1999). Efficacy and safety of rivastigmine in patients with Alzheimer's disease: international randomized controlled trial. *British Medical Journal*, 318, 633–638.

Salloway, S., Ferris, S., Kluger, A., *et al.* (2004). Efficacy of donepezil in mild cognitive impairment: a randomized placebo-controlled trial. *Neurology*, 63, 651–657.

Sano, M., Ernesto, C., Klauber, M., *et al.* (1996). Rationale and design of a multicenter study of selegiline and A-tocopherol in the treatment of Alzheimer disease using novel clinical outcomes. *Alzheimer Disease & Associated Disorders*, 10, 132–140.

Sano, M., Ernesto, C., Thomas, R., *et al.* (1997). A controlled trial of selegiline, alpha-tocopherol, or both as treatment for Alzheimer's disease. *New England Journal of Medicine*, 336, 1216–1222.

Scharf, S., Mander, A., Ugoni, A., *et al.* (1999). A double-blind, placebo-controlled trial of diclofenac/misoprostol in Alzheimer's disease. *Neurology*, 53, 197–201.

Schneider, L., Olin, J., Doody, R., *et al.* (1997). Validity and reliability of the Alzheimer's disease cooperative study-Clinical Global Impression of change. *Alzheimer Disease & Associated Disorders*, 11 (Suppl. 2), S22–S32.

Schneider, L., Tariot, P., Lyketsos, C., *et al.* (2001). National Institute of Mental Health Clinical Antipsychotic Trial of Inervention Effectiveness (CATIE): Alzheimer disease trial methodology. *American Journal of Geriatric Psychiatry*, 9, 346–390.

Schoenmaker, N. & Van Gool, W. (2004). The age gap between patients in clinical studies and in the general population: a pitfall for dementia research. *Lancet Neurology*, 3, 627–630.

Tariot, P., Erb, R., Podgorski, C., *et al.* (1988). Efficacy and tolerability of carbamazepine for agitation and aggression in dementia. *American Journal of Psychiatry*, 155, 54–61.

Tariot, P., Mack, J., Patterson, M., *et al.* **and the CERAD Behavioral Pathology Committee** (1995). The CERAD Behavior Rating Scale for Dementia (BRSD). *American Journal of Psychiatry*, 152, 1349–1357.

Tariot, P., Solomon, P., Morris, J., *et al.* (2000). A 5-month, randomized, placebo-controlled trial of galantamine in AD. *Neurology*, 54, 2269–2276.

Thal, L., Carta, A., Clarke, W., *et al.* (1996). A 1-year multicenter placebo-controlled study of acetyl-L-carnitine in patients with Alzheimer's disease. *Neurology*, 47, 705–711.

Tierney, M., Fisher, R., Anthony, J., *et al.* (1988). The NINCDS–ADRDA Work Group criteria for the clinical diagnosis of probable Alzheimer's disease: a clinicopathologic study of 57 cases. *Neurology*, 38, 359–364.

Weiner, M., Koss, E., Wild, K., *et al.* (1996). Measures of psychiatric symptoms in Alzheimer patients: a review. *Alzheimer Disease & Associated Disorders*, 10, 20–30.

Whitehouse, P. (1997). Pharmacoeconomics of dementia. *Alzheimer Disease & Associated Disorders*, 11 (Suppl. 5), S22–S33.

Wimo, A., Wetterholm, A., Mastey, Y., *et al.* (1998). Evaluation of the healthcare resource utilization and caregiver time in anti-dementia drug trials. In: Wimo, A., Jonsson, B., Karlson, G., Wilblad, B. (eds.), *Health Economics of Dementia*. Chichester, England: John Wiley, 465–499.

Winblad, B., Wimo, A. & Almkvist, O. (2000). Outcome measures in Alzheimer's disease: Do they go far enough? *Dementia and Geriatric Cognitive Disorders*, 11 (Suppl. 1), 3–10.

Winblad, B., Engedal, K., Soininen, H., *et al.* (2001). A 1-year, randomized, placebo-controlled study of donepezil in patients with mild to moderate AD. *Neurology*, 57, 489–495.

World Health Organization (1993). *The ICD-10 Classification of Mental and Behavioral Disorders. Diagnostic Criteria for Research*. Geneva, Switzerland: World Health Organization.

Zhong, K., Tariot, P., Minkwitz, M.C., *et al.* (2004). Quetiapine for the treatment of agitation in the elderly institutionalized patients with dementia: a randomized, double blind trial. International Conference on Alzheimer's Disease and Related Disorders meeting, Poster # P2-442.

Progress in Neurotherapeutics and Neuropsychopharmacology, 2:1, 79–96 © 2007 Cambridge University Press
DOI: 10.1017/S1748232106000061   Printed in the United Kingdom

Comparative Neuropsychological Effects of Lamotrigine and Topiramate in Healthy Volunteers

Kimford J. Meador

Department of Neurology, McKnight Brain Institute, University of Florida, Gainesville, FL, USA;
Email: kimford.meador@neurology.ufl.edu

Key words: anticonvulsant, lamotrigine, topiramate, cognition, neuropsychology.

Introduction and Overview

Neuropsychological problems are common in patients with epilepsy. Although a variety of factors contribute to neuropsychological dysfunction (Meador, 2004a), antiepileptic drugs (AEDs) are an important consideration since they are the main therapeutic modality for epilepsy. AEDs reduce neuronal irritability and thus may also reduce neuronal excitability. Thus, it is not surprising that all AEDs can produce adverse cognitive and behavioral side-effects. In general, these adverse effects are greater when the AED is first initiated (especially if the dose escalation is rapid), greater at higher dosages and blood levels (especially when the blood levels are above the standard therapeutic ranges), and greater with polytherapy (Meador, 2004a). The overall effectiveness of an AED is a combination of its efficacy and its tolerability. Further, there are individual idiosyncratic neuropsychological effects of AEDs such that some patients are particularly sensitive to certain AEDs and will suffer adverse effects even at low dosages. Across AEDs with a similar spectrum of efficacy, tolerability is commonly a more important factor in determining AED effectiveness. Further, adverse neuropsychological effects of AEDs can have adverse effects on a patient's perceived quality of life. Thus, the differential neuropsychological effects of AEDs are an important factor in drug selection.

AEDs clearly differ in their propensity to produce adverse neuropsychological effects; however, the evidence base is far from complete across all AEDs. Further, complicating interpretation of the literature is the presence of methodological

Correspondence should be addressed to: Kimford J. Meador MD, Department of Neurology, McKnight Brain Institute (L3-100), University of Florida, 100 South Newell Drive, Gainesville, FL 32611, USA; Ph: +1 352 273 5550; Fax: +1 352 273 5575; Email: kimford.meador@neurology.ufl.edu.

limitations in many neuropsychological studies of AEDs (Meador, 2004a; 1998). Concerns involve both issues of experimental design as well as flaws in statistical analysis and interpretation. Examples include subject selection bias, non-equivalence of clinical variables, failure to control for anticonvulsant dose and blood levels, failure to control for seizure frequency, non-equivalence of dependent variables, inadequate sample size, test-retest effects, inadequate sensitivity and scope of neuropsychological tests, type I error, non-orthogonal contrasts, comparison of studies with non-equivalent designs/statistics, and failure to differentiate between statistical versus clinical significance (Meador, 1998).

Two of the most commonly used of the newer AEDs are lamotrigine (LTG) and topiramate (TPM). Both have a wide spectrum of efficacy across seizure disorders, and both have approved indications beyond epilepsy. The differential neuropsychological effects of LTG and TPM in monotherapy were uncertain because they had not been established in a well-controlled, direct head-to-head comparison.

Prior studies have suggested that LTG is well-tolerated with few cognitive side-effects. A small double-blind, placebo-controlled cross-over study of patients with refractory partial epilepsy using a limited neuropsychological battery found that LTG exhibited no adverse cognitive effects and produced positive effects on the patients' perceived quality of life (Smith *et al.*, 1993). A double-blind, randomized, cross-over study of healthy volunteers reported significantly better performance on 48% of neuropsychological variables for LTG compared to carbamazepine (Meador *et al.*, 2001). LTG has been tolerated better than carbamazepine and phenytoin in studies of epilepsy patients (Brodie *et al.*, 1999; Steiner *et al.*, 1999; Gillham *et al.*, 1996), and produced fewer neuropsychological side-effects compared to carbamazepine, diazepam, phenytoin, and valproate in other studies (Aldenkamp *et al.*, 2002; Hamilton *et al.*, 1993; Cohen *et al.*, 1985).

Reports for TPM have been more mixed. Although generally well-tolerated, TPM has been reported to impair concentration, produce word-findings difficulties, and cause emotional liability (Jette, 2002; Glauser, 1999; Martin *et al.*, 1999; Burton & Harden, 1997). As noted earlier, the cognitive side-effects of AEDs are increased with faster initiation titration, higher dosages/blood levels, and polytherapy. The cognitive effects of TPM appear to be particular sensitive to these effects. Thus, the fast titration rate in a healthy volunteer study comparing the cognitive effects of TPM to LTG and gabapentin likely contributed to some of the observed effects (Martin *et al.*, 1999). Although TPM has been found to impair word fluency, list learning, processing speed, or working memory in two adjunctive studies of epilepsy patients (Lee *et al.*, 2003a; Thompson *et al.*, 2000), much less adverse effects were found in two studies comparing TPM and valproate as adjunctive therapy (Meador *et al.*, 2003; Aldenkamp *et al.*, 2000). TPM produced significantly greater impairment on only 1 of the 17 variables in one study (Aldenkamp *et al.*, 2000) and only 2 of 24 variables in the other study (Meador *et al.*, 2003).

Purpose of Trial

Since the relative neuropsychological effects of LTG and TPM were uncertain, our trial directly compared the cognitive and behavioral effects of LTG and TPM. The study was conducted in healthy volunteers using a double-blind, randomized cross-over design in order to control for confounding factors such as the cognitive effects produced by changes in seizures and to allow extrapolation of the results to patient populations without epilepsy, who are treated with these agents (e.g. pain and psychiatric disorders).

Agents

LTG is a phenyltriazine derivative which is approved for the treatment of epilepsy and bipolar disorder (Physicians' Desk Reference, 2005; LaRoche & Helmers, 2004). Although its exact mechanisms of action as an anticonvulsant and in bipolar disorder are unknown, LTG is known to inhibit voltage-sensitive sodium channels and thus modulate pre-synaptic release of excitatory amino acids. LTG also weakly inhibits calcium channels and serotonin 5-HT$_3$ receptors.

TPM is a sulfamate-substituted monosaccharide which is approved for the treatment of epilepsy and migraine prophylaxis (*Physicians' Desk Reference*, 2005; LaRoche & Helmers, 2004). Although its exact mechanisms of action as an anticonvulsant and in migraine are unknown, TPM is known to have four mechanistic properties:

1. inhibits voltage-dependent sodium channels,
2. augments gamma amino butyric acid (GABA) activity at some subtypes of the GABA-A receptor,
3. antagonizes the AMPA/kainite subtype of the glutamate receptor,
4. inhibits the carbonic-anhydrase enzyme.

Clinical Trial

Results of this study were originally published in *Neurology* (Meador *et al.*, 2005).

Subjects

The subjects were healthy paid volunteers who agreed to participate after informed consent according to the declaration of Helsinki. Subjects were free of centrally active prescription medications throughout the study and did not use over-the-counter medications or alcohol for 72 h prior to each neuropsychological test session.

Trial Methods

A multicenter, double-blind, randomized cross-over design was employed. The study was conducted at the Medical College of Georgia (MCG), Washington University (WU) and Case Western Reserve University (CWRU). Each AED was administered in monotherapy for a 12-week period including a 7 week initiation to target dose, 4 week maintenance treatment, and one week taper off AED. A 4 week washout period followed each AED treatment (see Figure 1). Neuropsychological testing was conducted on four occasions over 32 weeks including the initial non-drug baseline, end of treatment phase for each AED, and end of final washout phase. Neuropsychological tests were performed in a fixed order at the same time of day (approximately 3 h after morning dose). Anticonvulsant blood levels (2 h after morning dose) were obtained at the end of each maintenance phase. Physical exam and blood work (hematology and chemistry panel) were conducted at the non-drug baseline, end of each titration phase, end of each maintenance phase, and end of each washout phase. Urine drug screen was obtained at the initial baseline.

Subjects received a constant number of matched capsules (LTG 25 mg, TPM 25 mg, or placebo) for each day in pillboxes containing 1 weeks' supply during AED treatment phases. AED dosages were gradually increased to the target dose of

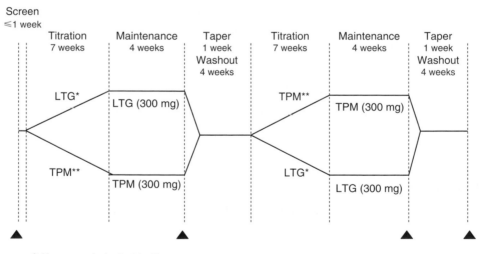

Fig. 1.
Study Design. *LTG titration: 25 mg/day × 2 weeks; 50 mg × 2 weeks; 100 mg × 2 weeks; 200 mg × 1 week. **TPM titration: 25 mg/day × 1 week, increase by 25 mg thru week 4, increase by 50 mg thru week 8. Neuropsychological testing denoted by black triangles. (Reproduced, with permission from *Neurology* 2005; 64: 2108–2114.)

300 mg/day over the 7 week initiation by replacing placebos with active capsules. LTG was given at 25 mg/day for 2 weeks, then 25 mg bid for 2 weeks, then 50 mg bid for 2 weeks, then 100 mg bid for the 7th week, and 150 mg bid for the 4 week maintenance phase. TPM was begun at 25 mg/day and increased by 25 mg/day each week over the first month, increased 50 mg/day each week for weeks 5–8 to a maintenance dose of 150 mg bid beginning the 8th week for the 4 week maintenance. AEDs were tapered off over 7 days at the end of each AED treatment phase by replacing the active drug capsules with placebos.

Instruments/Measures

Neuropsychological Tests: The Peabody Picture Vocabulary Test was used to assess IQ at enrollment (Dunn & Dunn, 1997). Neuropsychological effects of AEDs were evaluated by battery consisting of 17 tests yielding a total of 41 variables. The majority of the tests have been shown to be sensitive to AED effects in prior studies (Meador *et al.*, 2001; 1999; 1995; 1993; 1991). The battery assessed five neurobehavioral domains:

1. *Attention/Vigilance*: Continuous Performance Task (Ray *et al.*, 1992), Digit Cancellation Test (Dodrill *et al.*, 1995), Visual Serial Addition Test (Meador *et al.*, 1995).

2. *Memory*: MCG paragraph memory (Meador *et al.*, 1993), Selective Reminding Test (Buschke & Fuld, 1974).

3. *Language*: Controlled Oral Word Association Test (Spreen & Strauss, 1998), Boston Naming Test (Kaplan *et al.*, 1983), Semantic Fluency Test (Henry & Crawford, 2004).

4. *Cognitive & Motor Speed*: Lafayette Grooved Pegboard (Lezak, 1995), Choice Reaction Time: initiation, movement, and total time (Lachman *et al.*, 1979).

5. *Other Cognitive Tests*: Stroop (Golden, 1978), Symbol Digit Modalities Test (Smith, 1973).

6. *Subjective Behavioral Measures*: A-B Neurotoxicity Scale (Aldenkamp *et al.*, 1995), Adverse Events Profile (Abbetz *et al.*, 2000), Profile of Mood States (subscales for the POMS include tension/anxiety, depression, anger/hostility, vigor, fatigue, and confusion/bewilderment) (Lorr *et al.*, 1971) cognitive scales (i.e. attention, language, and memory) from the Quality of Life in Epilepsy-89 (QOLIE-89) (Devinsky *et al.*, 1995), side-effects and life satisfaction (subscales for the SEALS include dysphoria, tiredness, cognition, anger/temper and worry) (Gillham *et al.*, 1996), and SF-12 (generic 12 item quality of life scale) (Ware *et al.*, 1996).

Primary and Secondary Outcomes

The primary outcome variables were the test scores for the 41 neuropsychological variables at the end of the LTG and TPM treatments for each subject. Secondary outcomes included the difference scores for these same variables comparing the average of the non-drug conditions (i.e. baseline and final washout condition) to each drug condition.

Analyses and Results

Of the 94 subjects were enrolled (44 at MCG, 30 at WU and 20 at CWRU), 75 were randomized to drug and 47 completed the entire study. Reasons for the 19 who withdrew prior to drug randomization included: withdrew consent ($n = 6$), lost to follow-up ($n = 4$), excluded for protocol violations ($n = 8$), and started a new job ($n = 1$). Of those randomized to AED, 28 subjects withdrew from the study (13 on LTG, 12 on TPM, and 3 during washout period between AEDs). The 13 who withdrew on LTG included: skin rash ($n = 5$), depression ($n = 1$), nausea ($n = 1$), tachycardia ($n = 1$), withdrew consent ($n = 2$), protocol violations ($n = 2$, i.e. non-compliance), and started new job ($n = 1$). The 12 who withdrew on TPM included: skin rash ($n = 1$), depression ($n = 2$), psychosis ($n = 1$), paranoia/irritability ($n = 1$), hypertension ($n = 2$), dizziness ($n = 1$), memory problems ($n = 1$), withdrew consent ($n = 1$), fear of developing visual problem ($n = 1$), and one was randomized but never received drug and was lost to follow-up. The three who withdrew during the washout included: one withdrew consent, one was lost to follow-up, and one started a new job. Mean doses at the time of premature discontinuation were: TPM $= 129$ mg/day and LTG $= 117$ mg/day. Median doses were: TPM $= 100$ mg/day and LTG $= 25$ mg/day.

Table 1 lists the adverse events occurring in at least 10% of the subjects. Two serious adverse events occurred:

1. a traumatic fracture of the tibia and fibula in week 4 on LTG 50 mg/day,

2. psychosis requiring hospitalization in week 4 on TPM 100 mg/day that subsequently resolved when TPM was discontinued.

Demographics for 47 subjects who completing the entire study were: mean age $= 37$ years (range $= 22$–58); 28 women; 19 men. Mean (range) IQ of the subjects was 106 (85–138). The mean ($\pm$ range) anticonvulsant blood levels on the day of neuropsychological testing were: LTG $= 4.7$ mcg/ml (1.6–7.0) and TPM $= 9.3$ mcg/ml (2.8–15.8). Mean doses were: LTG $= 298$ mg/day (one subject was titrated to 200 mg/day in error) and TPM $= 300$ mg/day.

Table 1. **Adverse Events Occurring in at Least 10% of Subjects on LTG or TPM. Reproduced, with Permission from *Neurology* 2005; 64: 2108–2114**

ADVERSE EVENT	LTG (%)	TPM (%)
Appetite or weight change	4	11
Dizziness	6	14
Emotional changes	9	30
Fatigue	11	26
Digestive	14	38
Headache	13	11
Memory/concentration	10	35
Respiratory	11	18
Skin problems	10	6
Sleep difficulties	14	12
Tingling	7	61

Neuropsychological Outcomes

The primary analysis was a series of *t*-tests comparing scores on the neuropsychological variables for LTG versus TPM. Table 2 lists the means for LTG, TPM, and the non-drug average (ND) standard deviation ($\pm$SD) with significant differences denoted. LTG was statistically better than TPM on 33/41 (80%) of the variables including both objective and subjective neuropsychological measures; TPM was significantly better on none of the variables. Secondary analyses compared each AED to the average of the non-drug states (i.e. baseline and final non-drug assessment) (see Table 2). Performance on the ND was statistically better on 36/41 (88%) of the variables compared to TPM and 7/41 (17%) for LTG. In contrast, TPM was significantly better on none of the variables compared to non-drug, and LTG was better on 4/41 (10%) of the variables. Although doses of the two AEDs were matched, TPM had higher mean blood levels than LTG. Subjects with levels above 8 mcg/ml were excluded yielding a sample of 15 subjects who had the following mean (SD) blood levels: LTG = 4.4 (1.4), TPM = 6.7 (1.7). Comparison of LTG and TPM in this sample revealed 19 of 41 variables (46%) were significantly better for LTG, none in favor of TPM.

An important question is the magnitude of the observed effects. Figure 2 depicts the average number of neuropsychological tests with $\pm$ change scores in different SD ranges for each AED compared to the average non-drug condition. Basically, no change (i.e. change scores between $-1/2$ and $+1/2$ SD) compared to non-drug were seen for 54% of the variables during LTG treatment and for 34% during TPM. However, there was a skew to negative scores for TPM with 40% of the variables having ≥ -1 SD worsening compared to non-drug overall. In contrast, 12% of the variables had ≥ -1 SD worsening for LTG compared to non-drug. Figure 3 depicts the individual variability of the AED effects by plotting the percentage of

Table 2. **Means (SD) of Neuropsychological Measures for LTG and TPM and ND (*n* = 47). Reproduced, with Permission from *Neurology* 2005; 64: 2108–2114**

NEUROPSYCHOLOGICAL VARIABLE	LTG	TPM	ND
Attention/vigilance			
Continuous performance task	96.7 (5.2)^T	90.5 (11.6)	97.2 (3.7)^T
Digit Cancellation	205.1 (45.4)^T	188.8 (41.9)	204.0 (40.7)^T
Trial 1 Visual Serial Addition Test	57.1 (3.6)^{T,N}	49.1 (9.2)	56.0 (4.0)^T
Trial 2 Visual Serial Addition Test	55.6 (4.3)^T	47.7 (11.0)	54.7 (4.4)^T
Trial 3 Visual Serial Addition Test	53.7 (6.0)^{T,N}	45.3 (11.9)	52.6 (5.4)^T
Trial 4 Visual Serial Addition Test	48.4 (8.0)^T	41.3 (12.7)	48.1 (7.1)^T
Total Visual Serial Addition Test	212.7 (22.3)^T	183.4 (38.2)	211.3 (19.1)^T
Memory			
Selective Reminding Task CLTR	48.5 (14.8)^T	36.4 (13.2)	46.8 (11.0)^T
Selective Reminding Task Delay Recall	10.9 (6.3)	9.2 (2.4)	10.9 (5.5)^T
MCG Paragraphs: Immediate Recall 1	37.1 (14.3)^T	23.7 (14.0)	35.9 (13.1)^T
MCG Paragraphs: Immediate Recall 2	58.9 (18.3)^T	40.5 (16.4)	57.1 (15.6)^T
MCG Paragraphs: Delay Recall	60.4 (19.1)^T	42.7 (16.8)	58.1 (16.4)^T
Language			
Boston Naming Test	57.4 (3.2)^T	56.3 (4.0)	57.1 (2.8)^T
Semantic Fluency Test	24.1 (5.1)^T	17.6 (4.8)	25.4 (4.4)^{T,L}
COWA	47.1 (12.2)^{T,N}	28.7 (9.3)	45.0 (10.5)^T
Cognitive/motor Speed			
Grooved Pegboard*	61.9 (10.6)^T	66.4 (16.6)	59.8 (10.2)^{T,L}
Choice Reaction Time – Initiation*	458.7 (93.3)^T	516.7 (111.6)	448.3 (85.9)^T
Choice Reaction Time – Reaction*	210 (87)	215 (141)	220 (88)
Choice Reaction Time – Total*	673 (112)^T	739 (167)	673 (104)^T
Other Cognitive			
Stroop: Word	108.0 (16.2)^T	96.2 (14.1)	110.4 (13.1)^T
Stroop: Color	80.0 (14.6)^T	71.4 (12.3)	79.0 (10.8)^T
Stroop: Interference	43.7 (8.7)	43.8 (11.6)	45.4 (9.2)^L
Symbol Digit Modalities Test	61.3 (10.9)^T	46.3 (9.2)	62.1 (10.3)^T
Subjective Measures			
AB Neurotoxicity*	6.5 (8.7)^T	11.4 (12.2)	4.3 (4.7)^{T,L}
QOLIE – Memory	85.7 (13.7)^T	74.7 (19.3)	87.2 (11.1)^T
QOLIE – Attention/concentration	90.8 (11.3)^T	78.7 (16.5)	92.1 (6.8)^T
QOLIE – Language	93.7 (9.8)^T	85.6 (12.9)	94.9 (6.0)^T
SEALS – Dysphoria*	1.8 (2.1)^T	3.6 (2.6)	1.8 (1.5)^T
SEALS – Tiredness*	2.4 (1.9)^T	3.3 (2.3)	2.5 (1.7)^T
SEALS – Temper*	1.7 (1.5)^T	2.3 (1.6)	1.5 (1.1)^T
SEALS – Cognition*	4.9 (4.5)^T	8.6 (5.5)	4.7 (3.0)^T
SEALS – Worry*	2.9 (1.9)	3.4 (2.0)	3.2 (1.7)
POMS – Tension*	6.8 (7.2)	7.4 (5.9)	4.6 (3.0)^{T,L}
POMS – Depression*	6.0 (9.3)	6.6 (8.7)	4.0 (4.1)^T
POMS – Anger*	5.8 (6.3)	4.4 (6.0)	3.5 (3.4)^L
POMS – Vigor*	22.4 (5.7)^{T,N}	15.9 (8.5)	21.1 (5.0)^T
POMS – Fatigue*	5.8 (6.7)^T	7.9 (6.7)	4.4 (3.9)^T
POMS – Confusion*	4.8 (5.7)^T	7.2 (5.0)	3.6 (2.0)^T
POMS – Total*	9.3 (32.6)^T	18.8 (33.0)	−0.2 (18.6)^{T,L}
SF-12 Physical summary	54.6 (3.2)	53.9 (6.1)	54.8 (2.7)
SF-12 Mental summary	53.5 (6.8)^T	50.7 (8.9)	54.3 (4.7)^T

*Variables for which lower mean values indicate better performance.
MCG = Medical college of Georgia; POMS = Profile of mood states; QOLIE-89 = quality of life in epilepsy-89; SEALS = side-effects and life satisfaction; CLTR = consistent long-term retrieval; COWA = controlled oral word association.
Suprascripts refer to statistical differences: L = better than lamotrigine, T = better than topiramate, N = better than non-drug average.

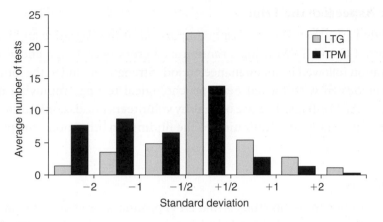

Fig. 2.
Average number of neuropsychological tests with change scores in each SD range for LTG and TPM compared to ND conditions. Reproduced, with permission from *Neurology* 2005; 64: 2108–2114.

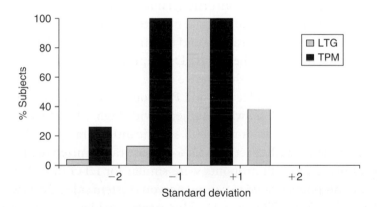

Fig. 3.
Percent of subjects with greater than 25% of neuropsychological change scores in each SD range for LTG and TPM compared to ND conditions.

subjects with >25% of their neuropsychological variables exhibiting ± change scores in different SD ranges for each AED compared to the ND. All 41 subjects had more than a forth of their variables reduced ≥ −1 SD for TPM compared to 13% for LTG. Furthermore, 26% of the subjects had over half of their variables reduced ≥ −1 SD for TPM compared to none for LTG. Improved change scores ≥ +1 SD in over a forth of the variables was seen in 38% of subjects on LTG, but none for TPM.

Unique Aspects of the Trial

This study is the first head-to-head comparison of the cognitive and behavioral effects of LTG and TPM using a randomized cross-over design and slow initiation tritration followed by maintenance period. Strengths included the randomized, cross-over design with formal neuropsychological testing employing measures sensitive to AED effects. The use of healthy volunteers avoids confounding effects of seizures and allows generalization of the findings to other non-epilepsy patient groups.

Conclusions

The main finding from this study is that LTG produces fewer cognitive and behavioral side-effects than TPM. Statistical differences were found in 80% of the variables statistically different, all in favor of LTG. Differences were present across a broad spectrum of measures including both objective and subjective measures. Both LTG and TPM had some adverse neuropsychological side-effects compared to the ND, but the effects of TPM were more marked. Compared to non-drug conditions, TPM was statistically worse on 88% of the variables, and LTG on 17%. TPM was better than non-drug on none, and LTG was better on 10%.

Several limitations of this study should be noted. The findings apply to dosages (in monotherapy), initiation titrations and timeframes employed in this investigation. Although the dosages of the two AEDs employed in this study are within the effective range for both AEDs, the relative efficacy of LTG and TPM at this dose is unknown. The higher blood levels for TPM could have exaggerated the relative effect of TPM. Nevertheless, when subjects with high TPM blood levels were excluded, 46% of the variables were still significantly in favor of LTG. Another limitation of this study is the fact that 37% of those randomized did not complete the study. However, overall dropouts were similar for LTG ($n = 13$) and TPM ($n = 12$), and dropouts related to central nervous system side-effects were greater for TPM ($n = 6$) than LTG ($n = 1$). The greater incidence of central nervous system side-effects for TPM is also apparent in the reported adverse events (see Table 1). Thus, the dropouts for central nervous system toxicity in this study would actually bias in favor of TPM.

Influence on the Field

This investigation provides a direct comparison of the neuropsychological effects of LTG and TPM controlling for a variety of confounding factors. The observed cognitive and behavioral effects of LTG and TPM are consistent with several other studies. A prior study from our group using a similar design in healthy adults demonstrated significantly better performance on 48% of the neuropsychological variables for LTG (150 mg/day) to versus carbamazepine (mean dose = 696 mg/day; mean blood level = 7.6 µg/ml) (Meador *et al.*, 2001). Other healthy volunteer studies have shown fewer cognitive side-effects with LTG compared with carbamazepine, diazepam, phenytoin, placebo, or valproate (Aldenkamp *et al.*, 2002; Hamilton *et al.*, 1993; Cohen *et al.*, 1985). Several studies in epilepsy patients have found that perceived quality of life is improved by LTG compared to placebo or carbamazepine (Brodie *et al.*, 1999; Brodie *et al.*, 1995; Smith *et al.*, 1993). Thus, LTG possesses a favorable profile in terms of cognitive and behavioral side-effects compared to several commonly used AEDs.

In contrast, concerns have been raised over the cognitive effects of TPM although the frequency and magnitude of the effects are debated. The variability in the magnitude of TPM's cognitive effects across studies is due to a variety of factors including: initiation titration, dose, maintenance duration, adjunctive versus monotherapy, measures employed to assess cognitive effects, and variation in idiosyncratic responses to TPM. The cognitive effects of all AEDs are affected by these issues, but TPM appears to be particularly sensitive to these factors. In the early clinical trials, sedation, psychomotor slowing, memory deficits, and language problems (e.g. word-finding difficulty) were reported. However, the magnitude of effects was increased because TPM was quickly titrated to high dosages in adjunctive therapy in these early clinical trials. TPM was found to have markedly more cognitive effects than gabapentin and LTG in a small, single-blind, randomized, parallel-group study of healthy volunteers, but the rapid titration rate likely increased the magnitude of TPM effects (Martin *et al.*, 1999). A small study of non-randomized epilepsy patients tested on and off TPM reported reductions in verbal fluency, attention, processing speed, and working memory (Lee *et al.*, 2003b). A small, open, randomized adjunctive trial in epilepsy patients significantly more cognitive declines for TPM compared to tiagabine (Fritz *et al.*, 2005). A double-blind, randomized, placebo-controlled parallel, healthy volunteer study comparing TPM (330 mg/day) to gabapentin (3600 mg/day) found significantly worse neuropsychological performance for TPM on half of the variables (Salinsky *et al.*, 2005). In contrast, two multicenter, randomized, parallel-group, double-blind adjunctive trials comparing TPM to valproate as adjunctive therapy to carbamazepine in epilepsy patients revealed only a few significant differences at the end of the 8 week maintenance phase following a slow titration (Meador *et al.*, 2003; Aldenkamp *et al.*, 2000). Only one of 17 variables (i.e. verbal memory) worse for TPM in one study (Aldenkamp *et al.*, 2000), and only two of 30 variables (i.e. verbal fluency and a graphomotor task) were worse for TPM in the other study (Meador *et al.*, 2003). Thus, TPM possesses a less favorable profile in terms of cognitive and behavioral side-effects compared to several commonly used AEDs.

Several questions remain unanswered by the presently available data. Additional studies are needed to more fully delineate the relative neuropsychological effects of most other newer AEDs to the older AEDs and to other newer AEDs. Fewer central nervous system adverse events are reported for TPM at lower dosages, but the objective cognitive effects of TPM at lower dosages have not been formally assessed with detailed neuropsychological testing to determine the frequency and magnitude of these effects. The cognitive effects of AEDs at the age extremes are poorly studied even though the elderly and very young have increased susceptibility to the cognitive effects of AEDs. LTG has been shown to be better tolerated than carbamazepine in two studies of elderly patients with new onset epilepsy, but formal neuropsychological data have not been reported (Rowan *et al.*, 2005; Brodie *et al.*, 1999). In fact, there is very little formal neuropsychological data for any AEDs in the elderly. At the other age extreme, there is also inadequate data on the cognitive effects of AEDs in children and the effects of in utero exposure on subsequent cognitive development (Meador, 2004b; Loring & Meador, 2004). Despite the relatively poorer cognitive profile for TPM in adults, it is possible that it possesses a different profile in the very young. For example, TPM appears to be protective against hypoxia and seizures in neonatal animal models. It reduces white matter damage hypoxic-ischemic injury and decreases subsequent neuro-motor deficits in neonatal rats when administered post injury (Follett *et al.*, 2004). In contrast to phenobarbital which worsen cognitive outcomes, TPM improves subsequent water maze performance compared to saline in rats treated after a series of 25 neonatal seizures (Zhao *et al.*, 2005). Unlike several older AEDs (i.e. benzodiazepines, phenobarbital, phenytoin, and valproate), TPM does not produce neuronal apoptosis in neonatal rats (Glier *et al.*, 2004). This finding may have important implications for the human fetus given that the developmental stage of the neonatal rat brain has been related to the third trimester fetal brain. Thus, additional studies of the cognitive effects of AEDs are needed in the elderly and children including in utero exposure.

The drug approval process assesses efficacy and tolerability. Safety is also evaluated, but this effort is directed primarily at serious adverse effects although it also assesses the frequency of subjective adverse events. However, this process may miss important factors related to drug choice. For example, TPM was tolerated in the majority of subjects in the present study, but 26% of those tolerating titration and maintenance had more than a forth of their neuropsychological scores lower than the non-drug conditions by two SD. This is certainly a clinically significant effect, and the magnitude of the effect may well be missed by simple subjective reports. There needs to be more attention paid to formal assessment of adverse cognitive effects in clinical drug trials, especially in those groups at particular risk.

A limitation of all clinical research trials is the problem associated with data analysis for subjects who fail to complete the study to the final endpoint, either because they fail the randomized therapy or because they are lost to follow-up.

An intention-to-treat analysis of the primary treatment outcome is preferred when a randomized clinical trial examines therapeutic efficacy (Lee *et al.*, 1991). This approach is problematic, however, if the major outcome for the study is adverse neuropsychological side-effects of a drug. When a subject discontinues a study early due to an adverse event, it is difficult to perform the neuropsychological testing before the drug is stopped or the dosage is reduced. Thus, the neuropsychological test results would include subjects on lower drug dosages or not on the drug at all. If the last observation is "brought forward" in these cases and used as the value for the final endpoint, then analysis would include results for patients on lower drug dosages or not on the drug at all. If negative AED adverse cognitive effects cause study termination, then that AED appear to have a more favorable cognitive tolerability profile based on the neuropsychological test results. Even if the patient experiencing adverse effects severe enough to cause termination is tested before AED change, unequivalent data may occur due to mismatches in the following:

1. dose if the patient is in the titration phase,
2. time for habituation if before the end of maintenance phase,
3. shorter test-retest interval which would alter practice effects.

The net effect of including neuropsychological data from such patients in the analysis would be to add noise to the analysis. There are several other methods for handling missing values (e.g. multiple imputation, weighted estimation procedures, maximum-likelihood estimates). Such methods are not without their limitations. For example, the statistical adjustment might be based on baseline characteristics. However, the baseline characteristics might bear little relationship to the adverse event or likelihood of adverse neuropsychological effect, especially in a rather homogenous sample. The method employed should be chosen for the specific problem. In the present study, we felt that a logical approach was to assess non-equivalence of tolerability during initiation/maintenance phases and then perform neuropsychological evaluation of the study completers, analyzing the data with the view that the results apply to patients who tolerate the drug initiation and maintenance. This is a practical approach as it relates to clinical practice where the clinician is concerned about the cognitive effects of those tolerating the drug, not in those who have already terminated the drug due to adverse effects. Assessing the cognitive effects in those tolerating initiation and maintenance is particularly important, given the weak relationship of objective cognitive performance to subjective perception of cognitive effects (Perrine *et al.*, 1995). In the current study, TPM had a worse dropout rate due to central nervous system adverse events and a worse profile on formal neuropsychological testing in the subjects completing the study.

Translation to Clinical Practice

Clinicians must assess and balance a variety of factors in treating patients with epilepsy. Factors affecting the choice of AED include efficacy, negative neuropsychological side-effects systemic side-effects, cormorbid disorders (e.g. depression), dosage forms, and cost. Adverse effects on neuropsychological function are an important factor, especially for those patients who have jobs, school, or other daily activities requiring attention, speed and learning. LTG has fewer adverse neuropsychological side-effects than TPM and the older AEDs. The magnitude of the difference between LTG and TPM in some individuals in the present study would certainly be of clinical significance. Many neuropsychological effects of AEDs are frequently unrecognized in clinical practice, but can have clinical impact even when relatively modest. There is a consistent highly significant inverse correlation of neurotoxicity symptoms to a patient's perception of their quality of life, which is present even in the absence of overt toxicity on clinical examination (Gilliam, 2003). In addition to its lower adverse cognitive profile, LTG may also produce positive effects on perceived health-related quality of life. TPM has been demonstrated to have slightly worse cognitive side-effects than valproate in adjunctive therapy when titrated slowly (Meador *et al.*, 2003; Aldenkamp *et al.*, 2000). Since the cognitive effects of valproate are similar to carbamazepine and phenytoin (Meador, 2004a), TPM would appear to have slightly worse cognitive effects than the most commonly used older AEDs. The magnitude of TPM's effect increases with faster initiation and higher dosages. However, the effects may be less at dosages lower than those formally tested thus far. Although TPM is more likely to produce cognitive effects overall, it may be the most effective and best tolerated AED for the individual patient. This information should be considered by the clinician and communicated to the patient when making treatment decisions. The ultimate goal is to obtain seizure freedom, minimize side-effects, and maximize the patient's quality of life.

Acknowledgements

This study was supported by a grant from Glaxo SmithKline. Original results were published in *Neurology* 2005; 64: 2108–2114. My thanks to F.G. Gilliam for his advice in study design and my co-investigators in conducting the study: D.W. Loring, V.J. Vahle, P.G. Ray, M.A. Werz, A.J. Fessler, P. Ogrocki, M.R. Schoenberg, J.M. Miller, and R.P. Kustra.

References

Abbetz, L., Jacoby, A., Baker, G.A., & McNulty, P. (2000). Patient based assessments of quality of life in newly diagnosed epilepsy patients: validation of the NEWQOL. *Epilepsia*, 41, 1119–1128.

Aldenkamp, A.P., Baker, G., Pieters, M.S., Schoemaker, H.C., Cohen, A.F., & Schwabe, S. (1995). The neurotoxicity scale: the validity of a patient-based scale assessing neurotoxicity. *Epilepsy Research*, 20, 229–239.

Aldenkamp, A.P., Baker, G., Mulder, O.G., *et al.* (2000). A multicenter, randomized clinical study to evaluate the effect on cognitive function of topiramate compared with valproate as add-on therapy to carbamazepine in patients with partial-onset seizures. *Epilepsia*, 41, 1167–1178.

Aldenkamp, A.P., Arends, J., Bootsma, H.P., *et al.* (2002). Randomized double-blind parallel-group study comparing cognitive effects of a low-dose lamotrigine with valproate and placebo in healthy volunteers. *Epilepsia*, 43, 19–26.

Brodie, M.J., Richens, A., & Yuen, A.W.C. (1995). Double-blind comparison of lamotrigine and carbamazepine in newly diagnosed epilepsy. *Lancet*, 345, 476–479.

Brodie, M.J., Overstall, P.W., Giorgi, L., & UK Lamotrigine Elderly Study Group (1999). Multicentre, double-blind, randomized comparison between lamotrigine and carbamazepine in elderly patients with newly diagnosed epilepsy. *Epilepsy Researh*, 37, 81–87.

Burton, L.A., & Harden, C. (1997). Effect of topiramate on attention. *Epilepsy Research*, 27, 29–32.

Buschke, H., & Fuld, P.A. (1974). Evaluating storage, retention, and retrieval in disordered memory and learning. *Neurology*, 24, 1019–1025.

Cohen, A.F., Ashby, L., Crowley, D., Land, G., Peck, A.W., & Miller, A.A. (1985). Lamotrigine (BW430C) potential anticonvulsant. Effects on the central nervous in comparison with phenytoin and diazepam. *British Journal of Clinical Pharmacology*, 29, 619–629.

Devinsky, O., Vickrey, B.G., Cramer, J., *et al.* (1995). Development of the quality of life in epilepsy (QOLIE) Inventory. *Epilepsia*, 36, 1089–1104.

Dodrill, C.B., Arnett, J.L., Sommerville, K.W., & Sussman, N.M. (1995). Effects of differing dosages of vigabatrin (Sabril) on cognitive abilities and quality of life in epilepsy. *Epilepsia*, 36, 164–173.

Dunn, L.M., & Dunn, L.M. (1997). *Peabody Picture Vocabulary Test* (3rd ed.). Circle Pines, MN: American Guidance Services.

Follett, P.L., Deng, W., Dai, W., Talos, D.M., Massillon, L.J., Rosenberg, P.A., Volpe, J.J., & Jensen, F.E. (2004). Glutamate receptor-mediated oligodendrocyte toxicity in periventricular leukomalacia: a protective role for topiramate. *Neurosci*, 24, 4412–4420.

Fritz, N., Glogau, S., Hoffmann, J., Rademacher, M., Elger, C.E., & Helmstaedter, C. (2005). Efficacy and cognitive side effects of tiagabine and topiramate in patients with epilepsy. *Epilepsy and Behavior*, 6, 373–381.

Gillham, R., Baker, G., Thompson, P., *et al.* (1996). Standardization of self-report questionnaire for use in evaluating cognitive, affective and behavioral side-effects of antiepileptic drug treatments. *Epilepsy Research*, 24, 47–55.

Gilliam, F. (2003). The impact of epilepsy on subjective health status. *Current Neurology and Neuroscience Reports*, 3, 357–362.

Glauser, T.A. (1999). Topiramate. *Epilepsia*, 40, S71–S80.

Glier, C., Dzietko, M., Bittigau, P., *et al.* (2004). Therapeutic doses of topiramate are not toxic to the developing rat brain. *Experimental Neurology*, 187, 403–409.

Golden, C.J. (1978). *Stroop Color and Word Test. A Manual for Clinical and Experimental Uses.* Chicago: Stoelting.

Hamilton, M.J., Cohen, A.F., Yuen, A.W.C., *et al.* (1993). Carbamazepine and lamotrigine in healthy volunteers: relevance to early tolerance and clinical trial dosages. *Epilepsia*, 34, 166–173.

Henry, J.D., & Crawford, J.R. (2004). A meta-analytic review of verbal fluency performance following cortical lesions. *Neuropsychology*, 18, 284–295.

Jette, N.J., Marson, A.G., & Hutton, J.L. (2002). Topiramate add-on for drug-resistant partial epilepsy. *Cochrane Database Systematic Reviews*, 3, CD001417.

Kaplan, E., Goodglass, H. & Weintraub, S. (1983). *The Boston Naming Test.* Philadelphia: Lea & Febiger.

Lachman, R., Lachman, J.L., & Butterfield, E.C. (1979). *Cognitive Psychology and Information Processing: An Introduction*. Hillsdale, NJ: Lawrence Erlbaum.

LaRoche, S.M., & Helmers, S.L. (2004). The new antiepileptic drugs: scientific review. *Journal of the American Medical Association*, 291, 605–614.

Lee, Y.J., Ellenberg, J.H., Hirtz, D.G., & Nelson, K.B. (1991). Analysis of clinical trials by treatment actually received: is it really an option? *Statistics in Medicine*, 10, 1595–1605.

Lee, S., Sziklas, V., Andermann, F., *et al.* (2003a). The effects of adjunctive topiramate on cognitive function in patients with epilepsy. *Epilepsia*, 44, 339–347.

Lee, S., Sziklas, V., Andermann, F., *et al.* (2003b). The effects of adjunctive topiramate on cognitive function in patients with epilepsy. *Epilepsia*, 44, 339–347.

Lezak, M.D. (1995). *Neuropsychological Assessment* (3rd ed.). New York: Oxford University Press.

Loring, D.W., & Meador, K.J. (2004). Cognitive side effects of antiepileptic drugs in children. [Review]. *Neurology*, 62, 872–877.

Lorr, M., McNair, D.M., & Droppleman, L.F. (1971). *Manual: Profile of Mood States*. San Diego, CA: Educational and Industrial Testing Service.

Martin, R., Kuzniecky, R., Ho, S., *et al.* (1999). Cognitive effects of topiramate, gabapentin, and lamotrigine in healthy young adults. *Neurology*, 52, 321–327.

Meador, K.J. (1998). Cognitive and behavioral assessments in AED trials. *Antiepileptic Drug Development. Advances in Neurology*, 23, 231–237.

Meador, K.J. (2004a). Cognitive effects of epilepsy and of antiepileptic medications. In: Wyllie, E. (ed.), *The Treatment of Epilepsy: Principles and Practice* (4th ed.). Philadelphia: Lippincott Williams & Wilkins, pp. 1215–1226.

Meador, K.J. (2004b). Cognitive deficits from in utero AED exposure. *Epilepsy Currents*, 4, 196–197.

Meador, K.J., Loring, D.W., Allen, M.E., *et al.* (1991). Comparative cognitive effects of carbamazepine and phenytoin in healthy adults. *Neurology*, 41, 1537–1540.

Meador, K.J., Loring, D.W., Abney, O.L., *et al.* (1993). Effects of carbamazepine and phenytoin on EEG and memory in healthy adults. *Epilepsia*, 34, 153–115.

Meador, K.J., Loring, D.W., Moore, E.E., *et al.* (1995). Comparative cognitive effects of phenobarbital, phenytoin and valproate in healthy subjects. *Neurology*, 45, 1494–1499.

Meador, K.J., Loring, D.W., Ray, P.G., *et al.* (1999). Differential cognitive effects of carbamazepine and gabapentin. *Epilepsia*, 40, 1279–1285.

Meador, K.J., Loring, D.W., Ray, P.G., *et al.* (2001). Differential cognitive and behavioral effects of carbamazepine and lamotrigine. *Neurology*, 8, 1177–1182.

Meador, K.J., Loring, D.W., Hulihan, J.F., Kamin, M., & Karim, R. (2003). Differential cognitive and behavioral effects of topiramate and valproate. *Neurology*, 60, 1483–1488.

Meador, K.J., Loring, D.W., Vahle, V.J., Ray, P.G., Werz, M.A., Fessler, A.J., Ogrocki, P. Schoenberg, M.R., Miller, J.M., & Kustra, R.P. (2005). Cognitive and behavioral effects of lamotrigine and topiramate in healthy volunteers. *Neurology*, 64, 2108–2115.

Perrine, K., Hermann, B.P., Meador, K.J., Vickrey, B.G., Cramer, J.A., Hays, R.D., & Devinsky, O. (1995). The relationship of neuropsychological functioning to quality of life in epilepsy. *Archives of Neurology*, 52, 997–1003.

Physicians' Desk Reference. (2005) (60th ed.). Montvale, NJ: Thomson PDR.

Ray, P.G., Meador, K.J., Loring, D.W., Zamrini, E.Y., Yang, X.H., & Buccafusco, J.J. (1992). Central anticholinergic hypersensitivity in aging. *Journal of Geriatric Psychiatry and Neurology*, 5, 72–77.

Rowan, A.J., Ramsay, R.E., Collins, J.F., Pryor, F., Boardman, K.D., Uthman, B.M., Spitz, M., Frederick, T., Towne, A., Carter, G.S., Marks, W., Felicetta, J., Tomyanovich, M.L., & VA Cooperative Study 428 Group. (2005). New onset geriatric epilepsy: a randomized study of gabapentin, lamotrigine, and carbamazepine. *Neurology*, 64, 1868–1873.

Salinsky, M.C., Storzbach, D., Spencer, D.C., Oken, B.S., Landry, T., & Dodrill, C.B. (2005). Effects of topiramate and gabapentin on cognitive abilities in healthy volunteers. *Neurology*, 64, 792–798.

Smith, A. (1973). *Symbol Digit Modalities Test. Manual*. Los Angeles: Western Psychological Services.

Smith, D., Baker, G., Davies, G., Dewey, M., & Chadwick, D.W. (1993). Outcomes of add-on treatment with lamotrigine in partial epilepsy. *Epilepsia*, 34, 312–322.

Spreen, O., & Strauss, E. (1998). *A Compendium of Neuropsychological Tests: Administration, Norms and Commentary*. New York: Oxford University Press.

Steiner, T.J., Dellaportas, C.I., Findley, L.J., *et al.* (1999). Lamotrigine monotherapy in newly diagnosed untreated epilepsy: a double-blind comparison with phenytoin. *Epilepsia*, 40, 601–607.

Thompson, P.J., Baxendale, S.A., & Duncan, J.S., Sander, J.W.A.S. (2000). Effects of topiramate on cognitive function. *Journal of Neurology Neurosurgery and Psychiatry*, 69, 636–641.

Ware, J.E., Kosinski, M., & Keller, S.D. (1996). A 12-item short-form health survey: construction of scales and preliminary tests of reliability and validity. *Medical Care*, 34, 220–233.

Zhao, Q., Hu, Y., & Holmes, G.L. (2005). Effect of topiramate on cognitive function and activity level following neonatal seizures. *Epilepsy Behavior*, 6, 529–536.

Progress in Neurotherapeutics and Neuropsychopharmacology, 2:1, 97–108 © 2007 Cambridge University Press
DOI: 10.1017/S1748232106000073   Printed in the United Kingdom

Pilot Clinical Trial of NT-3 in CMT1A Patients

Zarife Sahenk

Department of Neurology and Pediatrics, The Ohio State University, Columbus Children's Research Institute, Neuromuscular program, Columbus, OH, USA; Email: sahenkz@ccri.net

Key words: CMT disease, NT-3, regeneration, Schwann cell

Introduction and Overview

In Charcot-Marie-Tooth type 1A (CMT1A), despite the primary genetic abnormality in the myelin producing Schwann cell (SC), the clinical phenotype is characterized by axonal damage in the distal limbs leading to muscle atrophy below the knees and in the hands, foot drop, and distal sensory loss. This typical clinical presentation, a length dependent axonal disease correlates well with the major pathological component, a preferential distal axonal loss, an important feature of almost all CMT neuropathies. Impaired regeneration in CMT neuropathies could also be a contributing factor to the decreased nerve fibers distally in nerve. Our studies of the xenografts from patients with CMT1A have shown delay in onset of myelination and impairment in the regeneration capacity of nude mice axons passing through the grafted segments and that this defect is most pronounced for the large diameter axons (Sahenk *et al.*, 2003; 1999).

The long term outcome of a length dependent distal axonal disease depends on two seemingly opposing, but intimately associated processes: (1) the degree or rate of axonal degeneration, progressing centripetally towards cell body and (2) the ability of the nascent axon tips to regenerate efficiently. In conditions such as diabetic or hereditary neuropathy where there is defect in regeneration, a slow progressive course is seen, because the ongoing degeneration, even at a low rate, will be unopposed. One strategy to alter these processes in favor of anatomical and functional integrity of the nerve would be to improve the efficiency of regeneration. Experimental studies revealed that the regeneration outcome is poor following prolonged axotomy and denervation, which simulates a chronic longstanding neuropathic process in humans (Sulaiman, 2000; Li *et al.*, 1997; Sunderland, 1952). Factors that might influence this decreased regeneration capacity include

Correspondence should be addressed to: Zarife Sahenk, MD, PhD, Department of Neurology and Pediatrics, The Ohio State University, Columbus Children's Research Institute, Neuromuscular program, Columbus, OH, USA; Tel: +614 722 2202; Fax: +614 355 5247; Email: sahenkz@ccri.net

a reduction in the expression of neurotrophic factors and their receptors in SCs and the eventual atrophy and loss of the denervated SCs and the breakdown of the bands of Bungner, with their SC basal lamina scaffoldings. Therefore, for efficient regeneration, SCs distal to the axonal injury site must remain competent to support axonal growth for prolonged periods. Some of the experimental strategies used to improve functional recovery after peripheral nerve injury with potential from bench to bedside have been reviewed elsewhere (Boyd, 2003). One potentially promising approach is the exogenous supply of neurotrophic factors that are part of the SC autocrine survival loop such as neurotrophin-3 (NT-3), which we used in our studies of experimental models of CMT and in patients with CMT1A (Sahenk *et al.*, 2005; Mirsky *et al.*, 2002; Meier *et al.*, 1999; Syroid *et al.*, 1999).

Purpose of the Trial

To conduct a double-blind, placebo-controlled, randomized pilot clinical study to assess the effects of subcutaneously administered recombinant methionyl human NT-3 (r-metHuNT-3) on motor and sensory symptoms in patients with CMT1A.

Agent

NT-3 is expressed in SCs, promotes nerve regeneration, and is an important component of the autocrine survival loop, ensuring SC survival and differentiation in adult nerves in the absence of axons (Mirsky *et al.*, 2002; Meier *et al.*, 1999; Syroid *et al.*, 1999; Frostick *et al.*, 1998; Sterne *et al.*, 1997). We hypothesized that NT-3 would promote SC survival and competency in the denervated distal segment of the CMT nerve and establish a favorable microenvironment for nerve regeneration in the distal limb of the CMT patient (Mirsky *et al.*, 2002; Meier *et al.*, 1999; Syroid *et al.*, 1999). NT-3 is also particularly attractive because it acts synergistically with other members of the SC autocrine survival loop, insulin-like growth factors (IGFs) and platelet-derived growth factor-BB (PDGF-BB) to promote nerve regeneration and enhance autocrine survival (Oya *et al.*, 2002; Lobsiger *et al.*, 2000; Meier *et al.*, 1999). For this trial r-metHuNT-3 or identical-appearing placebo was supplied by Regeneron Pharmaceuticals, Inc. (Tarrytown, NY) in single-use vials.

Relevant Past Clinical Experience, Phase I or Preclinical Data

In our preclinical studies, we tested the ability of mutant SCs to respond to NT-3 in two different paradigms: a xenograft model of SCs with the common PMP22 duplication of CMT1A and with a naturally occurring animal model, *Trembler-J* (*Tr^J*) mice, which carry a point mutation in the PMP22 gene. Nude mice harboring CMT1A xenografts and *Tr^J* mice with sciatic crush injury were treated with NT-3 and the myelinated fiber (MF) and SC numbers were quantitated.

The NT-3 treatment augmented axonal regeneration and the associated myelination process in both animal models (Sahenk *et al.*, 2005).

The results of a prior phase I safety trial involving about 80 people demonstrate that subcutaneous administration of r-metHuNT-3 at doses of 25, 75 and 150 μg/kg three times a week (TTW) has been well tolerated. The most common side effects were redness, pain and itching at the injection site, a feeling of pins and needles-like tingling in the arms and legs, and change in bowel habits. Administration of 300 μg/kg/TTW is associated with a marked increase in gastrointestinal motility. The only major adverse effect of concern, seen only at the highest dose studied (300 μg/kg TTW) was sinus bradycardia, which was asymptomatic in one patient and associated with findings of light-headedness in another. Data from preclinical and clinical Phase I studies suggested a possible relationship between r-metHuNT-3 administration and mild elevations in alamine aminotransferase (ALT), and aspartate aminotransferase (AST) levels without abnormalities in other indicators of liver function. Similar elevations were not observed in the more recent study when NT-3 was administered to normal volunteer patients or constipated patients at a dose of 300 μg/kg TTW. Thus, there appear to be no significant safety concerns with regard to elevated transaminase levels when r-metHuNT-3 is administered at doses between 25 and 300 μg/kg TTW for up to 6 months.

Clinical Trial

A double-blind, placebo-controlled exploratory safety and bioeffect study, assessing the efficacy of subcutaneously administered r-metHuNT-3 in patients with CMT1A, was carried over 28 weeks following approval by the Institutional Review Board for the use of human subjects. Randomization was done by a research pharmacist using a random number table. Following a 2-week observation period, patients received injections of either placebo, or 50 μg/kg r-metHuNT-3, TTW for 2 weeks. The dose was increased to 100 and 150 μg/kg at 2-week intervals by increasing the volume of injection. Safety assessments were done monthly. The subjects were interviewed by the study coordinator according to the study protocol. All adverse events were reported to a safety monitor separate from the clinical evaluator. Assessments of peripheral nerve function was obtained twice at an interval of not more than 2 weeks prior to initiating NT-3 or placebo treatment, and at the end of treatment at 24 weeks. Fascicular sural nerve biopsies were obtained before and after treatment. A final study visit occurred 4 weeks after withdrawal of the study drug.

Subjects

Males and nonpregnant, nonlactating females (age >18 and ≤45 years) with CMT1A, proven with DNA diagnosis of PMP22 duplications were recruited. Eight patients were randomly assigned to receive either recombinant human NT-3 or identical-appearing placebo in single-use vials. The placebo group consisted of one female and three males, ages 21–44 (33.25 ± 4.73) versus the NT-3 group, three females and one male, ages 30–45 (39.00 ± 3.185).

Trial Methods, Instruments/Measures

Fascicular sural nerve biopsies (the lateral half of nerves), were obtained before the start of treatment (from left sural) and at the end of the study (from right sural) to assess the effects of NT-3 on the MF regeneration and SC density. Assessments of peripheral nerve function were obtained twice at 2-week intervals prior to initiating NT-3 or placebo treatment, and again at the end of treatment. Neuropathy impairment score (NIS) was completed according to Dyck *et al.* (Dyck *et al.*, 1995; 1980). A standard group of muscles were evaluated for weakness and muscle stretch reflexes. Perceptions of touch-pressure, pricking pain, temperature (hot and cold), vibration and joint position were graded on the index finger and the great toe as normal (0), decreased (1), or absent (2). In addition, the level of discrimination change for sensory modalities was recorded in each limb as normal (0), diminished or absent in fingers or toes (1), between fingers/toes and wrist or ankle (2), between wrist/ankle and elbow or knee (3), and above the level of elbow or knee (4). A Rydel-Seiffer graduated tuning fork was used to assess the vibration level (average of three repeat tests) (Martina *et al.*, 1998). Response scores for each subject were obtained by averaging right and left side values from two baseline and two post-treatment evaluations. Neuropathy functional rating scale, electrophysiologic measurements of sural, superficial peroneal, radial, median and ulnar sensory nerves and peroneal, median and ulnar motor nerves, maximum voluntary isometric contraction testing (MVICT) of biceps, hand grip, knee flexors, and ankle dorsiflexors bilaterally and pegboard performance were also assessed. No further data was collected on subjects after they exited the study.

Primary and Secondary Outcomes

The biological effect of NT-3 was assessed by sural nerve biopsies before and after treatment. MF regeneration in sural nerve biopsies before and after treatment served as the primary outcome measure. The clinical outcome measures included the Mayo Clinic NIS, electrophysiologic measurements, quantitative muscle testing and pegboard performance.

Analysis

Morphological Analyses of Sural Nerves

A 1 μm thick plastic embedding of nerve specimens were used for morphometric analyses. Entire cross-sectional fascicular areas from all available nerve fascicles were serially photographed and were assembled using prints at a final magnification of $\times 900$. Using a grid system, each fascicle was systematically screened to determine the number of MFs within each "unit", defined as single or clusters of MFs partially or completely surrounded by SC processes, and those solitary MFs without associated SC processes. Each fascicular area was determined using image analysis software. The number of MF per unit per mm^2 of endoneurial area, the number of solitary MFs per mm^2 of endoneurial area and the total MF density for each fascicle were determined. In five randomly selected areas from each biopsy, the SC densities were estimated as outlined previously using the Bioquant TCW98 image analysis software.

Statistical Analyses

Statistical analyses were performed using SAS JMP version 5 (SAS Institute, Cary, NC). Mixed effect statistical models were used for repeated measure data. A two-way analysis of variance (ANOVA) model was used with time and treatment group as predictors in most analyses. Interaction effects were included when found significant and associated p-values are reported. They indicate that the change in the mean response for the NT-3 group is significantly different from the change for the placebo group. Residuals were examined for model validity. *Post-hoc* t-tests were used to determine significance of specific comparisons. Summary statistics are reported as least squares mean $\pm$ standard error. Two sample t-tests for means were employed for cross-sectional comparisons. The t-tests were two-sided and normality was checked for each situation and equality of variance assumptions were tested using Levene's test. Appropriate (pooled Welch's) t-tests were then employed.

Results

Nerve Regeneration in Sural Nerves

Sural nerves from the NT-3 treated group showed an increase in the number of thinly MFs forming regeneration units, clustered with fibers containing thicker myelin (Figure 1a–c). Occasional units contained over 10 MFs and were partially surrounded by SC processes. In addition, thinly myelinated small diameter solitary fibers appeared more commonly in the NT-3 group. These fibers were not surrounded with SC processes but located in close vicinity to onion bulbs. These observations and ultrastructural studies suggested that clustered SCs that form onion bulbs serve as trails for axonal regeneration similar to Bünger's bands, and that as the new axonal growth occurs, they lose their classic multi-layered appearance and unravel. To test this, each fascicle was systematically screened to determine the number of MFs within each "unit", the frequency of each unit with the same number of MFs, and the solitary MFs.

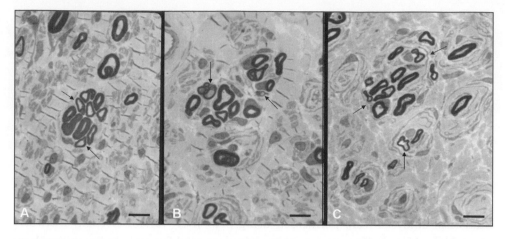

Fig. 1 (a–c).
A 1 μm thick, toluidine blue stained cross-sections of sural nerves from NT-3 treated subjects showing multiple thinly myelinated axons within regeneration units (arrows) clustered with fibers with thicker myelin. Bar = 10 μm.

Statistical analysis revealed that the changes in the NT-3 group were different from that observed in the placebo group for the mean number of small MFs within regeneration units ($p = 0.0001$), solitary MFs, ($p = 0.0002$). Significant improvements in these variables were detected in the NT-3 group, but not in the placebo group (Figure 2a and b).

Tukey's HSD (honesty significant differences) test was carried out to see whether any of the means is different from the rest at 5% level. It confirmed these findings in both cases. Figure 2c is the relative frequency histogram, averaged over all fascicles within group and time, shows the mean density of units (number/mm^2) containing 1, 2, and 3 or more MFs before and after treatment in the NT-3 or placebo groups. NT-3 treatment resulted in a decrease in the number of units with 1 MF (the classic onion bulbs), while the units containing 2, 3, or more increased. ANOVA comparison of the relative frequency on the log scale revealed significant interaction effects. The units with 2 ($p = 0.0002$) and with 3 or more ($p = 0.0041$) MFs increased in the NT-3 group while there was no change for the placebo group. For the mean SC density, changes in the NT-3 group was different from that was observed in the placebo ($p < 0.0001$). Similar to our observations in Tr^J mice, there was an increase in the mean SC density for the treatment group (2131/mm^2 or 36%; $p < 0.0001$, by paired t-test) and a decrease for the placebo group (1204/mm^2 or 18%; $p < 0.0001$, by paired t-test). The SC density decrease in placebo over the treatment period could be explained with the progressive nature of the disease process.

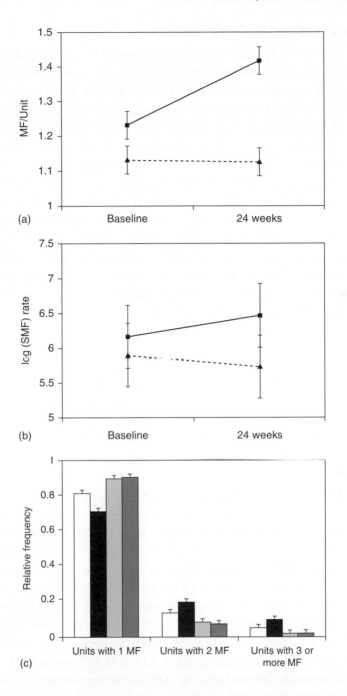

Fig. 2.
Least square means and standard errors of (a) mean MF number/unit and (b) solitary MF density, number per mm^2 (in log scale) at baseline and 24 weeks for NT-3 treated (■) and placebo (▲) . (c) Average relative frequencies of units with different MF numbers and their standard errors [NT-3 group at baseline (□) and 24 weeks (■), placebo group at baseline (▦)and 24 weeks (▩)].

Efficacy (NIS and Sensory Function)

Summary statistics for the NIS variables, grouped by the visit numbers are provided in Table 1. Pre- and post-treatment values for placebo and the pre-treatment value for the NT-3 group were not significantly different from each other (Figure 3). ANOVA, carried out on the mean composite score data on a log scale with groups, time and their interactions as predictors, revealed that the improvement in NT-3 group is different from that observed in the placebo group ($p = 0.0041$). Further, it also showed that NT-3 treatment improved the total score ($p = 0.0017$; ANOVA followed by Tukey's HSD test). When motor, sensory and reflex scores were analyzed separately, NT-3 treatment had a different improvement on mean sensory ($p = 0.0051$) and reflex scores ($p = 0.0366$), but not on motor score ($p = 0.409$), when compared to the changes in the placebo group. In the NT-3 group the mean of sensory score went up by 1.54 and the reflex score went up and 2.38.

The lack of effect of NT-3 on motor function was confirmed with MVICT, which showed no significant change over treatment period whereas vibratory sensation, tested using the Rydel-Seiffer graduated tuning fork-generated data, revealed a significant increase of vibration at big toe in the NT-3 group. Summary measures for the pre- and post-treatment mean toe values were 3.666 ± 1.465 and 5.260 ± 1.465, and the difference from baseline to 24 weeks, was 1.594 ± 0.364 ($p = 0.0002$). The least squares mean values for Rydel-Seiffer values for the index finger were above 7 (8/8 is being exquisitely normal) and did not change over the treatment period. No significant change in the placebo group was seen although there was a trend toward worsening at 24 weeks. Between group comparisons were not carried out since there were several absent (0) vibrations recorded in the placebo group.

Trends for improvement were found in the NT-3 group but not in the placebo for the change in the level of discrimination for sensory modalities in the distal limbs for pin, vibration and cold-temperature modalities. The perception of prickling pain in the index fingers was unchanged (1.25 ± 0.425 for the pre-treatment and 0.125 ± 0.125 for the post-treatment; $n = 4$). The vibration level was normal at baseline and remained unchanged in the upper extremities, but the impairment level receded distally in the lower extremities (1.25 ± 0.48 pre-treatment versus 0.5 ± 0.29 post-treatment; $n = 4$). Similar changes for pre- and post-treatment of cold appreciation levels were observed in both upper (1.75 ± 0.25 versus 0.56 ± 0.21) and lower extremities (1.875 ± 0.315 versus 1.31 ± 0.235). Each change in scores for all modalities is clarified as improvement, no change or worsening condition. Since the sample size is small, the data are ordinal and dependent, formal comparisons were not carried out.

Pegboard performance was significantly worsened in the placebo group. Summary measures for the pre- and post-treatment time points were 13.375 ± 1.364 and 12.500 ± 1.364 ($p = 0.0354$). NT-3 did not affect the

Table 1. **NISs (Mean ± SD) in NT-3 and Placebo**

GROUP	VISIT NUMBER	MOTOR	REFLEX	SENSORY	TOTAL
NT-3	V1	6.125 ± 2.69	6 ± 2.69	9.625 ± 3.64	21.75 ± 8.47
	V2	6.125 ± 2.69	6 ± 2.83	9.125 ± 3.61	21.25 ± 8.23
	V10	5.5 ± 2.86	2.5 ± 2.65	5.125 ± 2.59	13.125 ± 6.70
	V11	5.375 ± 3.01	2.75 ± 2.75	7 ± 2.92	15.125 ± 8.00
Placebo	V1	5.25 ± 4.03	3.5 ± 2.89	9 ± 4.81	17.75 ± 9.73
	V2	5.375 ± 4.27	3.75 ± 2.87	8.5 ± 3.98	17.625 ± 9.22
	V10	5 ± 4.97	4.5 ± 3.32	9.25 ± 2.87	18.75 ± 9.95
	V11	5.5 ± 4.51	4.25 ± 3.10	9.25 ± 4.41	19 ± 10.95

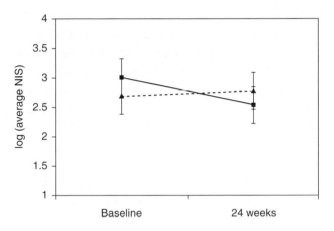

Fig. 3.

Least-square estimates of the means of natural log (average NIS-INS) for NT-3 treated (■) and placebo (▲) and associated standard errors at baseline and 24 weeks.

pegboard performance over the study period. Post-treatment nerve conduction velocities and amplitude of nerve action potentials showed no change from baseline values.

Tolerability

NT-3 was well tolerated. Adverse events did not necessitate dose reduction.

Safety

The adverse events reported by the patients are shown in Table 2. In the NT-3 group, all subjects reported minor irritation at the injection site and mild diarrhea or constipation which responded to changes in diet. Two women reported episodes of delayed or irregular menstruation, which resolved while they were still on the study drug.

Table 2. **Adverse Events**

	NT-3	PLACEBO
Fatigue	2	2
Diarrhea	3	
Constipation	1	
Soreness at injection site	3	
Redness, itching at injection site	1	1
Pins and needles	3	
Menstrual irregularity	2	

Unique Aspects of Trial

This is the first clinical study demonstrating possible benefit for CMT1A. In the four subjects who received NT-3, large- and small-fiber sensory modalities improved, and sural nerve fascicular biopsies showed increased numbers of thinly myelinated axons and increased numbers of SC nuclei. Results of this study needs to be substantiated with a large multi-center clinical trial. Several *in vivo* and *in vitro* studies show that exogenous NT-3 increase the level of nerve regeneration through a direct effect on neurons (Sterne *et al.*, 1997; Mohiuddin *et al.* 1995). Observations that NT-3 treatment increased the numbers of SCs in both sural nerves from CMT1A patients and in Tr^J sciatic nerve segments distal to a crush provide support for an alternative possibility that NT-3 improves mutant SC survival and differentiation, resulting in increases in the available SC pool, which in turn increases the number of MFs. Based on these biological properties of NT-3, it might be predict that other inherited or acquired neuropathies such as diabetes may benefit as well. These promising results may stimulate future studies to include potential combinations with other growth factors and with different routes of NT-3 administration including delivery of recombinant NT-3 by viral vectors such as adeno-associated virus(AAV) that can be taken from banch to bedside.

Disclosure

NT-3 and matching placebo were supplied by Regeneron Pharmaceuticals at no cost to the patients or the investigator. The clinical trial was supported by a grant from Neuropathy Association.

References

Boyd, J.G., & Gordon, T. (2003). Neurotrophic factors and their receptors in axonal regeneration and functional recovery after peripheral nerve injury. *Molecular Neurobiology*, 27(3), 277–324.

Dyck, P.J., Sherman, W.R., Hallcher, L.M., *et al.* (1980). Human diabetic endoneurial sorbitol, fructose, and myo-inositol related to sural nerve morphometry. *Annals of Neurology*, 8(6), 590–596.

Dyck, P.J., Litchy, W.J., Lehman, K.A., Hokanson, J.L., Low, P.A., & O'Brien, P.C. (1995). Variables influencing neuropathic endpoints: the Rochester Diabetic Neuropathy Study of Healthy Subjects. *Neurology*, 45(6), 1115–1121.

Frostick, S.P., Yin, Q., & Kemp, G.J. (1998). Schwann cells, neurotrophic factors, and peripheral nerve regeneration. *Microsurgery*, 18(7), 397–405.

Li, H., Terengi, G., & Hall, S.M. (1997). Effects of delayed re-innervation on the expression of c-erbB receptors by chronically denervated rat Schwann cells in vivo. *Glia*, 20, 333–347.

Lobsiger, C.S., Schweitzer, B., Taylor, V., & Suter, U. (2000). Platelet-derived growth factor-BB supports the survival of cultured rat Schwann cell precursors in synergy with neurotrophin-3. *Glia*, 30(3), 290–300.

Martina, I.S., van Koningsveld, R., Schmitz, P.I., van der Meche, F.G., & van Doorn, P.A. (1998). Measuring vibration threshold with a graduated tuning fork in normal aging and in patients with polyneuropathy. European Inflammatory Neuropathy Cause and Treatment (INCAT) group. *Journal of Neurology Neurosurgery and Psychiatry*, 65(5), 743–747.

Meier, C., Parmantier, E., Brennan, A., Mirsky, R., & Jessen, K.R. (1999). Developing Schwann cells acquire the ability to survive without axons by establishing an autocrine circuit involving insulin-like growth factor, neurotrophin-3, and platelet-derived growth factor-BB. *Journal of Neuroscience*, 19, 3847–3859.

Mirsky, R., Jessen, K.R., Brennan, A., *et al.* (2002). Schwann cells as regulators of nerve development. *Journal of Physiology Paris*, 96(1–2), 17–24.

Mohiuddin, L., Fernandez, K., Tomlinson, D.R., & Fernyhough, P. (1995). Nerve growth factor and neurotrophin-3 enhance neurite outgrowth and up-regulate the levels of messenger RNA for growth-associated protein GAP-43 and T alpha 1 alpha-tubulin in cultured adult rat sensory neurones. *Neuroscience Letter*, 185(1), 20–23.

Oya, T., Zhao, Y.L., Takagawa, K., *et al.* (2002). Platelet-derived growth factor-b expression induced after rat peripheral nerve injuries. *Glia*, 38(4), 303–312.

Sahenk, Z., Chen, L., & Mendell, J.R. (1999). Effects of PMP22 duplication and deletions on the axonal cytoskeleton [see comments]. *Annals of Neurology*, 45, 16–24.

Sahenk, Z., Serrano-Munuera, C., Chen, L., Kakabadze, I., & Najagara, H.N. (2003). Evidence for impaired axonal regeneration in PMP22 duplication: studies in nerve xenografts. *Journal of the Peripheral Nervous System*, 8(2), 116–127.

Sahenk, Z., Nagaraja, H., McCracken, B.S., King, W.M., Freimer, M.L., Cederbaum, J.M., & Mendell, J.R. (2005). Neurotrophin-3 promotes nerve regeneration and sensory improvement in CMT1A mouse models and in patients. *Neurology*, 54, 681–689.

Sulaiman, O.A., & Gordon, T. (2000). Effects of short and long term Schwann cell denervation on peripheral nerve regeneration, myelination and size. *Glia*, 32, 234–246.

Sunderland, S. (1952). Factors influencing the course of regeneration and quality of recovery after nerve suture. *Brain*, 75, 19–54.

Sterne, G.D., Brown, R.A., Green, C.J., & Terenghi, G. (1997). Neurotrophin-3 delivered locally via fibronectin mats enhances peripheral nerve regeneration. *European Journal of Neuroscience*, 9(7), 1388–1396.

Syroid, D.E., Zorick, T.S., Arbet-Engels, C., Kilpatrick, T.J., Eckhart, W., & Lemke, G. (1999). A role for insulin-like growth factor-I in the regulation of Schwann cell survival. *Journal of Neuroscience*, 19, 2059–2068.

Progress in Neurotherapeutics and Neuropsychopharmacology, 2:1, 109–122 © 2007 Cambridge University Press
DOI: 10.1017/S1748232106000085   Printed in the United Kingdom

New Directions in Pediatric Neuro-Oncology Practice: Impact of the Children's Cancer Group Study 9933, a Phase II Study of High-Dose Chemotherapy Before Radiation in Children with Newly Diagnosed High-Grade Astrocytoma

----

Tobey J. MacDonald

Hematology-Oncology, Children's National Medical Center, NW, Washington, DC, USA;
Email: tmacdona@cnmc.org

ABSTRACT

Background: Despite the use of surgery, radiotherapy (RT) and standard chemotherapy, childhood high-grade astrocytoma (HGA) continues to carry a dismal prognosis. In an attempt to identify effective drug combinations and an alternative treatment strategy, the Children's Cancer Group (CCG) conducted a nationwide clinical trial that prospectively evaluated 102 children with HGA and post-operative residual disease for efficacy and toxicity of four courses of high-dose chemotherapy (HDCT) before RT. Design and methods: Patients were randomly assigned to one of three couplets of drugs: carboplatin/etoposide (Regimen A); ifosfamide/etoposide (Regimen B); or cyclophosphamide/etoposide (Regimen C). After HDCT, all patients received local RT followed by lomustine and vincristine. Results: Of 76 evaluable patients (median age 11.95 years, range 3–20 years), 30 patients relapsed during HDCT and 11 others did not complete HDCT due to toxicity. Non-hematologic serious toxicities were common (29%) and 21% of patients did not receive RT. Objective response rates were not associated with amount of residual disease and did not statistically differ between regimens: 27% (Regimen A), 8% (Regimen B), and 29% (Regimen C). Overall survival (OS) was $24 \pm 5\%$ at 5 years and did not differ between groups. The 5-year, event-free survival (EFS) for all patients was $8 \pm 3\%$ and $14 \pm 7\%$ for Regimen A ($p = 0.07$). Patients who responded to HDCT had a nominally higher survival rate ($p = 0.03$ for trend). Interpretation: HDCT prior to RT provides no additional clinical benefit to conventional treatment in HGA, regardless of the amount of measurable residual tumor, and adversely effects ability to complete RT.

Correspondence should be addressed to: Tobey J. MacDonald MD, Hematology-Oncology, Children's National Medical Center, 111 Michigan Avenue, NW, Washington, DC 20010, USA; Tel: 202 884 2146; Fax: 202 884 5685; Email: tmacdona@cnmc.org

Strong consideration should be given to investigating alternative strategies and novel biologic agents for this disease.

Key words: Children's Cancer Group, High-Dose Chemotherapy, High-Grade Astrocytoma.

Introduction and Overview

Despite significant improvements in outcomes of most childhood central nervous system (CNS) tumors, the prognosis of HGA has remained poor (Rilliet, 2000). Extensive resection of HGA frequently improves neurologic function and correlates with more favorable outcome, yet is rarely curative due to local recurrence (Wisoff *et al.*, 1998; van den Hauwe *et al.*, 1995).The addition of post-operative involved-field RT has yielded at best a 6–18% 5-year survival rate (Marchese, 1990; Sheline, 1990; Sposto *et al.*, 1989; Dohrmann *et al.*, 1976; Leibel *et al.*, 1975). Although children with HGA appear to benefit from adjuvant chemotherapy with post-operative RT, the extent of this benefit remains unclear. The CCG study 943 compared post-operative RT alone with post-operative RT plus adjuvant chemotherapy that consisted of prednisone, lomustine (CCNU), and vincristine (pCV regimen) in a cohort of 58 patients (Sposto *et al.*, 1989). In this study, the 5-year EFS reported initially was 46% for the group that received RT and adjuvant chemotherapy compared with 18% for those with RT alone. However, in a subsequent trial (CCG-945) that compared pCV to eight drugs in one day (8-in-1) there was no significant difference in OS between groups (39 ± 7% compared with 29 ± 8%, respectively), and the EFS associated with pCV (26%) was substantially inferior to that noted in the original study (Finlay *et al.*, 1995). Further review of the histology of patients in CCG-943 suggested that a significant proportion (69/250, 37.7%) did not fit the central consensus definition of HGA.

Finlay *et al.* first reported a 60% response rate with myeloablative alkylator-based chemotherapy in 10 pediatric patients with recurrent or primary HGA, suggesting that HDCT may be effective for previously untreated primary HGA (Finlay *et al.*, 1990). A few small studies were subsequently performed using HDCT in children with primary HGA. Although most of these studies utilized similar alkylator-based regimens, the results have been mixed. Furthermore, the conclusions drawn from these studies are substantially limited by the relatively small number of patients investigated, and in most cases, a lack of a centralized data review. It is also unclear from these prior studies whether the amount of post-operative residual disease has a significant impact on HDCT efficacy. Heideman *et al.* initially reported no improvement in the survival of 11 pediatric patients with newly diagnosed HGA who had bulky residual disease treated with high-dose thiotepa and cyclophosphamide followed by autologous bone marrow rescue (Heideman *et al.*, 1993). Kedar *et al.* also reported that survival of three patients with newly diagnosed HGA treated with a similar HDCT regimen was no better than that seen with conventional therapy (Kedar *et al.*, 1994). Likewise, Abrahams *et al.* concluded from a study of 15 patients that dose-intensified cyclophosphamide was inactive against HGA (Abrahamsen *et al.*, 1995). However, two separate reports more recently suggested modest activity and acceptable toxicity of high-dose cyclophosphamide in newly diagnosed HGA, in cohorts of 10 and 14 pediatric patients, respectively, and Grovas *et al.* reported the feasibility of HDCT in 11 patients treated with BCNU, thiotepa and etoposide for newly diagnosed HGA (Grovas *et al.*, 1999; McCowage *et al.*, 1998; Yule *et al.*, 1997). Thus, the efficacy and safety of HDCT for newly diagnosed childhood HGA remained controversial.

Purpose of the CCG-9933 Trial

The primary aims of CCG-9933 were to determine the efficacy and safety of four courses of HDCT before RT within a 12-week phase II therapeutic window. A major obstacle in optimizing chemotherapy for HGA has been the paucity of data on efficacy of single agents or combinations, especially in untreated patients. Because most phase II studies were with patients who were heavily pretreated, which might have conferred resistance to new agents after recurrence, testing agents before RT or other chemotherapy in CCG-9933 was intended to identify agents that could be given with standard treatment to improve outcome.

Agents Administered

This study tested three promising combinations of agents in the therapeutic window between surgery and RT. Patients with post-operative residual disease that measured >1.5 cm^2 were assigned randomly to receive one of three chemotherapeutic regimens: carboplatin/etoposide (VP-16) (Regimen A); ifosfamide/VP-16 (Regimen B); and cyclophosphamide/VP-16 (Regimen C), all given at maximal dose-intensity. The rationale for these agents was supported by objective response rates as high as 50% in patients with recurrent HGA treated with high-dose cyclophosphamide and the observed activity of high-dose carboplatin and ifosfamide in pediatric brain tumors, particularly in combination with VP-16 (Kuhl *et al.*, 1998; Heideman *et al.*, 1995; Castello *et al.*, 1990; Allen, 1981).

CCG-9933 Clinical Trial

After HDCT, patients were treated with involved-field RT for a total dose of 5940 cGy and weekly vincristine, then maintenance chemotherapy with CCNU and vincristine. Patients whose disease progressed during HDCT proceeded directly to RT and maintenance therapy.

Subjects

CCG-9933 opened in 1993 and closed to patient accrual in 1998. A total of 102 patients were registered. Patients were eligible if they had newly diagnosed, non-irradiated, pathologically proven HGA and measurable residual disease $\geqslant 1.5$ cm^2 documented by contrast-enhanced magnetic resonance imagery (MRI) or computed tomography (CT). They had to be greater than 3 years old at entry and less than 26 years old when diagnosed originally. Patients with brain-stem tumors, primary spinal cord tumors, or oligodendrogliomas were not eligible; however, those with mixed tumors that included a major component of HGA and oligodendroglioma were eligible. Patients were eligible if they had low-grade astrocytomas that were believed to have evolved to high-grade tumors without exposure to RT or chemotherapy, if the tumors were biopsy proven. Patients who had documented disseminated disease to the cerebrospinal fluid (CSF) or spinal cord also were eligible. Patients were required to begin induction chemotherapy within 12 weeks of initial surgery.

Trial Design and Methods

Patients were assigned randomly at entry. Randomization was stratified by glioblastoma multiforme, anaplastic astrocytoma, and other HGA. Patients were assigned to one of three induction chemotherapy regimens to begin after initial diagnostic resection or biopsy and before radiation. All tumor specimens were subjected to a primary and secondary independent neuropathology review by two separate neuropathologists. If diagnoses of primary and secondary review neuropathologists were discrepant, the reviewers consulted to reach a final consensus diagnosis.

Induction Therapy

Induction therapy consisted of one 12-week course comprising four 3-week cycles beginning as soon as the patient had recovered sufficiently from surgery according to the neurosurgeon and neuro-oncologist, but no later than 12 weeks from definitive surgery. Patients were assigned randomly to receive one of three induction regimens: carboplatin, VP-16 (Regimen A); ifosfamide, mesna, VP-16 (Regimen B); or cyclophosphamide, mesna, VP-16 (Regimen C). Regimen A cycles consisted of intravenous (IV) carboplatin at 600 mg/m^2 × 2 days and IV VP-16 at 166 mg/m^2 × 3 days. Regimen B cycles consisted of ifosfamide at 2400 mg/m^2 × 5 days and IV VP-16 at 100 mg/m^2 × 5 days. Regimen C cycles consisted of IV cyclophosphamide at 2100 mg/m^2 × 2 days and IV VP-16 at 166 mg/m^2 × 3 days. For each regimen, granulocyte colony-stimulating factor (G-CSF) (5 µg/kg) was given subcutaneously beginning 24 h after the last dose of VP-16 and until ANC $\geqslant$ 10 000/mm^3 to protect against severe myelosuppression. Each subsequent cycle started when patient's APC > 750/mm^3 and platelet count > 100 000 mm^3 without transfusion and at least 3 weeks from the start of the previous cycle.

If hematologic recovery was not sufficient to allow the next cycle to begin by week 4 at the recommended dose, doses of each chemotherapeutic agent were reduced in 20% decrements with re-escalation to previous dose for recovery in 3 weeks. Patients who developed signs or symptoms of tumor progression during induction were evaluated with MRI or CT, and if progression was proven conclusively, induction chemotherapy was discontinued and interim therapy was initiated.

Interim Therapy

Interim therapy was identical for all regimens, consisting of one 12-week course of weekly IV vincristine at 1.5 mg/m^2 (2 mg maximum) for 8 weeks, concomitant with a 6-week course of RT, followed by a 4-week rest.

Maintenance Therapy

Maintenance therapy was identical for all regimens, comprising eight 4-week cycles beginning 6 weeks after the completion of RT and each subsequent course starting when patient's ANC >750/mm^3 and platelet count $>100\,000$ mm^3 without transfusion, and at least 4 weeks had passed from the start of the previous cycle. Each cycle consisted of oral CCNU at 100 mg/m$^2 \times 1$ day and IV vincristine 1.5 mg/m^2 (2 mg maximum) weekly for 4 weeks. CCNU dose was reduced in 25% decrements if cycles could not be given at least every 6 weeks due to delayed hematologic recovery.

Radiation Therapy

RT was initiated at the completion of the 12-week induction course, provided the patient had hematologic recovery (defined as ANC >750/mm^3 and platelet count $>75\,000$/mm^3). Interim therapy with RT also was initiated immediately for any patient with conclusive tumor progression during induction. The total dose delivered to the original tumor site, defined by contrast-enhanced MRI or CT, plus a 2.0-cm margin, was 5400 cGy in 30 fractions of 180 cGy each. An additional boost field included the whole tumor volume after surgery or after chemotherapy, whichever was larger, plus a 1.0-cm margin, a final total tumor dose of 5940 cGy (three fractions of 180 cGy each). The dose volume to spinal cord lesions included the documented disease, one vertebral body above and below the disease and 1.0 cm beyond the entire width of the vertebral body. The tumor dose in the spinal cord was 4680 cGy unless $>50\%$ of the spinal cord was to be treated, then the dose was 4500 cGy with a boost to 4680 cGy to areas of gross disease.

Instruments/Measures

Physical or neurologic examination was performed at least every 3 weeks during induction and interim therapy. Neuroimaging (contrast-enhanced MRI or CT) was done at completion of induction and interim therapy, then at 1-year intervals or at the time of progressive disease (PD) or relapse. There were 50 (66%) patients evaluated for residual disease and tumor progression by MRI, 17 (22%) by CT, and 9 (12%) by MRI/CT.

Independent and blinded central radiographic review was performed by two separate neuroradiologists to evaluate response. Complete response (CR) was defined as resolution of tumor on CT or MRI scan or CSF examination. Partial response (PR) was defined as >50% reduction in the product of the greatest tumor diameter and its perpendicular diameter measured on CT or MRI scan. Minor response (MR) and stable disease (SD) were defined as 25–50% reduction and <25% reduction over a 4-month interval, respectively, by the parameters described above. PD was defined as >25% increase in tumor size by CT or MRI scan or the appearance of tumor in a previously uninvolved area.

Primary and Secondary Outcomes

The primary endpoint for statistical analysis was tumor response to chemotherapy. Secondary endpoints included OS, which is time from entry to death from any cause, and EFS, defined as the minimum time from entry to disease progression, relapse, a second malignant neoplasm, or death from any cause.

Analysis

All analyses were based on intent-to-treat, whereby patients were not censored for deviations from protocol therapy. Non-parametric estimates of EFS and OS probabilities were obtained using the product limit estimate, with standard errors computed using the Greenwood formula (Cox, 1984).

Results

Of 102 patients registered on CCG-9933, 76 were eligible after review. The overall median age on study for the 76 eligible patients was 11.95 years (range 3–20 years); the median age by regimen was 12.4 years for A, 11.1 for B, and 12.3 for C. Most patients (86.8%) had supratentorial tumors; of the 66 patients with supratentorial tumors, 39 primarily were in the cerebral hemisphere. Five percent of the 76 eligible patients had M1 + disease. The percentage of supratentorial tumors for regimens A, B, and C were 91%, 85%, and 85%, respectively. Table 1 gives the breakdown by regimen of the composite diagnosis based on the reviewer pathology.

Efficacy

Table 2 shows the objective response status of the 72 evaluable patients by regimen by the end of chemotherapy. Based on overall response at the end of induction, post-operative chemotherapy with carboplatin/VP-16 (regimen A) had the lowest rate of PD (32%) compared with ifosfamide/VP-16 (regimen B) (50%) and cyclophosphamide/VP-16 (regimen C) (42%). The rate of objective response

Table 1. **Pathology for Eligible Patients (*N* = 76)**

	REGIMEN			
DIAGNOSIS	A	B	C	TOTAL
GBM	10 (43%)	14 (52%)	16 (62%)	40 (53%)
AA	9 (39%)	11 (41%)	10 (38%)	30 (39%)
Other	4 (17%)	2 (7%)	0	6 (8%)
Total	23	27	26	76

Table 2. **Status of Evaluable Patients at the End of Chemotherapy**

STATUS	A	B	C	TOTAL
PR	2 (9%)	0	5 (21%)	7 (10%)
MR	4 (18%)	2 (8%)	2 (8%)	8 (11%)
SD	6 (27%)	7 (27%)	2 (8%)	15 (21%)
PD	7 (32%)	13 (50%)	10 (42%)	30 (42%)
Withdrawn/died/toxicity	3 (14%)	3 (12%)	5 (21%)	11 (15%)
Unknown	0	1 (4%)	0	1 (1%)
Total	22	26	24	72

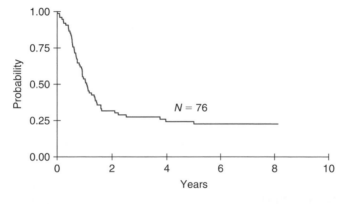

Fig. 1.
OS for eligible patients.

(CR, PR, MR) for the three regimens was 27% for A, 8% for B, and 29% for C; there were no CRs. There was no significant difference in the rate of objective response between the regimens by Fisher Exact test ($p = 0.10$). Also, there was no significant association between regimens and failure during induction ($p = 0.48$); the percentage who failed induction was 45% for A, 62% for B, and 63% for C. Also, there was no significant association between response and amount of residual tumor (1.5–3.0 versus >3.0 cm^2) by Fisher Exact test ($p = 0.72$); the percentage of patients with tumors exceeding 3.0 cm^2 was 87% for PR/MR, 73% for SD, and 73% for PD.

The 5-year OS based on the 76 eligible patients was 24 ± 5% (Figure 1); the survival rate for regimens A, B, and C was 18 ± 8%, 39 ± 10%, and 16 ± 7%,

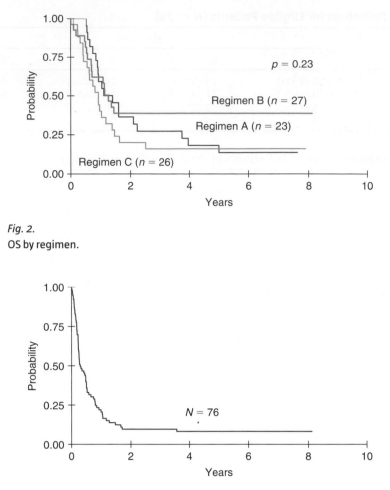

Fig. 2.
OS by regimen.

Fig. 3.
EFS for eligible patients.

respectively ($p = 0.23$) (Figure 2). The 5-year EFS was 8 ± 3% (Figure 3). The EFS for regimens A, B, and C was 14 ± 7%, 4 ± 4%, and 8 ± 6%, respectively ($p = 0.07$) (Figure 4). The median time to relapse, progression, or death based on eligible patients was 105 days, regimen A with the longest (283 days) compared with B (83 days), and C (91 days).

By composite pathology for the eligible patients, 5-year OS was 25 ± 8% for AA, 22 ± 7% for GBM and 40 ± 22% for other eligible ($p = 0.47$) (Figure 5). The 5-year EFS was 7 ± 5% for AA, 8 ± 4% for GBM, and 21 ± 18% for other eligible ($p = 0.28$) (Figure 6). By institutional response for evaluable patients, the OS at 5 years was 57 ± 19% for PRs, 38 ± 17% for MRs, 21 ± 11% for SDs, and 20 ± 7% for PDs ($p = 0.10$ for homogeneity and $p = 0.03$ for trend) (Figure 7).

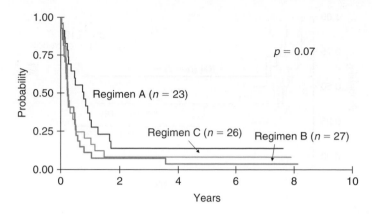

Fig. 4.
EFS by regimen.

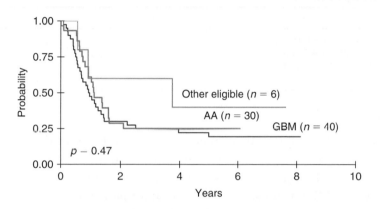

Fig. 5.
OS by composite pathology.

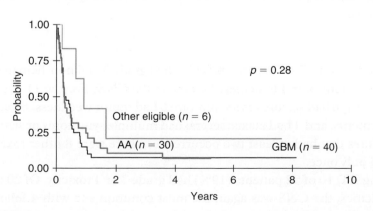

Fig. 6.
EFS by composite pathology.

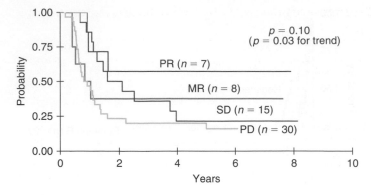

Fig. 7.
OS by institutional response.

Table 3. **RT by Regimen**

	A	B	C	TOTAL
Protocol RT after chemotherapy or PD	17	18	17	52 (68%)
Non-protocol RT after PD and w/d or toxicity	2	4	2	8 (11%)
No known RT – off protocol therapy	4	5	7	16 (21%)
Total	23	27	26	76

Tolerability

More than half of eligible patients relapsed during HDCT or did not complete HDCT due to toxicity. Non-hematologic grade 3 or 4 toxicities were common and only 68% of all eligible patients received protocol-directed RT and 21% did not receive any RT. The most common reason for patients not receiving RT was PD or the patient was too sick for it. After chemotherapy or progression, 52 of 76 eligible patients (68%) went to RT, as prescribed by protocol. The median time from surgery to beginning of RT was 114 days (range 27–154 days). Table 3 summarizes by regimens.

Safety

During induction, 22 of 76 patients (29%) had grade 3 or 4 non-hematologic toxicity. Of 43 grade 3 or 4 toxicities, 11 were in the CNS. For the 11 patients with CNS toxicity, 6 had seizures as a symptom, 6 had motor weakness, 6 had adventitial movements, and 4 had ataxia; several had multiple symptoms or signs. Table 4 lists the sites that had at least two occurrences; there were 8 other toxicities that occurred only once.

During RT, 10 of 52 patients (19%) had grade 3 or 4 toxicity. Of 20 of grade 3 or 4 toxicities, the CNS was again the most common site with 4 followed by 3 infections. The median days hospitalized during this course were 13, 21, and 25.5 for regimens A, B, and C, respectively.

Table 4. **Occurrence of Grade 3 or 4 Non-Hematologic Toxicity during Chemotherapy**

SITE – MEASURE	A	B	C	TOTAL
Nervous system – central	3	5	3	11
Infection	2	3	1	6
Allergy	1	0	2	3
Gastro-intestinal – nausea/vomiting	0	3	0	3
Renal/genitourinary – Hematuria	0	3	0	3
Nervous system – peripheral	1	2	0	3
Renal/genitourinary – BP diastolic	1	0	1	2
Electrolytes – Na	0	0	2	2
Performance (Karnofsky %)	1	1	0	2
Other toxicity	4	2	2	8
Total	13	19	11	43

Translation to Clinical Practice

Amongst pediatric neuro-oncologists, there has been long-standing controversy regarding the efficacy and safety of HDCT for the treatment of primary HGA, particularly in patients with evidence of significant residual disease. In this clinical trial of three different HDCT regimens in 76 pediatric patients with confirmed newly diagnosed HGA and post-operative residual disease, HDCT did not significantly improve survival and did not provide additional clinical benefit, regardless of the amount of residual tumor present, in comparison to conventional treatment regimens. Furthermore, compared to similar strategies in adults, the toxicities in this study were more severe and included more neurologic toxicity, and based on the final analysis, it appears that HDCT before RT markedly affected the number of patients who received RT and the ability to complete treatment (Vinolas *et al.*, 2002; Bottom *et al.*, 2000; Jeremic *et al.*, 1999; Finlay *et al.*, 1994). Taken together, CCG-9933 provides the first compelling evidence that HDCT strategies do not appear to be useful for primary HGA of childhood, and in fact, may lead to deleterious complications when given prior to RT. As a result of this study, the field is now turning away from this approach in this disease, despite its apparent success in infants with malignant brain tumors (Kalifa, 2005). While it is possible that the use of less HDCT cycles before RT, or less toxic approaches (i.e. stem cell support) may reduce HDCT treatment-related toxicity, it does not appear that this strategy will be translated into clinical practice due to its limited effectiveness.

How the Trial Results Fit into the Emerging Treatment and Research Framework

Current clinical trials for childhood HGA are now focusing on biologic-based therapy against tumor-derived molecular targets. For instance, recent reports have shown that HGA patients treated with the alkylator temozolomide have a better outcome if the tumor does not expresses the DNA repair enzyme, O6-methylguanine-DNA methyltransferase (MGMT) (Pollack *et al.*, 2006). Although the sample size in CCG-9933 would be too small to conclude definitively, it may be worthwhile to determine whether patients who had objective responses and prolonged EFS had tumors with relatively low levels of MGMT, since each regimen in CCG-9933 contained an alkylating agent. If this is the case, it may be better to use strategies that deplete MGMT levels rather than intensify or modify the type of alkylator used (Bobola *et al.*, 2001; Esteller *et al.*, 2000; Silber *et al.*, 1999; Hongeng *et al.*, 1997). This strategy could also allow for dose-reduction and limit toxicity.

Summary

Beyond complete surgical resection and post-operative RT, it still remains unclear how to best treat primary childhood HGA. The CCG-9933 study demonstrated no significant clinical advantage of HDCT regimens containing the most commonly used agents for the treatment of pediatric solid tumors over conventional therapeutic regimens in patients with newly diagnosed HGA, regardless of the amount of post-operative residual disease. These results strongly suggest that HDCT strategies be abandoned and that alternative strategies and/or newer cytotoxic or cytostatic agents specifically targeting HGA biology should be investigated for the treatment of primary HGA in children.

References

Abrahamsen, T.G., Lange, B.J., Packer, R.J., *et al.* (1995). A phase I and II trial of dose-intensified cyclophosphamide and GM-CSF in pediatric malignant brain tumors. *Journal of Pediatric Hematology Oncology*, 17, 134–139.

Allen, J.C., & Helson, L. (1981). High-dose cyclophosphamide chemotherapy for recurrent CNS tumors in children. *Journal of Neurosurgery*, 55, 749–756.

Bobola, M.S., Berger, M.S., Ellenbogen, R.G., *et al.* (2001). O6-Methylguanine-DNA methyltransferase in pediatric primary brain tumors: relation to patient and tumor characteristics. *Clinical Cancer Research*, 7, 613–619.

Bottom, K.S., Ashley, D.M., Friedman, H.S., *et al.* (2000). Evaluation of pre-radiotherapy cyclophosphamide in patients with newly diagnosed glioblastoma multiforme. Writing Committee for The Brain Tumor Center at Duke. *Journal of Neurooncology*, 46, 151–156.

Castello, M.A., Clerico, A., Deb, G., *et al.* (1990). High-dose carboplatin in combination with etoposide (JET regimen) for childhood brain tumors. *American Journal of Pediatric Hematology Oncology*, 12, 297–300.

Cox, D.R., & Oakes, D. (1984). *Analysis of Survival Data*. London: Chapman and Hall.

Dohrmann, G.J., Farwell, J.R., Flannery, J.T., *et al.* (1976). Glioblastoma multiforme in children. *Journal of Neurosurgery*, 44, 442–448.

Esteller, M., Garcia-Foncillas, J., Andion, E., *et al.* (2000). Inactivation of the DNA-repair gene MGMT and the clinical response of gliomas to alkylating agents. *New England Journal of Medicine*, 343, 1350–1354.

Finlay, J.L., Boyett, J.M., Yates, A.J., *et al.* (1995). Randomized phase III trial in childhood high-grade astrocytoma comparing vincristine, lomustine, and prednisone with the eight-drugs-in-1-day regimen. Childrens Cancer Group. *Journal of Clinical Oncology*, 13, 112–123.

Finlay, J.L., Geyer, J.R., Turski, P.A., *et al.* (1994). Pre-irradiation chemotherapy in children with high-grade astrocytoma: tumor response to two cycles of the '8-drugs-in-1-day' regimen. A Childrens Cancer Group study, CCG-945. *Journal of Neurooncology*, 21, 255–265.

Finlay, J.L., August, C., Packer, R., *et al.* (1990). High-dose multi-agent chemotherapy followed by bone marrow rescue for malignant astrocytomas of childhood and adolescence. *Journal of Neurooncology*, 9, 239–248.

Grovas, A.C., Boyett, J.M., Lindsley, K., *et al.* (1999). Regimen-related toxicity of myeloablative chemotherapy with BCNU, thiotepa, and etoposide followed by autologous stem cell rescue for children with newly diagnosed glioblastoma multiforme: report from the Children's Cancer Group. *Medical Pediatric Oncology*, 33, 83–87.

Heideman, R.L., Douglass, E.C., Langston, J.A., *et al.* (1995). A phase II study of every other day high-dose ifosfamide in pediatric brain tumors: a Pediatric Oncology Group Study. *Journal of Neurooncology*, 25, 77–84.

Heideman, R.L., Douglass, E.C., Krance, R.A., *et al.* (1993). High-dose chemotherapy and autologous bone marrow rescue followed by interstitial and external-beam radiotherapy in newly diagnosed pediatric malignant gliomas. *Journal of Clinical Oncology*, 11, 1458–1465.

Hongeng, S., Brent, T.P., Sanford, R.A., *et al.* (1997). O6-Methylguanine-DNA methyltransferase protein levels in pediatric brain tumors. *Clinical Cancer Research*, 3, 2459–2463.

Jeremic, B., Shibamoto, Y., Grujicic, D., *et al.* (1999). Pre-irradiation carboplatin and etoposide and accelerated hyperfractionated radiation therapy in patients with high-grade astrocytomas: a phase II study. *Radiotherapy Oncology*, 51, 27–33.

Kalifa, C., & Grill, J. (2005). The therapy of infantile malignant brain tumors: current status? *Journal of Neurooncology*, 75(3), 279–285. (review).

Kedar, A., Maria, B.L., Graham-Pole, J., *et al.* (1994). High-dose chemotherapy with marrow reinfusion and hyperfractionated irradiation for children with high-risk brain tumors. *Medical Pediatric Oncology*, 23, 428–436.

Kuhl, J., Muller, H.L., Berthold, F., *et al.* (1998). Preradiation chemotherapy of children and young adults with malignant brain tumors: results of the German pilot trial HIT'88/'89. *Klinische Padiatrie*, 210, 227–233.

Leibel, S.A., Sheline, G.E., Wara, W.M., *et al.* (1975). The role of radiation therapy in the treatment of astrocytomas. *Cancer*, 35, 1551–1557.

Marchese, M.J., & Chang, C.H. (1990). Malignant astrocytic gliomas in children. *Cancer*, 65, 2771–2778.

McCowage, G.B., Friedman, H.S., Moghrabi, A., *et al.* (1998). Activity of high-dose cyclophosphamide in the treatment of childhood malignant gliomas. *Medical Pediatric Oncology*, 30, 75–80.

Pollack, I.F., Hamilton, R.L., Sobol, R.W., *et al.* (2006). O6-methylguanine-DNA methyltransferase expression strongly correlates with outcome in childhood malignant gliomas: results from the CCG-945 Cohort. *Journal of Clinical Oncology*, 24(21), 3431–3437.

Rilliet, B., & Vernet, O. (2000). Gliomas in children: a review. *Childs Nervous System*, 16, 735–741.

Sheline, G.E. (1990). Radiotherapy for high grade gliomas. *International Journal of Radiation Oncology Biology Physics*, 18, 793–803.

Silber, J.R., Blank, A., Bobola, M.S., *et al.* (1999). O6-methylguanine-DNA methyltransferase-deficient phenotype in human gliomas: frequency and time to tumor progression after alkylating agent-based chemotherapy. *Clinical Cancer Research*, 5, 807–814.

Sposto, R., Ertel, I.J., Jenkin, R.D., *et al.* (1989). The effectiveness of chemotherapy for treatment of high grade astrocytoma in children: results of a randomized trial. A report from the Childrens Cancer Study Group. *Journal of Neurooncology*, 7, 165–177.

van den Hauwe, L., Parizel, P.M., Martin, J.J., *et al.* (1995). Postmortem MRI of the brain with neuropathological correlation. *Neuroradiology*, 37, 343–349.

Vinolas, N., Gil, M., Verger, E., *et al.* (2002). Pre-irradiation semi-intensive chemotherapy with carboplatin and cyclophosphamide in malignant glioma: a phase II study. *Anticancer Drugs*, 13, 163–167.

Wisoff, J.H., Boyett, J.M., Berger, M.S., *et al.* (1998). Current neurosurgical management and the impact of the extent of resection in the treatment of malignant gliomas of childhood: a report of the Children's Cancer Group Trial No. CCG-945. *Journal of Neurosurgery*, 89, 52–59.

Yule, S.M., Foreman, N.K., Mitchell, C., *et al.* (1997). High-dose cyclophosphamide for poor-prognosis and recurrent pediatric brain tumors: a dose-escalation study. *Journal of Clinical Oncology*, 15, 3258–3265.

Progress in Neurotherapeutics and Neuropsychopharmacology, 2:1, 123–136 © 2007 Cambridge University Press
DOI: 10.1017/S1748232106000097   Printed in the United Kingdom

Chemoradiotherapy for primary CNS lymphoma*

Antonio M.P. Omuro

*Division de Neurologie Mazarin – Groupe Hospitalier Pitie-Salpetriere, Paris, France; Email:
antonio.omuro@psl.ap-hop-paris.fr*

Joachim Yahalom

*Department of Radiotherapy – Memorial Sloan-Kettering Cancer Center, New York, NY, USA;
Email: yahalomj@mskcc.org*

Lauren E. Abrey

*Department of Neurology – Memorial Sloan-Kettering Cancer Center, New York, NY, USA;
Email: abreyl@mskcc.org*

Key words: primary central nervous system lymphone, Non-hodgkin's lymphs, brain neoplasm, chemotherapy, radiotherapy.

Introduction and Overview

Primary central nervous system lymphoma (PCNSL) is a non-Hodgkin's lymphoma (NHL) that arises within the brain, eyes, leptomeninges or spinal cord, in the absence of systemic disease. Despite being a relatively rare tumor, its incidence has been increasing in the immunocompetent patient population over the past several decades (Olson *et al.*, 2002; Eby *et al.*, 1988).

Numerous reports have shown that the addition of pre-irradiation methotrexate (MTX) in doses of 1 g/m^2 or higher significantly improves patient survival (Glass *et al.*, 1994; DeAngelis *et al.*, 1992; Gabbai *et al.*, 1989). Currently, multiple treatment regimens using high-dose MTX alone or in combination with other chemotherapeutic agents have been reported, with median overall survival (OS) rates ranging from 30 to 60 months (Batchelor *et al.*, 2003; Pels *et al.*, 2003; Abrey *et al.*, 2000). However, only a minority of these reports represents prospective

Correspondence should be addressed to: Antonio M.P. Omuro, MD, Groupe Hospitalier Pitie-Salpetriere, Federation de Neurologie Mazarin, 47, Bd de l'Hopital, 75661 Paris Cedex 13- France; Ph: +33 1 42 16 41 60; Fax: +33 1 42 16 03 75; Email: antonio.omuro@psl.ap-hop-paris.fr.

*Original article: Chemoradiotherapy for primary CNS lymphoma: An intent-to-treat analysis with complete follow-up. Published in NEUROLOGY 64 (1): 69–74, January 2005.

All authors have read and approved this chapter. Informed consent was obtained from all subjects and/or guardians involved in this study. The authors are responsible for the accuracy of the references.

clinical trials and long-term follow-up is rarely included. Moreover, treatment-related neurotoxicity is an increasingly recognized complication that impairs the quality of life in long-term survivors, but is rarely reported. In the present chapter we describe and discuss findings of a recently published trial of chemoradiotherapy for PCNSL (Omuro *et al.*, 2005b).

Purpose of the Trial

This prospective Phase II trial was designed in 1989 with the intent of increasing the efficacy of MTX by incorporating procarbazine and thiotepa into a new pre-radiotherapy (RT) chemotherapy regimen. These drugs penetrate the blood-brain barrier (BBB) well and have demonstrated activity in NHL (Lichtman *et al.*, 2001). Intra-ventricular (IV) MTX was also utilized to address the high rate of leptomeningeal dissemination seen with PCNSL at diagnosis by providing frequent and sustained therapeutic concentrations in the cerebrospinal fluid (CSF) (Khan *et al.*, 2002).

At the time of this report all patients have been followed for at least 10 years from completion of treatment, allowing for long-term characterization of disease control and treatment-related neurotoxicity.

Agents

High-dose MTX has been the most effective treatment for PCNSL and its importance in the upfront treatment has been widely accepted (Ferreri *et al.*, 2003). However, there is no agreement on the role of other agents. Procarbazine has been incorporated in a variety of proposed regimens for PCNSL (DeAngelis *et al.*, 2002; Abrey *et al.*, 2000; Chamberlain, 1990; 1992); thiotepa has also been tested in combination with other drugs, both in the setting of conventional chemotherapy (Sandor *et al.*, 1998) and as a component of high-dose chemotherapy followed by stem-cell rescue (Cheng *et al.*, 2003; Soussain *et al.*, 2001). However, because these drugs were used in combination, the individual impact of each agent is difficult to assess.

Retrospective experience with a chemotherapy protocol utilizing the combination of MTX, procarbazine and thiotepa has been previously reported (Sarazin *et al.*, 1995). The authors divided their heterogenous sample into three groups: Group A ($n = 13$ patients) had received IV (1 g/m^2) and intra-thecal (IT) MTX, followed by whole-brain radiotherapy (WBRT) and then thiotepa and procarbazine; Group B ($n = 4$) had received the same chemotherapy (without IT MTX) after WBRT and Group C ($n = 5$) had received chemotherapy only. Patient characteristics differed considerably, particularly because older patients were selected to receive chemotherapy only. As expected, best results were seen in Group A, which showed a median time to progression of 10 months. In that study, the chemotherapy regimen was well tolerated, but neurotoxicity was a serious complication, occurring in 4 patients in Group A. Further conclusions are limited because of the retrospective nature of the study and the short follow-up.

Subjects

Immunocompetent patients with a new diagnosis of PCNSL seen at Memorial Sloan-Kettering Cancer Center (MSKCC) between 1990 and 1992 were eligible for this treatment. The diagnosis was established by histologic sampling (brain tissue, CSF cytology, vitreous biopsy). Patients with typical magnetic resonance imaging (MRI) findings of PCNSL without histologic confirmation were also eligible for the trial. These findings were defined as diffusely enhancing periventricular lesions with indistinct borders and a reduction in the size of the lesions of at least 50% after 7 days of 32 mg/day dexamethasone treatment or its equivalent. All patients underwent baseline clinical and laboratory evaluation including brain MRI, lumbar puncture, ophthalmologic consultation and slit-lamp examination, abdominal computed tomographic (CT) scan, bone marrow biopsy, chest X-ray and HIV-1 serology. A leukocyte count >4000 cells and creatinine clearance >50 ml/min were required. An Ommaya reservoir was placed for IT MTX administration.

Trial Methods

This study was a prospective single center Phase II trial. All eligible patients were treated with chemotherapy, followed by WBRT. Chemotherapy consisted of IT MTX in a dose of 12 mg on days 1, 4, 11, 15, 22 and 29; IV MTX 1 g/m^2 diluted in 250 ml D5W infused over 1 h on days 1 and 15; thiotepa 30 mg/m^2 IV bolus on days 8 and 36; procarbazine 75 mg/m^2/day from days 8 to 15 and days 36 to 43. Leucovorin was started 24 h after IV MTX, at a dose of 10 mg every 6 h for 12 doses. WBRT followed completion of chemotherapy and was administered to a dose of 4140 cGy delivered in 23 treatments of 180 cGy each; the tumor bed area received an additional 1440 cGy boost divided in 8 sessions. The total tumor dose was 5580 cGy. When multifocal lesions could not be encompassed into a cone-down field, the whole brain was treated with an additional 900 cGy, divided in 5 doses.

The study was reviewed and approved by the Institutional Review Board at MSKCC. All patients signed written informed consent prior to treatment.

Instruments/Measures

Response to treatment was evaluated with brain MRI at the completion of pre-RT chemotherapy and at completion of the entire treatment regimen. A complete response (CR) was defined as resolution of enhancing tumor in patients who were not receiving steroids. Patients still receiving steroids with documented tumor resolution were classified as having uncertain complete response (uCR). A partial response (PR) was defined as a decrease of at least 50% in the tumor size in patients on stable or decreasing doses of steroids. Patients with unequivocal increase in tumor size or appearance of new lesions were classified as having progressive disease (PD); stable disease (SD) represented all other situations. In addition, patients with CSF or ocular involvement at diagnosis had to have complete resolution of disease in these compartments to qualify for a CR. Tumor in either the CSF or the eyes was classified as present or absent, and no PR was assigned to these locations. No patient had evidence of an objective response in one compartment with disease progression in another; therefore, no mixed responses were observed.

Patients were evaluated clinically and radiographically every 3 months for the first year, every 4 months for the second year and every 6 months thereafter; after 5 years, patients were evaluated annually. CSF was checked every 4–6 months for the first year or as clinically indicated. At recurrence, all patients underwent repeat neuroimaging, CSF cytologic examination and ophthalmologic evaluation.

Acute toxicity was evaluated with blood counts, renal and liver function assessments performed prior to each course of chemotherapy or as clinically indicated. Toxicity was graded by the National Cancer Institute (NCI) common toxicity criteria. Neurotoxicity was defined as deterioration of neurologic function in the absence of disease recurrence or other identifiable neurologic disease.

Primary and Secondary Outcomes

The primary end-point was OS; secondary end-points included response and progression-free survival (PFS). Time to progression and survival were measured from the date of diagnosis to the date of first relapse, death or last follow-up. Survival curves were drawn using the Kaplan–Meier product-limit method. The planned sample size was 36 patients, with a pre-specified goal of detecting a doubling in median survival from 18 months (previously reported with RT alone) to 36 months. All patients who began this treatment regimen were included in the analysis in an intent-to-treat fashion. Enrollment was prematurely discontinued in order to participate in a competing Radiation Therapy Oncology Group (RTOG) trial. Follow-up extended through December, 2003.

Results

Patient Characteristics

Seventeen patients (10 men, 7 women) were enrolled. Median age was 53 years, ranging from 26 to 71 years (Table 1). Median Karnofsky performance scale (KPS)

Table 1. **Examples of Treatment Regimens for PCNSL**

REFERENCE	REGIMEN	N	ORR	MEDIAN EFS/PFS	MEDIAN OS	COMMENTS
DeAngelis *et al.* (1992)	MTX 1 g/m^2, Ara-C + IT MTX with or without WBRT	31	64%	40 m	42 m	33% neurotoxicities
Abrey *et al.* (2000)	MTX 3.5 g/m^2, procarbazine, vincristine + IT MTX and Ara-C with or without WBRT	52	90%	NR	60 m	13 (25%) neurotoxicities; single-center study
DeAngelis *et al.* (2002)	MTX 2.5 g/m^2, procarbazine, vincristine + IT MTX (12 mg) + WBRT	98	94%	24 m	37 m	12 (15%) neurotoxicities; multi-center study
Pels *et al.* (2003)	MTX 5 g/m^2, vincristine, ifosfamide, cyclophosphamide, vindesine, dexamethasone + IT MTX and Ara-C; no WBRT	65	71%	21 m	50 m	6 (10%) toxic deaths; 2 neurotoxicities
Poortmans *et al.* (2003)	MTX 3 g/m^2, teniposide, carmustine, methylprednisolone + IT MTX, Ara-C and hydrocortisone + WBRT	52	81%	NA	46 m	5 (10%) toxic deaths; one death from neurotoxicity; short-term follow-up
Herrlinger *et al.* (2002, 2005)	MTX 8 g/m^2, no WBRT	37	30%	10 m	25 m	5 (20%) neurotoxicities
Batchelor *et al.* (2003)	MTX 8 g/m^2, no WBRT	25	74%	12 m	55 m	No data on long-term follow-up/ neurotoxicity
Hoang *et al.* (2003) (elderly patients)	MTX 1 g/m^2, Chloroethyl-cyclohexyl-nitrosourea (CCNU), procarbazine, prednisone + IT MTX Ara-C; no WBRT	50	48%	10 m	14 m	1 toxic death, 1 neurotoxicity.
Omuro *et al.* (2005b) (present study)	MTX 1 g/m^2, procarbazine, thiotepa + WBRT	17	88%	18 m	32 m	5 (30%) neurotoxicities

ORR: objective response rate; EFS: event-free survival; PFS: progression-free survival; OS: overall survival; MTX: methotrexate; IT: intra-thecal; NR: not reached; NA: not available.

was 70 (range: 50–90). Histologic confirmation was obtained from the brain in 12 (70.5%) patients, spinal cord in 1 (5.8%), CSF in 1 (5.8%) and vitrectomy specimen in 1 (5.8%) patient. Two patients did not have an initial histologic confirmation of PCNSL; both had the typical MRI findings of PCNSL and were eligible to participate in this trial. One of these patients had a CSF specimen suspicious for lymphoma; the other eventually died and autopsy confirmed the diagnosis of NHL confined to the CNS. Brain involvement was present in 16 (94.1%) patients; spinal involvement in 1 (5.8%) and ocular involvement in 2 (11.8%). CSF cytologic examination was positive in 3 (17.6%) and suspicious in 3 (17.6%) patients.

Chemotherapy started a median of 2 weeks (range: 1–5) after diagnosis. All patients completed the described course, with the exception of one who did not receive IT MTX because a large bifrontal mass did not permit placement of an Ommaya reservoir and the mass effect prohibited serial lumbar punctures. All patients completed WBRT with a median dose of 4140 cGy (range: 3600 to 5040 cGy) and total lesion dose of 5040 cGy (range: 4320–5580 cGy).

Response and Survival

At completion of chemotherapy, 3 patients (17.6%) achieved a CR, 4 (23.5%) an uCR and 7 (41.1%) a PR, for an objective response rate (ORR) of 82% (95% confidence interval (CI) 57,100). One (5.8%) patient was stable and 2 (11.8%) progressed during induction chemotherapy. After radiotherapy, 13 (76.5%; 95% CI 50,93) patients achieved a CR (including all patients with an uCR after chemotherapy) and 2 (11.8%) a PR for a response rate of 88.3% (95% CI 64,99). Disease progressed after RT in 2 (11.8%) patients.

Median PFS of the entire cohort was 18 months (Figure 1). Relapse occurred in 7 (41.2%) patients and all developed within the first 2 years. Recurrent disease developed in the brain in 3 (17.6%) patients and in the eyes in 2 (11.8%); neither patient had ocular involvement at presentation. CSF recurrence was seen in 2 (11.8%) patients, including the one patient who did not receive IT MTX. All patients with relapse received salvage therapy that may have included RT to the spine or eyes, IT and/or systemic chemotherapy.

Median OS (Figure 2) was 32 months (95% CI 8.3–57.4) and 2 (11.7%) patients remain alive after 12-years follow-up. PCNSL was the cause of death in 8 (47.1%) and neurotoxicity in 5 (29.4%) patients; 2 (11.8%) patients died from unknown causes. On univariate analysis, age was not a statistically significant predictor of survival ($p = 0.35$); however, only 4 patients were older than 60. Two of the patients who died of neurotoxicity had an autopsy revealing extensive leukoencephalopathy and no PCNSL was identified.

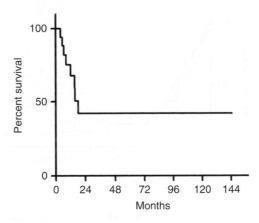

Fig. 1.
Progression-free survival. (Reprinted with permission from Omuro *et al.*, 2005b. Chemoradio-
therapy for primary CNS lymphoma: an intent-to-treat analysis with complete follow-up.
Neurology, 64, 69–74.)

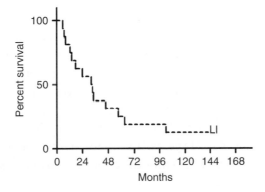

Fig. 2.
Overall survival. (Reprinted with permission from Omuro *et al.*, 2005b. Chemoradiotherapy
for primary CNS lymphoma: an intent-to-treat analysis with complete follow-up. Neurology,
64, 69–74.)

Toxicity

Myelotoxicity was the most common side effect, reaching a grade 3 in 3 (17.6%)
patients and grade 4 in 2 (11.8%). Renal side effects were not a major complication; 4 (23.5%) patients developed grade 1 nephrotoxicity. No patient died as a
result of acute treatment-related toxicity.

Neurotoxicity was defined as the presence of cognitive deterioration (mainly
executive dysfunction and decreased short-term memory), gait disturbance and

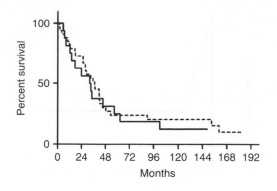

Fig. 3.

Comparison of survival between present study and previously reported regimen (DeAngelis et al., 1992) using MTX 1 g/m² ($p = 0.66$)

— — — IV MTX (1 g/m²) + IT MTX (12 mg) + RT + post-RT cytarabine (3 g/m²)

_____ IV MTX (1 g/m²) + IT MTX (12 mg) + thiotepa (30 mg/m²) + procarbazine (75 mg/m²) + RT (Reprinted with permission from Omuro *et al.*, 2005b. Chemoradiotherapy for primary CNS lymphoma: an intent-to-treat analysis with complete follow-up. Neurology, 64, 69–74.)

incontinence, in the absence of recurrent tumor. These symptoms developed in 5 (29.4%) patients. Cognitive deterioration was an early complaint and all 5 patients developed the full syndrome after progressing over the course of months. All patients with neurotoxicity eventually died as a result of neurologic deterioration, without PCNSL relapse. The median survival after the diagnosis of neurotoxicity was 8.3 (1–58) months. The median age at PCNSL diagnosis in this subgroup was 67 (range: 41–71) years. The median interval time for onset of neurotoxicity symptoms was 6 (4–26) months after the start of chemotherapy.

Conclusions

The regimen described in this study employed a relatively low IV dose of MTX in combination with IT MTX, procarbazine and thiotepa. Nonetheless, response rates, PFS and OS are comparable to other reported regimens utilizing higher MTX doses, although results must be interpreted carefully because of the small number of patients and large confidence intervals. Moreover, acceptable acute toxicity was observed, with particularly low rates of nephrotoxicity, suggesting that this regimen may be a suitable option for patients unable to tolerate higher doses of MTX. However, the combination with radiotherapy resulted in high rates of neurotoxicity, which eventually developed in 30% of patients. The first 2 years after treatment seem critical to define outcomes, since all unfavorable events (i.e. first relapse and neurotoxicity) were diagnosed within that time frame (Figure 3).

Influence on the Field

A significant focus of research in PCNSL has been the development of a more effective chemotherapy regimen that would provide increased response to initial treatment, as well as decreased incidence of relapse and neurotoxicity. However, authors disagree regarding the role of agents other than MTX, if any (Ferreri, 2003). The most appropriate way of answering this question would be to conduct Phase III trials comparing MTX alone versus the same dose of MTX combined with each of the candidate drugs. However, the application of such strict methodology is unrealistic for several reasons. First, the use of single-agent MTX has been questioned given the disappointing results of two recent Phase II results of very high-dose MTX regimens ($8 \, g/m^2$) (Herrlinger *et al.*, 2005; Batchelor *et al.*, 2003). Therefore, it would be difficult to accrual patients to a control arm utilizing a MTX-only regimen at doses suitable for combination such as 3–$5 \, g/m^2$, which in fact are even lower than the doses utilized in the recent single-agent MTX trials. Moreover, because the addition of a second drug is not expected to have a major impact on the primary end-point, the necessary sample size to adequately address this issue would be large, therefore rendering such studies unfeasible in this relatively rare disease. Thus, defining the role of other drugs rely on further analysis of existing Phase II data such as the present study; ongoing randomized Phase II studies may also provide insight into this question.

In this trial, MTX was used in a dose of $1 \, g/m^2$. Several studies looking at the pharmacokinetics of MTX and its penetration through the BBB have been performed by assessing CSF levels after IV infusions in patients with an intact BBB (Khan *et al.*, 2002; Borsi & Moe, 1987). CSF levels correlate with serum levels and higher concentrations are achieved with relatively rapid infusions of doses above $3 \, g/m^2$. Accordingly, many studies have employed higher doses, at the expense of higher toxicity, particularly renal failure (Herrlinger *et al.*, 2005; Batchelor *et al.*, 2003). The relatively low dose employed in this study does not follow this trend but, nonetheless, the achieved results are comparable to other combined modality treatments using much higher doses of MTX. Supplementation with IT MTX may have helped treat the CSF compartment and maintain therapeutic CSF levels. However, it is unlikely that adequate MTX levels were achieved within the parenchyma, except in bulky areas of tumor with a disrupted BBB. The combination with procarbazine and thiotepa may have been critical in treating any microscopic tumor residing behind an intact BBB.

To assess the importance of procarbazine and thiotepa, we performed a comparison with one of our earlier protocols using combined modality treatment (DeAngelis *et al.*, 1992). Long-term follow-up is also available for that study and patient characteristics were similar. That regimen incorporated IV and intra-ommaya (IO) MTX infusions at the same dose, as well as comparable RT doses and delivery. However, in that study, cytarabine-3 g/m^2 was added after completion of RT. The median OS observed was 42 months, compared to 32 months in the present study; this difference was not statistically significant (log-rank $p = 0.66$). However, response rates after induction chemotherapy and before RT were lower in the earlier study; no patient had a CR and 64% had a PR. The response differences suggest that the combination of MTX, procarbazine and thiotepa is superior to MTX alone when 1 g/m^2 doses are employed, highlighting the activity of procarbazine and thiotepa in PCNSL. Moreover, because survival was similar in both studies, we speculate that the addition of high-dose cytarabine played a role in prolonging survival in the initial study.

Another contribution of this study is to report a long follow-up (>10 years), which provides a unique opportunity to characterize long-term outcomes, rarely reported in the literature. This is particularly relevant for regimens involving WBRT, since immature data may underestimate the importance of long-term complications, such as neurotoxicity (Omuro *et al.*, 2005b; Correa *et al.*, 2004; Abrey *et al.*, 2000; O'Neil *et al.*, 1999). The mechanisms underlying the development of neurotoxicity are poorly understood. Radiation effects are thought to play a key role, since chemotherapy-only regimens have achieved lower neurotoxicity rates (Omuro *et al.*, 2005a). Because patients older than 60 years of age are thought to be at particular risk, many authors have been deferring RT to avoid neurotoxicity in that population. However, this may compromise disease control and many intensified chemotherapy-only regimens are associated with increased life-threatening toxicity, particularly myelotoxicity (Abrey *et al.*, 2003; Hoang-Xuan *et al.*, 2003; Pels *et al.*, 2003). In our study, we confirmed that the overall incidence of neurotoxicity is approximately 30% and that it results in a significant decrease in quality of life among long-term survivors, and caused the death of all affected patients. However, we also observed that the development of neurotoxicity was not a "late-delayed" event, since the onset can be as early as 4 months. Therefore, some patients did not benefit from the response of their tumor to treatment because their function was rapidly compromised by neurotoxicity. Moreover, we found that neurotoxicity developed in 2 patients younger than 60 years, demonstrating that neurotoxicity is not restricted to older patients. This finding supports the necessity of developing treatment regimens that could be safely delivered to patients of all ages.

The long-term follow-up in this study also provides some insight in terms of pattern of relapses and history of disease in PCNSL. We demonstrated that the first 2 years are critical, with all first relapses and the majority of neurotoxicity occurring within that period. Some of the relapsing patients responded to salvage therapy but eventually they all recurred again, as late as 7 years after first relapse. Therefore, our data demonstrate that both first relapse and neurotoxicity within the first 2 years are predictors of unfavorable outcome. This suggests that 2-year event-free survival (EFS) may be an important end-point in PCNSL trials, with neurotoxicity categorized as an unfavorable event in addition to relapse and death.

Translation to Clinical Practice

This study was a Phase II trial and therefore this regimen was not directly compared to other established regimens. However, in the absence of Phase III studies in this disease and no defined standard of care, these results can help to define and validate some of the general principles that should guide the treatment for PCNSL:

- *Choice of chemotherapy*: This study helps to support the use of a combination of drugs rather than single-agent high-dose MTX. Further analyses suggest that regimens incorporating procarbazine, thiotepa or cytarabine may be reasonable options. A list of proposed regimens is shown in Table 1.

- *Addition of radiotherapy*: These results contribute to validate the concept that the combination of chemotherapy and radiotherapy may result in a significant risk of neurotoxicity and suggest that patients younger than 60 years are also at risk. Therefore, all patients should be made aware of such risk.

- *Follow-up issues*: Close follow-up during the first 2 years is necessary for monitoring relapses and cognitive deterioration secondary to neurotoxicity. Patients event-free after 2 years appear to have a better overall prognosis.

Summary of How to Treat the Disorder Incorporating the Results of the New Trial Data

The treatment for PCNSL should be individualized and prognostic factors such as age should be taken into consideration. Patients over 60 years are at significant risk of neurotoxicity and, therefore, should probably receive chemotherapy alone as initial treatment. Regimens associated with less acute toxicity are preferable. Patients under 60 years should be made aware of the potential risks and benefits of adding radiotherapy to chemotherapy and decisions should be made on an individual basis. Chemotherapy should encompass high-dose MTX, combined with other drugs (commonly utilized regimens summarized in Table 1). Treating these patients in tertiary centers with large experience in this disease is preferable over community-based hospitals. Although occasional cures are seen in PCNSL, the overall prognosis remains dismal and enrollment in clinical trials is strongly recommended.

References:

Abrey, L.E., Yahalom, J., & DeAngelis, L.M. (2000). Treatment for primary CNS lymphoma: the next step. *Journal of Clinical Oncology*, 18, 3144–3150.

Abrey, L.E., Moskowitz, C.H., Mason, W.P., *et al.* (2003). Intensive methotrexate and cytarabine followed by high-dose chemotherapy with autologous stem-cell rescue in patients with newly diagnosed primary CNS lymphoma: an intent-to-treat analysis. *Journal of Clinical Oncology*, 21, 4151–4156.

Batchelor, T., Carson, K., O'Neill, A., *et al.* (2003). Treatment of primary CNS lymphoma with methotrexate and deferred radiotherapy: a report of NABTT 96-07. *Journal of Clinical Oncology*, 21, 1044–1049.

Borsi, J.D., & Moe, P.J. (1987). Systemic clearance of methotrexate in the prognosis of acute lymphoblastic leukemia in children. *Cancer*, 60, 3020–3024.

Chamberlain, M.C., & Levin, V.A. (1990). Adjuvant chemotherapy for primary lymphoma of the central nervous system. *Archives of Neurology*, 47, 1113–1116.

Chamberlain, M.C., & Levin, V.A. (1992). Primary central nervous system lymphoma: a role for adjuvant chemotherapy. *Journal of Neuro-Oncology*, 14, 271–275.

Cheng, T., Forsyth, P., Chaudhry, A., *et al.* (2003). High-dose thiotepa, busulfan, cyclophosphamide and ASCT without whole-brain radiotherapy for poor prognosis primary CNS lymphoma. *Bone Marrow Transplantation*, 31, 679–685.

Correa, D.D., DeAngelis, L.M., Shi, W., Thaler, H., Glass, A., & Abrey, L.E. (2004). Cognitive functions in survivors of primary central nervous system lymphoma. *Neurology*, 62, 548–555.

DeAngelis, L.M., Yahalom, J., Thaler, H.T., & Kher, U. (1992). Combined modality therapy for primary CNS lymphoma. *Journal of Clinical Oncology*, 10, 635–643.

DeAngelis, L.M., Seiferheld, W., Schold, S.C., Fisher, B., & Schultz, C.J. (2002). Combination chemotherapy and radiotherapy for primary central nervous system lymphoma: Radiation therapy oncology group study 93-10. *Journal of Clinical Oncology*, 20, 4643–4648.

Eby, N.L., Grufferman, S., Flannelly, C.M., Schold Jr, S.C., Vogel, F. S., & Burger, P.C. (1988). Increasing incidence of primary brain lymphoma in the US. *Cancer*, 62, 2461–2465.

Ferreri, A.J., Abrey, L.E., Blay, J.Y., *et al.* (2003). Summary statement on primary central nervous system lymphomas from the eighth international conference on malignant lymphoma, Lugano, Switzerland, June 12 to 15, 2002. *Journal of Clinical Oncology*, 21, 2407–2414.

Gabbai, A.A., Hochberg, F.H., Linggood, R.M., Bashir, R., & Hotleman, K. (1989). High-dose methotrexate for non-aids primary central nervous system lymphoma. Report of 13 cases. *Journal of Neurosurgery*, 70, 190 194.

Glass, J., Gruber, M.L., Cher, L., & Hochberg, F.H. (1994). Preirradiation methotrexate chemotherapy of primary central nervous system lymphoma: long-term outcome. *Journal of Neurosurgery*, 81, 188–195.

Herrlinger, U., Schabet, M., Brugger, W., *et al.* (2002). German Cancer Society Neuro-Oncology Working Group NOA-03 multicenter trial of single-agent high-dose methotrexate for primary central nervous system lymphoma. *Annals of Neurology*, 51, 247–252.

Herrlinger, U., Kuker, W., Uhl, M., *et al.* (2005). NOA-03 trial of high-dose methotrexate in primary central nervous system lymphoma: final report. *Annals of Neurology*, 57, 843–847.

Hoang-Xuan, K., Taillandier, L., Chinot, O., *et al.* (2003). Chemotherapy alone as initial treatment for primary CNS lymphoma in patients older than 60 years: a multicenter phase II study (26952) of the European Organization for Research and Treatment of Cancer Brain Tumor Group. *Journal of Clinical Oncology*, 21, 2726–2731.

Khan, R.B., Shi, W., Thaler, H.T., DeAngelis, L.M., & Abrey, L.E. (2002). Is intrathecal methotrexate necessary in the treatment of primary CNS lymphoma? *Journal of Neuro-Oncology*, 58, 175–178.

Lichtman, S.M., Kolitz, J., Budman, D.R., *et al.* (2001). Treatment of aggressive non-hodgkin's lymphoma in elderly patients with thiotepa, novantrone (mitoxantrone), vincristine, prednisone (TNOP). *American Journal of Clinical Oncology*, 24 , 360–362.

Olson, J.E., Janney, C.A., Rao, R.D., *et al.* (2002). The continuing increase in the incidence of primary central nervous system non-Hodgkin lymphoma: a surveillance, epidemiology and end results analysis. *Cancer*, 95, 1504–1510.

Omuro, A.M., Ben-Porat, L.S., Panageas, K.S., *et al.* (2005a). Delayed neurotoxicity in primary central nervous system lymphoma. *Archives of Neurology*, 62, 1595–1600.

Omuro, A.M., DeAngelis, L.M., Yahalom, J., & Abrey, L.E. (2005b). Chemoradiotherapy for primary CNS lymphoma: an intent-to-treat analysis with complete follow-up. *Neurology*, 64, 69–74.

O'Neill, B.P., Wang, C.H., O'Fallon, J.R., *et al.* (1999). The consequences of treatment and disease in patients with primary CNS non-Hodgkin's lymphoma: Cognitive function and performance status. North Central Cancer Treatment Group. *Journal of Neuro-Oncology*, 1, 196–203.

Pels, H., Schmidt-Wolf, I.G.H., Glasmacher, A., *et al.* (2003). Primary central nervous system lymphoma: results of a pilot and phase II study of systemic and intraventricular chemotherapy with deferred radiotherapy. *Journal of Clinical Oncology*, 21, 4489–4495.

Poortmans, P.M., Kluin-Nelemans, H.C., Haaxma-Reiche, H., *et al.* (2003). High-dose methotrexate-based chemotherapy followed by consolidating radiotherapy in non-aids-related primary central nervous system lymphoma: European Organization for Research and Treatment of Cancer Lymphoma Group phase II trial 20962. *Journal of Clinical Oncology*, 21, 4483–4488.

Sandor, V., Stark-Vancs, V., Pearson, D., *et al.* (1998). Phase II trial of chemotherapy alone for primary CNS and intraocular lymphoma. *Journal of Clinical Oncology*, 16, 3000–3006.

Sarazin, M., Ameri, A., Monjour, A., Nibio, A., Poisson, M., Delattre, J.Y. (1995). Primary central nervous system lymphoma: treatment with chemotherapy and radiotherapy. *European Journal of Cancer*, 31A, 2003–2007.

Soussain, C., Suzan, F., Hoang-Xuan, K., *et al.* (2001). Results of intensive chemotherapy followed by hematopoietic stem-cell rescue in 22 patients with refractory or recurrent primary CNS lymphoma or intraocular lymphoma. *Journal of Clinical Oncology*, 19, 742–749.

Progress in Neurotherapeutics and Neuropsychopharmacology, 2:1, 137–154 © 2007 Cambridge University Press
DOI: 10.1017/S1748232106000103   Printed in the United Kingdom

A Double-Blind, Randomized Clinical Trial to Assess the Augmentation with Nimodipine of Antidepressant Therapy in the Treatment of "Vascular Depression"

F.E. Taragano

Department of Neuropsychiatry, CEMIC University, Buenos Aires, Argentina; Nuestra Señora de las Nieves, Geriatric Institute, Buenos Aires, Argentina; E-mail: ftaragano@arnet.com.ar

P.M. Bagnati

Consultants Clinic, Mar del Plata, Argentina; E-mail: pablo.bagnati@consultantsmedicina.com

R.F. Allegri

Department of Neuropsychiatry, CEMIC University, Buenos Aires, Argentina; E-mail: rallegri@fibertel.com.ar

Key words: vascular depression, treatment augmentation, nimodipine, cerebrovascular disease, recurrence, therapeutic possibilities.

Introduction and Overview

There is evidence for an association between vascular disease and depression, and in particular between cerebrovascular disease and depression, especially that occurring later in life. Among the diverse psychiatric diseases, the one which is most widely studied concerning the relationship with the vascular system, is depression. The risk relationship between depression and vascular events is a two-way road: the presence of depression increases the cerebrovascular and cardiovascular event risk (worsening its evolution and prognosis, as well) and a patient evidencing cerebrovascular or heart disease, will also show an increase in the risk of suffering depression (Taragano *et al.*, 2005). Depression is a common cause of disability in the elderly. It reduces quality of life and represents a serious public health problem (Beekman *et al.*, 2001; Steffens *et al.*, 2000). Its prevalence in late life is 2–3% for major depression and 12–15% for all depressive syndromes (Beekman *et al.*, 1999). In Argentina, according to data of the National Institute of Statistics and Census (INDEC), between 1950 and 2000, the general population increased by

Correspondence should be addressed to: Fernando E. Taragano, MD, PhD, Instituto Universitario CEMIC, Av. E. Galván 4102, 1431 Buenos Aires, Argentina; Email: ftaragano@cemic.edu.ar

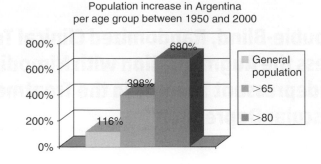

Fig. 1.
Population increase in Argentina: dramatic increase in people over 80 years old.

116%, whereas people other than age 65 years increased by 398% and people over 80 years old *increased by 682%* (Arizaga, 2003); these percentages show the considerable presence that late life depressive syndromes can have in elderly people community (Figure 1). Ageing- and disease-related processes may cause vulnerability to depression. Cerebrovascular disease might predispose, precipitate or perpetuate depressive syndromes, especially in older people (Alexopoulos *et al.*, 1997). The acceptance of the term "vascular depression (VaD)" results from the accruing evidence of the relationship of cerebrovascular disease to depression. Alexopoulos defined that VaD may represent a distinct syndrome, characterized by depressive symptoms that co-occur with vascular disease such as hypertension, diabetes and heart disease (Mast *et al.*, 2004). The term "vascular depression" is currently used to define a subgroup of elderly patients with depression who exhibit clinical or imaging evidence of brain vascular disease. Many cases of late onset depression are related to overt stroke, silent infarction or subcortical white matter ischemic injury (Cummings & Mega, 2003). This comorbidity of depression with cerebrovascular lesions and cerebrovascular risk factors, together with the fact that depression is a common consequence after stroke, support the idea of vascular disease as one potential etiological factor in late life depression (Alexopoulos, 2005; Robinson, 2003).

The VaD clinical picture typically includes (Table 1): a late age at onset (after age of 65) or there is a change in the course of an early onset depressive disorder; persistent symptoms; the association of such depression with clinical and/or neuroimaging evidence of cerebrovascular disease, or risk factors and diffuse or multifocal cerebrovascular lesions; executive dysfunction, psychomotor retardation and associated neuropsychological disturbances (e.g. delay in responding verbally, impaired concentration and decision-making); poor insight; absence of a family history of mood disorder; limited depressive ideation and less guilt than early onset depression or elderly depressed without vascular risk factors (Alexopoulos, 2005; Kales *et al.*, 2005; Cummings & Mega, 2003).

Table 1. **Characteristics of VaD**

- A late age at onset (after age of 65 years)
- The association of depression with clinical and/or neuroimaging evidence of cerebrovascular disease, or risk factors and diffuse or multifocal cerebrovascular lesions
- Executive dysfunction and more neuropsychological disturbances
- Less guilt than early onset depression or elderly depressed without vascular risk factors
- Poor insight. More apathy and retardation
- Absence of a family history of mood disorder
- Persistent symptoms

Evidence has been found for an excess of atheromatous disease, related to the aortic and cerebral vessels, in late life depression (Tiemeier *et al.*, 2003; Thomas *et al.*, 2001). Occurrence of symptoms of depression has been associated with small lesions in the basal ganglia, large cortical white matter lesions and severe subcortical white matter grade (Taylor *et al.*, 2003a; Nebes *et al.*, 2002; Steffens *et al.*, 2002). It is postulated that the presence of silent or overt vascular ischemic changes in the subcortical and frontal circuits may raise the vulnerability for late-age onset depression (Townsend *et al.*, 2002) and that depression is often a direct consequence of brain damage caused by stroke (Lyketsos *et al.*, 1998). White matter hyperintensities on magnetic resonance imaging (MRI) are increased in deep white matter, especially in frontal areas in major depression. Deep white matter hyperintensities are more frequently located at the level of dorsolateral prefrontal cortex in depressed subjects (Thomas *et al.*, 2002). More severe hyperintensity ratings in the deep white matter have been found in older people with late life depression than those with early onset depression (de Groot *et al.*, 2000). Neuroimaging studies have shown an association between subcortical lesions and depressive symptoms in late life with the VaD hypothesis (Steffens *et al.*, 2002; Campbell & Coffey, 2001; Krishnan *et al.*, 1997). Atherosclerosis could lead to events such as cerebral lesions. Two pathophysiological pathways of ischemic brain injury can occur: occlusion (complete infarct) or stenosis and hypoperfusion involving the microcirculation. In practice, both pathological pathways can overlap, coexisting in the same patient (Román *et al.*, 2002). Five circuits connecting the frontal lobes and subcortical structures are involved: a motor circuit originating in the supplementary motor area, an oculomotor circuit and three circuits originating in prefrontal cortex (dorsolateral prefrontal cortex, lateral orbital cortex and anterior cingulate cortex) (Coffey & Cummings, 1994). Vascular disconnection of these striatofrontal areas produces executive dysfunction and changes in mood regulation. Two mechanisms for these pathways disconnection have been proposed (Alexopoulos *et al.*, 1997): small direct lesions might themselves disrupt pathways involved in mood process, or accumulation of lesions exceeding a certain threshold might be required. One recent study showed that atherosclerosis is strongly

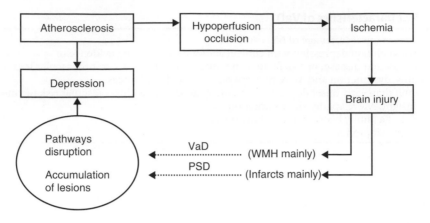

Fig. 2.
Pathophysiological mechanisms postulated in VaD (WMH: white matter hyperintensities; PSD: post-stroke depression).

associated with a late life depression (Tiemeier *et al.*, 2004). Other evidence of vascular disconnection was provided by Taylor *et al.* (2003b): in his study, elderly depressed patients exhibited white matter hyperintensities in bilateral frontal and left parieto-temporal regions, whereas control subjects had significant white matter lesions mainly in parieto-temporal regions (not frontal regions); frontal white matter lesions (presented in depressed subjects) may produce a disruption of frontal–striatal white matter tracts. The pathophysiological and clinical constructions described above are summarized in Figure 2. The term *subcortical ischemic depression* has been proposed because it is illustrative as regards the etiological mechanisms and anatomical areas involved in late life depression (Krishnan *et al.*, 2004).

Subcortical ischemic depression and VaD with executive dysfunction (Alexopoulos *et al.*, 2002) are new categorizations of depressive disorder (Robinson, 2005). Alexopoulos has suggested that many patients with late onset depression have cerebrovascular disease, which leads to ischemia, and consequent white matter tract injury, causing changes in mood and executive function (Vataja *et al.*, 2005).

One study showed that for patients with VaD, nimodipine treatment led to improved outcomes of the depression and to a lower likelihood of recurrence (Taragano *et al.*, 2001). These findings support the etiopathogenetic hypotheses surrounding VaD and have implications for the treatment of patients with VaD. Whatever its underlying mechanism, VaD should also serve as a reminder that psychiatric diagnoses are syndromes that can have different pathogenetic pathways (Breitner, 2001). This rule helps us to understand that cerebrovascular disease is probably an outstanding aggravating element for major depression in late life and this condition may differ importantly from early life depressive disorders.

The late life disorders usually have a different clinical appearance and tend toward chronicity and refractoriness to treatments that commonly succeed with younger patients, including in particular the use of selective serotonin reuptake inhibitors (SSRIs).

A randomized, controlled study by Taragano *et al.* (2001) showed that VaD is probably pathophysiologically linked to cerebrovascular disease. As a consequence of using nimodipine, a calcium-channel blocker agent, to augment the standard antidepressant treatment there was an improvement in the course of depression and a decrease in the rates of recurrence.

Objective

Our aim was to evaluate the efficacy and tolerability of fluoxetine plus nimodipine in the treatment of VaD. We tested the hypothesis that this intervention would produce more patients with a positive response, full remission and lower rates of recurrence. This trial was based on the relationship between depression and vascular disease. Our intention was to modify the underlying vascular mechanisms contributing to depression in late life. We sought to improve the clinic picture, to achieve a full remission and avoid recurrence as long as possible.

Methods

Design

This was a, double-blind, randomized, parallel, multicenter clinical trial. The senior author (FET) conceived of the project and developed the protocol.

Participants

One hundred and one outpatients with VaD by the Alexopoulos criteria (see Appendix), who also met DSM-IV (Diagnostic and Statistical Manual of Mental Disorders, Fourth Edition) criteria for "major depressive episode" using the Structured Clinical Interview for DSM-IV Axis I Disorders, were included. Patients were recruited from geriatric neuropsychiatry outpatient units in Argentina, at the following centers: CEMIC University ($n = 38$), Colon Clinic ($n = 34$) and Nuestra Señora de Las Nieves Geriatric Institute ($n = 29$). At each center a senior neuropsychiatrist with experience in caring for geriatric patients was in charge of the study at their site.

All patients underwent a neuropsychiatric examination to verify that they met the study inclusion criteria. This included rating of the Hamilton Depressive Rating Scale ($HDRS_{17}$), the Mini-Mental State Examination (MMSE), laboratory studies and brain computed tomography (CT) or magnetic resonance imaging (MRI) to investigate for vascular disease of the brain, including extensive leukoareosis. Patients were excluded if their MMSE was ≤ 18 points, their HDRS was ≤ 15, or if they were clinically too ill to be treated safety with fluoxetine and/or nimodipine or to participate in the study. According to local ethical regulations, all participants gave informed consent to take part in the study.

Clinical Trial Methods

All patients were treated with fluoxetine at the usually effective minimum dose. In general, patients were started on a low dose and slowly titrated upward to the doses decided by the investigator.

The intervention of interest was as follows. At the same time that patients began with fluoxetine they started on nimodipine. Patients were randomly assigned in blocks of two to either nimodipine ($n = 50$) or placebo ($n = 51$) and the allocation was concealed. All personnel associated with the study were blind to treatment condition; the codes could be broken only in the event of serious adverse events or at the conclusion of the clinical trial. A clinic pharmacy prepared the medication and placebo capsules according to established double-blind procedures. Numbered containers were used to implement the random allocation sequence.

Medications were dispensed directly to patients by non-physician staff at each site and the same staff members received the unused pills and conducted pill counts for the purpose of assessing adherence to treatment at each follow-up visit.

The dose of nimodipine was 90 mg three times per day because, in general, dosing in elderly patients should be cautious, reflecting the greater frequency of decreased hepatic, renal or cardiac function, and of concomitant disease or other drug therapy. The initial dose was based on whether patients were already taking antihypertensive medication(s). For patients taking none the starting dose were 30 mg (one tablet of nimodipine or placebo) three times per day. Patients taking any antihypertensive were started on 15 mg three times per day and increasing after 10 days to 30 mg three times per day. If hypotension developed, then the research assistant decreased the other antihypertensive medication(s), titrated to the optimal blood pressure. On average, 91% of doses were taken in both groups.

Eight participants (7.9%) did not complete the study because of adverse events ($n = 6$, 5.9%) and withdrawal of consent ($n = 2$, 1.9%). There was no significant difference between nimodipine or control participants in dropout rates.

OUTCOME ASSESSMENT

Patients were assessed on the $HDRS_{17}$ for outcome by a research assistant at baseline and at days 15, 30, 61, 122, 183 and 244 after treatment initiation or when needed with the authorization of the principal investigator. The scores were known and followed only by the research assistant. Study outcome measures were as follows:

1. Mean score on the $HDRS_{17}$ at each follow-up time point.

2. Rate of positive response of depression. Positive response was defined as 50% reduction in $HDRS_{17}$ score at the 61-day study follow-up visit.

3. Rate of full remission of depression. Full remission was defined as an $HDRS_{17}$ score $\leqslant 12$ at the 61-day study follow-up visit *and* a 50% reduction in $HDRS_{17}$ score.

4. Rate of recurrence of depression after remission. Recurrence was defined as full remission followed by the return of a DSM-IV "major depressive episode" at any point in the study interval between 61 and 244 days of follow-up.

5. Rates of adverse events were documented at every follow-up point of the study.

ANALYSES

All analyses were "intent-to-treat" with the last observation carried forward. The following statistical analyses were conducted. First, a repeated measures analysis of covariance (ANCOVA) was performed. The dependent variables were $HDRS_{17}$ scores at each follow-up point, starting at day 15. This analysis covaried for the baseline $HDRS_{17}$ score and for treatment assignment groups. The second analysis compared, between the groups, the rates of positive response and full remission at day 61 and the rates of recurrence from days 61 and 244. Finally, the analysis compared the rates of adverse events between the two groups at any time point of the study. χ^2-tests were used to assess the statistical significance of the difference in rates between the two groups (with Fisher's exact test when needed).

The estimated sample size for two sample comparison of proportions (positive response of depression) was obtained: test $H_o: p_1 = p_2$, where p_1 is the proportion in population 1 and p_2 is the proportion in population 2. Assumptions: alpha = 0.05 (two-sided), power = 0.80, $p_1 = 0.60$, $p_2 = 0.30$, $N_2/N_1 = 1.00$. Estimated required sample sizes: $N_1 = 49, N_2 = 49$.

Results

Figure 3 is a flow diagram of the progress through the stages of the trial. The recruitment period was from July to December 2001 and follow-up period until August 2002. Table 2 presents a comparison of the study groups at baseline for several variables. No statistically significant differences were found between them.

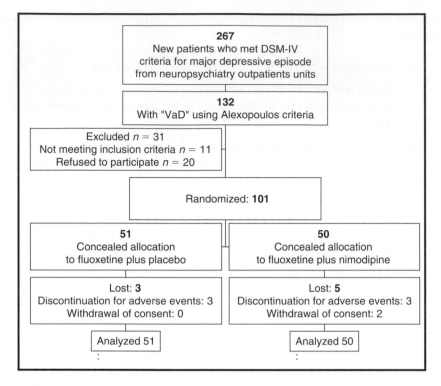

Fig. 3.
Flow diagram.

Table 2. **Comparison of the Study Groups at Baseline on Several Variables**

	PLACEBO (N = 51)	NIMODIPINE (N = 50)	COMPARISON
Age (mean, SD)	69.6 (7.4)	70.2 (8.1)	t (d.f. 81) $= 0.32, p = 0.80$
Gender (female n)	24 (47%)	21 (42%)	χ^2 (d.f. 1) $= 0.26, p = 0.609$
Concurrent GMC[a] (n)	44 (86%)	41 (82%)	χ^2 (d.f. 1) $= 0.34, p = 0.556$
Number of medicines for GMC[a] (mean, SD)	1.3 (0.73)	1.4 (0.8)	t (d.f. 80) $= 1.4, p = 0.14$
Age depression onset (mean, SD)	66.7 (7.6)	65.2 (7.2)	t (d.f. 78) $= 1.03, p = 0.38$
Days current episode (mean, SD)	95.6 (77)	101 (105)	t (d.f. 82) $= 0.4, p = 0.78$
Baseline HDRS$_{v17}$ (mean, SD)	27.3 (4)	28.8 (5.2)	t (d.f. 80) $= 1.2, p = 0.35$
Baseline MMSE (mean, SD, max, min)	24.7 (2.9; 29; 20)	23.9 (2.3; 28; 20)	t (d.f. 82) $= 0.3, p = 0.85$
Dose of fluoxetine (mean, SD)	19.9 (3.3)	19.1 (2.7)	t (d.f. 80) $= 1.2, p = 0.51$

[a]GMC: general medical condition.

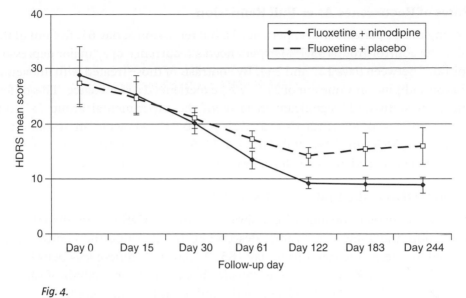

Fig. 4.
Mean on the HDRS at baseline and each follow-up visit for the nimodipine and control groups.

HDRS Scores at Follow-Up

Figure 4 shows the mean scores of the two groups at baseline and at each follow-up time point. Both groups exhibited substantial reductions in HDRS scores, with most improvements occurring within the first 122 days. The improvements in the nimodipine-treated group were more rapid after day 30, and in the consecutive days there always was a better antidepressive response. Additionally, at the end of the trial the nimodipine group showed a steady decline while the control group showed an increase in HDRS scores. The differences in outcome between the two groups were statistically significant ($F(1,80) = 9.76$, $p = 0.001$) during repeated measures ANCOVA, with baseline HDRS score as the within-subjects covariate.

Rates of Positive Response and Full Remission

At the 61-day time point there was a statistically significant difference in favor of the nimodipine group, with 37 patients on nimodipine (74%) as compared to 27 (53%) on placebo meeting the criteria for a positive response (χ^2 (d.f. 1) $= 4.82$, $p = 0.028$). The analysis shows a clinically significant treatment effect in favor of the nimodipine group, with an absolute benefit increase (ABI) of 21% (95%CI 2.7–39.3%) and the number needed to treat (NNT) equal to 5 (95%CI 3–37). At the same point, 27 patients on nimodipine (54%) and 14 patients on placebo (27%) met criteria for full remission, demonstrating a statistically significant difference in favor of the nimodipine group (χ^2 (d.f. 1) $= 7.3$, $p = 0.006$) and a clinically significant treatment effect showing an ABI of 27% (95%CI 8.1–44.9%) and an NNT of 4 (95%CI 2–12).

Rates of Recurrence After Full Remission

Among the 41 patients who experienced a full remission at day 61, five out of the 14 in the control group (35.7%) experienced a recurrence of a "major depressive episode" between days 122 and 244. By contrast, of those treated with fluoxetine plus nimodipine only one out of 27 (3.7%) experienced a recurrence. This difference was statistically significant in favor of the experimental group (χ^2 (d.f. 1) = 7.56, p = 0.006; Fisher's exact test p = 0.012) showing an absolute risk reduction (ARR) of 32% (95%CI 11.4–52.6%) and an NNT of 3 (95%CI 2–9), with clear evidence of a clinically important treatment effect.

Mean HDRS at the End of the Trial

After day 30 patients on nimodipine always had lower HDRS scores than the control group and showed a steadily descending trend, while the control group showed an increasing trend from day 183. At day 244, differences between the two groups on HDRS scores were statistically significant in analysis of variance ($F(1.25)$ = 9.8, p = 0.001). Hence, at the end of the trial, nimodipine seemed to be preventing the recurrence of depression.

Tolerability

The frequency of side-effects was also compared between the two groups (Table 3). Any side-effects at any time of the study was registered in 17 patients in the control group (33.3%) and 24 patients (48%) on fluoxetine plus nimodipine. This difference was not statistically significant (χ^2 (d.f. 1) = 2.25, p = 0.133). The most common side effect in the experimental group was mild hypotension occurring in 9 patients (18%) compared with 3 (5.8%) in the control group and showing a significant difference between them (Fisher's exact test p = 0.043). The absolute risk increase (ARI) of 12.2% (95%CI -0.2–24.5%) and the number needed to harm (NNH) of 8 (95%CI 4 to infinity) indicates that the differences may be of low impact.

With regard to withdrawal for adverse events: in the control group 1 patient dropped out because of exacerbation of anorexia and diarrhea, and 2 because of nausea, while in the experimental group one patient left the study because of headache and dizziness, one for epigastric pains and one for nausea. The difference in dropouts was not significant (Fisher's exact test p = 0.322). Neither severe nor serious adverse events were reported.

Discussion

This study contributes to the growing literature on VaD (Table 4). The strongest point of our trial is the observation that better clinical treatment and risk reduction in the recurrence of depression can be achieved by managing the underlying

Table 3. **Number of Patients in Each Group Reporting Specific Side-Effects at Any Follow-Up Visit and the Causes of Dropout**

SIDE-EFFECTS	CONTROL ($N = 51$)	NIMODIPINE ($N = 50$)	P-VALUE FISHER'S EXACT TEST	DROPOUT CONTROL ($N = 51$)	DROPOUT NIMODIPINE ($N = 50$)	P-VALUE FISHER'S EXACT TEST
Hypotension	3	9	0.043	0	0	–
Nausea	4	2	0.241	2	1	0.382
Headache	4	2	0.241	0	1	0.495
Dizziness	2	2	0.382	0	0	–
Retarded ejaculation	2	1	0.382	0	0	–
Facial rash	0	2	0.242	0	0	–
Epigastric pains	0	2	0.242	0	1	0.495
Anorexia	2	0	0.252	1	0	0.505
Insomnia	0	1	0.5	0	0	–
Diarrhea	0	1	0.5	0	0	–
Total	17	24	χ^2 (d.f. 1) $= 2.25, p = 0.133$	3	3	0.322

Table 4. **Topics in VaD**

IN FOCUS	LESS STUDIED
• Clinical picture	• Mortality
• Vascular risk factors	• Other etiologies (besides vascular)
• White matter hyperintensities	• Psychosocial factors
• New categorizations	• Prevention
• Cognitive impairment and development of dementia	• Functional neuroimaging
• Treatment response	• New treatments strategies

From Robinson (2005) and Baldwin (2004).

cerebrovascular disease. This approach was encouraged by knowledge of the neuroanatomical areas involved (frontal–subcortical–thalamic circuits) and the idea that vascular disease can cause the disruption of mood regulation pathways (Alexopoulos *et al.*, 1997). Thus, we are advancing toward the ambitious objective of operating on an etiologically specific target for a depressive disorder.

Nimodipine has lipophilic properties and can easily cross the blood–brain barrier. Its primary action is to reduce the number of open channels, thereby restricting influx of calcium ions into cells. It also has an antivasoconstrictive and a vasodilatatory action on arterioles. In experimental situations this inhibition suggests that nimodipine may have neuroprotective potential, particularly against transient ischemia and hypoxia. A recent *Cochrane Review* found evidence of some short-term benefit mainly in measures of cognitive function and global assessments for

Table 5. **Nimodipine in VaD: Possible Additional Benefits**

- Reducing stroke incidence
- Short-term benefit cognitive function
- Neuroprotective potential

patients with degenerative, mixed and vascular dementia (López Arrieta & Birks, 2004). Nimodipine may be treating the underlying pathophysiology in VaD.

There is not total consensus that the generalized atherosclerosis is a risk factor for depressive symptoms (Vinkers *et al.*, 2005). Ischemic lesions in the brain can also be a result of low tissue perfusion, and we think that nimodipine might be useful from this point of view. VaD can be conceptualized as a cumulative model of *vascular burden* on the brain (Mast *et al.*, 2004): patients with greater chronic vascular disease may be at risk for greater cerebrovascular changes and nimodipine may reduce this risk.

A longitudinal study found a positive association between vascular burden and depressive symptoms in geriatric patients (Mast *et al.*, 2004). Mast *et al.* examined the cumulative effects of multiple cerebrovascular risk factors on depression: when the number of them increases from one to two or more, the frequency of depression increases strongly. In spite of the difficulties establishing the relationship between cerebrovascular risk factors and late life depression, the role of cerebrovascular risk factors in relation of treatment considerations is increasingly relevant: for example, pharmacological control of hypertension, was shown to reduce white matter hyperintensities progression (Dufouil *et al.*, 2001), and so might also reduce the risk of depression. Calcium antagonists are particularly useful in reducing the incidence of stroke (Weir & Izzo, 2003). Both observations (probability to reduce white matter hyperintensities and incidence of stroke) support the use of nimodipine, a calcium-channel antagonist agent with hypotensor effect (Table 5).

In a recent study, the investigators measured the impact of cardiovascular risk factors on the outcome of antidepressant treatment in major depressive disorder (age, smoking, family history, hypertension, diabetes and hypercholesterolemia). Although in this work the ages were 19–65 years, the cardiovascular risk score was significantly associated with treatment non-response and lack of remission when adjusting for age of onset of major depressive disorder and baseline severity of depression. Elevated total cholesterol also was a significant predictor of treatment non-response and lack of remission (Iosifescu *et al.*, 2005). Another study showed no significantly affected sertraline antidepressant effect by the presence of comorbid vascular illness (e.g. hypertension) (Krishnan *et al.*, 2001). Less efficient antidepressant response has been described in late life depression linked to vascular disease: there is initial treatment resistance, poor long-term outcome (O'Brien *et al.*, 1998; Simpson *et al.*, 1998; 1997) and increased relapse risk (Kales *et al.*, 2005).

According to these features, adding nimodipine to a standard antidepressant therapy (fluoxetine) makes sense, allowing treatment of one the causes (vascular disease), which may produce resistance and recurrence. The results of our research strengthen this hypothesis. There was a low risk of recurrence, which was evidenced among treatment responders.

Symptoms of depression precede cognitive decline and dementia (Jorm, 2001; Yaffe *et al.*, 1999). Patients with late life depression have increased risk of developing dementia (Green *et al.*, 2003). Vascular risk factors may have considerable negative effects on brain and cognitive performance. Among people older than 65 years, hypertension prevalence is estimated to be about 65% (two of every three elderly people) (Kearney *et al.*, 2005). Hypertension may be linked to cognitive impairment by a number of mechanisms including white matter disease, brain atrophy and endothelial dysfunction (Gorelick, 2005).

Evidence has emerged to support the hypothesis that vascular factors may be involved in Alzheimer's disease (de la Torre, 2004). Both high and low blood pressure plays a role in the development and progression of cognitive impairment and dementia. High blood pressure in middle age is a risk factor for late life cognitive impairment and dementia. Very high blood pressure (e.g. >180 mmHg) can be a risk factor for dementia in elderly people. Chronic hypertension-induced atherosclerosis and cerebral ischemic conditions may mediate the associations of midlife high blood pressure and late life low blood pressure with dementia (Qiu *et al.*, 2005).

These complex relations among depression, vascular disease and cognitive impairment led us to the possible benefits of augmentation treatment with nimodipine in VaD.

Translation to Clinical Practice

Our aim has been to describe VaD stressing its treatment resistance, recurrence, poor long-term outcome and associated cognitive impairment. Late onset depressive disorder is associated with a high rate of mortality and possible dementia (Baldwin, 2006). Poorer outcomes are produced partly by executive dysfunction and consequent disability (Kiosses *et al.*, 2001). In this trial we found that more patients achieved a positive response with fluoxetine plus nimodipine, thus improving the outcomes of VaD. Intrinsically, an NNT of 5 indicates that few patients need to be treated to achieve one additional positive response, demonstrating a substantial clinical treatment effect. In addition, nimodipine was associated with a risk reduction in the recurrence of depression. In general, fluoxetine plus nimodipine was well tolerated, although there was mild hypotension, possibly due to the effects on arterial smooth muscle.

We are aware of the limitations of our study. First, the power calculation was performed for the rates of positive response (which undoubtedly showed a statistically significant effect) but not for the rates of recurrence. Thus, even if the

Table 6. **Possible Therapeutic Limitations**

- Non-vascular mechanisms
- Hypotension (worsening cognition and functional level)
- Drug intolerance
- Treatment non-adherence
- Non-responder group

Table 7. **Therapeutic Possibilities**

- Primary prevention
- Psychosocial interventions
- Other neuropharmacological alternatives (e.g. memantine, cholinesterase inhibitors)

differences in rates of recurrence of depression are statistically significant, the data for nimodipine preventing recurrence need to be better established. Second, the rules for treating patients with VaD are limited because of insufficient trials. In Table 6 we have described other possible limitations of this treatment (Baldwin, 2005; Qiu *et al.*, 2005) and in Table 7 other therapeutics possibilities which might improve VaD (Kales *et al.*, 2005; Alexopoulos *et al.*, 2003).

The findings in our investigation in patients who meet VaD criteria may suggest this strategy of augmentation as a useful tool in the therapeutic algorithm of late life depressive syndromes. The patient suffering from VaD who evidences cognitive impairment and clinical–neuropsychological manifestations of emerging dementia might be considered as another indication for this augmentation approach.

In VaD high rates of relapse and poor long-term outcome are observed. For this reason, it is necessary to identify crucial pathophysiological aspects, still unknown, which could offer a greater power of predicting the course of the disease (Keller, 2003). We conclude that this trial as implications in practice; treatment of underlying cerebrovascular factors in depression has the effect of expanding the selection of potential treatment. This suggests the possibility of new beneficial interventions analogous to the treatments of cardiocerebrovascular diseases, allowing new approaches designed not only for treatment but also for prevention.

Acknowledgments

This work was supported partially by CEMIC University and by an NSDLN-1-01 Research Grant (Dr. F.E. Taragano).

References

Alexopoulos, G.S. (2005). Depression in the elderly. *Lancet*, 365, 1961–1970.
Alexopoulos, G.S., Meyers, B.S., Young, R.C., Campbell, S., Sibersweig, D., & Charlson, M. (1997). The "vascular depression" hypothesis. *Archives of General Psychiatry*, 54, 15–22.

Alexopoulos, G.S., Kiosses, D.N., Klimstra, S., *et al.* (2002). Clinical presentation of the "depression-executive dysfunction syndrome" of late life. *American Journal of Geriatric Psychiatry*, 10, 98–106.

Alexopoulos, G.S., Raue, P., & Arean, P. (2003). Problem-solving therapy versus supportive therapy in geriatric major depression with executive dysfunction. *American Journal of Geriatric Psychiatry*, 11, 46–52.

Arizaga, R. (2003). *Enfermedad de Alzheimer y otras demencias*, Chapter 1. Editorial Polemos, Buenos Aires, Argentina, p. 24.

Baldwin, R. (2005). Is vascular depression a distinct sub-type of depressive disorder? A review of causal evidence. *International Journal of Geriatric Psychiatry*, 20(1), 1–11.

Baldwin, R.C. (2006). Prognosis of late life depression: a three year cohort study of outcome and potential predictors. *International Journal of Geriatric Psychiatry*, 21(1), 57–63.

Beekman, A.T., Copeland, J.R., & Prince, M.J. (1999). Review of community prevalence of depression in later life. *British Journal of Psychiatry*, 174, 307–311.

Beekman, A.T.F., *et al.* (2001). Emergence and persistence of late life depression: a 3 year follow-up of the longitudinal aging study, Amsterdam. *Journal of Affective Disorders*, 65, 130–138.

Breitner, J.C. (2001). Vascular depression: new light on an established idea? *Journal of Neurology, Neurosurgery and Psychiatry*, 70, 3.

Campbell, J.J., & Coffey, C.E. (2001). Neuropsychiatric significance of subcortical hyperintensity. *Journal of Neuropsychiatry and Clinical Neurosciences*, 13, 261–288.

Coffey, C.E., & Cummings, J.L. (1994). *Textbook of Geriatric Neuropsychiatry*, Chapter 4. The American Psychiatric Press, Washington, DC, p. 86.

Cummings, J.C., & Mega, M.S. (2003). *Neuropsychiatry and Behavioral Neuroscience*, Chapter 14. Oxford University Press, New York, pp. 206–207.

de Groot, J.C., de Leeuw, F.E., Oudkerk, M., *et al.* (2000). Cerebral white matter lesions and depressive symptoms in elderly adults. *Archives of General Psychiatry*, 57, 1071–1076.

de la Torre, J.C. (2004). Is Alzheimer's disease a neurodegenerative or a vascular disorder? Data, dogma and dialectics. *Lancet Neurology*, 3, 184–190.

Dufouil, C., de Kersaint-Gilly, A., Besancon, V., *et al.* (2001). Longitudinal study of blood pressure and white matter hyperintensities. *Neurology*, 56, 921–926.

Gorelick, P.B. (2005). William M. Feinberg lecture: cognitive vitality and the role of the stroke and cardiovascular disease risk factors. *Stroke*, 36, 875–879.

Green, R.C., Cupples, L.A., Kurz, A., *et al.* (2003). Depression as a risk factor for Alzheimer's disease: The MIRAGE Study. *Archives of Neurology*, 60, 753–759.

Iosifescu, D.V., Clementi-Craven, N., Fraguas, R., *et al.* (2005). Cardiovascular Risk Factors May Moderate Pharmacological Treatment Effects in Major Depressive Disorder. *Psychosomatic Medicine*, 67, 703–706.

Jorm, A.F. (2001). History of depression as a risk factor for dementia: an updated review. *Australian New Zealand Journal of Psychiatry*, 35, 776–781.

Kales, H.C., Maixner, D.F., & Mellow, A.M. (2005). Cerebrovascular disease and late-life depression. *American Journal of Geriatric Psychiatry*, 13, 88–98.

Kearney, P.M., Whelton, M., Reynolds, K., *et al.* (2005). Global burden of hypertension: analysis of worldwide data. *Lancet*, 365, 217–223.

Keller, M. (2003). Past, present, and future directions for defining optimal treatment outcome in depression. *Journal of the American Medical Association*, 289, 23.

Kiosses, D.N., Klimstra, S., Murphy, C., *et al.* (2001). Executive dysfunction and disability en elderly patients with major depression. *American Journal of Geriatric Psychiatry*, 9, 269–274.

Krishnan, K.R., Hays, J.C., & Blazer, D.G. (1997). MRI defined vascular depression. *American Journal of Psychiatry*, 154, 497–501.

Krishnan, K.R., Doraiswamy, P.M., & Clary, C.M. (2001). Clinical and treatment response characteristics of late life depression associated with vascular disease: a pooled analysis of two multicenter trials with sertraline. *Progress in Neuro-Psychopharmacology and Biological Psychiatry*, 25, 247–361.

Krishnan, K.R., Taylor, W.D., McQuoid, D.R., *et al.* (2004). Clinical Characteristics of magnetic resonance imaging-defined subcortical ischemic depression. *Biological Psychiatry*, 55, 390–397.

López Arrieta, J.M., & Birks, J. (2004). Nimodipine for primary degenerative, mixed and vascular dementia (Cochrane Review). In *The Cochrane Library*, Issue 2. Chichester, UK: John Wiley & Sons, Ltd.

Lyketsos, C.G., Treisman, G.C., Lipsey, J.R., Morris, P.L., & Robinson, R.G. (1998). Does stroke cause depression? *Journal of Neuropsychiatry and Clinical Neurosciences*, 10, 103–107.

Mast, B.T., MacNeill, S.E., & Lichtenberg, P.A. (2004). Post-stroke and clinically-defined vascular depression in geriatric rehabilitation patients. *American Journal of Geriatric Psychiatry*, 12, 84–92.

Mast, B.T., Neufeld, S., MacNeill, S.E., *et al.* (2004). Longitudinal support for the relationship between vascular risk factors and late life depressive symptoms. *American Journal of Geriatric Psychiatry*, 12, 93–101.

Nebes, R.D., *et al.* (2002). Longitudinal increase in the volume of white matter hyperintensities in late-onset depression. *International Journal of Geriatric Psychiatry*, 17, 526–530.

O'Brien, J., Ames, D., Chiu, E., *et al.* (1998). Severe deep white matter lesions and outcome in elderly patients with major depressive disorder: follow up study. *British Medical Journal*, 317, 982–984.

Qiu, C., Winbland, W., & Fratiglioni, L. (2005). The age-dependent relation of blood pressure to cognitive function and dementia. *Lancet Neurology*, 4, 487–499.

Robinson, R.G. (2003). Post stroke depression: prevalence, diagnosis, treatment and disease prevention. *Biological Psychiatry*, 54, 376–387.

Robinson, R.G. (2005). Vascular depression and poststroke depression. *American Journal of Geriatric Psychiatry*, 13(2), 85–87.

Román, G.C., Erkinjuntti, T., Wallin, A., Pantoni, L., & Chui, H.C. (2002). Subcortical ischaemic vascular dementia. *Lancet Neurology*, 1, 426–436.

Simpson, S.W., Jackson, A., Baldwin, R.C., *et al.* (1997). Subcortical hyperintensities in late life depression: acute response to treatment and neuropsychological impairment. *International Psychogeriatrics*, 9, 257–275.

Simpson, S.W., Baldwin, R.C., Jackson, A., *et al.* (1998). Is subcortical disease associated with a poor response to antidepressants? Neurological, neuropsychological and neuroradiological findings in late life depression. *Psychological Medicine*, 28, 1015–1026.

Steffens, D.C., *et al.* (2000). Prevalence of depression and its treatment in an elderly population. The Cache Country Study. *Archives of General Psychiatry*, 57, 601–607.

Steffens, D.C., Krishnan, K.R.R., Crump, C., & Burke, G.L. (2002). Cerebrovascular disease and depression in the Cardiovascular Health Study. *Stroke*, 33, 1633–1644.

Taragano, F.E., Allegri, R., Bagnati, P.M., Vicario, A., & Lyketsos, C.G. (2001). A double blind randomized clinical trial assessing the efficacy and safety of augmenting standard antidepressant therapy with nimodipine in the treatment of vascular depression. *International Journal of Geriatric Psychiatry*, 16, 254–260.

Taragano, F.E., Allegri, R.F., Vicario, A., Bagnati, P.M., Pereira Redondo, J.C., Kremer, J.L., Serrano, C.M., Sarasola, D., & Loñ, L. (2005). *Arterias, Corazón y Cerebro: Fisiopatología Vascular de los Trastornos Neuropsiquiátricos* (2nd ed.). Editorial Ediser, Buenos Aires, pp. 63–103.

Taylor, W.D., *et al.* (2003a). White matter hyperintensity progression and late life depression outcomes. *Archives of General Psychiatry*, 60, 1090–1096.

Taylor, W.D., MacFall, J.R., Steffens, D.C., *et al.* (2003b). Localization of age-associated white matter hyperintensities in late life depression. *Progress in Neuro-Psychopharmacology and Biological Psychiatry*, 27(3), 539–544.

Thomas, A.J., *et al.* (2001). A neuropathological study of vascular factors in late life depression. *Journal of Neurology, Neurosurgery and Psychiatry*, 70, 83–87.

Thomas, A.J., *et al.* (2002). Ischemic basis for deep white matter hyperintensities in major depression: a neuropathological study. *Archives of General Psychiatry*, 59, 785–792.

Tiemeier, H., Breteler, M.M., van Popele, N.M., Hofman, A., & Witteman, J.C. (2003). Late life depression is associated with arterial stiffness: a population-based study. *Journal of the American Geriatrics Society*, 51, 1105–1110.

Tiemeier, H., van Dijck, W., Hofman, A., *et al.* (2004). Relationship between atherosclerosis and late life depression. *Archives of General Psychiatry*, 61, 369–376.

Townsend, B.A., Petrella, J.R., & Doraiswamy, P.M. (2002). The role of neuroimaging in geriatric psychiatry. *Current Opinion in Psychiatry*, 15, 427–432.

Vataja, R., Pohjasvaara, T., Mantyla, R., *et al.* (2005). Depression-executive dysfunction syndrome in stroke patients. *American Journal of Geriatric Psychiatry*, 13, 99–107.

Vinkers, D.J., Stek, M.L., van der Mast, R.C., *et al.* (2005). Generalized atherosclerosis, cognitive decline, and depressive symptoms in old age. *Neurology*, 65, 107–112.

Weir, M.R., & Izzo, J.L. (2003). Calcium antagonists. In: *Hypertension Primer*, Chapter 146c, from the Council on High Blood Pressure Research, American Heart Association, Lippincott Williams & Wilkins, Philadelphia, pp. 433–436.

Yaffe, K., Blackwell, T., Gore, R., Sands, L., Reus, V., & Browner, W. (1999). Depressive symptoms and cognitive decline in nondemented elderly: a prospective study. *Archives of General Psychiatry*, 56, 425–430.

Appendix

The Alexopoulos criteria for Vascular Depression as operationalized for this study :

1. Major depressive episode by DSM IV criteria *plus*.

2. Vascular risk factors and/or

3. Cerebrovascular disease (evidenced by characteristic history, alterations in the neurologic examination typical of cerebrovascular disease, and/or typical brain imaging findings, including extensive white matter hyperintensities on MRI) *plus*.

4. Late-life depression (ocurring alter 65 years of age) or worsening of depression after the onset of cerebrovascular disease.

Progress in Neurotherapeutics and Neuropsychopharmacology, 2:1, 155–172 © 2007 Cambridge University Press
DOI: 10.1017/S1748232106000115   Printed in the United Kingdom

Repetitive Transcranial Magnetic Stimulation: A Novel, Noninvasive Add-on Treatment for Medication-Resistant Depression

Tung-Ping Su

Faculty of Medicine, National Yang-Ming University, Taipei, Taiwan;
Email:tpsu@vghtpe.gov.tw

Chih-Chia Huang

Department of Psychiatry, Taipei Veterans General Hospital; Institute of Clinical Medicine, National Yang-Ming University, Taipei, Taiwan

Key words: transcranial magnetic stimulation; prefrontal cortex; depression.

Introduction

Over the past two decades, research in antidepressant therapy has been directed toward improving the response to antidepressants, treatment of refractory depressed patients, and prevention of relapse of depressive episodes. In addition to advances in pharmacological treatment, studies have lead to a new realization that both normal and abnormal behavior arise from chemical processes that occur within parallel neural networks in specific brain regions. Tremendous attention has been directed toward the depression-generating role of neurotransmitter and central nervous system (CNS) neuropeptide dysfunction and of disturbances in brain neural networks. More recently, there has been an explosion of new nonpharmacological techniques that allow for direct stimulation of these brain circuits. These novel approaches include transcranial magnetic stimulation (TMS) (Padberg *et al.*,

Correspondence should be addressed to: Tung-Ping Su, MB, MD, No. 201, Sec 2, Shih-Pai Rd, Taipei, Taiwan 112; Ph: +886 2 - 28757027, Ext 302; Fax: +886 2 28733113; Email:tpsu@vghtpe.gov.tw.

2002; Wassermann & Lisanby, 2001; Lisanby *et al.*, 2000; George *et al.*, 1999), vagus nerve stimulation (Sackeim, 2004; Sackeim *et al.*, 2001), deep brain stimulation (Greenberg, 2004), and magnetic seizure therapy (Lisanby, 2004; Lisanby *et al.*, 2001).

TMS was originally introduced in 1985 by Barker *et al.* as a noninvasive tool of brain stimulation. TMS uses magnetic fields to induce electric currents in the cerebral cortex, thereby depolarizing neurons (Barkere *et al.*, 1985) without being attenuated by the resistances of scalp, skull, and cerebrospinal fluid (CSF). Round and figure eight-shaped coil designs have been widely applied in TMS studies. The induced magnetic field declines exponentially with the increasing distance from the coil. Thus, direct depolarization of neurons is mostly restricted to cortical areas of the brain. An action on deep brain structures, however, may occur transsynaptically within cortico-subcortical circuits (George *et al.*, 1999). Results in animal models suggest that this electric field might cause several changes in the target cortex, including changes in metabolism, neurotransmitters release, and induction of gene expression (Padberg & Möller 2003; Hausmann *et al.*, 2000). Single-pulse TMS was first used as a possible therapeutic tool for depression in 1993 (Hasey, 2001). Pascual-Leone *et al.* described increased excitability of neurons with high frequency repetitive TMS (rTMS) (Pascual-Leone *et al.*, 1994; Pascual-Lenoe *et al.*, 1993). Three studies have found that left prefrontal rTMS resulted in slight increases in subjective sadness whereas right prefrontal rTMS caused increased happiness (Martin *et al.*, 1997; George *et al.*, 1996; Pascual-Leone *et al.*, 1996), raising the possibility that rTMS could affect circuits that modulate mood. The application of rTMS to depression has become the most studied of its applications. Additionally, rTMS has been developed into a novel vehicle of antidepressant treatment for medication-refractory patients (Pascual-Leone *et al.*, 1996; George *et al.*, 1995).

Numerous open trials investigating rTMS as a putative antidepressant treatment were conducted in 1990s. A recent meta-analysis revealed that rTMS reduces depression score on average a modest 37% (range: 26–60%) from baseline (Jennifer, 2005; Burt *et al.*, 2002). These open studies should be interpreted with caution as subjects with depression are highly susceptible to placebo effects (range: 30–50% in drug trial) (Schatzberg & Kraemer, 2000; Brown, 1994). Device-based treatments, like rTMS, may result in even higher placebo response rates because of the elaborate rituals and sophisticated technology involved (Kaptchuk *et al.*, 2000).

In a systematic review (Jennifer, 2005), 19 of 87 randomized controlled trials (RCTs) investigating the efficacy of rTMS involved treatment of a major depressive episode. Among them, six met more specific inclusion criteria including the use of rapid-rate stimulation, application to the left dorsolateral prefrontal cortex (DLPFC), evaluation with 21-item Hamilton Rating Scale for Depression (HAMD-21), and use of an intent-to-treat analysis. A random-effects model was chosen for the meta-analysis. Three studies indicated that mood symptoms were significantly more improved in an rTMS treatment group than a sham treatment group (George *et al.*, 2000, 1997; Avery *et al.*, 1999), while the other three studies did not (Eschweiler *et al.*, 2000; Kimbrell *et al.*, 1999; Padberg *et al.*, 1999). Further, the test for overall effect (i.e. overall weighted mean difference) after combining these six studies was also not statistically significant (Jennifer, 2005). This meta-analysis suggested that rapid-rate rTMS was no different from sham treatment in major depression. However, the power within these studies to detect a difference was generally low. RCTs with sufficient power to detect a clinically meaningful difference are required.

Despite the fact that technical parameters used in a variety of TMS studies differ widely and have lead to disparate results (Gershon *et al.*, 2003), patient characteristics, such as younger age, previous response to rTMS, and less depression at baseline (Gershon *et al.*, 2003; Grunhaus *et al.*, 2002) may still be used to predict rTMS treatment success. Negative predictors were psychotic depression, nonresponse to electroconvulsive therapy (ECT), prefrontal atrophy in older patients, and inadequate dose of TMS (Janicak *et al.*, 2002; McConnell *et al.*, 2001; Kpzel *et al.*, 2000; Figiel *et al.*, 1998). Knowledge of these influencing factors might help us not only to explain the disparity of results among different trials investigating rTMS, but also to elucidate the possible mechanism of rTMS and to understand more about the nature of depression (Su *et al.*, 2005).

Clinical Trial of rTMS

To further explore the effectiveness of rTMS in major depression using the specific inclusion criteria mentioned above such as similar parameters of rapid-rate rTMS, stimulation location and rating scales, we first performed a RCT of this novel treatment in the Chinese population.

Aims

The aims of this trial were (1) to investigate whether 2 weeks of rTMS applied to the left DLPFC can alleviate medication-resistant depression, and (2) to examine some demographic variables and clinical characteristics that might predict the antidepressant effects of rTMS.

Methods

SUBJECTS

A 2-week, randomized, double-blind, sham-controlled trial of rTMS was conducted on patients with the DSM-IV (American Psychiatric Association, 1994) diagnosis of major depressive episode or of bipolar disorder, depressive episode, based on the MINI (Mini International Neuropsychiatric Interview) (Sheehan *et al.*,

1998). In addition, all subjects selected were medication-resistant and had failed to respond to at least two adequate trials of antidepressant medications prior to rTMS treatment. An adequate medication trial was defined as a minimum of 6-week treatment with a dosage adequate for treatment of depression in the majority of patients. Severity of depression was determined to be above the moderate level (i.e. HAM-D-21 (Hamilton, 1960) scores greater than 18) at entry. Exclusion criteria were (1) history of epilepsy, (2) history of major head trauma, (3) any significant physical and neurological abnormalities, (4) having an implanted pacemaker, (5) history of any signs of substantial risk of suicide during the trial, (6) psychotic symptoms, and (7) previous history of rTMS or ECT.

All patients continued their current antidepressant medications during the 2-week course of rTMS administration and no medication changes were allowed for at least 4 weeks preceding rTMS and throughout the period of rTMS treatment. The concomitant administered medications were as follows: (1) serotonin-noradrenaline reuptake inhibitor (venlafaxine [$n = 9$], mirtazapine [$n = 3$]); (2) purely serotonin reuptake inhibitors (paroxetine [$n = 5$], fluoxetine [$n = 2$], citalopram [$n = 1$], sertraline [$n = 1$], fluvoxamine [$n = 1$]; and (3) combination treatments either with antipsychotics ($n = 4$: two with olanzapine and venlafaxine, one with risperidone and sertraline, and one with quetiapine, valporic acid, and fluoxetine); or with the mood stabilizer, valporic acid ($n = 3$: two with venlafaxine and one with citalopram); or with the stimulant, ritalin ($n = 1$: with venlafaxine). All subjects signed a consent form, approved by the Institutional Review Board of Veterans General Hospital-Taipei, and by the National Health Department of Taiwan, after receiving a full explanation of the procedure.

Thirty-three patients enrolled in this study and were randomly assigned to either sham treatment ($N = 11$) or active treatment ($N = 22$) with one of two different active treatment frequencies, faster $= 20\,\text{Hz}$ ($N = 10$) or slower $= 5\,\text{Hz}$ ($N = 12$) at 100% motor threshold (MT). Thirty patients completed the study and three dropped out. In the active lower frequency rTMS group, two patients had to stop the trial during the first three treatment sessions because of pain induced by rTMS. One patient in the sham group withdrew from the study due to worsening of clinical depression. At the end of the 2-week treatment, the blind label was broken. The patients who were initially randomized to the sham treatment group were offered the option of a course of active 20 Hz rTMS treatment. Seven out of ten patients completed this open-label active trial, but the results were not used in the analysis of primary outcome data.

Menopause is the permanent cessation of menstruation resulting from loss of ovarian follicular activity (World Health Organization Scientific Group, 1981). By convention, we defined perimenopausal status as having irregular menstrual cycles (fewer than six menstrual cycles per year), and postmenopausal status as being amenorrhea for 12 months or more (Sowers & La Pietra, 1995).

rTMS PARAMETERS

A Magstim super rapid magnetic stimulator (Wales, UK) with four booster modules equipped with a 70-mm air-cooled figure-eight-shaped coil was used for stimulation. Subjects were seated upright in a comfortable chair, and foam earplugs were used during TMS to diminish the noise from the discharging coil.

On the initial treatment visit, we determined the MT at rest for the contralateral (right) *abductor pollicus brevis* muscle, as described previously (Pridmore *et al.*, 1998). All stimulations were applied to the DLPFC, which was defined as the region 5 cm rostral and in a parasagittal plane from the site of maximal *abductor pollicus brevis* stimulation (George *et al.*, 2000; Pascual-Leone *et al.*, 1996). Muscle contractions were observed visually and no stereotaxic apparatus was used to determine stimulation location. MT was determined daily and the dose was adjusted accordingly before the rTMS therapy and all stimulations were done by the same psychiatrist (CCH).

Subjects received 5 Hz stimulation in 40, 8-second trains over 20 minutes for 10 weekdays (total 16 000 pulses) at 100% of MT for the active lower frequency treatment and 20 Hz stimulation in 40, 2-second trains over 20 minutes for 10 weekdays (total 16 000 pulses) at 100% of MT for the active higher frequency treatment. For sham stimulation, the coil was turned to 90°, with coil edge on the left DLPFC.

SYMPTOM SEVERITY ASSESSMENTS

Severity of depression at baseline and at the end of each week was assessed by a psychiatrist (TPS), blinded to treatment arm, using the 21-item HAM-D-21, Hamilton Anxiety Rating Scale (HAM-A) (Hamilton, 1967), and the Clinical Global Impressions (CGI) (Guy, 1976) scale. The Beck Depression Inventory (BDI) (Beck *et al.*, 1961) was used to assess the patient's subjective feelings. Clinical response to rTMS was evaluated by calculating percent improvement in HAM-D-21 scores from the baseline to the end of treatment. Responder was defined as more than 50% reduction of HAM-D-21 scores and remitter was defined as HAM-D-21 scores less than 8 at the end of trial.

STATISTICAL ANALYSES

Demographic variables and clinical features at entry were compared for the three groups (5 Hz, 20 Hz, and sham) using one-way analysis of variance (ANOVA) or the χ^2 test. ANOVA with repeated measures (ANOVA-R) was performed using treatment group (sham, 5 Hz, and 20 Hz) as the between-subjects factor and time point (baseline, week 1, week 2) as the within-subjects factor to compare the rTMS efficacy in the three different groups. If the *F* value was significant for any of the aforementioned mood rating scales, two-way ANOVA-R was then used to assess differences between each pair of groups, that is, sham versus 5 Hz, sham versus 20 Hz and 5 Hz versus 20 Hz. Final outcome ratings were calculated by subtracting mood ratings at the end of the trial from the baseline values. One-way ANOVA with Bonferroni correction was then performed to elicit differences of the final delta ratings between treatment groups.

In seeking predictors of clinical responsiveness to rTMS, characteristics of the active rTMS treatment groups (5 and 20 Hz), such as demographic variables and clinical features at entry, were compared between responders and nonresponders using the nonparametric Wilcoxon test or the χ^2 with Fisher exact test. All statistical tests were two-sided and at the 5% significance level.

Results

DEMOGRAPHIC, DIAGNOSIS AND CLINICAL FEATURES

Thirty patients who had completed 2-week trials were included in the final analysis. There were no significant differences of age, gender ratio or education levels among these three treatment groups (Table 1). The mean age was 43.1 (SD 10.8)

Table 1. **Demographic Data, Clinical Features, and Mood Symptom Ratings at Entry of Trial[a]**

VARIABLE	ALL SUBJECTS ($n = 30$)	20 Hz rTMS ($n = 10$)	5 Hz rTMS ($n = 10$)	SHAM ($n = 10$)	P
Age, years	43.1 (10.8)	43.6 (12.0)	43.2 (10.6)	42.6 (11.0)	NS
Gender, n					NS
Male	8	3	2	3	
Female	22	7	8	7	
Menopausal status, n					NS
Premenopausal	13	5	4	4	
Perimenopausal	2	0	1	1	
Postmenopausal	7	2	3	2	
Education, grade	12.2 (4.3)	13.4 (5.2)	11.1 (5.0)	12.2 (2.4)	NS
Duration of current episode of depression, mo	11.0 (10.3)	10.2 (13.1)	7.0 (3.7)	15.8 (10.7)	NS
No. of total depression episodes	5.2 (5.1)	5.2 (3.7)	4.5 (1.1)	5.9 (8.2)	NS
Diagnosis, n					NS
Major depressive episode	25	9	8	8	
Bipolar I disorder, depressed episode	2	0	1	1	
Bipolar II disorder, depressed episode	3	1	1	1	
MT[b]	67.2 (9.2)	68.2 (8.0)	68.6 (13.1)	64.8 (5.0)	NS
HAM-D score	24.1 (6.0)	23.2 (7.5)	26.5 (5.2)	22.7 (4.7)	NS
CGI-S score	4.6 (0.7)	4.5 (0.7)	4.7 (0.8)	4.7 (0.5)	NS
BDI score	31.8 (9.0)	28.0 (9.1)	33.9 (7.6)	33.4 (9.6)	NS
HAM-A score	18.6 (5.2)	16.5 (7.1)	20.6 (3.5)	18.8 (3.9)	NS

[a] Data are given as mean (SD) unless otherwise indicated.
[b] MT indicates minimal amount of machine power that induces movement of *abductor pollicus brevis* muscle.
BDI: Beck Depression Inventory, CGI-S: Clinical Global Impressions – Severity of Illness, HAM-A: Hamilton Rating Scale for Anxiety, HAM-D: Hamilton Rating Scale for Depression, NS: not significant, rTMS: repetitive transcranial magnetic stimulation.
Source: (Su & Huang, 2005 with permission of *Journal of Clinical Psychiatry*)

years and there were 3 times as many female patients as males. The data in Table 1 also demonstrated no significant group differences in the clinical features of major depression, in terms of duration of illness, number of depressive episodes, and mood symptom ratings at entry. The MTs used for locating the rTMS site were also comparable. Among the 15 female subjects, 5 were postmenopausal, 1 was perimenopausal, and the other 9 were premenopausal.

EFFICACY

Figure 1 illustrates the severity of objective (HAM-D-21) and subjective depressive symptom rating (BDI) at baseline and post-rTMS trial over time in the three treatment groups.

Hamilton Rating Scale for Depression.   ANOVA-R revealed a significant interaction of treatment group (sham, 5Hz and 20Hz) with time (baseline, week 1, week 2) on changes of HAM-D-21 ratings ($F_{4,54} = 4.8, p < 0.01$) (Figure 1). ANOVA-R also disclosed a significant time by group effect on changes of HAM-D-21 ratings when comparing sham versus 5Hz ($F_{2,36} = 6.6, p < 0.005$) or sham versus 20Hz

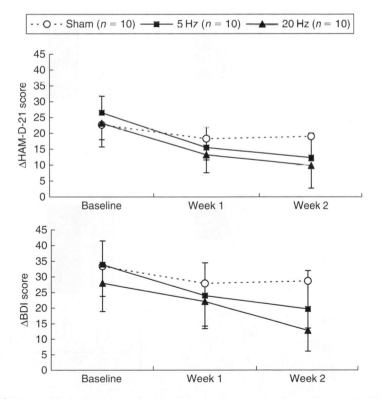

Fig. 1.
Mean score of HAM-D-21 and BDI in patients with treatment-resistant major depression receiving rTMS overtime. Each bar represents standard deviation (SD).

($F_{2,36}$ = 6.5, p < 0.005) but not of 5Hz versus 20Hz ($F_{2,36}$ = 0.1, p = NS). These data suggest that the active rTMS treatments for reducing depression are significantly better than sham treatment but are not different from each other.

The mean baseline HAM-D-21 scores ranged from 22.7 (SD 4.7) to 26.5 (SD 5.2) but were not different (one-way ANOVA, p = NS) between groups (sham, 5, and 20 Hz). However, in Figure 2, changes of HAM-D-21 scores from baseline to week 1 were significant (one-way ANOVA, $F_{2,27}$ = 4.4, p < 0.05) as were those from baseline to week 2 (one-way ANOVA, $F_{2,27}$ = 7.0, p < 0.005). Post hoc tests showed that a significant reduction of HAM-D-21 scores in the 5 Hz group (p < 0.05) and a trend toward reduction in the 20 Hz group (p < 0.1), compared with sham treatment, was found at week 1. At the week-2 endpoint, the reductions in HAM-D-21 score by 5 Hz and 20 Hz treatments were both significantly greater than for the sham treatment ($p \leq 0.01$) (Figure 2). The improvement rates for

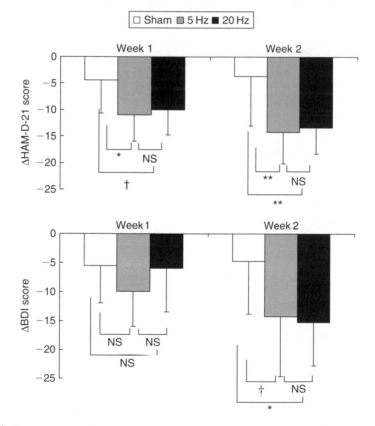

Fig. 2.

Changes in mean score of HAM-D-21 and BDI was from the baseline to end of trial. Each bar represents standard deviation (SD). **p < 0.01, *p < 0.05, [†]p < 0.1, NS = nonsignificant.

sham, 5 Hz, and 20 Hz were found to be 19.1%, 41.5%, and 43.1% after the 1-week treatment and 16.3%, 53.5%, and 57.8% at the end of trial, respectively.

Beck Depression Inventory.   Figure 1 showed a similar significant interaction of treatment group (sham, 5 Hz, and 20 Hz) with time (baseline, week 1, week 2) on changes in the BDI scores ($F_{4,54} = 3.5, p = 0.01$). When the sham versus active treatments were compared, the 5 Hz and 20 Hz trials exerted significant time by group effects on changes of BDI ratings ($F_{2,36} = 3.7$ & $5.8, p < 0.05$ and < 0.01, respectively) suggesting that both slower and faster rTMS may reduce subjective symptoms of depression.

There were no significant differences in baseline BDI ratings or of changes in BDI scores from baseline to week 1 among these 3 groups ($F_{2,27} = 1.4$ and 1.3, $p = $ NS, respectively). However, significantly different reductions of BDI scores from baseline to week 2 were demonstrated among the 3 treatment groups (one-way ANOVA : $F_{2,27} = 4.1, p < 0.05$). Post hoc tests showed a trend to decrease in the 5 Hz group and a significant reduction in the 20 Hz group, compared to sham treatment ($p < 0.1$ and $p < 0.05$, respectively) (Figure 2). The improvement rates for subjective feelings of decreased mood symptoms for the sham, 5 Hz, and 20 Hz groups were 16.4%, 29.2%, and 21.1% after the 1-week treatment and 20%, 41.9%, and 36% at the end of trial, respectively.

Clinical Global Impressions.   Analysis by ANOVA-R revealed a significant time effect (baseline, week 1, and week 2) for reduction of CGI scores ($F_{2,54} = 39.7$, $p < 0.001$), but no group effect (sham, 5 Hz, and 20 Hz) ($F_{2,27} = 2.1, p = $ NS) or group by time interaction ($F_{4,54} = 1.2, p = $ NS) were observed. This finding indicates a significant global improvement of CGI rating (23% to 42.6%) at the end of treatment for the three groups, but the differences among groups did not reach significance.

The Hamilton Anxiety Rating Scale.   Results similar to those for the CGI were found for anxiety ratings. There was a significant time effect (baseline, week 1, and week 2) for reducing HAM-A scores ($F_{2,54} = 27.1, p < 0.001$), but no group (sham, 5 Hz, and 20 Hz) effect ($F_{2,27} = 0.42, p = $ NS) and no group by time interaction ($F_{4,54} = 1.2, p = $ NS). The improvement in anxiety symptoms by rTMS varied from 32% to 48%, but the differences between the three treatments were not significant.

Two-Week Extended Active rTMS for the Sham Treatment Patients.   Among 10 patients with the sham treatment, 3 discontinued further active rTMS (one became remitted; one developed mania (Huang *et al.*, 2004); another patient refused). The remaining 7 patients received another 2-week course of 20 Hz active rTMS, and 3 of them (43%) became responders at the end of the trial, further supporting the outcome of the original active rTMS trial groups.

Factors to Predict rTMS Responders and Nonresponders.   With active rTMS treatment, responder rate was 60% and remission rate was 50% for each 5 Hz and

20 Hz treatment group while it was only 10% (1 out of 10 patients) for the sham treatment group. Fisher exact test revealed that the responder rates for active rTMS patients were significantly higher than for the sham treatment group ($\chi^2 = 6.8$, df = $1, p = 0.01$).

In the search for predictors of clinical outcome, Table 2 illustrates significant differences in age, age at disease onset, menopausal status, and scores of depression and anxiety ratings at entry between responders and nonresponders. Most of the responders were younger than 50 years, with onset of disease before 35 years, and of premenopausal status, suggesting a relationship between the age and hormonal status of females and their clinical treatment response. All 5 menopausal patients and only 1 out of 9 premenopausal patients did not respond to rTMS, suggesting that menopausal status may play an important role in the prediction of clinical response. In addition, less severe baseline ratings on the HAM-D-21, the BDI, and the HAM-A were associated with better clinical outcome. Factors that showed no ability to predict clinical response were gender, types of depression (unipolar versus bipolar disorder), number of previous depressive episodes, and duration of current episode.

Table 2. **Characteristics of Responders and Nonresponders Among Patients Receiving Double-Blind Active rTMS[a]**

VARIABLE	RESPONDERS ($n = 12$)	NONRESPONDERS ($n = 8$)	z/χ^2	p
Gender, N			1	NS
Female	9	6		
Male	3	2		
Age, y	38.8 (9.3)	50.3 (10.1)	−2.6	<.05
Age at disease onset, y	29.8 (9.3)	43.6 (9.7)	−2.5	<.05
Menopausal status, N			9.4	<.05
Premenopausal	8	1		
Perimenopausal	1	0		
Postmenopausal	0	5		
Duration of current episode, mo	6.2 (3.8)	12.3 (14.1)	−0.51	NS
No. of previous episodes	4.9 (2.6)	4.8 (3.0)	−0.08	NS
MT [b] (%)	67.7 (8.6)	69.4 (13.6)	−0.04	NS
HAM-D score at entry	22.2 (4.0)	28.9 (7.6)	−2.2	<0.05
CGI-S score at entry	4.4 (0.51)	4.9 (0.99)	−0.99	NS
BDI score at entry	27.6 (9.5)	36.0 (3.9)	−2.1	<0.05
HAM-A score at entry	16.2 (4.3)	22.1 (6.2)	−2.3	<0.05
Type of depression, N			0.8	NS
Major depressive episode	10	7		
Bipolar disorder, depressed episode	2	1		

[a] Data are given as mean (SD) unless otherwise indicated.
[b] MT indicates minimal amount of machine power that induces movement of abductor pollicus brevis muscle.
BDI: Beck Depression Inventory, CGI-S: Clinical Global Impressions–Severity of Illness, HAM-A: Hamilton Rating Scale for Anxiety, HAM-D: Hamilton Rating Scale for Depression, NS: not significant, rTMS: repetitive transcranial magnetic stimulation.
Source: (Su and Huang, 2005 with permission of *Journal of Clinical Psychiatry*)

SAFETY AND TOLERABILITY

Generally, there was no safety problem, and patients withstood the procedure well. The rate of completing the study was high. As noted earlier, three subjects dropped out of the study because of pain and worsening of clinical symptoms. In addition, among the 30 subjects who completed the study, 4 in the active rTMS group (2 for faster, 2 for slower), and 1 in the sham group reported headaches. Most of them were relieved by rest and one patient needed acetylsalicylic acid to diminish his headaches. In the open-label active treatment group, one patient suffered from a panic episode, which had happened before and during her long course of major depression. One of the bipolar I depression patients developed hypomania after three sessions of rTMS treatment (Huang *et al.*, 2004).

Unique Aspects of this Clinical Trial

The positive result of our clinical study, if considered with the positive results of the three previously mentioned RCTs with positive outcome (Jennifer, 2005), greatly strengthens the conclusion that rTMS is an effective treatment for refractory depression. Our study identified depression without psychosis, younger age, onset of depression at an earlier age, a shorter duration of depression episode, less severity of depression, and premenopausal status as factors that increase the likelihood of better response to rTMS therapy. Menopausal status to predict response to rTMS has rarely been mentioned in previous studies. In our study, none of the 5 menopausal females (0%) were responders, whereas 8 out of 9 premenopausal women (77%) were, suggesting that menopausal status may play an important role in the antidepressant effect of TMS. However, since menopausal status was highly associated with age, and age was found to be a predictor of TMS effectiveness, any conclusion relating menopause to the efficacy of rTMS cannot be drawn. To see if age impacts the efficacy of TMS more than menopause does, a study of male subjects will need to be conducted. The number of male patients in our present study was too small to be tested. The effect of menopausal status may therefore need to be investigated in the future. Since one of the bipolar I depression patients developed hypomania after three sessions of active rTMS (Martin *et al.*, 1997), caution should be observed when enrolling bipolar patients. Finally, our study revealed no ethnic difference in response to rTMS using the same technical parameters and also that rTMS posed no safety problem.

Limitations and Further Questions

Like previous studies, our study had limitations. First, the small sample size might have prevented the detection of real differences between treatment arms, and therefore the finding of no differences between the two active treatments may be a type II error. Second, although the sham rTMS treatment was inferior to the active ones, the sham treatment still showed a minimal clinical effect as it involved considerable clinical contact and attention to potentially therapeutic activities or might also be a meaningfully active stimulation effect (Gershon et al., 2003). Third, all of our patients received only a 2-week trial of rTMS. The clinical response of reduction in both the subjective (BDI) and the objective (HAM-D-21) mood ratings seemed not to appear in the first week, unlike the acute effect within 5 days demonstrated by Figiel et al. (1998) and Pascual-Leone et al. (1996). In our study, the significant clinical response was seen by the second week, reflecting that the lag time for significant effect to occur is shorter than for most antidepressant medications. Does this mean that the optimal duration for rTMS treatment is 2 weeks or do the treatment sessions need to be extended to increase the potential for clinical effect? Fourth, our study also could not assess how long the clinical effects of TMS might last in responders. Long-term outcome and safety follow-up studies on this cohort are needed. Fifth, assessing ovarian function concomitantly with taking the patient's history might be a more reliable way to measure menopausal status.

Conclusions of the Current Clinical Trial

To our knowledge, this is the first study using rTMS to treat depression in Chinese patients. The results of our study support those of some previous reports that show high-frequency rTMS over the left dorsal prefrontal cortex may exert a significant antidepressant effect in medication-refractory patients and identify a number of potential predictors (e.g. younger age, earlier onset of depression, a shorter duration of depression episode, less severity of depression, and premenopausal status) of better outcome with rTMS treatment. Nevertheless, not all the rTMS trials were positive. Many were negative (Holtzheimer et al., 2004; Loo C.K. et al., 2003; Boutros et al., 2002; Manes et al., 2001; Berman et al., 2000; Loo C. et al., 1998) and even in those with the positive results, the antidepressant effect of rTMS was not robust, suggesting the efficacy of rTMS should be judged with caution.

Recent Advances in rTMS Research

Two recent RCT studies reported better response to active rTMS treatment than sham treatment. One study (Koerselman et al., 2004) disclosed no difference between treatments by the end of a 2-week trial, but a significant decrease in depression severity in the active trial group did not occur until 3 months later, strongly indicating that active rTMS may have a late effect on mood regulation. The other add-on RCT trial (Rumi et al., 2005) to compare the effect of rTMS versus sham in depressed patients with underlying amitriptyline treatment revealed that rTMS at 5 Hz accelerated onset of action and augmented the response to amitriptyline. This result conflicts with the report of Garcia-Tro (Garcia-Toro et al., 2001), who found that high frequency rTMS did not increase the effectiveness of underlying sertraline treatment. A recent RCT study repeated the failure of rTMS treatment in the elderly depressed patients (Mosimann *et al.*, 2004). Failure in these cases has been attributed to age-related brain atrophy leading to greater distance between the scalp and prefrontal cortex (Kozel *et al.*, 2000), suggesting the dose of rTMS was inadequate and could be corrected by increasing intensity (McConnell *et al.*, 2001). However, in an open pilot study (Nahas *et al.*, 2004), rTMS successfully decreased depression severity about 37%, and 27% of the elderly depressed group responded after the duration and MT intensity of the rTMS treatment was increased. This pilot study finding supports the need for RCT studies that test rTMS treatment in the elderly by comparing the effectiveness of rTMS delivered at stimulation intensities calculated to overcome atrophy with that of TMS without adjusting for atrophy.

Besides clinical testing of rTMS, functional brain imaging study is an important tool to understand the underlying mechanisms of interaction between rTMS and depression and further elucidate the relationships among brain regions. Recent studies using combined imaging techniques (positron emission tomography [PET], single photon emission computerized tomography [SPECT], and functional MRI) demonstrated that rTMS of prefrontal cortex modulated brain activity at both stimulation site and in several distal regions presumably connected with the stimulation cortex (e.g., anterior cingulate) (Kimbrell *et al.*, 2002; Shajahan *et al.*, 2002; Paus *et al.*, 2001; Teneback *et al.*, 1999). These findings substantiate the hypothesis that prefrontal rTMS modulates the activity in fronto-cingulate circuits, which has been found to be altered in major depression (Drevets, 2000). Findings of functionally reversible hypoactivity of the prefrontal cortex in major depression (Baxter *et al.*, 1989) suggest that patterns of activity in different brain cortex regions may be predictors of clinical response to rTMS. Studies have shown: (1) patients with a reduced metabolism underneath the coil in prefrontal cortex respond better to high frequency (20 Hz) rTMS treatment (Kimbrell *et al.*, 1999), whereas patients with regionally increased metabolism benefit more from low frequency (1 Hz) rTMS; (2) reduction in inferior lobe blood flow perfusion is less in responders than nonresponders and the inferior lobe perfusion is normalized after rTMS (Eschweiler *et al.*, 2000); and (3) baseline regional cerebral blood flow (rCBF) in several limbic structures is negatively correlated with the clinical outcome while baseline rCBF in some neocortical areas is positively correlated with clinical outcome (Mottaghy *et al.*, 2002). More data are needed to support the notion that some brain activity patterns can serve as an aid to effective rTMS treatment.

Status of Clinical Practice of rTMS

Prefrontal cortex rTMS has already been approved in Canada for indication of treatment in pharmacotherapy-resistant depression. However, owing to some concerns about the small numbers of patients in majority of clinical trials, inconsistency of clinical study designs, short of duration of treatment, sham applications and parameters used, rTMS is still considered experimental, investigational, and unproven by the FDA of the United States (CIGNA HealthCare Coverage Position: TMS, July 15, 2005).

Guidelines of rTMS Treatment and Future Perspectives

Though most depressed patients are currently given pharmacological treatment, nonpharmacological alternatives or adjuncts are under consideration, with rTMS being a possible important novel component of the nonpharmacological treatment of major depression. rTMS has a smaller range of clinical applications than antidepressant pharmacotherapy. Guidelines for rTMS treatment may utilize: (1) selection of cases with positive predictors; (2) exclusion of cases with negative predictors (such as psychotic depression, old age, perimenopausal or menopausal status, and resistance to ECT or previous TMS) or cases with contraindications for TMS (such as seizure disorder or CNS diseases); (3) precision placement of rTMS on the left DLPFC *via* use of MRI-based neuronavigation procedures (Herwig *et al.*, 2001); and (4) selection of cases with certain brain activity patterns revealed by imaging study.

Further systematic study of the effect of rTMS on depression should consider evaluating rTMS in large, controlled multicentre trials, extending treatment sessions, conducting longer-term follow-up, optimizing parameters (e.g. stimulation intensity) to improve rTMS effectiveness, and investigating the influence of age and menopausal status. Through these efforts, the underlying mechanisms of rTMS can be elucidated and broader clinical use of rTMS can be expected in the foreseeable future.

Acknowledgment

This work was supported by a grant from Taipei Veterans General hospital (VGH-91-237).

References

American Psychiatric Association (1994). *Diagnostic and Statistical Manual of Mental Disorder* (4th ed.). Washington, DC: American Psychiatric Association.

Avery, D.H., Claypoole, K., Robinson, L., Neumaier, J.F., Dunner, D.L., Scheele, L., Wilson, L., & Roy-Byrne, P. (1999). Repetitive transcranial magnetic stimulation in the treatment of medication-resistant depression: preliminary data. *Journal of Nervous and Mental Disease*, 187, 114–117.

Barkere, A.T., Jalinous, R., & Freeston, I.L. (1985). Noninvasive magnetic stimulation of human motor cortex. *Lancet*, 2, 1106–1107.

Baxter, L.R., Schwartz, J.M., Phelps, M.E., Schwartz, J.M., Jeffrey, M., Phelps, M.E., Mazziotta, J.C., Guze, B.H., Selin, C.E., Gerner, R.H., & Sumida, R.M. (1989). Reduction of prefrontal cortex glucose metabolism common to three types of depression. *Archives of General Psychiatry*, 46, 243–250.

Beck, A.T., Ward, C.H., Mendelson, M., Mock, J., & Erbaugh, J. (1961). An inventory for measuring depression. *Archives of General Psychiatry*, 4, 561–571.

Berman, R.M., Narasimhan, M., Sanacora, G., Miano, A.P., Hoffman, R.E., Hu, X.S., Charney, D.S., & Boutros, N.N. (2000). A randomized clinical trial of repetitive transcranial magnetic stimulation in the treatment of major depression. *Biological Psychiatry*, 47, 332–337.

Boutros, N.N., Gueorguieva, R., Hoffman, R.E., Oren, D.A., Feingold, A., & Berman, R.M. (2002). Lack of a therapeutic effect of a 2-week sub-threshold transcranial magnetic stimulation course for treatment-resistant depression. *Psychiatry Research*, 113, 245–254.

Brown, W. (1994). Placebo as a treatment for depression. *Neuropsychopharmacology*, 10, 265–269.

Burt, T., Lisanby, S.H., & Sackeim, H.A. (2002). Neuropsychiatric applications of transcranial magnetic stimulation: a meta analysis. *International Journal of Neuropsychpharmacology*, 5, 73–103.

Drevets, W.C. (2000). Functional anatomical abnormalities in limbic and prefrontal cortical structures in major depression. *Progress in Brain Research*, 126, 413–431.

Eschweiler, G.W., Wegerer, C., Spandl, C., Stevens, A., Bartels, M., Bartels, M., & Buchkremer, G. (2000). Left prefrontal activation predicts therapeutic effects of repetitive transcranial magnetic stimulation (rTMS) in major depression. *Psychiatry Research*, 99, 161–172.

Eschweiler, G.W., Wegerer, C., Schotter, W., Spandl, C., Stevens, A., Bartels, M., & Buchkremer, G. (2000). Left prefrontal activation predicts therapeutic effects of repetitive transcranial magnetic stimulation (rTMS) in major depression. *Psychiatry Research*, 99, 161–172.

Figiel, G.S., Epstein, C., McDonald, W.M., Amazon-Leece, J., Figiel, L., Saldivia, A., & Glover, S. (1998). The use of rapid-rate transcranial magnetic stimulation (rTMS) in refractory depressed patients. *The Journal of Neuropsychiatry and Clinical Neurosciences*, 10, 20–25.

Garcia-Toro, M., Pascual-Leone, A., Romera, M., Gonzalez, A., Mico, J., Ibarra, O., Arnillas, H., Capllonch, I., Mayol, A., & Tormos, J.M. (2001). Prefrontal repetitive transcranial magnetic stimulation as add-on treatment in depression. *Journal of Neurology, Neurosurgery, and Psychiatry*, 71, 546–548.

George, M.S., Lisanby, S.H., & Sackeim, H.A. (1999). Transcranial magnetic stimulation. *Archives of General Psychiatry*, 56, 300–311.

George, M.S., Nahas, Z., Molloy, M., Speer, A.M., Oliver, N.C., Li, B.X., Arana, G.W., Risch, S.C., & Ballenger, J.C. (2000). A controlled trial of daily left prefrontal cortex TMS for treating depression. *Biological Psychiatry*, 48, 962–970.

George, M.S., Wassermann, E.M., Kimbrell, T.A., Little, J.T., Williams, W., Danielson, A.L., Greenberg, B.D., Hallett, M., & Post, R.M. (1997). Mood improvement following daily left prefrontal repetitive transcranial magnetic stimulation in patients with depression: a placebo-controlled crossover trial. *American Journal of Psychiatry*, 154, 1752–1756.

George, M.S., Wassermann, E.M., Williams, W.A., Callahan, A., Ketter, T.A., Basser, P., Hallett, M., & Post, R.M. (1995). Daily repetitive transcranial magnetic stimulation (rTMS) improves mood in depression. *NeuroReport*, 6, 1853–1856.

George, M.S., Wassermann, E.M., Williams, W.A., Steppel, J., Pascual-Leone, A., Basser, P., Hallett, M., & Post, R.M. (1996). Changes in mood and hormone levels after rapid-rate transcranial magnetic stimulation (rTMS) of the prefrontal cortex. *The Journal of Neuropsychiatry and clinical Neurosciences*, 8, 172–180.

Gershon, A.A., Dannon, P.N., & Grunhaus, L. (2003). Transcranial magnetic stimulation in the treatment of depression. *The American Journal of Psychiatry*, 160, 835–845.

Greenberg, B.D. (2004). Deep Brain stimulation in psychiatry. In: Lisanby, S.H. (ed.), *Brain Stimulation in Psychiatric Treatment*. Arlington, VA: American Psychiatric Publishing, Inc., pp. 53–65.

Grunhaus, L., Dolberg, O.T., Polak, D., & Dannon, P.N. (2002). Monitoring the response to rTMS in depression with visual analog scales. *Human Psychopharmacology*, 17, 349–352.

Guy, W. (1976). Early drug evaluation (ECDEC). In: Guy, W. (ed.), *Assessment Manual for Psychopharmacology*. Rockville: NIMH, pp. 217–222.

Hamilton, M. (1960). A rating scale for depression. *Journal of Neurology, Neurosurgery, and Psychiatry*, 12, 56–62.

Hamilton, M. (1967). Development of a rating scale for primary depressive illness. *The British Journal of Social and Clinical Psychology*, 6, 278–296.

Hasey, G. (2001). Transcranial magnetic stimulation in the treatment of mood disorder: a review and comparison with electroconvulsive therapy. *Canadian Journal of Psychiatry-Revue Canaduenne de Psychiatrie*, 46, 720–727.

Hausmann, A., Weis, C., Marksteiner, J., Hinterhuber, H., & Humpel, C. (2000). Chronic repetitive transcranial magnetic stimulation enhances c-fos in the parietal cortex and hippocampus. *Brain Research. Molecular Brain Research*, 76, 355–362.

Herwig, U., Padberg, F., Unger, J. Spitzer, M., & Schonfeldt-Lecuona, C. (2001). Transcranial magnetic stimulation in therapy studies: examination of the reliability of "standard" coil positioning by neuronavigation. *Biological Psychiatry*, 50, 58–61.

Holtzheimer, P.E., Avery, D., & Schlaepfer, T.E. (2004). Antidepressant effects of repetitive transcranial magnetic stimulation. *The British Journal of Psychiatry*, 184, 541–542.

Huang, C.C., Su, T.P., & Shan, I.K. (2004). A case report of repetitive transcranial magnetic stimulation-induced mania. *Bipolar Disorders*, 6, 444–445.

Janicak, P.G., Dowd, S.M., Martis, B., Alam, D., Beedle, D., Krasuski, J., Strong, M.J., Sharma, R., Rosen, C., & Viana, M. (2002). Repetitive transcranial magnetic stimulation versus electroconvulsive therapy for major depression: preliminary results of a randomized trial. *Biological Psychiatry*, 51, 659–667.

Jennifer, L. (2005). Efficacy of rapid-rate repetitive transcranial magnetic stimulation in the treatment of depression: a systematic review and meta-analysis. *Journal of Psychiatry and Neuroscience*, 30, 83–90.

Kaptchuk, T.J., Goldman, P., Stason, D.A., & Stason, W.B. (2000). Do medical devices have enhanced placebo effects? *Journal of Chemical Epidemiology*, 53, 786–792.

Kimbrell, T.A., Little, J.T., Dunn, R.T., Frye, M.A., Greenberg, B.D., & Wassermann, E.M. (1999). Frequency dependence of antidepressant response to left prefrontal repetitive transcranial magnetic stimulation (rTMS) as a function of baseline cerebral glucose metabolism. *Biological Psychiatry*, 46, 1603–1613.

Kimbrell, T.A., Little, J.T., Dunne, R.T., & Frye, M.A. (1999). Frequency dependence of antidepressant response to left prefrontal repetitive transcranial magnetic stimulation (rTMS) as a function of baseline cerebral glucose metabolism. *Biological Psychiatry*, 46, 1603–1613.

Kimbrell, T.A., Dunn, R.T., George, M.S., Danielson, A.L., Willis, M.W., Repella, J.D., Benson, B.E., Herscovitch, P., Post, R.M., & Wassermann, E.M. (2002). Left prefrontal-repetitive transcranial magnetic stimulation (rTMS) and regional cerebral glucose metabolism in normal volunteers. *Psychiatry Research*, 115, 101–113.

Koerselman, F., Laman, D.M., van Duijn, H., van Duijn, M.A., & Willems, M.A. (2004). A 3-month, follow-up, randomized, placebo-controlled study of repetitive transcranial magnetic stimulation in depression. *The Journal of Clinical Psychiatry*, 65, 1323–1328.

Kozel, F.A., Nahas, Z., deBrux, C., Molloy, M., Lorberbaum, J.P., Bohning, D., Risch, S.C., & George, M.S. (2000). How coil-cortex distance relates to age, motor threshold, and antidepressant response to repetitive transcranial magnetic stimulation. *The Journal of Neuropsychiatry and Clinical Neurosciences*, 12, 376–384.

Lisanby, S.H. (2004). Magnetic seizure therapy: development of a novel convulsive technique. In: Lisanby, S.H. (ed.), *Brain Stimulation in Psychiatric Treatment*. Arlington, VA: American Psychiatric Publishing, Inc., pp. 67–98.

Lisanby, S.H., Luber, B., Perera, T., & Sackeim, H.A. (2000). Transcranial magnetic stimulation: applications in basic neuroscience and neuropsychopharmacology. *International Journal of Neuropsychopharmacology*, 3, 259–273.

Lisanby, S.H., Schlaepfer, T.E., Fisch, H.-U., & Sackeim, H.A. (2001). Magnetic seizure induction for the treatment of major depression. *Archives of General Psychiatry*, 58, 303–305.

Loo, C., Mitchell, P., & Sachdev, P. (1998). rTMS: a sham-controlled trial in medication-resistant depression. *Biological Psychiatry*, 43, 95.

Loo, C.K., Mitchell, P.B., Croker, V.M., Malhi, G.S., Wen, W., Gandevia, S.C., & Sachdev, P.S. (2003). Double-blind controlled investigation of bilateral prefrontal transcranial magnetic stimulation for the treatment of resistant major depression. *Psychological Medicine*, 33, 33–40.

Manes, F., Jorge, R., Morcuende, M., Yamada, T., Paradiso, S., & Robinson, R.G. (2001). A controlled study of repetitive transcranial magnetic stimulation as a treatment of depression in the elderly. *International Psychiatries*, 13, 225–231.

Martin, J.D., George, M.S., & Greenberg, B.D. (1997). Mood effects of prefrontal repetitive high-frequency TMS in healthy volunteers. *International Journal of Psychiatry in Medicine*, 2, 53–68.

McConnell, K.A., Nahas, Z., Shastri, A., Lorberbaum, J.P., Kozel, F.A., Bohning, D.E., & George, M.S. (2001). The transcranial magnetic stimulation motor threshold depends on the distance from coil to underlying cortex: a replication in healthy adults comparing two methods of assessing the distance to cortex. *Biological Psychiatry*, 49, 454–459.

Mosimann, U.P., Schmitt, W., Greenberg, B.D., Kosel, M., Muri, R.M., Berkhoff, M., Hess, C.W., Fisch, H.U., & Schlaepfer, T.E. (2004). Repetitive transcranial magnetic stimulation: a putative add-on treatment for major depression in elderly patients. *Psychiatry Research*, 126, 123–133.

Mottaghy, F., Keller, C., Gangitano, M., Ly, J., Thall, M., Parker, J.A., & Pascual-Leone, A. (2002). Correlation of cerebral blood flow and treatment effects of repetitive transcranial magnetic stimulation in depressed patients. *Psychiatry Research*, 115, 1–14.

Nahas, Z., Li, X., Kozel, F.A., Mirzki, D., Memon, M., Miller, K., Yamanaka, K., Anderson, B., Chae, J.H., Bohning, D.E., Mintzer, J., & George, M.S. (2004). Safety and benefits of distance-adjusted prefrontal transcranial magnetic stimulation in depressed patients 55–57 years of age: a pilot study. *Depression and Anxiety*, 19, 249–256.

Padberg, F., & Möller, H.J. (2003). Repetitive transcranial magnetic stimulation dose it have potential in the treatment of depression? *CNS Drugs*, 17, 383–403.

Padberg, F., Zwanzger, P., Thoma, H., Kathmann, N., Haag, C., Greenberg, B.D., Hampel, H., & Moller, H.J. (1999). Repetitive transcranial magnetic stimulation (rTMS) in pharmacotherapy-refractory major depression: comparative study of fast, slow and sham rTMS. *Psychiatry Research*, 88, 163–171.

Padberge, F., Zwanzger, P., Keck, K.E., Kathmann, N., Mikhaiel, P., Ella, R., Rupprecht, P., Thoma, H., Hampel, H., Toschi, N., & Moller, H.J. (2002). Repetitive transcranial magnetic stimulation (rTMS) in major depression: relation between efficacy and stimulation intensity. *Neuropsychopharmacology*, 27, 638–645.

Pascual-Leone, A., Rubio, B., Pallardo, F., & Catala, M.D. (1996). Rapid-rate transcranial magnetic stimulation of left dorsolateral prefrontal cortex in drug-resistant depression. *Lancet*, 348, 233–237.

Pascual-Leone, A., Houser, C.M., Reese, K., Shotland, L.I., Greafman, J., Seto, S., Valls-Sole, J., Brasil-Neto, J.P., Wassermann, E.M., & Cohen, L.G. (1993). Safety of rapid-rate transcranial magnetic stimulation in normal volunteers. *Electroencephalography and Clinical Neurophysiology*, 89, 120–130.

Pascual-Leone, A., Valls-Sole, J., Wassermann, E.M., & Hallett, M. (1994). Responses to rapid-rate transcranial stimulation of the human motor cortex. *Brain*, 4, 847–858.

Paucual-Leone, A., Catala, M.D., & Pascual, A.P. (1996). Lateralized effect of rapid-rate transcranial magnetic stimulation of the prefrontal cortex. *The Journal of Neuropsychiatry and Clinical Neurosciences*, 8, 499–502.

Paus, T., Castro-Alamancos, M.A., & Petrides, M. (2001). Cortico-cortical connectivity of the human mid-dorsolateral frontal cortex and its modulation by repetitive transcranial magnetic stimulation. *European Journal of Neuroscience*, 14, 1405–1411.

Pridmore, S., Fernandes, J.A., Nahas, Z., Liberatos, C., & George, M.S. (1998). Motor threshold in transcranial magnetic stimulation: a comparison of a neurophysiological method and a visualization of movement method. *The Journal of ECT*, 14, 25–27.

Rumi, D.O., Gattaz, W.F., Rigonatti, S.P., Rosa, M.A., Fregni, F., Rosa, M.O., Mansur, C., Myczkowski, M.L., Moreno, R.A., & Marcolin, M.A. (2005). Transcranial magnetic stimulation accelerates the antidepressant effect of amitriptyline in severe depression: a double-blind placebo-controlled study. *Biological Psychiatry*, 57, 162–166.

Sackeim, H.A. (2004). Vagus nerve stimulation. In: Lisanby, S.H. (ed.), *Brain Stimulation in Psychiatric Treatment*. Arlington, VA: American Psychiatric Publishing, Inc., pp. 99–142.

Sackeim, H.A., Rush, A.J., George, M.S., Marangell, L.B., Husain, M.M., Nahas, Z., Johnson, C.R., Seidman, S., Giller, C., Haines, S., Simpson Jr., R.K., & Goodman, R.R. (2001). Vagus nerve stimulation (VNS) for treatment-resistant depression: efficacy, side-effects, and predictors of outcome. *Neuropsychopharmacology*, 25, 713–728.

Schatzberg, A., & Kraemer, H.C. (2000). Use of placebo control groups in evaluating efficacy of treatment of unipolar major depression. *Biological Psychiatry*, 47, 736–744.

Shajahan, P.M., Glabus, M.F., Steele, J.D., Doris, A.B., Anderson, K., Jenkins, J.A., Gooding, P.A., & Ebmeier, K.P. (2002). Left dorso-lateral repetitive transcranial magnetic stimulation affects cortical excitability and functional connectivity, but does not impair cognition in major depression. *Progress in Neuropsychopharmacology and Biological Psychiatry*, 26, 945–954.

Sheehan, D.V., Lecrubier, Y., Sheehan, K.H., Amorim, P., Janavs, J., Weiller, E., Hergueta, T., Baker, R., & Dunbar, G.C. (1998). The Mini-International Neuropsychiatric Interview (M.I.N.I.): the development and validation of a structured diagnostic psychiatric interview for DSM-IV and ICD-10. *The Journal of Clinical Psychiatry*, 59, 22–33.

Sowers, M.R., & La Pietra, M.T. (1995). Menopause: its epidemiology and potential association with chronic diseases. *Epidemiologic Reviews*, 17, 287–302.

SU T.-P., Huang C-.C., Wei I-.H. (2005). Add-on rTMS for medication-resistant depression: a randomized, double-blind, sham-controlled trial in Chinese patients. *The Journal of Clinical Psychiatry*, 66, 930–937.

Teneback, C.C., Nahas, Z., Speer, A.M., Molloy, M., Stallings, L.E., Spicer, K.M., Risch, S.C., & George, M.S. (1999). Changes in prefrontal cortex and paralimbic activity in depression following two weeks of daily left prefrontal TMS. *The Journal of Neuropsychiatry and Clinical Neurosciences*, 11, 426–435.

Wassermann, E.M., & Lisanby, S.H. (2001). Therapeutic application of repetitive transcranial magnetic stimulation: a review. *Clinical Neurophysiology*, 112, 1367–1377.

World Health Organization Scientific Group (1981). WHO Technical Services Report Series. In: *Research on the Menopause*, Geneva, Switzerland: World Health Organization, p. 670.

Progress in Neurotherapeutics and Neuropsychopharmacology, 2:1, 173–186 © 2007 Cambridge University Press
DOI: 10.1017/S1748232106000127   Printed in the United Kingdom

The NIMH MATRICS Initiative: Development of a Consensus Cognitive Battery

Robert S. Kern, Michael F. Green and Stephen R. Marder

Department of Psychiatry and Biobehavioral Sciences, Geffen School of Medicine at UCLA, Department of Veterans Affairs VISN 22 Mental Illness Research, Education, and Clinical Center, Los Angeles, California, USA; Email: rkern@ucla.edu; mgreen@ucla.edu; marder@ucla.edu

ABSTRACT

A key obstacle to the development of new drugs to treat the cognitive deficits of schizophrenia was the absence of a standard by which to measure their efficacy. Before granting approval for any new drug for this condition, the US Food and Drug Administration wanted a standard cognitive endpoint based on a broad consensus-based method. To address this obstacle, the Measurement and Treatment Research to Improve Cognition in Schizophrenia (MATRICS) intiative oversaw a process to develop a consensus neurocognitive battery. Its development included a ten-step process that is described in this article.

Key words: cognition, schizophrenia, tests and measurement.

Introduction

Despite an ever-increasing knowledge of the scope, severity, and functional relevance of cognitive impairment in schizophrenia (Green *et al.*, 2000; Heinrichs & Zakzanis, 1998; Saykin *et al.*, 1991) no drug has gained Food and Drug Administration (FDA) approval for this purpose. The National Institute of Mental Health (NIMH). Measurement and Treatment Research to Improve Cognition in Schizophrenia (MATRICS) initiative was charged with obtaining a consensus on a number of key issues relevant to stimulating drug discovery for the treatment of cognitive dysfunction in schizophrenia (Marder & Fenton, 2004). The initiative sponsored a series of consensus-oriented conferences over a 2-year period. The topics included selection of molecular targets, prioritization of compounds, clinical trials design, and government/industry/academia interactions (for further information see the June, 2004 Special Issue in *Psychopharmacology*; Buchanan *et al.* (2005); Marder (2006), and the MATRICS website at www.matrics.ucla.edu).

Correspondence should be addressed to: Robert S. Kern, Ph.D, VA Greater Los Angeles Healthcare Center (MIRECC 210 A), 11301 Wilshire Blvd., Los Angeles, CA 90073, USA; Ph: +310 478 3711, x.49229; Fax: +310 268 4056; Email: rkern@ucla.edu

One specific obstacle for drug development was the absence of a measurement standard to evaluate the efficacy of new compounds developed for this purpose. The FDA stated that it would not grant approval for new drugs to treat the cognitive deficits of schizophrenia in the absence of a consensus end point. Drug companies would be unlikely to devote significant resources to drug development in an area that could not gain FDA approval. Hence, there was a clear need for a consensus-based method to assess cognition (Green & Nuechterlein, 2004; Green *et al.*, 2004). This paper describes the process by which the NIMH MATRICS initiative addressed this obstacle.

Background and Rationale

Cognitive deficits are common to the vast majority of persons with schizophrenia with estimates that 90% of affected persons have a clinically meaningful level of impairment in at least one cognitive domain and 75% have impairment in at least two (Palmer *et al.*, 1997). These figures may be underestimates when one considers pre-morbid levels of functioning. For example, a person with a pre-morbid IQ of 130 (two standard deviations above the mean; 96th percentile) may continue to function within normal limits after the onset of illness, for example IQ of 100, but this level would reflect a considerable drop from their pre-morbid status. This example illustrates that average cognitive performance levels can result from a clinically meaningful decline from previous higher levels.

There is a compelling rationale for developing treatments to target the cognitive deficits of persons with schizophrenia. First, it is widely held that cognitive deficits are a core feature of the illness (Gold, 2004). That is, they reflect a primary deficit, not secondary to other aspects of the illness (clinical symptoms) or other treatment-related factors (medication effects).

Considerable evidence suggests that the cognitive impairments associated with schizophrenia are relatively independent from the clinical symptoms of the disorder. Although one might suspect that positive symptoms of psychosis (e.g. hallucinations, delusions) should produce adverse effects on cognitive performance, there is little evidence to support such a relationship. Most cross-sectional studies and meta-analytic reviews show a minimal relationship between the two (Heydebrand *et al.*, 2004; Nieuwenstein *et al.*, 2001; Bilder *et al.*, 2000; Mohamed *et al.*, 1999). On the other hand, cognitive deficits show a somewhat stronger and more consistent relationship with disorganized and negative symptoms (e.g. avolition, apathy, anhedonia), but the amount of shared variance is relatively small (5–10%). The relative independence of the two is further supported by data from studies that reveal the presence of cognitive impairment in patients in psychotic and remitted states (Nuechterlein *et al.*, 1998) and family studies of "at-risk" children and adolescents that reveal the presence of cognitive deficits well before the onset of illness (Cornblatt *et al.*, 1992).

In general, the first-line drugs to treat the psychotic symptoms of schizophrenia are not associated with negative effects on cognition, and in fact, appear to convey modest benefits. The primary effects of first generation antipsychotic medications on cognition are modest-to-moderate when compared with placebo or no medication (Mishara & Goldberg, 2004). Second generation antipsychotic agents (SGAs) have typically been compared against conventional agents. Interpretation of the findings is not straightforward. Databased articles and meta-analyses show advantages for SGAs compared with conventional agents with effect sizes generally in the small to medium range (Woodward *et al.*, 2005; Bilder *et al.*, 2002; Harvey & Keefe, 2001; Keefe *et al.*, 1999). However, it is not clear that SGAs actually exert a procognitive advantage over conventional agents. It is possible that the observed differences are due to dose levels of the conventional agents used in many studies or a reduction in extrapyramidal symptoms associated with SGAs. In a study by Green *et al.* (2002) no significant overall difference was found between risperidone and low-dose haloperidol treatment on cognition over a 2-year follow-up period that included six assessment points. Although anticholinergic agents used to treat extrapyramidal symptoms can produce adverse effects on memory (Perlick *et al.*, 1986; Tune *et al.*, 1982) the scope of these effects is limited and does not account for the broader cognitive dysfunction seen in many persons with schizophrenia.

The second reason to target cognitive deficits for treatment is that there is considerable evidence to show their link to functional outcome. Three reviews of the literature (Green *et al.*, 2004; Green *et al.*, 2000; Green, 1996) show cross-sectional and prospective links between cognition and functional outcome (e.g. work and social functioning, rehabilitation success) in persons with schizophrenia. For individual cognitive measures, the magnitude of the correlation tends to yield effect sizes that fall within the small to medium range. However, when multiple domains are included in a summary score, the effect sizes can be large, sometimes explaining 20–50% of the variance (Green *et al.*, 2000). Though much of the earlier literature examined cross-sectional relationships, a recent review of prospective studies indicated that cognitive functioning predicted functional status years later (Green *et al.*, 2004).

A third reason for viewing cognition as an intervention target stems from evidence obtained from pre-clinical studies of neurobiology, psychopharmacology, and cognition. These studies identify promising molecular targets for the development of pharmacological treatments for schizophrenia. For example, results from animal and non-human primate studies reveal a direct relationship between prefrontal dopamine function and cognition. Perhaps, the most compelling evidence has been for a link between D_1 receptor activity and working memory functioning

(Goldman-Rakic *et al.*, 2004). Pre-clinical studies have demonstrated that insufficient D_1 receptor signaling in the prefrontal cortex is associated with working memory impairment, and these deficits can be ameliorated by treatments that augment D_1 receptor stimulation (Fernandez-Ruiz *et al.*, 1999; Williams & Goldman-Rakic, 1995; Schneider *et al.*, 1994).

The glutamate system has also received a fair amount of attention. Examination of targets within the glutamate system has yielded mixed results. Two classes of receptors within the glutamatergic system have been studied for their effects on cognition, NMDA and AMPA receptors. Two small controlled trials found that addition of agonists at the glycine site of the NMDA receptor failed to improve cognitive functioning (Goff *et al.*, 2005; Goff *et al.*, 1999). The recent development of compounds that act as positive modulators at the glutamatergic AMPA receptor complex (ampakines) has made it possible to examine the clinical effects of positive modulation of AMPA receptors in animals and humans. Early animal studies with ampakines demonstrated enhancement of learning and problem-solving ability on a number of experimental tasks (Hampson *et al.*, 1998; Staubli *et al.*, 1994). Pre-clinical and clinical studies involving persons with schizophrenia are currently being conducted. In sum, the results of the dopamine and glutamate pre-clinical studies identify potential molecular targets for drug development aimed at addressing impairments in learning and memory.

Despite a clear rationale for developing treatments that target the cognitive deficits of schizophrenia, drug development in this area has been limited due to certain obstacles. MATRICS was created to use a consensus building process to address potential barriers to drug development.

The "Measurement" Obstacle

One of the first identified tasks for MATRICS was to establish a consensus-based method for measuring cognition in clinical trials (Green & Nuechterlein, 2004; Green *et al.*, 2004). Previous clinical trials assessed cognition using a variety of different tests and measures. Some studies used clinical scales that included a gross measure of cognition (e.g. Positive and Negative Symptom Scale, PANSS). Other studies used highly specialized computer-based batteries that were not widely used. Even when clinical trials used more conventional neurocognitive batteries with the same or similar measures, there was a surprising degree of inconsistency in the categorization of tests by cognitive domain. For example, tests like category fluency are sometimes listed as a measure of semantic memory, speed of processing, or language functioning leaving the findings ambiguous as to which area of cognition was affected. Further, there is little agreement about which measures to use in tests that yield more than a single index of performance. For example, some memory tests include over 15 separate performance measures. The FDA expressed concern that, given such a wide array of options for assessment, it could not be determined if the findings of procognitive agents were idiosyncratic to the method of measurement.

The Consensus-Building Process: Ten Steps Towards Development of the MATRICS Consensus Cognitive Battery

MATRICS was guided by the principle that the consensus development process should be transparent, perceived as fair, include input from experts representing diverse points of view, and be grounded in the best available scientific data. For development of the MATRICS Consensus Cognitive Battery (MCCB) the consensus process was overseen by the MATRICS Neurocognition Committee. This 14-member group (K. Nuechterlein and M. Green, Co-Chairpersons) was formulated to provide oversight of the MATRICS process and act as the final decision-making body on issues central to development of the battery. Members included persons from academia, NIMH, and patient advocacy and are listed on the MATRICS website (www.matrics.ucla.edu).

The first step of the ten-step process towards developing a consensus-based cognitive battery required the identification of cognitive domains to be represented in the battery and prioritization of criteria used to evaluate candidate cognitive tests. The first of the six MATRICS consensus meetings was used to address these two needs. The third meeting was used to evaluate candidate tests and involved use of the RAND Panel Method to attain consensus (described later in this paper). The other four meetings addressed other MATRICS goals that were not directly related to the selection of the MCCB. Information about these meetings can be found on the MATRICS website.

1: Identifying Cognitive Domains

Prior to the first consensus meeting, experts in selected content areas were asked to participate in a survey. Participants included experts in the following areas: cognitive deficits in schizophrenia, clinical neuropsychology, cognitive science, cognitive neuroscience, neuropharmacology, clinical trials methodology, outcome assessment, psychometrics/test development, and biostatistics. The purpose of the survey was to gather input on the selection of cognitive targets and the criteria for evaluating candidate tests. For cognitive targets, the experts were asked to rank order a broad set of cognitive domains according to their importance to the treatment of schizophrenia. Results showed that executive functioning, attention/vigilance, short- and long-term memory, and problem-solving ability were ranked highest with speed of processing and social cognition ranked slightly below these domains (Kern *et al.*, 2004). This group was also asked to nominate tests to be considered for the consensus battery. Experts who participated in the survey were invited to attend the in-person meeting. Sixty-eight experts completed the survey (including six members of the MATRICS Neurocognition Committee).

Prior to the meeting, a subgroup of the MATRICS Neurocognition Committee reviewed existing available evidence for the purpose of identifying separable cognitive constructs relevant to schizophrenia. Thirteen factor analytic studies were reviewed. Based on the review, the subgroup concluded that six separable cognitive factors could be identified (Nuechterlein *et al.*, 2004). The six cognitive factors included: working memory, attention/vigilance, verbal learning, visual learning, reasoning and problem-solving, and speed of processing. The selection of these six factors largely overlapped with the findings from the survey of experts, except that the construct of memory was split differently (verbal and visual versus short- and long-term) based on the factor analytic results, and executive functioning and reasoning and problem-solving ability were collapsed into one domain.

At the in-person meeting, a decision was reached based on presentation of the factor analytic data, the survey findings, and group discussion. There was a clear consensus among participants in the meeting that a seventh cognitive domain, social cognition, should be included in the battery because it was seen as an important new domain in schizophrenia research that is related to functional outcome.

2: Selecting Test Criteria for Evaluating Neurocognitive Tests

Two steps were involved in establishing essential test criteria for evaluating candidate tests. First, experts were asked in the pre-conference survey to rate and rank order the importance of a variety of test qualities (Kern *et al.*, 2004). Second, the first MATRICS consensus meeting included presentations and discussion on biostatistics and psychometrics as they related to selecting measures for the battery. Based on the survey results, and presentations and discussion at the in-person meeting, the MATRICS Neurocognition Committee decided upon five test criteria. These included: test-retest reliability, high utility as a repeated measure (i.e. minimal influence from practice effects), relationship to functional outcome, potential response to pharmacologic agents, and tolerability and practicality. Tolerability in this case refers to how well a patient likes taking a test; practicality refers to ease of administration and scoring for the examiner/tester. These criteria for test selection applied to clinical trials in which there would be a need to observe change in performance over a relatively brief time period (e.g. 1–6 months).

3: Soliciting Nominations for Cognitive Tests

Nomination of candidate tests was solicited from persons who participated in the pre-conference survey, and additionally, from attendees at the first MATRICS consensus meeting. Over 90 cognitive tests were nominated for consideration in the MATRICS battery, including measures from neuropsychology, experimental psychopathology, cognitive neuroscience, and psychophysiology.

4: Narrowing the List of Nominated Tests

The MATRICS Neurocognition Committee held a series of meetings with the aim of reducing the large number of nominated tests to a more manageable number for review by the RAND Panel (Step 6 below). Initially, the MATRICS Neurocognition Committee assigned each of the nominated tests to one of the seven cognitive domains. Then, the committee dropped tests that were not practical for use in clinical trials, had notable practice effects, lacked reliability data, or were not good representatives of one of the seven cognitive domains. The committee used their knowledge and expertise and the available literature to inform their decisions. The list was narrowed to 36 tests across the seven cognitive domains.

5: Creating a Database for Candidate Tests

The MATRICS staff compiled a database on each of the 36 tests according to the five test selection criteria. A comprehensive review of the literature was conducted that was supplemented by information solicited from test developers, test manuals, and published and unpublished data. The data for each test were organized into a standard format and cataloged by cognitive domain. Copies of the resulting document were provided to each RAND panelist prior to the in-person meeting in Los Angeles, CA, USA.

6: Evaluating Tests with the RAND Panel Method

The next step was to formally evaluate the narrowed list of 36 tests based on the selection criteria in an unbiased, open format, with input from experts representing diverse points of view. The RAND Panel Method (Fitch *et al.*, 2001) has been used in other settings, primarily medical ones, to reach consensus that require agreement among key stakeholders. The process begins with development of a standard database that is provided to panel members for review. Panelists are typically selected to represent diverse points of view of key stakeholders in the process. After review of the database material, panelists provide ratings on a series of Likert-scale questions developed specifically for this purpose. The panelists' ratings are compiled and large discrepancies identified. An in-person meeting of the panelists is then conducted with the focus on resolution of discrepancies.

For the purpose of reaching agreement on a cognitive battery, a 14-member RAND Panel was created. Members were selected who represented different perspectives in the process and included members from cognitive science, clinical neuropsychology, clinical trials design, biostatistics, cognitive deficits in schizophrenia, and patient advocacy. Prior to the meeting, the individual members rated each test within its respective cognitive domain on four of the five test selection criteria using the database material mailed to them and their personal expertise/ unique perspective. The ratings of the panelists were then submitted and compiled by UCLA MATRICS staff for presentation and review at the in-person meeting.

To streamline the discussion, areas of disagreement among the group were identified prior to the meeting so that these could be the focus of discussion at the in-person meeting. Discrepancies among raters were resolved or narrowed through discussion and further review of database material. RAND Panel members rated these tests again on the test selection criterion. One of the five criterions, response to pharmacological treatment, was dropped because the panelists considered it to be too difficult to evaluate given the existing database. The final ratings for all tests across all test criteria were summarized and presented to the MATRICS Neurocognition Committee.

7: Selecting Tests for the Beta Battery

After the RAND Panel meeting, the MATRICS Neurocognition Committee reviewed the ratings of panel members with the purpose of narrowing the number of tests within each cognitive domain. Tests within a domain were ranked based on consideration of the RAND Panel ratings on the five test selection criteria and the tests' mean overall rating. Though test–retest reliability was typically considered pre-requisite, any of the other criteria could tilt the ranking either upward or downward. The highest ranked tests were selected for inclusion in the "beta" version of the battery. This resulted in a range of two to five tests per domain (total = 20). More tests were included in the speed of processing domain because all of these measures had brief administration times and several had comparable overall ratings. The beta version was purposefully over-inclusive. It included roughly twice as many tests as would be ideal in the final battery so that tests within a domain could be directly compared with one another in the next stage.

8: Conducting a Psychometric Study with the Beta Battery

MATRICS sponsored a five-site Psychometric and Standardization Study (PASS) to formally evaluate the beta version of the battery in a sample of 176 schizophrenia and schizoaffective disorder (depressed type) outpatients. The sites included UCLA, Kansas University, University of Maryland Psychiatric Center, Duke University, and Harvard University. Patients were tested twice, 4 weeks apart. The purpose of the study was to run a head-to-head comparison of the tests within each cognitive domain on their psychometric properties (e.g. test–retest reliability, practice effects), relationship to functional outcome (work status, social functioning, and independent living), and practicality and tolerability in a patient sample representative of that typical of clinical trials designs.

9: Selecting the Final Battery

The psychometric data on all tests from PASS were compiled and the MATRICS Neurocognition Committee evaluated the tests on the essential test selection criteria, ranking the tests within their respective cognitive domain. The highest ranked tests within each cognitive domain were selected for inclusion in the final battery. The final MCCB included ten tests with one to three tests representing each of the seven cognitive domains (see Table 1).

10: Co-norming of Tests in a Community Sample

Though normative data are available on most of the tests included in the final battery, the samples are sometimes difficult to compare due to differences in sample size, gender and ethnic make-up, education, and geographical representation. Also, some tests were normed on more than one sample, making interpretation further complicated. Co-norming of the 10 tests in a single community sample would provide a single normative database for the MCCB and provides clear advantages for interpretation (Palmer *et al.*, 2004; Tulsky & Price, 2003). Data collection was conducted at five sites (the same ones that participated in PASS Phase I), and included 300 community residents who were recruited through survey sampling methods and stratified on age, sex, and education. The data from this study were used to establish a common metric for the 10 individual tests, the seven cognitive domains, and an overall composite index of cognitive functioning. Because calculating the composites as a mean of the standardized test scores does not yield a standard deviation of 10, the T-scores for the individual tests comprising the composite were summed and this index was standardized to yield a mean of 50 with a standard deviation of 10.

Papers describing the RAND Panel process, PASS Phase I, and PASS Phase II are currently in preparation. The end product from this effort was the development of the MCCB to be used in clinical trials of cognition-enhancing drugs and other related uses. The MCCB became available for distribution in April 2006, and includes nine paper-and-pencil tests and one computer-based measure. The ten tests comprising the MCCB are presented in the Table 1.

Table 1. **MCCB Tests Listed by Cognitive Domain**

COGNITIVE DOMAIN	TEST NAME
Speed of processing	Brief Assessment of Cognition in Schizophrenia (BACS): Symbol-Coding
	Category Fluency: Animal naming
	Trail Making Test: Part A (TMT)
Attention/vigilance	Continuous Performance Test – Identical Pairs (CPT-IP)
Working memory	Wechsler Memory Scale – Third Edition (WMS-III): Spatial Span
	Letter-Number Span (LNS)
Verbal learning	Hopkins Verbal Learning Test – Revised (HVLT-R)
Visual learning	Brief Visuospatial Memory Test – Revised (BVMT-R)
Reasoning and problem solving	Neuropsychological Assessment Battery (NAB): Mazes
Social cognition	Mayer-Salovey-Caruso Emotional Intelligence Test (MSCEIT): Managing Emotions

The MCCB test kit includes a computerized scoring program that provides T-scores and percentiles for each test, cognitive domain, and the overall composite score. The test data can be scored according to the following scoring methods: (a) age- and gender-correction, (b) age-, gender-, and education-correction, or (c) without any demographic-correction. Age- and gender-correction is the default and is the recommended scoring method for use in clinical trials of cognition-enhancing drugs for schizophrenia and related disorders. Age-, gender-, and education-correction may be preferred for assessment of neurological or psychiatric conditions that occur after expected educational level has been achieved (e.g. traumatic brain injury in adulthood). The no demographic-correction method may be desirable in situations in which one wishes to examine scores relative to the same broad normative sample to allow comparison of absolute performance levels. The MCCB can be purchased from Psychological Assessment Resources, Inc., Harcourt Assessment, Inc., or Multi-Health Systems, Inc.

The "Measurement" Obstacle Resolved

One charge of the MATRICS Initiative was to create a uniform way to measure cognition for use in clinical trials of cognition-enhancing agents, thereby helping to construct a pathway for FDA approval of such medications. The final decisions regarding the composition and use of the MCCB were submitted to the NIMH National Mental Health Advisory Council in April 2005 and they were accepted unanimously. These recommendations were then forwarded to the FDA where they were accepted. The outcome is that the MCCB is now recommended as the standard battery for all clinical trials of cognition-enhancing agents in schizophrenia that will be submitted to the FDA.

The MCCB is comprised of older (Trails A, category fluency) and newer (NAB Mazes, MSCEIT Managing Emotions, BACS Symbol Coding) tests. In the nomination of tests for the battery, there was a conscious decision to consider newer measures that may advance the measurement of cognition in schizophrenia. There was also consideration of other complete batteries in the process, but the Neurocognition Committee failed to find any batteries that adequately measured all of the cognitive domains identified as important to the assessment of cognitive function in clinical trials of cognition-enhancing drugs.

An unanticipated issue that surfaced from the meetings with the FDA was the need for a co-primary measure of outcome. There was concern that neurocognitive measures lacked ecological validity. That is, it was not clear what improvement on a neurocognitive test (e.g. list learning measure) meant in terms of real world functioning. For the results from a clinical trial to be clinically meaningful, there was a perceived need for inclusion of a second measure, a co-primary, with the consensus battery. To this end, MATRICS formed an outcomes committee to review existing measures of functional outcome relevant to schizophrenia. The committee acknowledged that this was a relatively immature area that required further development, but agreed upon the selection of four measures based on the available evidence. The psychometric properties of these measures were evaluated in the PASS with patients and will be described in an upcoming paper.

The next step in the process is to test promising compounds in clinical trials. The Treatment Units for Research on Neurocognition in Schizophrenia (TURNS) contract with NIMH (S.R. Marder, PI) is designed to facilitate investigation of new cognition-enhancing agents for use in schizophrenia. TURNS is a clinical trial network that includes seven participating sites and is currently evaluating nominated compounds from pharmaceutical industry and biotech companies for use in pharmacodynamic/pharmacokinetic and proof-of-concept studies.

References

Bilder, R.M., Goldman, R.S., Robinson, D., Reiter, G., Bell, L., Bates, J.A., *et al.* (2000). Neuropsychology of first-episode schizophrenia: initial characterization and clinical correlates. *American Journal of Psychiatry*, 157, 549–559.

Bilder, R.M., Goldman, R.S., Volavka, J., Czobor, P., Hoptman, M., Sheitman, B., Lindenmayer, J.P., Citrome, L., McEvoy, J., Kunz, M., Chakos, M., Cooper, T.B., Horowitz, T.L., & Lieberman, J.A. (2002). Neurocognitive effects of clozapine, olanzapine, risperidone, and haloperidol in patients with chronic schizophrenia or schizoaffective disorder. *American Journal of Psychiatry*, 159, 1018–1028.

Buchanan, R.W., Davis, M., Goff, D., Green, M.F., Keefe, R.S., Leon, A.C., Nuechterlein, K.H., Laughren, T., Levin, R., Stover, E., Fenton, W., & Marder, S.R. (2005). A summary of the FDA-NIMH-MATRICS workshop on clinical trial design for neurocognitive drugs for schizophrenia. *Schizophrenia Bulletin*, 31, 5–19.

Cornblatt, B., Lenzenweger, M.F., Dworkin, R., & Erlenmeyer-Kimling, L. (1992). Childhood attentional dysfunction predicts social deficits in unaffected adults at risk for schizophrenia. *British Journal of Psychiatry*, 161, 59–64.

Fernandez-Ruiz, J., Doudet, D., & Aigner, T.G. (1999). Spatial memory improvement by levodopa in parkinsonian MPTP-treated monkeys. *Psychopharmacology*, 147, 104–107.

Fitch, K., Bernstein, S.J., Aguilar, M.D., Burnand, B., LaCalle J.R., Lazaro, P., van het Loo, M., McDonnell, J., Vader, J.P., & Kahan J.P. (2001). *The RAND/UCLA Appropriateness Method User's Manual*. Santa Monica, California: RAND.

Goff, D.C., Herz, L., Posever, T., Shih, V., Tsai, G., Henderson, D.C., Freudenreich, O., Evins, A.E., Yovel, I., Zhang, H., & Schoenfeld, D.A. (2005). A six-month, placebo-controlled trial of D-cycloserine co-administered with conventional antipsychotics in schizophrenia patients. *Psychopharmacology*, 179, 144–150.

Goff, D.C., Tsai, G., Levitt, J., Amico, E., Manoach, D., Schoenfeld, D.A., Hayden, D.L., McCarley, R., & Coyle, J.T. (1999). A placebo-controlled trial of D-cycloserine added to conventional neuroleptics in patients with schizophrenia. *Archives of General Psychiatry*, 56, 21–27.

Gold, J.M. (2004). Cognitive deficits as treatment targets in schizophrenia. *Schizophrenia Research*, 72, 21–28.

Goldman-Rakic, P.S., Castner, S.A., Svensson, T.H., Siever, L.J., & Williams, G.V. (2004). Targeting the dopamine D_1 receptior in schizophrenia: insights for cognitive dysfunction. *Psychopharmacology*, 174, 3–16.

Green, M.F. (1996). What are the functional consequences of neurocognitive deficits in schizophrenia? *American Journal of Psychiatry*, 153, 321–330.

Green, M.F., & Nuechterlein, K.H. (2004). The MATRICS initiative: developing a consensus cognitive battery for clinical trials. *Schizophrenia Research*, 72, 1–3.

Green, M.F., Kern, R.S., & Heaton, R.K. (2004). Longitudinal studies of cognition and functional outcome in schizophrenia: implications for MATRICS. *Schizophrenia Research*, 72, 41–51.

Green, M.F., Kern, R.S., Braff, D.L., & Mintz, J. (2000). Neurocognitive deficits and functional outcome in schizophrenia: Are we measuring the "right stuff"? *Schizophrenia Bulletin*, 26, 119–136.

Green, M.F., Marder, S.R., Glynn, S.M., McGurk, S.R., Wirshing, W.C., Wirshing, D.A., Liberman, R.P., & Mintz, J. (2002). The neurocognitive effectts of low-dose haloperidol: a two-year comparison with risperidone. *Biological Psychiatry*, 51, 972–978.

Green, M.F., Nuechterlein, K.H., Gold, J.M., Barch, D., Cohen, J., Essock, S., Fenton, W.S., Frese, F., Goldberg, T.E., Heaton, R.K., Keefe, R.S.E., Kern, R.S., Kraemer, H., Stover, E., Weinberger, D.R., Zalcman, S., & Marder, S.R. (2004). Approaching a consensus cognitive battery for clinical trials in schizophrenia: The NIMH-MATRICS conference to select cognitive domains and test criteria. *Biological Psychiatry*, 56, 301–307.

Hampson, R.E., Rogers, G., Lynch, G., & Deadwyler, S. (1998). Facilitative effects of the Ampakine CX516 on short term memory in rats: correlations with hippocampal neuronal activity. *Journal of Neuroscience*, 18, 2748–2763.

Harvey, P.D., & Keefe, R.S.E. (2001). Studies of the cognitive change in patients with schizophrenia following novel antipsychotic treatment. *American Journal of Psychiatry*, 158, 176–184.

Heinrichs, R.W., & Zakzanis, K.K. (1998). Neurocognitive deficit in schizophrenia: a quantitative review of the evidence. *Neuropsychology*, 12, 426–445.

Heydebrand, G., Weiser, M., Rabinowitz, J., Hoff, A.L., DeLisi, L.E., & Csernansky, J.G. (2004). Correlates of cognitive deficits in first episode schizophrenia. *Schizophrenia Research*, 68, 1–9.

Keefe, R.S.E., Silva, S.G., Perkins, D.O., & Lieberman, J.A. (1999). The effects of atypical antipsychotic drugs on neurocognitive impairment in schizophrenia: a review and meta-analysis. *Schizophrenia Bulletin*, 25, 201–222.

Kern, R.S., Green, M.F., Nuechterlein, K.H., & Deng, B.-H. (2004). NIMH-MATRICS survey on assessment of neurocognition in schizophrenia. *Schizophrenia Research*, 72, 11–19.

Marder, S.R. (2006). The NIMH-MATRICS project for developing cognition-enhancing agents for schizophrenia. *Dialogues in Clinical Neuroscience*, 8, 109–113.

Marder, S.R., & Fenton, W. (2004). Measurement and treatment research to improve cognition in schizophrenia: NIMH MATRICS initiative to support the development of agents for improving cognition in schizophrenia. *Schizophrenia Research*, 72, 5–9.

Mishara, A.L., & Goldberg, T.E. (2004). A meta-analysis and critical review of the effects of conventional neuroleptic treatment on cognition in schizophrenia: opening a closed book. *Biological Psychiatry*, 55, 1013–1022.

Mohamed, S., Paulsen, J.S., O'Leary, D.S., Arndt, S., & Andreasen, N.C. (1999). Generalized cognitive deficits in schizophrenia. *American Journal of Psychiatry*, 156, 749–754.

Nieuwenstein, M.R., Aleman, A., & de Haan, E.H.F. (2001). Relationship between symptom dimensions and neurocognitive functioning in schizophrenia: a meta-analysis of WCST and CPT studies. *Journal of Psychiatric Research*, 35, 119–125.

Nuechterlein, K.H., Asarnow, R.F., Subotnik, K.L., Fogelson, D.L., Ventura, J., Torquato, R., *et al.* (1998). Neurocognitive vulnerability factors for schizophrenia: convergence across genetic risk studies and longitudinal trait/state studies.

In: Lenzenweger, M.F. & Dworkin, R.H.(ed.), *Origins and Development of Schizophrenia: Advances in Experimental Psychopathology.* Washington, DC: American Psychological Association, pp. 299–327.

Nuechterlein, K.H., Barch, D.M., Gold, J.M., Goldberg, T.E., Green, M.F., & Heaton, R.K. (2004). Identification of separable cognitive factors in schizophrenia. *Schizophrenia Research,* 72, 29–39.

Palmer, B.W., Appelbaum, M.I., & Heaton, R.K. (2004). Rohling's interpretive method and inherent limitations on the flexibility of "flexible batteries". *Neuropsychology Review,* 14, 171–176.

Palmer, B.W., Heaton, R.K., Paulsen, J.S., Kuck, J., Braff, D., Harris, M.J., *et al.* (1997). Is it possible to be schizophrenic yet neuropsychologically normal? *Neuropsychology,* 11, 437–446.

Perlick, D., Stastny, P., Katz, I., Mayer, M., & Mattis, S. (1986). Memory deficits and anticholinergic levels in chronic schizophrenia. *American Journal of Psychiatry,* 143, 230–232.

Saykin, A.J., Gur, R.E., Gur, R.C., & Mozley, P.D. (1991). Neuropsychological function in schizophrenia: selective impairment in memory and learning. *Archives of General Psychiatry,* 48, 618–622.

Schneider, J.S., Sun, Z.Q., & Roeltgen, D.P. (1994). Effects of dopamine agonists on delayed response performance in chronic low-dose MPTP-treated monkeys. *Pharmacology Biochemistry and Behavior,* 48, 235–240.

Staubli, U., Rogers, G., & Lynch, G. (1994). Facilitation of glutamate receptors enhances memory. *Proceedings of the National Academy of Sciences, USA,* 91, 777–781.

Tulsky, D.S., & Price, L.R. (2003). The joint WAIS-III and WMS-III factor structure: development and cross-validation of a six-factor model of cognitive functioning. *Psychological Assessment,* 15, 149–162.

Tune, L.E., Strauss, M.E., Lew, M.F., Breitlinger, E., & Coyle, J.T. (1982). Serum levels of anticholinergic drugs and impaired recent memory in chronic schizophrenic patients. *American Journal of Psychiatry,* 139, 187–190.

Williams, G.V., & Goldman-Rakic, P.S. (1995). Modulation of memory fields by dopamine D_1 receptors in prefrontal cortex. *Nature,* 376, 549–550.

Woodward, N.D., Purdon, S.E., Meltzer, H.Y., & Zald, D.H. (2005). A meta-analysis of neuropsychological change to clozapine, olanzapine, quetiapine, and risperidone in schizophrenia. *International Journal of Neuropsychopharmacology,* 8, 457–472.

Progress in Neurotherapeutics and Neuropsychopharmacology, 2:1, 187–192 © 2007 Cambridge University Press
DOI: 10.1017/S1748232106000139   Printed in the United Kingdom

Review of a Randomized-Controlled Trial of Adjunctive Bupropion in the Treatment of SSRI-Induced Sexual Dysfunction

Anna Lembke and Charles DeBattista

Department of Psychiatry and Behavioral Sciences, Stanford University School of Medicine, Stanford, CA, USA

Key words: bupropion, sexual, side-effects, serotonin, antidote, dysfunction

Introduction and Overview

Selective serotonin reuptake inhibitors (SSRIs) commonly cause sexual side-effects. The range of sexual side-effects associated with SSRIs include decreased *libido*; delayed, reduced, or absent orgasm; diminished sensation and arousal; and erectile and ejaculatory dysfunction. Some studies have reported that up to 70% of individuals taking SSRIs will experience sexual side-effects (Lane, 1997). Sexual side-effects are among the most common reasons that patients discontinue SSRIs, even when they are effective (Harvey & Balon, 1995).

Many antidotes to SSRI-induced sexual dysfunction have been proposed over the years; most of them are 5-hydroxytryptamine (serotonin) (5-HT) modulators. However, few antidotes have been rigorously studied in a double-blind comparative fashion, and even then, studies have provided conflicting and/or discouraging results. For example, buspirone, a partial agonist of the 5-HT1A receptor, showed an advantage over placebo in one double-blind trial (Landen *et al.*, 1999), and no advantage over placebo in another (Michelson *et al.*, 2000). Granisetron, a 5-HT3 antagonist, failed to show benefit over placebo in two double-blind trials (Nelson *et al.*, 2005; Jespersen *et al.*, 2004). Other agents that have shown benefit in case reports and case series, but have yet to be tested in randomized-controlled trial, include yohimbine (Balon, 1993), sildenafil (Rosenberg, 1999; Schaller & Behar, 1999), amantadine (Balon, 1996), amphetamines (Bartlik *et al.*, 1995), cyproheptadine (Gitlin, 1994).

Correspondence should be addressed to: Anna Lembke, MD and Charles DeBattista, MD, Department of Psychiatry and Behavioral Sciences, 401 Quarry Road, Stanford University School of Medicine, Stanford, CA 94305, USA; Ph: 650 723 8335; Email: alembke@stanford.edu; debattista@stanford.edu.

Purpose of Our Trial

We set out to measure whether adjunctive bupropion might improve SSRI-induced sexual dysfunction, when given in a fixed morning dose of 150-mg sustained release (SR), over a 6-week period.

Agent: Bupropion

Bupropion is an Food and Drug Administration (FDA)-approved antidepressant and smoking cessation medication, which works via dopamine and norepinephrine reuptake inhibition. Bupropion does not have sexual side-effects, and may even enhance sexual function.

Numerous case reports and open label trials endorse improvement in SSRI-induced sexual side-effects when bupropion is added to the SSRI (Ashton & Rosen, 1998; Labbate *et al.*, 1997; Labbate & Pollack, 1994), but controlled trials are less encouraging. Two double-blind placebo-controlled trials have examined the effect of adjunctive bupropion on SSRI-induced sexual dysfunction (Clayton *et al.*, 2004; Masand *et al.*, 2001). Masand *et al.* found no difference between placebo and bupropion 150 mg given at night over a 3-week period (Masand *et al.*, 2001). Clayton *et al.* found an improvement over placebo in desire and frequency of sexual functioning with adjunctive bupropion (150 mg, given twice a day for 4 weeks), but no differences in orgasm or arousal between bupropion and placebo (Clayton *et al.*, 2004). Orgasm and arousal improved in both treatment groups, as did Hamilton Depression Rating Scale (HAM-D21) scores, leading one to speculate that improvement in sexual function may have been attributable to improvement in mood, rather than due to a physiologic change in sexual function *per se*.

Clinical Trial

Subjects were recruited from clinic populations and by advertisements. Subjects gave written, informed consent prior to enrollment. Criteria for inclusion included: ages between 18 and 60 years; taking a fixed therapeutic dose of fluoxetine (at least 20 mg/day), paroxetine (at least 20 mg/day), citalopram (at least 20 mg/day), or sertraline (at least 50 mg/day) for at least 6 weeks; and endorsing complaints of sexual side-effects which they believed to be temporally related to their antidepressant use. Arizona Sexual Experiences Scale (ASEX) scores of at least 15 out of 30 were required for participation (McGahuey *et al.*, 2000).

Subjects were randomized to one of two groups. In one group placebo was added to their current SSRI for 6 weeks, and in the other group, bupropion SR 150 mg every morning was added to their current SSRI for 6 weeks. Subjects were seen weekly for 2 weeks, and then every 2 weeks for the remaining 4 weeks.

Instrument measures included the ASEX, male and female (McGahuey *et al.*, 2000), the Brief Index of Sexual Functioning (BISF) (Taylor *et al.*, 1994), and a 10-point visual analog scale that assessed interest and satisfaction for both the previous week and prior to taking an SSRI. Items taken from the BISF for men included level of arousal during masturbation, during insertion of penis, during thrusting of penis; frequency of nocturnal erections, frequency of ejaculation during sleep and intercourse, and frequency of difficulty with ejaculation during masturbation and intercourse. Items from the BISF for women included frequency of desire to engage in masturbation or intercourse, frequency of arousal during masturbation or intercourse, frequency of orgasm during masturbation, sleep, and intercourse; frequency of lack of vaginal lubrication, and frequency of difficulty reaching orgasm. Items from the BISF for both men and women included frequency of masturbation and intercourse and level of pleasure from sexual experience. Secondary measures included a Hamilton Depression Rating Scale (HAM-D) (Hamilton, 1960), a Beck Depression Inventory (BDI) (Beck *et al.*, 1961), and a Clinician Global Impression-improvement scale (CGI) (Guy, 1976) focusing on sexual dysfunction.

In the overall assessment of change in sexual function, both total ASEX scores and individual items were assessed. Thirty-six individual items were treated as separate dependent variables: 3 CGI items, 6 items on each of the male and female versions of the ASEX (total 12), 21 items of the BISF, item number 14 from the HAM-D, and item number 22 from the BDI. Total HAM-D and BDI scores were assessed over time. Significant improvement in sexual function was defined as a 50% reduction in total ASEX score. Two-way repeated measures analyses of variance were conducted on these variables, with treatment group and time as factors. Significance level was set at $p = 0.05$. Corrections for multiple comparisons were made using a stepwise Bonferroni procedure.

Twenty-four women and 17 men, for a total of 41 patients, entered and completed the 6-week trial. There were no dropouts. The mean age of participants was 46 years (sd = 10.79). Sixteen patients were taking fluoxetine, 12 were taking paroxetine, 12 were taking sertraline, and one was taking citalopram. Duration of use of SSRI prior to enrollment in our trial ranged between 6 and 34 weeks. Baseline ASEX mean score prior to enrollment was 22 (sd = 4). Baseline mean HAM-D and BDI scores were 11 (sd = 6) and 10 (sd = 6), respectively. The intervention was well tolerated, with not a single dropout for the duration of the study.

No assessments of sexual function were found to be significantly different over time between bupropion and placebo. Only 5 of 15 patients in the bupropion SR group showed 25% or more improvement on the total ASEX score. Only 6 of 15 patients in the placebo group showed 25% or more improvement on the total ASEX score. HAM-D and BDI scores did not change significantly over time in either group. In short, bupropion was not more effective than placebo in improving sexual function in patients with SSRI-induced sexual dysfunction, and neither bupropion nor placebo imparted much benefit in the majority of patients.

The fact that bupropion did not differentiate from placebo suggests that bupropion is not an effective antidote for SSRI-induced sexual dysfunction. On the other hand, a number of factors may have contributed to the lack of difference between treatment groups, other than non-efficacy. The dose of bupropion at only 150 mg in the morning may have been sub-therapeutic. Although a prior double-blind study used bupoprion 300 mg/day and found no difference from placebo in orgasm or sexual function, this study dosed bupropion in the evening. It is theoretically possible that a higher dose of bupropion given in the morning might be more effective. It is also possible that the intermediate release form of buproprion may be superior to longer acting forms. The small number of participants also might have contributed to the negative findings. A sample size of 41 is underpowered to evaluate a small effect size of the active drug. The frequency of visits and the use of the same assessments at every visit might have contributed to a higher placebo response rate.

Despite these study limitations, the available evidence garnered from randomized-controlled trial, to support the use of adjunctive bupropion to counteract sexual side-effects caused by SSRIs.

Influence on the Field

Most psychiatrists prescribe adjunctive bupropion as first line treatment for SSRI-induced sexual dysfunction (Perlis *et al.*, 2002). This method has become common practice for a number of reasons: numerous case reports and open label studies endorse its benefit; and there is no clear viable alternative, except perhaps sildenafil (Viagra). In our opinion, the placebo-controlled trials, which are the gold standard for efficacy, offer only modest evidence that bupropion is useful for SSRI-induced sexual dysfunction. Bupropion does not appear to reverse the SSRI-induced physiologic changes that lead to anorgasmia and other forms of sexual dysfunction. Bupropion may confer some indirect enhancement of sexual interest and frequency, but these changes may be more related to improvements in mood rather than sexual function *per se*.

Summary of how to treat the disorder incorporating the results of the new trial data

In conclusions, we would like to summarize how to treat SSRI-induced sexual dysfunction, based on the data available. The evidence does not necessarily support the addition of bupropion to an SSRI for sexual dysfunction caused by the SSRI. However, if the patient has some residual symptoms of depression, which might otherwise benefit from the addition of bupropion, as well as suffers from

SSRI-induced sexual dysfunction, then bupropion might be the best adjunctive treatment. This is further supplied by additional studies (DeBattista *et al.*, 2004; Triveda *et al.*, 2006) that suggest that bupropion effectively augments antidepressant response. In this case, bupropion might indirectly improve sexual interest and frequency, by improving overall depressive symptoms.

Acknowledgement

Dr. DeBattista is a speaker for (GSK) GlaxoSmtihKlin, and both Dr. DeBattista and Dr. Lembke have received funding from GSK.

References

Ashton, A.K. & Roscn, R.C. (1998). Bupropion as an antidote for serotonin reuptake inhibitor-induced sexual dysfunction. *Journal of Clinical Psychiatry*, 59, 112–115.

Balon, R. (1993). Fluoxetine-induced sexual dysfunction and yohimbine. *Journal of Clinical Psychiatry*, 54, 161–162.

Balon, R. (1996). Intermittent amantadine for fluoxetine-induced anorgasmia. *Journal of Sex and Marital Therapy*, 22, 290–292.

Bartlik, B.D., Kaplan, P. & Kaplan, H.S. (1995). Psychostimulants apparently reverse sexual dysfunction secondary to selective serotonin re-uptake inhibitors. *Journal of Sex and Marital Therapy*, 21, 264–271.

Beck, A.T., *et al.* (1961). An inventory for measuring depression. *Archives of General Psychiatry*, 4, 561–571.

Clayton, A.H., *et al.* (2004). A placebo-controlled trial of bupropion SR as an antidote for selective serotonin reuptake inhibitor-induced sexual dysfunction. *Journal of Clinical Psychiatry*, 65, 62–67.

Gitlin, M.J. (1994). Psychotropic medications and their effects on sexual function: diagnosis, biology, and treatment approaches. *Journal of Clinical Psychiatry*, 55, 406–413.

Guy, W. (1976). *ECDEU Assessment Manual for Psychopharmacology*, E. US Department of Health, and Welfare Publications (ADM), Editor. National Institute of Mental Health: Rockville, Maryland. pp. 218–222.

Hamilton, M. (1960). A rating scale for depression. *Journal of Neurology Neurosurgery and Psychiatry*, 23, 56–62.

Harvey, K.V. & Balon, R. (1995). Clinical implications of antidepressant drug effects on sexual function. *Annal Clinical Psychiatry*, 7, 189–201.

Jespersen, S., *et al.* (2004). A pilot randomized, double-blind, placebo-controlled study of granisetron in the treatment of sexual dysfunction in women associated with antidepressant use. *International Clinical Psychopharmacology*, 19, 161–164.

Labbate, L.A. & Pollack, M.H. (1994). Treatment of fluoxetine-induced sexual dysfunction with bupropion: a case report. *Annal Clinical Psychiatry*, 6, 13–15.

Labbate, L.A., *et al.* (1997). Bupropion treatment of serotonin reuptake antidepressant-associated sexual dysfunction. *Annal Clinical Psychiatry*, 9, 241–245.

Landen, M., *et al.* (1999). Effect of buspirone on sexual dysfunction in depressed patients treated with selective serotonin reuptake inhibitors. *Journal Clinical Psychopharmacology*, 19, 268–271.

Lane, R.M. (1997). A critical review of selective serotonin reuptake inhibitor-related sexual dysfunction; incidence, possible aetiology and implications for management. *Journal of Psychopharmacology*, 11, 72–82.

Masand, P.S., *et al.* (2001). Sustained-release bupropion for selective serotonin reuptake inhibitor-induced sexual dysfunction: a randomized, double-blind, placebo-controlled, parallel-group study. *American Journal of Psychiatry*, 158, 805–807.

McGahuey, C.A., *et al.* (2000). The Arizona Sexual Experience Scale (ASEX): reliability and validity. *Journal Sex and Marital Therapy*, 26, 25–40.

Michelson, D., *et al.* (2000). Female sexual dysfunction associated with antidepressant administration: a randomized, placebo-controlled study of pharmacologic intervention. *American Journal of Psychiatry*, 157, 239–243.

Nelson, J.C., Portera, L. & Leon, A.C. (2005). Residual symptoms in depressed patients after treatment with fluoxetine or reboxetine. *Journal Clinical Psychiatry*, 66, 1409–1414.

Perlis, R.H., *et al.* (2002). Strategies for treatment of SSRI-associated sexual dysfunction: a survey of an academic psychopharmacology practice. *Harvard Review of Psychiatry*, 10, 109–114.

Rosenberg, K.P. (1999). Sildenafil citrate for SSRI-induced sexual side effects. *American Journal of Psychiatry*, 156, 157.

Schaller, J.L. & Behar, D. (1999). Sildenafil citrate for SSRI-induced sexual side effects. *American Journal of Psychiatry*, 156, 156–157.

Taylor, J., Rosen, R.C. & Leiblum, S. (1994). Self-report assessment of female sexual function: psychometric evaluation of the Brief Index of Sexual Functioning for Women. *Archives of Sexual Behavior*, 23, 627–643.

Progress in Neurotherapeutics and Neuropsychopharmacology, 2:1, 193–212 © 2007 Cambridge University Press
DOI: 10.1017/S1748232106000140   Printed in the United Kingdom

Trial-Based Advances in the Treatment of Bipolar Depression

David E. Kemp, Keming Gao, David J. Muzina,
Prashant Gajwani and Joseph R. Calabrese

NIMH Bipolar Disorder Research Center, Mood Disorders Program, University Hospitals of Cleveland/Case Western Reserve University School of Medicine, Cleveland, OH, USA

Key words: bipolar disorder, depression, antidepressant treatment, mood stabilizers, atypical antipsychotics.

Introduction and Overview

The burden of bipolar depression is particularly arduous as patients typically spend a greater amount of time in the depressed phase of the illness than in the manic phase (Post, 2005). Time to recovery is often more prolonged in depression than in mania (Judd *et al.*, 2002) with controlled studies of maintenance therapies finding the median time to full remission as long as 40.0 weeks for a depressive episode in contrast to 16.8 weeks for a manic episode (Hlastala *et al.*, 1997). In addition, the depressive phase of bipolar disorder results in greater occupational, family, and social dysfunction (Calabrese *et al.*, 2004). More strikingly, when compared to bipolar mania, bipolar depression is associated with increased rates of mortality by suicide (Dilsaver *et al.*, 1997).

Pharmacological agents for the treatment of bipolar depression have been understudied in comparison to research in bipolar mania. The only agent currently approved by the Food and Drug Administration (FDA) for the treatment of bipolar depression is a combination of olanzapine and fluoxetine (OFC; Symbyax®). Limited biological treatments have created an unmet need for more comprehensive trial-based assessments of safe and efficacious therapies for treating bipolar depression. Early studies of bipolar depression have included lithium (Baron *et al.*, 1975; Goodwin *et al.*, 1969), carbamazepine (Post *et al.*, 1986), and conventional antidepressants (Sachs *et al.*, 1994; Himmelhoch *et al.*, 1991; Cohn *et al.*, 1989), though many methodological problems exist with these trials hindering data interpretation and generalizability. Modern trials enrolling hundreds of patients have investigated

Correspondence should be addressed to: David E. Kemp, MD, 11400 Euclid Avenue, Suite 200, Cleveland, OH 44106, USA; Ph: 216 844 2865; Fax: 216 844 2875; Email: kemp.david@gmail.com

the antidepressant effects of lamotrigine, olanzapine, and an OFC in patients with bipolar depression. These recent studies have changed the approach to treatment in clinical practice. According to the 2004 expert consensus guideline for the treatment of bipolar disorder, lamotrigine was recommended as an initial monotherapy for bipolar depression (Keck *et al.*, 2004). In addition to lamotrigine monotherapy, a combination of lithium and lamotrigine or lithium plus an antidepressant was recommended for severe, nonpsychotic bipolar depression. The Texas Implementation of Medication Algorithms advises treatment with any antimanic agent plus lamotrigine for bipolar I depression and lamotrigine monotherapy in cases without a history of severe or recent mania (Suppes *et al.*, 2005). Lithium was equally recommended as lamotrigine for initial treatment of bipolar depression in the American Psychiatric Association guideline (2002).

The incomplete acute antidepressant effect of current available agents has propelled investigators to search for new drugs to manage this debilitating illness. Most recently, a multi-center trial evaluating the atypical antipsychotic quetiapine has been completed. The aim of this manuscript will be to review the first randomized, placebo-controlled, double-blind trial evaluating the efficacy and safety of quetiapine in the treatment of bipolar I and II subjects experiencing a major depressive episode (Calabrese *et al.*, 2005). A second follow-up study to this initial trial has only recently been completed and appears to confirm the results that suggest a role for quetiapine in the acute treatment of bipolar I or II depression. The results of other clinical trials that have influenced the treatment recommendations for bipolar depression and those of smaller trials that may shape future recommendations will also be reviewed. Clinical implications will be discussed including emerging evidence for the use of atypical antipsychotics in the treatment of the depressed phase of bipolar disorder.

Quetiapine in the Treatment of Bipolar Depression

Apart from olanzapine, the only atypical antipsychotic agent rigorously evaluated in clinical trials of bipolar depression is quetiapine (Calabrese *et al.*, 2005). These registration trials have been referred to as BOLDER I and II (BipOLar DEpRession). In the initial study, BOLDER I, enrolled subjects were outpatients ages 18–65 years old who met *Diagnostic and Statistical Manual for mental disorders-Fourth Edition* (DSM-IV) criteria for bipolar I or II disorder and were experiencing a major depressive episode. Diagnosis was confirmed using the Structured Clinical Interview for DSM-IV (SCID). Subjects were required to have a Hamilton Depression Rating Scale (HAM-D) 17-item score ≥ 20, a HAM-D item 1 score ≥ 2, and a Young Mania Rating Scale (YMRS) score ≤ 12 at both the screening and randomization visits. Subjects were excluded from the study if they were diagnosed with an axis I disorder other than bipolar disorder that was the primary focus of treatment within

6 months prior to screening, met criteria for substance use or dependence, had a significant medical illness, or met criteria for a mixed state of bipolar disorder. Subjects who posed a current serious suicidal or homicidal risk were also excluded.

Methodology

Subjects enrolled in this trial were treated for 8 weeks and randomly assigned to quetiapine 600 mg/day, quetiapine 300 mg/day, or placebo. The primary efficacy measure was the mean change in the Montgomery–Åsberg Depression Rating Scale (MADRS) total score from baseline to week 8. The proportion of subjects who achieved a response ($\geq$50% reduction from baseline score on the MADRS), the time to response, the proportion of patients who achieved remission (MADRS score $\leq$ 12), the time to remission, as well as a MADRS item analysis were reported. Secondary outcome measures included the Clinical Global Impression Severity of Illness and Improvement (CGI-S and CGI-I) scores, HAM-D, Quality of Life Enjoyment and Satisfaction Questionnaire (Q-LES-Q), Pittsburgh Sleep Quality Index, and the Hamilton Anxiety Rating Scale (HAM-A).

Primary and secondary efficacy analyses were performed on the intent-to-treat population. For patients who withdrew during the study, a last-observation carried-forward (LOCF) analysis was used to impute missing data. Effect size was determined with a mixed-model repeated-measures (MMRM) analysis. All secondary analyses were conducted at the significance level of 0.05, with no adjustment for multiple comparisons.

Results

A total of 838 patients were screened, and 542 patients with bipolar I ($N = 360$) or bipolar II ($N = 182$) disorder were randomly assigned to receive quetiapine, 600 mg/day ($N = 180$); quetiapine, 300 mg/day ($N = 181$); or placebo ($N = 181$). The ratio of patients who completed the study was 54% in the 600 mg/day quetiapine group, 67% in the 300 mg/day quetiapine group, and 59% in the placebo group, with no significant difference found between groups. Quetiapine at a dose of either 600 or 300 mg/day demonstrated significantly greater mean improvement in MADRS total scores compared with placebo at all time points (Figure 1), including as early as week 1, in the intent-to-treat group of patients with bipolar I or II depression ($p < 0.001$ for both quetiapine doses versus placebo). The effect sizes were 0.81 for 600 mg/day of quetiapine and 0.67 for 300 mg/day of quetiapine.

The median time to response was significantly shorter for both 600 mg/day (22 days) and 300 mg/day (22 days) of quetiapine compared with placebo (36 days). In the final assessment, both doses of quetiapine resulted in significantly higher response rates than placebo (58% versus 36.1%, $p < 0.001$). When examining remission rates, 52.9% of the 600 mg/day and 300 mg/day quetiapine groups entered into remission at the final assessment as compared to 28.4% in the

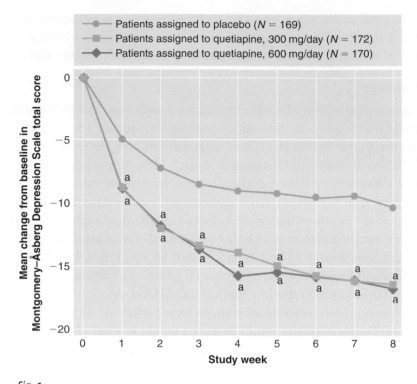

Fig. 1.
Change From Baseline in MADRS Total Score. [Reprinted with permission from Calabrese, J.R.
(*Am J Psychiatry* 2005; 162: 1351–1360)]

placebo group ($p < 0.001$). The median time to remission was also significantly shorter for both quetiapine 600 mg/day (27 days) and 300 mg/day (29 days) compared with placebo (65 days).

Significant improvement compared to placebo was observed in 9 out of 10 MADRS items in patients taking 600 mg/day of quetiapine and 8 out of 10 items in patients taking 300 mg/day of quetiapine ($p < 0.05$). The core mood symptoms of apparent sadness, reported sadness, and pessimistic thoughts were significantly improved in both quetiapine groups as early as week 1 compared with placebo ($p < 0.05$). Suicidal thoughts were reduced with both groups of quetiapine at a rate nearly twice that of placebo ($p < 0.001$). The effect size in the bipolar I subgroup was 1.09 for those assigned to 600 mg/day and 0.91 for those taking 300 mg/day of quetiapine. In the subgroup of patients with bipolar II disorder, change in MADRS did not reach statistical significance at the final assessment. A statistically significant change in MADRS total scores with quetiapine as compared to placebo was seen even in the presence of rapid cycling in the intent-to-treat group. Statistically significant improvement ($p < 0.001$) on the CGI severity scale was seen in quetiapine-treated patients as early as week 1 and was sustained to the end of the study for both quetiapine doses versus placebo. A larger percentage of patients at the final assessment were rated as "normal, not at all ill" or "borderline ill" in the 600 mg/day (42.4%) and 300 mg/day quetiapine groups (38.1%) compared with the placebo group (23.7%).

Secondary efficacy analyses showed significant improvement as early as week 1 in anxiety as measured by HAM-A total scores and was maintained to last assessment for both quetiapine doses versus placebo. Additionally, quality of sleep improved significantly among those treated with either dose of quetiapine compared with placebo. Quetiapine-treated patients also experienced improvements in quality of life as measured by the Q-LES-Q total score.

Safety

Common adverse events included dry mouth, sedation, somnolence, dizziness, and constipation. The overall rate of study discontinuation due to adverse events was 26.1% ($N = 47$) in the 600 mg/day group, 16.0% ($N = 29$) in the 300 mg/day group, and 8.8% ($N = 16$) in the placebo group. No significant difference was seen in the rates of serious adverse events across treatment groups. There were a total of two suicide attempts in this study (one in each of the active treatment groups) but no completed suicides or deaths occurred.

Rates of treatment-emergent mania were 2.2% for quetiapine 600 mg/day, 3.9% for quetiapine 300 mg/day, and 3.9% for placebo. Extrapyramidal symptoms were present in 8.9% of the 600 mg/day group, 6.7% of the 300 mg/day group, and 2.2% of the placebo group. Patients taking 600 mg/day of quetiapine experienced a mean weight gain of 1.6 kg by the final assessment compared with 1.0 kg in the 300 mg/day group and 0.2 kg in the placebo group. When comparing patients at final assessment, 16 patients (9.0%) treated with 600 mg/day of quetiapine, 15 patients (8.5%) treated with 300 mg/day of quetiapine, and 3 patients (1.7%) who received placebo had a weight gain of $\geq 7\%$ of their baseline measurement. There was no significant change in mean fasting serum glucose at final assessment between both quetiapine groups and placebo.

Additional Advances in the Treatment of Bipolar Depression

BOLDER II

A replication study to verify the validity and reliability of BOLDER I has also been undertaken (Calabrese, October 24, 2005). Data from this confirmatory study, BOLDER II, has recently been released and showed for a second time that quetiapine monotherapy (both 600 mg/day and 300 mg/day) was superior to placebo as early as week 1 on the MADRS and HAM-D. A notable difference in the BOLDER II study was that the bipolar II subgroup showed statistically significant improvement over placebo in both quetiapine arms, similar to the magnitude of improvement observed in the bipolar I subgroup. These results lend mounting evidence to support the use of quetiapine in a dose range of 300–600 mg/day for the treatment of both acute bipolar I and II depression. This is the first time a large-scale, successful, bipolar depression study has ever been replicated.

Olanzapine and OFC

Tohen and colleagues (2003) presented data on the first placebo-controlled trial comparing the use of an atypical antipsychotic agent alone and in combination with an antidepressant for the treatment of bipolar depression. In this study, the efficacy and tolerability of olanzapine monotherapy was assessed in a randomized, placebo-controlled, double-blind fashion. A total of 833 adults with bipolar I depression were randomly assigned to receive either olanzapine monotherapy ($N = 370$), placebo ($N = 377$), or OFC ($N = 86$) for up to 8 weeks. The primary efficacy measure was the mean change from baseline to last assessment in the MADRS total score and was analyzed using both LOCF and MMRM methods. At study endpoint, significant improvements in MADRS total score were seen with olanzapine and OFC compared with placebo. Beginning at week 4 and to study endpoint, OFC was superior to olanzapine monotherapy. The effect size based on a MMRM analysis of the improvement in the MADRS scores was 0.32 for olanzapine and 0.68 for OFC.

Treatment-emergent mania was low revealing no statistically significant differences among groups. Treatment-emergent adverse events reported by 10% or more of patients in any group revealed a statistically higher rate of somnolence, weight gain, increased appetite, dry mouth, and asthenia with either olanzapine or OFC compared to placebo.

Recent data has also been released describing the maintenance effects of olanzapine as compared to lithium over a 12-month period (Tohen *et al.*, 2005). This was the first double-blind, controlled trial to investigate the ability of an atypical antipsychotic to prevent the recurrence of bipolar disorder in comparison with an active treatment. Patients who were recently manic received open-label co-treatment with olanzapine and lithium for 6–12 weeks ($N = 543$). Those meeting remission criteria were randomly assigned to double-blind maintenance treatment with either olanzapine ($N = 217$) or lithium ($N = 214$). Symptomatic recurrence for either mania or depression occurred in 30.0% of olanzapine-treated and 38.8% of lithium-treated patients. Significantly fewer patients in the olanzapine arm experienced recurrence of manic or mixed episodes in comparison to the lithium arm. However, olanzapine was unable to separate from placebo with regard to prophylaxis against a depressive recurrence.

Lamotrigine

The first randomized, parallel-group, placebo-controlled trial to evaluate any monotherapy treatment in bipolar depression utilized lamotrigine and was published by Calabrese and colleagues (1999). Currently, two published placebo-controlled monotherapy trials exist examining the use of lamotrigine in the acute treatment of depressed bipolar patients (Frye *et al.*, 2000; Calabrese *et al.*, 1999).

The first study evaluated the efficacy and safety of two dosages of lamotrigine in 195 patients with bipolar I disorder experiencing a major depressive episode. Adult outpatients were randomized to monotherapy treatment with lamotrigine 50 mg/day ($N = 66$), lamotrigine 200 mg/day ($N = 63$), or placebo ($N = 66$) for 7 weeks. Lamotrigine 200 mg/day was observed to be statistically superior to placebo using LOCF analysis on the HAM-D item 1 (core symptom of depression – depressed mood), MADRS total score, and the CGI-S and CGI-I subscale scores compared to placebo. Rate of response defined as a 50% reduction in MADRS total score was significantly greater in the lamotrigine 200 mg/day group (54%) and lamotrigine 50 mg/day group (48%) as compared to placebo (29%; $p < 0.05$ versus placebo). Only the lamotrigine 200 mg/day group was statistically superior to placebo at treatment endpoint on the CGI-I using LOCF ($p < 0.05$), though the lamotrigine 50 mg/day group approached statistical significance ($p < 0.1$). The most common adverse event in this trial was headache which was also the only event observed significantly more frequently in the lamotrigine groups than the placebo group.

Lamotrigine Maintenance in Bipolar Depression

In addition to being studied for the acute relief of bipolar depression, the efficacy of lamotrigine has also been examined in comparison to lithium and placebo for the maintenance treatment of patients with bipolar I disorder who had recently experienced a depressive episode ($N = 966$) (Calabrese *et al.*, 2003). Subjects received open-label lamotrigine (target dose 200 mg/day with a minimum dose of 100 mg/day) adjunctively or as monotherapy for a period of 8–16 weeks. Concomitant psychotropic drugs were gradually withdrawn, and patients stabilized on open-label treatment ($N = 463$) were then randomly assigned to lamotrigine (50, 200, or 400 mg/day; $N = 221$), lithium (0.8–1.1 mEq/l; $N = 121$), or placebo ($N = 121$) monotherapy for up to 18 months. The primary efficacy measure was the time to intervention for any mood (manic, hypomanic, mixed, or depressive) episode. Analysis of overall survival in the study revealed median times to treatment intervention were 46 days for placebo, 86 days for lithium, and 92 days for lamotrigine. Both lamotrigine and lithium were significantly superior to placebo in this regard. In those patients who required intervention for recurrence of mood symptoms, interventions for depressive symptoms predominated over manic symptoms in nearly a 3 : 1 ratio. Lamotrigine was significantly more effective than placebo at delaying intervention for depressive symptoms. In contrast, lithium was superior to placebo in delaying intervention for manic symptoms.

Analysis of median survival data demonstrated a significantly prolonged survival on all measures except time to intervention for an emerging manic or hypomanic episode in the lamotrigine 200 mg/day group. No significant change in mean score for suicide as assessed by the HAM-D was observed in the double-blind phase. The most common treatment-emergent adverse event occurring during the study was headache and the incidence was similar across all three treatment groups. The incidence of rash was significantly higher in the lamotrigine groups (7%) compared with the placebo group. One case of mild Stevens–Johnson syndrome was reported in a patient on open-label lamotrigine. Both tremor and somnolence were significantly elevated in the lithium group compared with placebo.

A similar trial to the maintenance study described in recently depressed patients was also undertaken in patients with bipolar I disorder who were recently manic or hypomanic (Bowden *et al.*, 2003). Both lamotrigine and lithium were superior to placebo in delaying time to intervention for any mood episode. Lamotrigine, but not lithium, was superior when compared to placebo at prolonging the time to a depressive episode. In contrast, lithium, but not lamotrigine, was superior to placebo at prolonging time to a manic, hypomanic, or mixed episode. The complementary pattern of results between this study and the one enrolling recently depressed patients suggests that the prophylactic efficacy of lamotrigine and lithium is not contingent on the phase of the most recent mood episode.

Putative Agents for Bipolar Depression

A number of studies enrolling smaller numbers of subjects with bipolar depression have been published involving a myriad of drug classes and novel mechanisms of action (Anand *et al.*, 2005; Davis *et al.*, 2005; Guelti & Calabrese, 2005; Zarate *et al.*, 2005; Goldberg *et al.*, 2004; Shelton & Stahl, 2004; Zarate *et al.*, 2004; Nahas *et al.*, 2003; McIntyre *et al.*, 2002; Winsberg *et al.*, 2001) (Table 1). The anticonvulsant topiramate and the non-SSRI antidepressant bupropion Sustained Release (SR) were studied over 8 weeks as add-on therapy to mood stabilizers in a single-blind (rater blind) fashion for the treatment of bipolar depression (McIntyre *et al.*, 2002). The percentage of responders was comparable for both topiramate (56%) and bupropion SR (59%). A significantly higher rate of sleeping difficulty was found in the bupropion-treated group than topiramate group (28% versus 16%). Weight loss was observed in both groups, but the topiramate group experienced a significantly greater mean weight loss, 5.8 kg with topiramate versus 1.2 kg in the bupropion SR group ($p = 0.061$ and $p = 0.043$, respectively).

Two studies have examined the use of pramipexole, a dopamine D2/D3 receptor agonist, in the treatment of bipolar depression. Pramipexole ($N = 10$) was compared to placebo ($N = 11$) in a group of bipolar II patients on therapeutic levels of a mood stabilizer and showed statistically higher response rates in the pramipexole group (Zarate *et al.*, 2004). In another study, pramipexole augmentation was assessed in patients with treatment-resistant bipolar depression (bipolar I = 15, bipolar II = 7) and revealed a higher percentage of responders in the pramipexole

Table 1. **Studies Addressing the Depressed Phase of Bipolar Disorder**

AUTHOR STUDY DURATION STUDY DESIGN	TREATMENTS	N-VALUE	RESPONSE (%)	REMISSION (%)	COMPLETION (%) (COMPLETED/ENROLLED)	EFFECT SIZE	SIDE-EFFECTS
Calabrese et al. (2005) 8 weeks	QUE	BP I = 360 BP II = 182	58 (600, 300 mg/day)[a] (600, 300 mg/day)[b]	52.9 (600, 300 mg/day)[a] (600, 30C mg/day)[b]	54 (98/180, 600 mg/day) 67 (121/181, 300 mg/day)	0.81 (600 mg/day) 0.67 (300 mg/day)	Dry mouth, sedation, somnolence, dizziness, weight gain, and constipation
Acute monotherapy	PBO		36.1 $p < 0.001$	28.4 $p < 0.001$	59 (107/181)		
Tohen et al. (2003) 8 weeks	OLZ OFC	BP I = 833	39.0[a] 56.1 $p = 0.02$, OLZ $p < 0.001$, OFC	32.8[b] 48.8 $p = 0.02$, OLZ $p < 0.001$, OFC	48 (179/370) 64 (55/86)	0.32 0.68	OLZ: somnolence, increased appetite, weight gain, asthenia
Acute monotherapy	PBO		30.4	24.5	38 (145/377)		OFC: asthenia, weight gain
Calabrese et al. (2003) 7 weeks	LTG	BP I = 195	48.0 (50 mg/day)[a] 54.0 (200 mg/day)	N/A	65 (43/66, 50 mg/day) 71 (45/63, 200 mg/day)	N/A	Headache
Acute monotherapy	PBO		29.0 $p < 0.05$		71 (47/66)		
Zarate et al. (2004) 6 weeks	PRM PBO	BP II = 21	60[a] 9 $p = 0.02$	40[b] 9 $p = 0.149$ (N/S)	90 (9/10) 90 (10/11)	N/A	Tremor
Add-on to lithium or divalproex							

(Continued)

Table 1. **(Continued)**

AUTHOR STUDY DURATION STUDY DESIGN	TREATMENTS	N-VALUE	RESPONSE (%)	REMISSION (%)	COMPLETION (%) (COMPLETED/ ENROLLED)	EFFECT SIZE	SIDE-EFFECTS
Goldberg et al. (2004) 6 weeks	PRM	BP I, II = 22	67[c]	58[d]	83 (10/12)	N/A	Nausea
	PBO		20	10	60 (6/10)		
Add-on to current mood stabilizer			p = 0.04	p = N/A			
Davis et al. (2004) 8 weeks	VPA	BP I = 25	N/A	46[e]	46 (6/13)	0.5	N/A
	PBO			25	50 (6/12)		
Acute monotherapy							
Winsberg et al. (2000) 12 weeks	VPA	BP II = 19	63[c]	63[e]	89 (17/19)	N/A	sedation, hair loss, diarrhea
				p = (N/S)			
Open-label acute monotherapy							
Shelton & Stahl (2004) 12 weeks	PAR + PBO	BP I, II=30	20[c]	20[d]	80 (8/10)	0.472	appetite increase, weight gain, diarrhea, somnolence, sexual dysfunction
	RIS + PBO		30	10	50 (5/10)	0.386	
Add-on to current mood stabilizer	PAR + RIS		30	30	60 (6/10)	0.463	
			p = N/S	p = N/S			

Study / design	Treatment	Diagnosis (n), %	p-value	Response / score	Response rate	Dropout	Side effects
Zarate *et al.* (2005) 8 weeks Open-label add-on to lithium	RLZ PBO	BP I, II = 14 50[a]		50[b]	57 (8/14)	N/A	Asymptomatic increase in liver function tests
McIntyre *et al.* (2002) 8 weeks Add-on (single-blind) to current mood stabilizer	TOP BUP	BP I, II = 36 56[c] 59	$p = 0.04$, TOP $p = 0.03$, BUP	24.8[d] 27.5 p = N/A	55.5 (10/18) 72.2 (13/18)	N/A	weight loss, paresthesia, tremor, insomnia, sweating, blurred vision
Anand *et al.* (2005) 8 weeks Open-label add-on to current mood stabilizer	ZON	BP I, II = 10 62.5[c]		N/A	80 (8/10)	N/A	rash, paresthesia, increased urinary frequency

Abbreviations: BUP: bupropion; LTG: lamotrigine; N/A: data not available; N/S: not statistically significant; OFC: olanzapine–fluoxetine combination; OLZ: olanzapine; PAR: paroxetine; PBO: placebo; PRM: pramipexole; QUE: quetiapine; RIS: risperidone; RLZ: riluzole; TOP: topiramate; VPA: divalproex sodium; ZON: zonisamide.
[a]Defined as $\geq$ 50% reduction in MADRS score; [b]Defined as $\geq$ 50% reduction in HAM-D score; [c]Defined as MADRS score $\leq$ 12; [d]Defined as HAM-D score $\leq$ 7; [e]Defined as HAM-D score $\leq$ 9.

group when compared with placebo (67% versus 20%) (Goldberg *et al.*, 2004). Both studies were small but suggest pramipexole may be useful as an adjunctive agent in the treatment of bipolar depression warranting more large-scale trials.

A 12-week open trial of divalproex in medication-naïve and mood-stabilizer-naïve bipolar II depression found that divalproex was well tolerated and that 63% of subjects responded (>50% decrease in HAM-D score) (Winsberg *et al.*, 2001). There was a trend towards a higher rate of antidepressant response to divalproex in medication-naïve patients (82%) compared to mood-stabilizer-naïve patients (38%). The clinical efficacy of divalproex was also tested in a placebo-controlled study ($N = 25$) in primarily male outpatients with bipolar I depression (Davis *et al.*, 2005). Using repeated measures analysis of variance (ANOVA) with LOCF, divalproex was more effective than placebo at improving symptoms of depression and anxiety.

Agomelatine, a melatonin receptor agonist with 5-hydroxytryptamine (serotonin) (5-HT_{2C}) antagonist properties, was added to lithium or valproate in an open-label study of bipolar depression (Guelti & Calabrese, 2005). Patients treated with lithium ($N = 14$) and valproate ($N = 7$) for at least 6 months, and who continued to suffer from depressive symptoms (HAMD $\geqslant 18$) received addition of agomelatine for 6 weeks. After 6 weeks of treatment, 81% of patients met response criteria. Eleven (52%) patients continued in an extension phase for up to 1 year. Agomelatine was well tolerated during the 6 weeks of treatment, though two cases of mania and one case of hypomania occurred during the 1-year extension period.

The glutamate modulating agent riluzole has been tested in an open-label, 8-week add-on study for depressed bipolar subjects (Zarate *et al.*, 2005). After being treated for 4 weeks with lithium, subjects who continued to have an MADRS score $\geqslant 20$ ($N = 14$) received riluzole up to 200 mg/day. Preliminary results were promising as analysis revealed a significant treatment effect with 50% of patients entering into remission upon completion of the trial.

A pilot study was performed using repetitive transcranial magnetic stimulation (rTMS) in patients with bipolar depression (Nahas *et al.*, 2003). A total of 23 patients (bipolar I depressed = 12, bipolar II depressed = 9, bipolar I mixed = 2) were randomly assigned to receive either daily left prefrontal rTMS (5 Hz, 110% motor threshold, 8 s on, 22 s off, over 20 min) or sham treatment for 2 weeks. No statistically significant difference was seen between the two groups in the number of antidepressant responders.

Translation into Clinical Practice

Bipolar disorder is a chronic, recurrent disease associated with significant morbidity and mortality, especially in the depressed phase of the illness. A review of trial-based advances support the efficacy of lamotrigine for the acute- and long-term treatment of bipolar I depression through adequately powered, placebo-controlled trials in both a 7-week acute study (Calabrese *et al.*, 1999) and two 18-month maintenance studies (Bowden *et al.*, 2003; Calabrese *et al.*, 2003). Considerable evidence also exists for the efficacy of lithium in the maintenance treatment of bipolar disorder, although lithium was not shown to be beneficial in delaying the relapse time to depression using survival analytic methods, suggesting that lithium is more effective to prevent manic relapse than depressive relapse. Early studies of lithium in bipolar depression have noted an advantage over placebo. However, the majority of these trials followed a crossover design in which subjects received lithium for short time intervals prior to abrupt discontinuation upon crossover to the placebo phase (Zornberg & Pope, 1993). This methodology may have contributed to a worse outcome with placebo treatment as the risk of recurrence is now known to increase when lithium is rapidly discontinued (Suppes *et al.*, 1991). Despite these limitations, lithium has been proven to delay the time to intervention for any mood episode in bipolar disorder in two 18-month studies (Bowden *et al.*, 2003; Calabrese *et al.*, 2003) and demonstrates antidepressant effects that are more prominent when serum levels are maintained >0.8 mEq/l (Nemeroff *et al.*, 2001).

The atypical antipsychotic olanzapine in monotherapy has also been shown to significantly improve depressive symptoms in patients with bipolar depression compared to placebo although the statistical effect size was relatively small (Tohen *et al.*, 2003). The OFC proved more effective than olanzapine or placebo alone and carried a moderately large effect size. Due to these positive findings, OFC was approved by the FDA in 2003 for the acute treatment of bipolar depression. Data from a head-to-head comparison of olanzapine and lithium appears to indicate that olanzapine works more like lithium than lamotrigine, as it prevents manic relapse more than depressive relapse (Tohen *et al.*, 2005). Quetiapine monotherapy demonstrated significant antidepressant effects in a group of bipolar I and II patients including those with features of rapid cycling (Calabrese *et al.*, 2005), but had a much larger effect size (1.09 and 0.91 for the 600- and 300-mg/day doses) in the treatment of bipolar I depression compared with olanzapine (0.32). Since there is no long-term data available for quetiapine in bipolar depression, it is difficult to determine whether quetiapine will work like lamotrigine. Quetiapine separated from 9 of 10 MADRS items including suicidal ideation, indicating quetiapine may be especially useful for those with severe depression. Due to the concern of metabolic syndrome from atypical antipsychotics, this drug class was recommended as first line with an antidepressant only in patients with psychotic depression (Keck *et al.*, 2004). However, it should be noted that the quetiapine data was not available when the expert consensus was conducted. It is possible that quetiapine will become a first-line agent for the acute treatment of bipolar depression, given the encouraging results from BOLDER II, the recently completed replication study.

When analyzing individual MADRS items between trials, only OFC, as opposed to olanzapine monotherapy, showed statistically significant improvement in core mood items such as apparent sadness, reported sadness, and inability to feel. However, the study of quetiapine monotherapy produced a significant improvement in all of the core mood symptoms of depression. Furthermore, both doses of quetiapine were roughly twice as effective as placebo in reducing suicidal ideation, providing evidence that quetiapine possesses inherent antidepressant properties. In the olanzapine study, change in suicidal thoughts was not statistically different compared to placebo in either the olanzapine monotherapy or OFC groups.

The approval of OFC for the management of acute bipolar I depression offers clinicians a first-line agent with proven short-term efficacy and safety. Initial treatment with OFC is reasonable; however, clinicians must remain vigilant for the emergence of significant weight gain or metabolic abnormalities associated with olanzapine. Lamotrigine has a role for the treatment of acute depressive episodes and given its more robust efficacy in the prophylaxis against depressive relapse, should be considered as a potential cornerstone in management. The validation of BOLDER I by BOLDER II results will likely lead to the approval of quetiapine for acute bipolar I and II depression. Since quetiapine is also efficacious for acute mania, it would seem that at present it possesses uniquely strong bimodal attributes for bipolar disorder. The combination of quetiapine with lamotrigine offers potentially great advantage in both the acute management of either bipolar mania or depression with benefits likely persisting into the continuation and maintenance phase. Although strong evidence exists for both lithium and divalproex in the maintenance treatment of bipolar disorder, it would seem that these agents should be considered secondary mood stabilizers in terms of preventing depressive relapses or treating acute bipolar depression.

Limitations

Apart from the positive effects on mood and reduction of suicidal thoughts, specific limitations should be appreciated in the BOLDER study presented in this review. Nearly half of participants taking 600 mg/day of quetiapine (46%) did not complete the 8-week trial. The most common reasons for withdrawal from the study were adverse events in the quetiapine groups (26.1% taking 600 mg/day and 16.0% taking 300 mg/day) and lack of efficacy in the placebo group (13.3%). Sedation was particularly prominent in both quetiapine groups affecting nearly one-third of participants (32.2% and 29.6%) as compared to placebo (6.1%). Weight gain must also be watched for, since despite a modest mean weight gain of 1.6 kg occurring in patients taking 600 mg/day of quetiapine as compared to 1.0 kg in the 300 mg/day group and 0.2 kg in the placebo group, the proportion of quetiapine-treated patients with significant weight change (gaining >7% of initial body weight) was greater than placebo. Similarly, a high rate of somnolence, weight gain, and increased appetite was observed in the olanzapine and OFC groups being treated for bipolar depression.

Hyperphagia and hypersomnia are symptoms of depression and constitute part of the criteria for atypical depression. Given that cross-sectional studies show atypical depression to be more common among patients with bipolar II disorder than unipolar disorder (Benazzi, 2000; Perugi *et al.*, 1998), an agent that could further potentiate weight gain and sedation may hinder long-term effectiveness in bipolar depression treatment. In the BOLDER study, patients with bipolar II disorder did not achieve a significant reduction in MADRS scores compared to placebo at the final assessment. This study may have been underpowered to detect a difference in subjects with bipolar II disorder. However, the incidence of bipolar II disorder and bipolar spectrum conditions is greater than bipolar I disorder (Benazzi, 2001; Angst, 1998). As many as 30–55% of all major depressions conform to a bipolar II pattern or its derivative reported in both academic centers and outpatient clinics (Akiskal *et al.*, 2000). Future studies should seek to enroll patients with bipolar conditions who have not necessarily experienced full criteria for mania, as these patients are frequently encountered in naturalistic settings.

Summary

Treatment guidelines for the management of bipolar depression have typically called for use of a mood stabilizer alone or in combination with an antidepressant. Unimodal antidepressant therapy in patients with bipolar depression should be avoided secondary to the risk of increasing relapse rates (Prien *et al.*, 1984) and inducing mania and cycle acceleration (Altshuler *et al.*, 1995). Even in patients taking mood stabilizers, antidepressants have not been shown to reduce the length of depressive episodes (Frankle *et al.*, 2002). Recent evidence substantiates the use of the atypical antipsychotics quetiapine or olanzapine as initial monotherapy for bipolar depression. No published bipolar depression studies currently exist for the atypical antipsychotics risperidone, ziprasidone, aripiprazole, or clozapine. Maintenance treatment for the prevention of depressive episodes supports the use of lamotrigine monotherapy.

Further research is warranted in discovering innovative agents to treat not only the acute phase of bipolar depression, but to prevent depressive episodes in an illness characterized by frequent relapse and recurrence. Limited investigations have assessed the continuation and maintenance treatment of bipolar disorder with atypical antipsychotics. Olanzapine has been studied for the longest duration, in a 12-month trial in comparison to lithium (Tohen *et al.*, 2005). In continuation studies involving aripiprazole (Keck *et al.*, 2006), quetiapine (McIntyre *et al.*, 2005), or risperidone (Smulevich *et al.*, 2005) for bipolar disorder, none has exceeded 6 months duration. Furthermore, no continuation or maintenance study has evaluated the use of an atypical antipsychotic in patients presenting with an index episode of depression.

Additional studies should be undertaken to determine more optimal treatments for bipolar depression that work rapidly, are well tolerated, and maintain efficacy beyond the range of 8 weeks assessed in the short-term studies of atypical antipsychotics. Greater emphasis should also be placed on managing depression in bipolar II and subsyndromal bipolar spectrum states. Monotherapy is often inadequate and multiple-drug regimens have become standardized in the treatment of bipolar disorder (Zarate & Quiroz, 2003). Controlled combination studies in bipolar depression need to be implemented. The question also exists if other atypical antipsychotics other than olanzapine and quetiapine likewise possess inherent antidepressant properties. Attention to these variables will address the unmet need which exists for the optimal management of bipolar depression. This will require greater investment in outcomes research and drug development targeting this challenging disorder.

References

Practice guideline for the treatment of patients with bipolar disorder (revision) (2002). *American Journal of Psychiatry*, 159 (Suppl. 4), 1–50.

Akiskal, H.S., Bourgeois, M.L., Angst, J., Post, R., Moller, H., & Hirschfeld, R. (2000). Re-evaluating the prevalence of and diagnostic composition within the broad clinical spectrum of bipolar disorders. *Journal of Affective Disorders*, 59 (Suppl. 1), S5–S30.

Altshuler, L.L., Post, R.M., Leverich, G.S., Mikalauskas, K., Rosoff, A., & Ackerman, L. (1995). Antidepressant-induced mania and cycle acceleration: a controversy revisited. *American Journal of Psychiatry*, 152, 1130–1138.

Anand, A., Bukhari, L., Jennings, S.A., Lee, C., Kamat, M., Shekhar, A., Nurnberger Jr., J.I., & Lightfoot, J. (2005). A preliminary open-label study of zonisamide treatment for bipolar depression in 10 patients. *Journal of Clinical Psychiatry*, 66, 195–198.

Angst, J. (1998). The emerging epidemiology of hypomania and bipolar II disorder. *Journal of Affective Disorders*, 50, 143–151.

Baron, M., Gershon, E.S., Rudy, V., Jonas, W.Z., & Buchsbaum, M. (1975). Lithium carbonate response in depression. Prediction by unipolar/bipolar illness, average-evoked response, catechol-O-methyl transferase, and family history. *Archives of General Psychiatry*, 32, 1107–1111.

Benazzi, F. (2000). Depression with DSM-IV atypical features: a marker for bipolar II disorder. *European Archives of Psychiatry and Clinical Neuroscience*, 250, 53–55.

Benazzi, F. (2001). Prevalence and clinical correlates of residual depressive symptoms in bipolar II disorder. *Psychotherapy and Psychosomatics*, 70, 232–238.

Bowden, C.L., Calabrese, J.R., Sachs, G., Yatham, L.N., Asghar, S.A., Hompland, M., Montgomery, P., Earl, N., Smoot, T.M., & DeVeaugh-Geiss, J. (2003). A placebo-controlled 18-month trial of lamotrigine and lithium maintenance treatment in recently manic or hypomanic patients with bipolar I disorder. *Archives of General Psychiatry*, 60, 392–400.

Calabrese, J. (October 24, 2005). Quetiapine monotherapy for the treatment of bipolar depression: the BOLDER II study. *Presented at the 2005 annual meeting of the European College of Neuropsychopharmacology* (Amsterdam, The Netherlands).

Calabrese, J.R., Bowden, C.L., Sachs, G.S., Ascher, J.A., Monaghan, E., & Rudd, G.D. (1999). A double-blind placebo-controlled study of lamotrigine monotherapy in outpatients with bipolar I depression. Lamictal 602 Study Group. *Journal of Clinical Psychiatry*, 60, 79–88.

Calabrese, J.R., Bowden, C.L., Sachs, G., Yatham, L.N., Behnke, K., Mehtonen, O.P., Montgomery, P., Ascher, J., Paska, W., Earl, N., & DeVeaugh-Geiss, J. (2003). A placebo-controlled 18-month trial of lamotrigine and lithium maintenance treatment in recently depressed patients with bipolar I disorder. *Journal of Clinical Psychiatry*, 64, 1013–1024.

Calabrese, J.R., Hirschfeld, R.M., Frye, M.A., & Reed, M.L. (2004). Impact of depressive symptoms compared with manic symptoms in bipolar disorder: results of a U.S. community-based sample. *Journal of Clinical Psychiatry*, 65, 1499–1504.

Calabrese, J.R., Keck Jr., P.E., Macfadden, W., Minkwitz, M., Ketter, T.A., Weisler, R.H., Cutler, A.J., McCoy, R., Wilson, E., & Mullen, J. (2005). A randomized, double-blind, placebo-controlled trial of quetiapine in the treatment of bipolar I or II depression. *American Journal of Psychiatry*, 162, 1351–1360.

Cohn, J.B., Collins, G., Ashbrook, E., & Wernicke, J.F. (1989). A comparison of fluoxetine imipramine and placebo in patients with bipolar depressive disorder. *International Clinical Psychopharmacology*, 4, 313–322.

Davis, L.L., Bartolucci, A., & Petty, F. (2005). Divalproex in the treatment of bipolar depression: a placebo-controlled study. *Journal of Affective Disorders*, 85, 259–266.

Dilsaver, S.C., Chen, Y.W., Swann, A.C., Shoaib, A.M., Tsai-Dilsaver, Y., & Krajewski, K.J. (1997). Suicidality, panic disorder and psychosis in bipolar depression, depressive-mania and pure-mania. *Psychiatry Research*, 73, 47–56.

Frankle, W.G., Perlis, R.H., Deckersbach, T., Grandin, L.D., Gray, S.M., Sachs, G.S., & Nierenberg, A.A. (2002). Bipolar depression: relationship between episode length and antidepressant treatment. *Psychological Medicine*, 32, 1417–1423.

Frye, M.A., Ketter, T.A., Kimbrell, T.A., Dunn, R.T., Speer, A.M., Osuch, E.A., Luckenbaugh, D.A., Cora-Ocatelli, G., Leverich, G.S., & Post, R.M. (2000). A placebo-controlled study of lamotrigine and gabapentin monotherapy in refractory mood disorders. *Journal of Clinical Psychopharmacology*, 20, 607–614.

Goldberg, J.F., Burdick, K.E., & Endick, C.J. (2004). Preliminary randomized, double-blind, placebo-controlled trial of pramipexole added to mood stabilizers for treatment-resistant bipolar depression. *American Journal of Psychiatry*, 161, 564–566.

Goodwin, F.K., Murphy, D.L., & Bunney Jr., W.E. (1969). Lithium-carbonate treatment in depression and mania. A longitudinal double-blind study. *Archives of General Psychiatry*, 21, 486–496.

Guelti, J., & Calabrese, J. (2005). Efficacy and safety of the new antidepressant agomelatine in combination with mood stabilizer in bipolar I patients with a major depressive episode. *Bipolar Disorders*, 7 (Suppl. 2), 63.

Himmelhoch, J.M., Thase, M.E., Mallinger, A.G., & Houck, P. (1991). Tranylcypromine versus imipramine in anergic bipolar depression. *American Journal of Psychiatry*, 148, 910–916.

Hlastala, S.A., Frank, E., Mallinger, A.G., Thase, M.E., Ritenour, A.M., & Kupfer, D.J. (1997). Bipolar depression: an underestimated treatment challenge. *Depression and Anxiety*, 5, 73–83.

Judd, L.L., Akiskal, H.S., Schettler, P.J., Endicott, J., Maser, J., Solomon, D.A., Leon, A.C., Rice, J.A., & Keller, M.B. (2002). The long-term natural history of the weekly symptomatic status of bipolar I disorder. *Archives of General Psychiatry*, 59, 530–537.

Keck, P.E., Perlis, R.H., Otto, M.W., Carpenter, D., Ross, R., & Docherty, J.P. (2004). *The Expert Consensus Guideline Series: Treatment of Bipolar Disorder 2004. Postgraduate Medicine Special Report*, December 1–19.

Keck, P.E. Jr., Calabrese J.R., McQuade, R.D., Carson, W.H., Carlson, B.X., Rollin, L.M., Marcus, R.N., & Sanchez, R. (2006). A randomized, double-blind, placebo-controlled 26-week trial of aripiprazole in recently manic patients with bipolar II disorder. *Journal of Clinical Psychiatry*, 67, 626–637.

McIntyre, R.S., Mancini, D.A., McCann, S., Srinivasan, J., Sagman, D., & Kennedy, S.H. (2002). Topiramate versus bupropion SR when added to mood stabilizer therapy for the depressive phase of bipolar disorder: a preliminary single-blind study. *Bipolar Disorders*, 4, 207–213.

McIntyre, R.S., Brecher, M., Paulsson, B., Huizar, K., & Mullen, J. (2005). Quetiapine or haloperidol as monotherapy for bipolar mania – a 12-week, double-blind, randomised, parallel-group, placebo-controlled trial. *European Neuropsychopharmacology*, 15, 573–585.

Nahas, Z., Kozel, F.A., Li, X., Anderson, B., & George, M.S. (2003). Left prefrontal transcranial magnetic stimulation (TMS) treatment of depression in bipolar affective disorder: a pilot study of acute safety and efficacy. *Bipolar Disorders*, 5, 40–47.

Nemeroff, C.B., Evans, D.L., Gyulai, L., Sachs, G.S., Bowden, C.L., Gergel, I.P., Oakes, R., & Pitts, C.D. (2001). Double-blind, placebo-controlled comparison of imipramine and paroxetine in the treatment of bipolar depression. *American Journal of Psychiatry*, 158, 906–912.

Perugi, G., Akiskal, H.S., Lattanzi, L., Cecconi, D., Mastrocinque, C., Patronelli, A., Vignoli, S., & Bemi, E. (1998). The high prevalence of "soft" bipolar (II) features in atypical depression. *Comprehensive Psychiatry*, 39, 63–71.

Post, R.M. (2005). The impact of bipolar depression. *Journal of Clinical Psychiatry*, 66 (Suppl. 5), 5–10.

Post, R.M., Uhde, T.W., Roy-Byrne, P.P., & Joffe, R.T. (1986). Antidepressant effects of carbamazepine. *American Journal of Psychiatry*, 143, 29–34.

Prien, R.F., Kupfer, D.J., Mansky, P.A., Small, J.G., Tuason, V.B., Voss, C.B., & Johnson, W.E. (1984). Drug therapy in the prevention of recurrences in unipolar and bipolar affective disorders. Report of the NIMH Collaborative Study Group comparing lithium carbonate, imipramine, and a lithium carbonate – imipramine combination. *Archives of General Psychiatry*, 41, 1096–1104.

Sachs, G.S., Lafer, B., Stoll, A.L., Banov, M., Thibault, A.B., Tohen, M., & Rosenbaum, J.F. (1994). A double-blind trial of bupropion versus desipramine for bipolar depression. *Journal of Clinical Psychiatry*, 55, 391–393.

Shelton, R.C., & Stahl, S.M. (2004). Risperidone and paroxetine given singly and in combination for bipolar depression. *Journal of Clinical Psychiatry*, 65, 1715–1719.

Smulevich, A.B., Khanna, S., Eerdekens, M., Karcher, K., Kramer, M., & Grossman, F. (2005). Acute and continuation risperidone monotherapy in bipolar mania: a 3-week placebo-controlled trial followed by a 9-week double-blind trial of risperidone and haloperidol. *European Neuropsychopharmacology*, 15, 75–84.

Suppes, T., Baldessarini, R.J., Faedda, G.L., & Tohen, M. (1991). Risk of recurrence following discontinuation of lithium treatment in bipolar disorder. *Archives of General Psychiatry*, 48, 1082–1088.

Suppes, T., Dennehy, E.B., Hirschfeld, R.M., Altshuler, L.L., Bowden, C.L., Calabrese, J.R., Crismon, M.L., Ketter, T.A., Sachs, G.S., & Swann, A.C. (2005). The Texas implementation of medication algorithms: update to the algorithms for treatment of bipolar I disorder. *Journal of Clinical Psychiatry*, 66, 870–886.

Tohen, M., Vieta, E., Calabrese, J., Ketter, T.A., Sachs, G., Bowden, C., Mitchell, P.B., Centorrino, F., Risser, R., Baker, R.W., Evans, A.R., Beymer, K., Dube, S., Tollefson, G.D., & Breier, A. (2003). Efficacy of olanzapine and olanzapine–fluoxetine combination in the treatment of bipolar I depression. *Archives of General Psychiatry*, 60, 1079–1088.

Tohen, M., Greil, W., Calabrese, J.R., Sachs, G.S., Yatham, L.N., Oerlinghausen, B.M., Koukopoulos, A., Cassano, G.B., Grunze, H., Licht, R.W., Dell'Osso, L., Evans, A.R., Risser, R., Baker, R.W., Crane, H., Dossenbach, M.R., & Bowden, C.L. (2005). Olanzapine versus lithium in the maintenance treatment of bipolar disorder: a 12-month, randomized, double-blind, controlled clinical trial. *American Journal of Psychiatry*, 162, 1281–1290.

Winsberg, M.E., DeGolia, S.G., Strong, C.M., & Ketter, T.A. (2001). Divalproex therapy in medication-naive and mood-stabilizer-naive bipolar II depression. *Journal of Affective Disorders*, 67, 207–212.

Zarate Jr., C.A., & Quiroz, J.A. (2003). Combination treatment in bipolar disorder: a review of controlled trials. *Bipolar Disorders*, 5, 217–225.

Zarate Jr., C.A., Payne, J.L., Singh, J., Quiroz, J.A., Luckenbaugh, D.A., Denicoff, K.D., Charney, D.S., & Manji, H.K. (2004). Pramipexole for bipolar II depression: a placebo-controlled proof of concept study. *Biological Psychiatry*, 56, 54–60.

Zarate Jr., C.A., Quiroz, J.A., Singh, J.B., Denicoff, K.D., De Jesus, G., Luckenbaugh, D.A., Charney, D.S., & Manji, H.K. (2005). An open-label trial of the glutamate-modulating agent riluzole in combination with lithium for the treatment of bipolar depression. *Biological Psychiatry*, 57, 430–432.

Zornberg, G.L., & Pope Jr., H.G. (1993). Treatment of depression in bipolar disorder: new directions for research. *Journal of Clinical Psychopharmacology*, 13, 397–408.

Progress in Neurotherapeutics and Neuropsychopharmacology, 2:1, 213–224 © 2007 Cambridge University Press
DOI: 10.1017/S1748232106000152   Printed in the United Kingdom

Symptomatic Remission in Patients with Bipolar Mania: Results from a Double-Blind, Placebo-Controlled Trial of Risperidone Monotherapy

----

Srihari Gopal

Johnson & Johnson Pharmaceutical Research and Development, LLC, Titusville, NJ, USA;
E-mail: SGopal2@PRDUS.JNJ.com

John L. Beyer & David C. Steffens

Department of Psychiatry and Behavioral Sciences, Duke University School of Medicine, Durham, NC, USA;
E-mail: beyer001@mc.duke.edu; steff001@mc.duke.due

Michelle L. Kramer

Johnson & Johnson Pharmaceutical Research and Development, LLC, Titusville, NJ, USA;
E-mail: mkramer@prdus.jnj.com

ABSTRACT

Background: The purpose of this analysis was to compare symptomatic remission rates between risperidone and placebo in a completed randomized controlled trial. **Design and Methods:**   Two hundred ninety (290) adult patients who met DSM-IV criteria for Bipolar I Disorder Manic or Mixed episode were randomized to flexible doses of risperidone or placebo for 3 weeks. An entry Young Mania Rating Scale (YMRS) score of > 20 was required at trial screening and baseline. Time to first onset of remission (as defined as a YMRS score of < 8)was assessed using Cox proportional hazards. Persence or absence of sustained remission was analyzed using logistic regression. Sustained remission was defined as maintaining a YMRS < 8 for the remainder of the trial or until censor. **Results:**   After adjusting for presence of psychosis, baseline YMRS, gender, number of mood cycles in the previous year and treatment, the odds of sustained remission for subjects on risperidone was 5.6 ($p < 0.0001$). Similarly the adjusted hazard or remission for subjects on rsiperidone was 4.0 ($p < 0.0001$). **Interpretaion:**   A statistically significant proportion of manic patients receiving risperidone monotherapy achieved symptomatic remission within 3 weeks as compared to placebo.

Key words: risperidone, mania, remission, bipolar.

Correspondence should be addressed to: Srihari Gopal, MD, MHS, Johnson & Johnson Pharmaceutical Research & Development, LLC, 1125 Trenton-Harbourton Road, Titusville, NJ 08560

Introduction and Overview

Throughout history bipolar disorder or manic depression has been one of the most clearly identifiable mental illnesses. Ancient Greek writers described of subjects with symptoms similar to bipolar illness and depression (Goodwin & Jamison, 1990). In 1913, Emil Kraeplin was the first to clearly delineate manic-depressive illness from other psychotic disorders. The American Psychiatric Association (APA) first designated the disease as "manic-depressive reaction" in its Diagnostic and Statistical Manual of Mental Disorders (DSM) in 1952. Currently, bipolar disorder is thought of as a collection of symptoms encompassing cycles of mania, depression, and psychosis. Current guidelines specify the following categories: Manic, Mixed, Hypomanic, Depressed, bipolar II disorder, and Cyclothymia (American Psychiatric Association, 2000).

Bipolar disorder is a chronic disease with a variety of different clinical symptoms. Patients may have inflated self-esteem, decreased need for sleep, pressured speech, racing thoughts, and/or mental distractibility. Studies of attempted suicide in bipolar patients show that 25–50% of patients attempted suicide at least once (Roy-Byrne *et al.*, 1988). The mortality rate for untreated bipolar patients is higher than most types of cardiovascular disease and many types of cancer (Goodwin & Jamison 1990).

Bipolar disorder was once thought to be relatively uncommon. Over the last several years, research has shown that the prevalence of bipolar I disorder is much higher than previously estimated: approximately 1–2% of the US population is afflicted by bipolar disorder (Weissman *et al.*, 1990).

Unfortunately, patients who have bipolar I disorder are often subject to a fairly debilitating course consisting of periods of extreme euphoria and depression. These recurring episodes have been shown to have a cumulative effect on patient functioning and recovery (Gelenberg *et al.*, 1996). The progressively worsening clinical course coupled with sub-optimal treatment options lead to a cumulative deteriorative effect on overall functioning and recovery.

Purpose of Trial

It has been postulated that achieving a clinical remission can reduce the lifetime severity of symptoms and prolong the time to relapse (Angst & Sellaro, 2000). More importantly, recent evidence has shown that patients who achieve full remission instead of mere partial symptom relief have less disability and better long-term prognosis (Judd *et al.*, 1998). Even though data from long-term follow-up studies of patients with bipolar disorder are scarce, it is important to find clinical predictors of response to treatment. Fleiss first described the life table method of analysis of survival data to determine usefulness of lithium prophylaxis in patients with bipolar disorder in 1976 (Fleiss *et al.*, 1976). The concept of remission of disease in affective disorders was first described by Frank in 1991 (Frank *et al.*, 1991).

Most current trials in psychopharmacology (including major depressive disorder and bipolar mania trials) distinguish between symptomatic responders and non-responders. Although the exact definition varies somewhat, a responder is typically defined as a ⩾50% reduction in the primary efficacy scale from baseline to endpoint. While this approach may be useful to assess relative efficacy of a reference compound, it is not particularly useful to practicing clinicians. The goal of treatment in bipolar patients is not to reduce symptoms by 50%, but instead to be symptom free (or as close to this as possible). A 50% reduction can still leave patients with residual symptoms that significantly affect functioning and are in need of treatment.

The study was undertaken to establish the efficacy and safety of risperidone monotherapy in the treatment of patients with acute mania. A *post hoc* multivariate analysis was attempted by us to establish clinical predictors of remission. Accordingly, it was also necessary to use appropriate statistical methods to identify and adjust for possible confounders in the prediction of remission.

Past clinical experience with risperidone in acute mania

To date, five randomized, double-blind placebo-controlled trials have been published utilizing risperidone in the treatment of acutely manic patients. Of these, three studies utilized risperidone monotherapy in the treatment of mania (Hirschfeld *et al.*, 2004; Khanna *et al.*, 2005; Smulevich *et al.*, 2005) and two studies involved risperidone as adjunctive therapy to mood-stabilizers (Sachs *et al.*, 2002; Yatham *et al.*, 2003).

This remission analysis focused on one of three randomized, double-blind, placebo-controlled, 3-week monotherapy trials. The study was conducted in India (Gopal *et al.*, 2005).

Clinical Trial Methods

Subjects

Adult male or female patients between the ages of 18 and 65 years who fulfilled DSM-IV criteria for bipolar disorder I manic or bipolar disorder I mixed were eligible to enter this trial.

Patients had to meet the following inclusion criteria in order to enter the study: signed informed consent, acceptable birth control for females, Young Mania Rating Scale (YMRS) score >20, and history of at least one prior manic episode. Patients who had the following conditions were excluded: schizoaffective disorder, rapid cycling bipolar disorder, borderline or antisocial personality disorder, pregnant or nursing females, unstable thyroid disorder, neuroleptic malignant syndrome, substance dependence, seizure disorder, significant suicidal/violent threat, or other serious and/or unstable illnesses.

Trial methods

This was a double-blind, parallel-group, multicenter placebo-controlled trial (protocol # RIS-IND-2). There were eight clinical sites participating in this trial from India. Initially, hospitalized patients with bipolar I disorder who were suffering a manic or mixed episode were screened for trial entry eligibility. Those who met the entry criteria entered a washout period of up to 3 days. The double-blind portion of the trial lasted 3 weeks. Patients were randomized to one of two treatment groups according to dynamic randomization procedure via interactive voice response system. The randomization was stratified according to the presence or absence of psychotic features associated with the manic episode and by center.

The treatment groups consisted of oral risperidone or placebo. Risperidone was dosed once daily and flexibly in a range of 1–6 mg/day, with a starting dose of 3 mg/day. Following randomization and the initiation of double-blind medication, a minimum of 7 full days of inpatient hospitalization was required. As early as day 8, patients could be discharged and followed as outpatients if they were believed by the investigator to be at no significant risk for suicidal or violent behavior and if their Clinical Global Impressions-Severity of Illness item (CGI-S) score was 3 (mildly ill) or less.

The antimanic efficacy of risperidone versus placebo after 3 weeks of treatment was determined primarily by the treatment group change in the YMRS scores from baseline. Most efficacy and safety assessments were made weekly although treatment-emergent adverse events and vital signs were assessed more frequently during the inpatient period and subsequently, as clinically indicated.

At the end of the treatment period, patients who completed 3 weeks of double-blind treatment were offered the opportunity to enter an open-label trial in which they received risperidone treatment for up to 9 weeks.

The following concomitant medications were allowed during the study: lorazepam for the treatment of agitation, beta-adrenergic blockers for treatment-emergent akathisia, and antiparkinsonian drugs for the treatment of Extrapyramidal Side Effects (EPS). Lorazepam dosing was limited to a maximum of 8 mg/day from days 1 to 3, 6 mg/day from days 4 to 7, and <4 mg/day from days 8 to 10. Lorazepam administration was not permitted within 8 h of a scheduled behavioral assessment.

Instruments/measures

The following instruments were used to assess efficacy and safety: YMRS, Clinical Global Impressions (CGI) Severity scale, the Global Assessment Scale (GAS), the Montgomery Asberg Depression Rating Scale (MADRS), the Positive and Negative Syndrome Scale for schizophrenia (PANSS), and the Extrapyramidal Symptoms

Rating Scale (ESRS). Investigators were trained in the use of each of these instruments and certification was required for the YMRS.

Primary and secondary outcomes

Two main statistical methods were used to test our hypothesis that risperidone treatment is associated with remission in bipolar I patients: survival analysis using Cox proportional hazards and multiple logistic regression analysis. The outcome variable of interest for the Cox model was the time to first onset of remission (YMRS < 8). The presence or absence of sustained remission (maintenance of YMRS < 8 for the trial duration) was examined using multiple logistic regression.

Analysis

The primary outcome variable tested in each statistical model was the dichotomous presence or absence of sustained remission (YMRS < 8) during all consecutive evaluations, or until time of censor. Intent-to-treat statistical (ITT) analyses were performed at the two-tailed 5% significance level. Subjects were included in the ITT population if they had at least one post-baseline assessment. Because survival analysis methods allow for varying lengths of follow-up time, we did not use any special imputation methods for missing values. All patients were censored at 21 days, or at the point of withdrawal from the trial, if earlier. All statistical analyses were performed using SAS Analyst Application 8.02, SAS Institute, Cary, NC, USA. Graphs were plotted using GraphPad Prism 3.02 for Windows, GraphPad Software, San Diego California, USA.

A 10% significance level was used to test for interactions. Univariate plots for all continuous predictor variables were used to assess for linearity. Collinearity diagnostics of tolerance, variance/inflation, and standard error were used to determine the existence of interrelationships among all of the variables. Log-minus-log survival plots were examined to assess assumptions of proportional hazards. The Cochran–Mantel–Haenszel test controlling for site was used to test for the homogeneity of odds ratios across the different investigational sites.

Results

Of the 324 patients screened for eligibility, a total of 291 patients were randomized. One subject was randomized to placebo and did not have any post-baseline assessments done. This subject was excluded from this efficacy analysis. Participants were mostly male (62%) and had a DSM-IV entry diagnosis of bipolar I disorder with psychotic features (56%). Baseline clinical characteristics and demographic data were similar for both groups. All subjects were of Indian descent except one. The mean duration of treatment was 17.9 ± 0.46 days for placebo and 19.9 ± 0.31 days in the risperidone group. The mean mode dose of risperidone used in this trial was 5.6 ± 0.08 mg/day (Table 1 and Figure 1).

Table 1. **Baseline Demographic Variables**

	PLACEBO	RISPERIDONE
Number of subjects randomized	145	146
Gender		
Male	81 (28%)	100 (34%)
Female	63 (22%)	46 (16%)
Age (years) ± SD	35.5 ± 12.3	34.7 ± 12.0
DSM-IV Diagnosis		
Manic with psychotic features	79 (27%)	84 (29%)
Manic without psychotic features	57 (20%)	58 (20%)
Mixed with psychotic features	4 (1.4%)	3 (1.0%)
Mixed without psychotic features	4 (1.4%)	1 (0.3%)
Mean # of prior manic episodes ± SD	4.8 ± 3.7	4.7 ± 4.5
Mean age at onset of bipolar disorder (years) ± SD	25.2 ± 10.4	24.6 ± 8.8
Mean age at time of first pharmacologic treatment (years) ± SD	25.4 ± 10.8	25.2 ± 9.1
Number of patients with history of treatment for substance abuse	2 (0.7%)	1 (0.3%)
Number of prior suicide attempts ± SD	0.2 ± 0.7	0.1 ± 0.5
Baseline GAS score ± SD	34.6 ± 10.3	35.2 ± 10.3
Baseline MADRS score ± SD	5.9 ± 4.5	5.1 ± 3.4
Baseline YMRS score ± SD	37.4 ± 7.9	36.9 ± 8.0

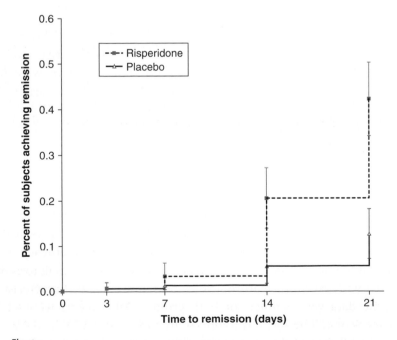

Fig. 1.
Kaplan–Meier estimates of the time to remission with risperidone or placebo.

Table 2. **Results of Statistical Analyses**

	LOGISTIC REGRESSION MODEL		COX PROPORTIONAL HAZARDS MODEL	
	ODDS RATIO (95% CI)	P VALUE (χ^2)	HAZARD RATIO (95% CI)	P VALUE (χ^2)
Unadjusted analyses				
Risperidone treatment	5.02 (2.78, 9.09)	<0.0001 (31.36)	3.68 (2.17, 6.22)	<0.0001 (23.5)
Adjusted analyses				
Risperidone treatment	5.60 (3.02, 10.40)	<0.0001 (29.85)	3.99 (2.34, 6.80)	<0.0001 (25.88)
Female gender	1.33 (0.74, 2.39)	0.34 (0.91)	1.22 (0.77, 1.94)	0.39 (0.73)
Baseline YMRS	0.99 (0.95, 1.03)	0.54 (0.38)	0.988 (0.96, 1.02)	0.41 (0.68)
Absence of psychotic features	2.08 (1.14, 3.78)	0.02 (5.69)	1.82 (1.14, 2.92)	0.013 (6.21)
# of cycles in the past year	0.96 (0.62, 1.47)	0.84 (0.04)	0.97 (0.68, 1.37)	0.84 (0.04)

Unadjusted analysis

Of the randomized population, 41.7% of subjects on risperidone and 6.2% of subjects on placebo achieved sustained remission. Similarly, 41.7% of risperidone subjects and 14.5% of placebo subjects had YMRS scores <8 at least once during the trial (unsustained remission). The risperidone treatment was significantly correlated with shorter time to remission; hazard ratio 3.7 (Table 2). Similarly, the unadjusted odds ratio for sustained remission in the risperidone group was 5.0 (Table 2). Odds ratios and hazard ratios >1 indicate that treatment with risperidone is statistically superior in achieving remission as compared to placebo.

Adjusted analyses

Our multivariate Cox model showed that risperidone treatment and absence of psychosis were significantly independent predictors of remission (adjusted hazard ratio = 1.8 and 4.0, respectively). In addition to the above two predictors, the following additional variables were added to our multivariate models: gender, baseline YMRS score, and number of manic or mixed mood cycles in the year prior to enrollment. Predictor variables were chosen *post hoc* based on the items that were believed to be of interest to practicing clinicians. Multiple logistic regression analysis confirmed that subjects treated with risperidone had significantly higher odds of sustained remission. The adjusted odds ratio for sustained remission in the risperidone group was 5.6. No significant interactions were found and only main effects were included in the multivariate models.

Influence on the Field

A total of 10 medications have been approved by the Federal Drug administration (FDA) for the treatment of acute bipolar mania. These include a metallic salt: lithium; two anticonvulsants: valproate and carbamazepine; and antipsychotics: conventional neuroleptics (chlorpromazine and haloperidol); and atypical antipsychotics: (aripiprazole, olanzapine, quetiapine, risperidone, and ziprasidone). This trial supports the effectiveness of risperidone, and the antipsychotic class of medications as effective agents for the treatment of acute bipolar mania. The use of oral risperidone as either monotherapy or adjunctive therapy in the treatment of patients with acute bipolar mania was approved by the FDA in December 2003.

The described analysis attempts to address two emerging issues facing researchers and clinicians working with patients having bipolar disorder: defining remission and predicting response.

The APA guidelines for the treatment of bipolar disorder state that the focus of acute treatment is stabilization with the eventual goal of remission (American Psychiatric Association, 2002). While this may seem apparent, defining the end-point of treatment "remission" can be difficult. Is remission the absence of mood symptoms? What if just a couple of symptoms remain (such as some questionable judgment, or a mildly elevated level of energy)? Is there a prioritized list defining those symptoms considered "major", and those considered "minor"? Should remission be defined functionally, as when the patient is able to return to work or engage in other social roles? Which roles? Or, should remission be defined at the point when the patient or family member states that he/she is "back to normal"?

In an effort to address this problem, various symptomatic scales for bipolar disorder have been developed to measure changes in the illness. In acute mania, the two most common scales are the YMRS and the Mania Rating Scale (MRS). Both have been validated as capable of capturing improvement or worsening of disease symptoms, but neither defines a number at which a patient may said to be "in remission". Indeed, since the scales may not measure all components of the experience of bipolar disorder, it is possible that a patient may score zero on the scale, but remain symptomatic from the perspective of the patient, family, and/or clinician.

The issue has been further confounded by the fact that while remission is the overall goal of the clinician and patient, it is not the goal for most published clinical trials. Rather, clinical trials are powered to demonstrate that over a defined period of time (usually 3–4 weeks for acute mania trials, and 6–8 weeks for acute depression trials) the medication is more effective than non-treatment (placebo). Superior clinical improvement versus placebo is not the same as effective remission, and should not be interpreted as such.

Why is there a disparity in goals between clinicians and clinical trialists? There are three primary issues. First, in order to receive approval from the FDA, a medication is required to show that it is safe and effective. From this viewpoint, a differentiation from placebo in symptomatic efficacy is required whereas remission is desirable but not necessary. Second, there are no agreed upon definitions of remission measured by the mood scales that consistently equate to what a clinician or patient may consider "remission". Finally, in many people's estimation, "remission" is equated with "cure". Since at this time there are no cures for bipolar disorder, it would stand to reason that remission may never be achievable and thus all medications would eventually fail.

Recently, reanalyses of many of the major clinical trials have attempted to measure clinically meaningful remission rates from mania. Although there has been no clear definition of remission in patients with bipolar mania, several of these reports defined remission as a score ≤12 on the YMRS at study endpoint. The limitation to this approach is that while many patients may no longer meet DSM-IV criteria for mania at this score, they may still exhibit disabling symptoms of mania. Nine acute mania monotherapy trials using this definition (or the similar definition of ≤10 on the MRS) have reported remission rates ranging from 27% to 61% (Tohen *et al.*, 2000; Bowden *et al.*, 2005; McIntyre *et al.*, 2005; Potkin *et al.*, 2005). In four of these trials a placebo was used with placebo remission rates reported between 20% and 36%. Interestingly, one clinical trial involving quetiapine showed significant separation on treatment response but did not show separation from placebo on remission. However, it should be remembered that the trials were not powered to demonstrate this difference; nor were they necessarily designed to demonstrate remission. Recently, a more stringent definition of remission has been proposed. Noting that a cutoff score of ≤7 on the Hamilton Depression Rating Scale (HAM-D) has been used to define remission in the unipolar depression literature, Chengappa *et al.* proposed to define remission similarly (Chengappa *et al.*, 2005). They proposed remission in acute mania trials should be defined as a total score of ≤7 on both the total YMRS and HAM-D at endpoint. This new definition was applied to two previously published olanzapine/placebo acute mania studies. Using the more standard definition (≤12 on the YMRS at study endpoint), they found the range of subjects meeting criteria for remission to be 50% for olanzapine and 27% for placebo. With the more stringent remission definition, olanzapine remained significantly superior to placebo ($p = 0.015$), but remission rates dropped to 18% for olanzapine and 7% for placebo.

Our study, using a similar but slightly different definition of remission (YMRS ≤ 8) demonstrated 41% of subjects on risperidone, and 6% of subjects on placebo-achieved remission. While these studies with the more stringent remission criteria cannot be compared directly, both suggest that some available treatments may be effective for remission of symptoms within a short period of time (3 weeks for all three studies) in a subset of patients. Longer trials may be useful to evaluate whether time impacts remission rates.

Tohen *et al.* found that approximately two-thirds of first episode manic patients achieved syndromal recovery (no longer meeting DSM-IV criteria for acute mania) within 3 months and nearly all (97.5%) achieved this status within 2 years (Tohen *et al.*, 2000). Recently, Chengappa reported further analyzes from the open, 1-year extension of the first olanzapine trial (Chengappa *et al.*, 2005). Here remission was defined using the more stringent criteria as well as adding a second criterion for sustained clinical recovery (remission for at least 8 weeks). The authors found that almost 70% of manic subjects eventually achieved remission within a year of treatment, but only 35% achieved sustained clinical recovery during that time.

The importance of this discussion about remission is reflected in the early data from the Systematic Treatment Enhancement Program for Bipolar Disorder (STEP-BD) trial. This prospective examination of bipolar disorder outcomes used a standard care pathway to evaluate effectiveness of current treatments. Recovery was defined as the presence of two or fewer syndromal features for at least 8 weeks (consistent with DSM-IV criteria for partial or full remission). Perlis *et al.* reported that 58.4% of the patients achieved recovery within the first 2 years of follow-up (Perlis *et al.*, 2006). However, the presence of residual mood symptoms early in recovery appeared to be a powerful predictor of recurrence. Perlis found that the risk of depression recurrence increased by 14% for every depressive symptom present at the time of "remission", and 20% for every manic/hypomanic symptom.

Once consensus regarding the definition and measurement of remission can be achieved, it may be possible to identify factors predicting who will respond to treatment and achieve such a remitted state. Identifying such factors may even allow for better-tailored treatments. In previous studies assessing predictors of good clinical response (usually diagnosed as ≥50% change from baseline rating scores rather than remission) disease severity, use of the active medication and absence of psychosis were identified as important, as well as good premorbid functioning, treatment compliance, absence of substance abuse, and limited dysphoric features. In our 3-week study, only treatment with the active medication (risperidone) and the absence of psychotic features predicted remission. Neither the number of prior mood cycles nor the gender was a contributor in treatment remission.

Translation to Clinical Practice

This analysis supports the importance of identifying improved methods for determining treatment response. The APA has focused on stabilization of symptoms as the primary treatment goal, with remission as a goal for the future. Thus, in acute manic states, decreasing overt symptoms of mania has been the major focus. Recent studies suggest that aggressive treatment with a goal of remission should be the target for treatment. Our study suggests that risperidone is effective to remission for up to 40% of the subjects within 3 weeks. The question of whether higher remission rates would be seen with longer trial durations remains unanswered, as does the question of maintained remission, a concept sometimes referred to as recovery (see Chengappa's "sustained clinical recovery" definition).

Summary

This study supports the use of the atypical antipsychotic risperidone as a treatment for acute mania. Further, it supports the effectiveness of risperidone as monotherapy in the treatment for acute mania when the goal of therapy is remission rather than just response. Due to the high recurrence rate of this disorder, and the increased risk that residual symptoms pose for those recurrences, clinicians are encouraged to evaluate a treatment's effectiveness in obtaining remission of symptoms as an outcome for therapy.

References

American Psychiatric Association (2000). *Diagnostic and Statistical Manual of Mental Disorders* (4th ed. – Text Revision). Washington, DC: American Psychiatric Association, p. 382.

American Psychiatric Association (2002). Practice guideline for the treatment of patients with bipolar disorder (revision). *American Journal of Psychiatry*, 159 (Suppl. 4), 1–50.

Angst, J., & Sellaro, R. (2000). Historical perspectives and natural history of bipolar disorder. *Biological Psychiatry*, 48(6), 445–457.

Bowden, C.L., Grunze, H., Mullen, J., Brecher, M., Paulsson, B., Jones, M., Vagero, M., & Svensson, K. (2005). A randomized, double-blind, placebo-controlled efficacy and safety study of quetiapine or lithium as monotherapy for mania in bipolar disorder. *Journal of Clinical Psychiatry*, 66(1), 111–121.

Chengappa, K.N., Hennen, J., Baldessarini, R.J., Kupfer, D.J., Yatham, L.N., Gershon, S., Baker, R.W., & Tohen, M. (2005). Recovery and functional outcomes following olanzapine treatment for bipolar I mania. *Bipolar Disorder*, 7(1), 68–76.

Fleiss, J.L., *et al.* (1976). The life table. A method for analyzing longitudinal studies. *Archives of General Psychiatry*, 33(1), 107–112.

Frank, E. *et al.* (1991). Conceptualisation and rationale for consensus definitions of terms in major depressive disorder. Remission, recovery, relapse, and recurrence. *Archives of General Psychiatry*, 48, 851–855.

Gelenberg, A.J., *et al.* (1996). Antipyschotics in bipolar disorder. *Journal of Clinical Psychiatry*, 57 (Suppl. 9), 49–52.

Goodwin, F.K., & Jamison, K.R. (1990). *Manic Depressive Illness* (1st ed.). New York: Oxford University Press; pp. 1–5.

Gopal, S., Steffens, D.C., Kramer, M.L., & Olsen, M.K. (2005). Symptomatic remission in patients with bipolar mania: results from a double-blind, placebo-controlled trial of risperidone monotherapy. *Journal of Clinical Psychiatry*, 66(8), 1016–1020.

Hirschfeld, R.M., Keck, Jr. P.E., Kramer, M., Karcher, K., Canuso, C., Eerdekens, M., & **Grossman, F.** (2004). Rapid antimanic effect of risperidone monotherapy: a 3-week multicenter, double-blind, placebo-controlled trial. *American Journal of Psychiatry*, 161(6), 1057–1065.

Judd, L.L., *et al.* (1998). A prospective 12-year study of subsyndromal and syndromal depressive symptoms in unipolar major depressive disorders 1998. *Archives of General Psychiatry*, 55, 694–700.

Khanna, S., Vieta, E., Lyons, B., Grossman, F., Eerdekens, M., & Kramer, M. (2005). Risperidone in the treatment of acute mania. Double-blind placebo-controlled study. *British Journal of Psychiatry*, 187, 229–234.

McIntyre, R.S., Brecher, M., Paulsson, B., Huizar, K., & Mullen, J. (2005). Quetiapine or haloperidol as monotherapy for bipolar mania – a 12-week, double-blind, randomised, parallel-group, placebo-controlled trial. *European Neuropsychopharmacology*, 15(5), 573–585.

Perlis, R.H., Ostacher, M.J., Patel, J.K., Marangell, L.B., Zhang, H., Wisniewski, S.R., Ketter, T.A., Miklowitz, D.J., Otto, M.W., Gyulai, L., Reilly-Harrington, N.A., Nierenberg, A.A., Sachs, G.S., & Thase, M.E. (2006). Predictors of recurrence in bipolar disorder: primary outcomes from the Systematic Treatment Enhancement Program for Bipolar Disorder (STEP-BD). *American Journal of Psychiatry*, 163(2), 217–224.

Potkin, S.G., Keck, Jr. P.E., Segal, S., Ice, K., & English, P. (2005). Ziprasidone in acute bipolar mania: a 21-day randomized, double-blind, placebo-controlled replication trial. *Journal of Clinical Psychopharmacology*, 25(4), 301–310.

Roy-Byrne, P.P., *et al.* (1988). Suicide and course of illness in major affective disorder. *Journal of Affective Disorders*, 15, 1–8.

Sachs, G.S., Grossman, F., Ghaemi, S.N., Okamoto, A., & Bowden, C.L. (2002). Combination of a mood stabilizer with risperidone or haloperidol for treatment of acute mania: a double-blind, placebo-controlled comparison of efficacy and safety. *American Journal of Psychiatry*, 159(7), 1146–1154.

Smulevich, A.B., Khanna, S., Eerdekens, M., Karcher, K., Kramer, M., & Grossman, F. (2005). Acute and continuation risperidone monotherapy in bipolar mania: a 3-week placebo-controlled trial followed by a 9-week double-blind trial of risperidone and haloperidol. *European Neuropsychopharmacology*, 15(1), 75–84.

Tohen, M., Jacobs, T.G., Grundy, S.L., McElroy, S.L., Banov, M.C., Janicak, P.G., Sanger, T., Risser, R., Zhang, F., Toma, V., Francis, J., Tollefson, G.D., & Breier, A. (2000). Efficacy of olanzapine in acute bipolar mania: a double-blind, placebo-controlled study. The Olanzipine HGGW Study Group. *Archives of General Psychiatry*, 57(9), 841–849.

Weissman, M.M., *et al.* (1990). Affective disorders. In: Robins, L.R.D. (ed.), *Psychiatric Disorders of America: The Epidemiologic Catchment Area Study*. New York, NY: Free Press, pp. 58–80.

Yatham, L.N., Grossman, F., Augustyns, I., Vieta, E., & Ravindran, A. (2003). Mood stabilisers plus risperidone or placebo in the treatment of acute mania. International, double-blind, randomised controlled trial. *British Journal of Psychiatry*, 182, 141–147.

Progress in Neurotherapeutics and Neuropsychopharmacology, 2:1, 225–238 © 2007 Cambridge University Press
DOI: 10.1017/S1748232106000164   Printed in the United Kingdom

Olanzapine as Maintenance Therapy in Patients with Bipolar I Disorder

Mauricio Tohen

Lilly Research Laboratories, Indianapolis, IN; Department of Psychiatry, Harvard Medical School, McLean Hospital, Belmont, MA, USA; Email: TOHEN_MAURICIO@Lilly.com

Daniel Yen Lin

Lilly Research Laboratories, Indianapolis, IN, USA; Email: dlin@lilly.com

ABSTRACT

Effective treatments for the prevention of relapse and recurrence of mood episodes in patients with bipolar disorder are essential to reduce the high mortality associated with this condition, and to improve long-term outcomes. While lithium is considered to be effective as a first line maintenance treatment, additional treatment options would provide clinicians with tools to address the needs of individual patients. The efficacy of olanzapine, an atypical antipsychotic, for the prevention of relapse in bipolar disorder has been demonstrated in several randomized controlled double-blind clinical trials, both as monotherapy and in combination with other agents. The data reviewed herein suggest a more robust efficacy of treatment with olanzapine in the prevention of relapse into manic episodes than into depressive episodes. The adverse events observed most frequently in patients treated with olanzapine relative to comparators were related to somnolence (somnolence, fatigue, or hypersomnia) and weight gain (weight gain, or increased appetite). Moreover, a larger proportion of olanzapine-treated patients than comparator-treated patients experienced clinically important weight gain.

Key words: bipolar disorder, atypical antipsychotic, maintenance, relapse, remission

Introduction

Given the chronic recurring nature of bipolar disorder, considerable attention has recently focused on developing therapeutic strategies for the long-term management of this condition. Treatments that prolong recovery from a mood episode and delay

Correspondence should be addressed to: Mauricio Tohen, MD, DrPH, Lilly Research Laboraories, Indianapolis, IN: Department of Psychiatry, Harvard Medical School, McLean Hospital, Belmont, MA, USA, tel: +317 277 9585; fax +317 276 7845; Email: tohen_mauricio@lilly.com

relapse into a new mood episode, should be considered cornerstones of any long-term strategy. Lithium has been studied extensively as a mood stabilizer and a recent meta-analysis of data from randomized controlled trials supported its efficacy relative to placebo in reducing the risk of relapse, particularly into manic episodes, although efficacy in preventing depressive relapse was less robust (Geddes *et al.*, 2004). It should be noted, however, that despite a reduced risk of relapse compared to placebo, a significant proportion of patients nevertheless experienced relapse of a mood episode within the limited timeframe of the studies, the longest of which was 2 years (40% for lithium versus 60% for placebo) (Geddes *et al.*, 2004). The heterogeneity of response to treatment may reflect the wide range of clinical presentations that are characteristic of bipolar disorder. Therefore, evidence-based treatment alternatives should provide clinicians with a broader array of therapeutic options to increase the likelihood of achieving long-term improvements in outcomes for individual patients.

The atypical antipsychotic olanzapine has been studied in randomized controlled trials for the prevention of relapse in bipolar disorder, both as monotherapy and in combination with other active treatments. These studies provide evidence for the efficacy of olanzapine monotherapy in relapse prevention relative to placebo, lithium, and divalproex. Based on the common clinical practice of combination therapy for the treatment of bipolar disorder (Lin *et al.*, 2006), the efficacy of olanzapine was also examined in combination with lithium and divalproex.

Olanzapine versus Placebo

The efficacy and safety of olanzapine as monotherapy was examined in the first placebo-controlled randomized double-blind study of an antipsychotic, typical or atypical, for relapse prevention in patients with bipolar I disorder (Tohen *et al.*, 2006b). Patients with an acute manic or mixed episode received open-label treatment with olanzapine (5–20 mg/day) for 6–12 weeks. Of the 731 patients who received open-label treatment with olanzapine, 361 (49%) reached criteria for symptomatic remission (Young Mania Rating Scale (YMRS) total score $\leq$ 12 and Hamilton Depression Rating Scale (HAM-D21) score $\leq$ 8) for at least 1 week and were randomized in a 2:1 ratio to double-blind maintenance treatment with either olanzapine 5–20 mg/day ($N = 225$) or placebo ($N = 136$) for 48 weeks. The primary measure of efficacy was time to symptomatic relapse into any mood episode, or hospitalization for the specific mood episode. Definitions for symptomatic relapse were YMRS score $\geq$ 15 and HAM-D score $<$ 15 for mania; HAM-D score $\geq$ 15 and YMRS score $<$ 15 for depression; and YMRS score $\geq$ 15 and HAM-D score $\geq$ 15 for a mixed episode.

Time to symptomatic relapse into any mood episode during double-blind maintenance treatment was significantly longer for patients who received olanzapine relative to those who received placebo. The median estimated time to symptomatic relapse into any mood episode was 174 days for the olanzapine treatment group and

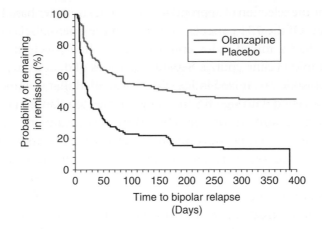

Fig. 1.
Kaplan-Meier survival analysis of time to symptomatic relapse into any mood episode for bipolar I disorder patients in the double-blind maintenance phase of a study of olanzapine in relapse prevention[a]. [a]Relapse based on Young Mania Rating Scale score $\geq$ 15, 21-item Hamilton Depression Rating Scale score $\geq$ 15, or hospitalization for a mood episode. Estimated median time to relapse was 174 days for olanzapine patients and 22 days for placebo patients (log-rank χ^2 = 56.3, df = 1, p < 0.001; hazard ratio = 2.67, 95% CI = 2.03–3.50).

22 days for the placebo treatment group (χ^2 = 56.3, df = 1, p < 0.001) (Figure 1). Rates of symptomatic relapse into any mood episode during the double-blind maintenance phase were 46.7% in the olanzapine treatment group, and 80.1% in the placebo treatment group (odds ratio = 4.61, 95% confidence interval (CI) = 2.81–7.58). Patients treated with olanzapine experienced significantly lower rates of relapse into a manic episode (olanzapine 16.4% versus placebo 41.2%; p < 0.001), or depressive episode (olanzapine 34.7% versus placebo 47.8%; p = 0.015) relative to placebo.

A large proportion of patients who received placebo experienced relapse during the early part of the double-blind maintenance phase, which may be attributed in part to the discontinuation of active treatment. Nevertheless, in order to determine if the separation from placebo was just a reflection of the treatment discontinuation, further analyses of data from patients who completed at least 8 weeks of the maintenance phase without relapse were conducted and revealed a significantly longer time to relapse for those treated with olanzapine relative to placebo (χ^2 = 9.0, df = 1, p < 0.003), which supports recurrence prevention rather than just relapse secondary to treatment discontinuation. Furthermore, rates of symptomatic relapse to any mood episode, excluding patients with relapses during the first 8 weeks of the double-blind phase, were 25.0% for patients who received olanzapine, and 52.9% for those who received placebo (p = 0.003, odds ratio = 3.38, 95% CI = 1.52–7.29).

The large sample size in this study permitted analyses of data from subpopulations of patients with different clinical presentations, which may provide useful information for the selection of appropriate treatment strategies based on individual patient profiles. Of the 731 patients who entered the open-label acute treatment phase, 41.6% had a mixed index episode, 21.5% had psychotic features, and 51.7% had a rapid cycling course. Separate analyses of data from patients with a manic index episode or a mixed index episode revealed that treatment with olanzapine was associated with significantly longer times to relapse in both subpopulations relative to treatment with placebo. Moreover, treatment with olanzapine significantly lengthened time to symptomatic relapse in patients with and without a history of rapid cycling course, as well as in those with and without psychotic features.

Rates of study completion were relatively low with 21.3% of olanzapine-treated and 6.6% of placebo-treated patients completing the 48-week double-blind maintenance phase. However, if the event of interest (relapse) is also considered study completion, the rates are 68.0% for olanzapine and 86.8% for placebo. The rate of discontinuation due to an adverse event was greater in the olanzapine group (7.6%) relative to the placebo group (0%). Weight gain was the most common treatment emergent adverse event observed during treatment with olanzapine during both the open-label (18.6% of patients) and double-blind (8.0% of patients) phases. During the acute-phase patients gained a mean of 3.0 kg $\pm$ SD 3.4 with open-label olanzapine treatment. After randomization, patients receiving placebo lost a mean of 2.0 kg $\pm$ SD 4.4 whereas those receiving olanzapine gained an additional 1.0 kg $\pm$ SD 5.2. During the open-label acute phase, 204 (29.1%) of the patients treated with olanzapine, experienced an increase of $\geqslant$ 7% of baseline body weight. During the double-blind maintenance phase, 36 (16.1%) of olanzapine-treated, and 3 (2.3%) of placebo-treated patients experienced an increase of $\geqslant$ 7% body weight from the point of randomization. The incidence rates of treatment-emergent high levels of prolactin, glucose, and cholesterol during the double-blind maintenance phase were 11.5%, 1.5%, and 3.1%, respectively, for the olanzapine treatment group, and 3.1%, 1.6%, and 0%, respectively for the placebo treatment group.

Olanzapine versus Lithium

The efficacy and safety of olanzapine for prevention of mood episode relapse was compared to lithium in a 12-month randomized, double-blind controlled trial (Tohen *et al.*, 2005). Patients with a diagnosis of bipolar disorder (manic or mixed) and YMRS total score > 20 received open-label co-treatment with olanzapine (5–20 mg/day) and lithium (dose optimized to reach a target blood level 0.6–1.2 meq/liter) for 6–12 weeks. Those who met symptomatic remission criteria (YMRS score $\leqslant$ 12; 21-item (HAMD-21) score $\leqslant$ 8) were randomly assigned in a 1:1 ratio to receive monotherapy with either olanzapine, 5–20 mg/day or lithium (target blood level: 0.6–1.2 meq/liter) for 52 weeks. The discontinued drug was gradually tapered over 4 weeks. The primary objective of this study was to test for non-inferiority of olanzapine relative to lithium in preventing relapse to any mood episode.

Of the 542 patients enrolled during the open-label period, 431 (79.4%) achieved symptomatic remission with lithium/olanzapine co-treatment, and were randomly assigned to double-blind maintenance monotherapy with olanzapine ($N = 217$) or lithium ($N = 214$). The primary objective of the study was to show the non-inferiority of olanzapine relative to lithium concerning the rate of symptomatic relapse (relapse to any mood episode based on a score $\geqslant 15$ on either the YMRS or HAMD, following pre-randomization remission of mania and depression), using a protocol-defined margin of non-inferiority of -7.3%. This margin of non-inferiority allows for olanzapine to be considered non-inferior to lithium if the relapse rate for olanzapine patients is not worse than the relapse rate for lithium-treated patients by 7.3 percentage points, based on a one-sided 97.5% CI about the relapse rate difference. With observed relapse rates of 30.0% ($n = 65$ of $N = 217$) for olanzapine-treated patients and 38.8% ($n = 83$ of $N = 214$) among lithium-treated patients, the non-inferiority of olanzapine relative to lithium was established (rate difference, 8.8%; limit for the one-sided 97.5% CI, -0.1%). In fact, the results of the study nearly show the superiority of olanzapine compared to lithium in terms of the difference in relapse rates ($p = 0.055$). Differences between the

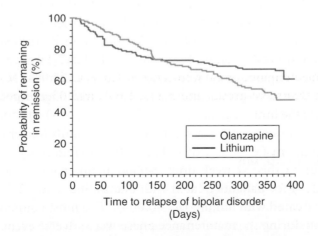

Fig. 2.

Time until mood episode relapse[a] among patients with bipolar disorder randomly assigned to double-blind olanzapine or lithium monotherapy following stabilization with olanzapine and lithium co-treatment. [a]Relapse defined as score $\geqslant 15$ on the Young Mania Rating Scale and/or Hamilton depression scale. Time until relapse longer for the olanzapine group than for the lithium group, but the difference was not significant ($\chi^2 = 3.4$, df = 1, $p = 0.07$, log-rank test).

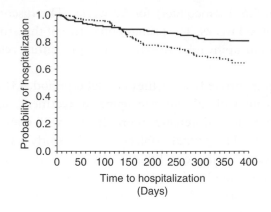

Fig. 3.
Time until hospitalization among patients with bipolar disorder randomly assigned to double-blind olanzapine or lithium monotherapy following stabilization with olanzapine and lithium co-treatment[a]. [a]Time until hospitalization significantly longer for the olanzapine group than for the lithium group ($\chi^2 = 6.2$, df = 1, $p = 0.01$, log-rank test).

olanzapine and lithium treatment groups with respect to time to symptomatic recurrence of any mood episode approached, but did not reach significance ($\chi^2 = 3.4$, df = 1, $p = 0.07$) (Figure 2). No significant differences between treatment groups were observed with respect to rates of depressive relapse, but significantly fewer patients treated with olanzapine (14.3%) experienced a relapse to mania or mixed episode relative to those treated with lithium (28.0%; $p < 0.001$). This finding is noteworthy in light of lithium's demonstrated superiority relative to placebo in preventing relapse to mania (Geddes *et al.*, 2004). Furthermore, significantly fewer olanzapine-treated patients (14.3% [$N = 31$ of 217]) were hospitalized for a mood episode compared to lithium-treated patients (22.9% [$N = 49$ of 214]; $p < 0.03$) and time to hospitalization was significantly longer for the olanzapine group relative to the lithium group ($\chi^2 = 6.2$, df = 1, $p < 0.01$) (Figure 3).

Time to discontinuation for any reason was significantly longer for olanzapine compared to lithium ($\chi^2 = 5.7$, df = 1, $p < 0.02$) (Figure 4). Rates of study completion during this 52-week double-blind maintenance trial were 46.5% ($N = 101$ of 217) for patients treated with olanzapine, and 32.7% ($N = 70$ of 214) for those treated with lithium ($p = 0.004$). The most common reasons for discontinuation during the maintenance phase were adverse events, lack of efficacy, and patient decision, with no significant differences between treatment groups. Mean weight change during the double-blind period was significantly greater for the olanzapine group (mean = 1.8 kg, SD = 5.8) than for the lithium group (mean = 1.4 kg, SD = 5.0, $p < 0.001$), and a significantly greater proportion of olanzapine-treated patients experienced $\geq 7\%$ increase in weight than

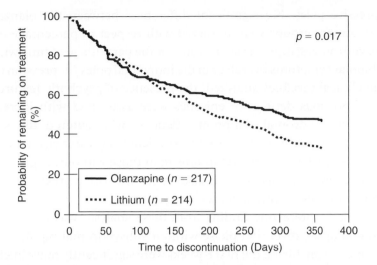

Fig. 4.
Time to discontinuation for any reason among patients with bipolar disorder randomly assigned to double-blind olanzapine or lithium monotherapy following stabilization with olanzapine and lithium co-treatment[a]. [a]Time to discontinuation differed significantly between the treatment groups ($\chi^2 = 5.7$, df = 1, $p < 0.02$) with a median length of 303 days for olanzapine and 207 days for lithium.

Table 1. **Categorical Definitions for Euthymia, Subsyndromal and Relapse**

	EUTHYMIA CRITERIA	SUBSYNDROMAL CRITERIA	RELAPSE CRITERIA
Mania	YMRS > 8	YMRS 9-14	YMRS > 15
Depression	HAMD-21 > 8	HAMD-21 9-14	HAMD-21 > 15
Mixed	YMRS > 8 and HAMD-21 > 8	YMRS 9-14 and HAMD-21 9–14	YMRS > 15 and HAMD-21 > 15
Bipolar Disorder	YMRS > 8 and HAMD-21 > 8	YMRS 9-14 or HAMD-21 9-14	YMRS > 15 or HAMD-21 > 15

lithium-treated patients (29.8% versus 9.8%, respectively; $p < 0.001$). No significant differences between treatment groups were observed in incidence rates of potentially clinically relevant increases in non-fasting glucose or cholesterol.

Secondary analyses of data from this trial examined factors that were associated with a greater percentage of time with subsyndromal symptoms and characterized how these symptoms influenced outcomes in bipolar I disorder (Tohen *et al.*, 2006a). The categorical definitions for euthymia, subsyndromal, and relapse used in these analyses are presented in Table 1. Relapse and subsyndromal were classified globally as bipolar (any mood symptom), and by their respective manic and depressive poles. No significant differences between the olanzapine and lithium treatment groups were observed with respect to percentage of patients with subsyndromal symptoms at any time, or the percentage of time with subsyndromal bipolar symptoms overall or in the individual poles (depression or mania).

Of the clinical variables analyzed, the presence of psychotic features and the number of previous depressive episodes were associated with increased time spent with subsyndromal symptoms. Patients who entered the study with psychotic features were more likely to experience a greater percentage of time with subsyndromal depressive symptoms than those without. A greater number of previous depressive episodes was also associated with a greater percentage of time spent with subsyndromal depressive symptoms.

A particularly interesting finding from these analyses was that patients who started the relapse prevention phase without subsyndromal bipolar symptoms, but developed them during the first 8 weeks were significantly more likely to experience bipolar relapse relative to those without subsyndromal symptoms during the same time frame (20 of 39 versus 75 of 253 patients; relative risk 1.73 [CI 1.21, 2.48]; $p = 0.01$). This was especially true of patients with subsyndromal depressive symptoms and subsequent relapse into the depressive pole (12 of 25 patients versus 31 of 314 patients, relative risk 4.86 [CI 2.87, 8.24]; $p < 0.0001$). By contrast, patients who had residual subsyndromal any mood symptoms at the outset of the double-blind phase and continued to experience symptoms during the first 8 weeks were not more likely to relapse relative to those without subsyndromal symptoms during this time frame (12 of 48 versus 75 of 253 patients, relative risk 0.84 [CI 0.50, 1.43], $p = 0.60$). These findings suggest that the longitudinal assessment of symptom severity, as opposed to just cross-sectional occurrence, may better determine the risk of subsequent relapse.

Olanzapine versus Divalproex

In a 47-week double-blind randomized-controlled trial, the efficacy and safety of olanzapine was compared with divalproex sodium for the treatment of acute mania and maintenance of remission (Tohen *et al.*, 2003a). Patients who met diagnostic criteria for a manic or mixed episode of bipolar disorder and had a baseline YMRS score > 20 were randomized to receive olanzapine 5–20 mg/day ($N = 125$) or divalproex 500–2500 mg/day ($N = 126$). Symptomatic remission of mania and depression was defined as an endpoint YMRS total score ≤ 12 and a HAMD score ≤ 8. Symptomatic relapse into an affective episode (mania, depression, mixed) was defined as YMRS score ≥ 15 or HAMD score ≥ 15 in a patient who previously met the criteria for symptomatic remission. Time to relapse was computed by prospectively examining the data for the patients who met the criteria for remission at week 3.

The median time to symptomatic remission of mania was significantly shorter for patients treated with olanzapine (14 days) relative to those treated with divalproex (62 days) ($\chi^2 = 3.96$, df $= 1$, $p = 0.05$). Rates of symptomatic remission of mania were similar (56.8% for olanzapine, 45.5% for divalproex; $p = 0.10$). There was no statistically significant difference in time to symptomatic relapse to an affective episode (mania, depression, or mixed) between the olanzapine and divalproex treatment groups ($\chi^2 = 0.22$, df $= 1$, $p < 0.64$). Symptomatic relapse to an affective episode occurred in 42.4% (14 of 33) of olanzapine-treated patients, and 56.5% (13 of 23) of divalproex-treated patients ($p = 0.42$).

Rates of completion during the 47-week trial among patients who achieved symptomatic remission at 3 weeks were 20.3% (12 of 59) for olanzapine-treated and 26.2% (11 of 42) for divalproex-treated patients. Discontinuations due to an adverse event did not differ significantly between treatment groups (24.8% [31 of 125] of olanzapine-treated patients, 19.8% [25 of 126] of divalproex-treated patients). Weight gain during the 47-week trial was significantly greater for the olanzapine group (2.79 kg, [SE $= 0.32$]) relative to the divalproex group (1.22 kg [SE $= 0.32$]; $p < 0.001$). The incidence of weight gain $>7\%$ did not differ significantly between olanzapine- and divalproex-treated patients (23.6% [29 of 123] versus 17.9% [22 of 123], respectively; $p = 0.35$). The incidence of treatment-emergent abnormally high levels of cholesterol or glucose did not differ significantly between treatment groups.

Olanzapine in Combination with Lithium or Valproate versus Lithium or Valproate Monotherapy

Patients with a diagnosis of bipolar disorder, manic or mixed episode, with or without psychotic features, received combination treatment with olanzapine plus lithium or valproate, or lithium or valproate monotherapy during a 6-week double-blind trial (Tohen *et al.*, 2004). Those who achieved syndromic remission (Mania: DSM-IV "A" criteria for current manic episode no worse than mild [$\leqslant 3$ in a range of 1–7], "B" criteria no worse than mild [$\leqslant 3$ in a range of 1–7], and no more than two "B" criteria were mild [score of 3 in a range of 1–7]; Depression: DSM-IV "A" criteria for current major depressive episode no worse than mild [3 in a range of 1–7], and no more than three "A" criteria mild [score of 3 in a range of 1–7]) were randomly assigned in a 1 : 1 ratio to receive an additional 18 months of double-blind treatment consisting of either olanzapine (5–20 mg/day) in combination with lithium or valproate, or placebo added to lithium or valproate monotherapy. During the relapse prevention phase, dosages were adjusted to achieve a therapeutic blood level range of 0.6–1.2 mmol/l for lithium, and 50–125 µg/ml for valproate. Patients continued to take the same mood stabilizer that they had received during the acute phase. Relapse was assessed as: (1) syndromic, meeting DSM-IV criteria for a

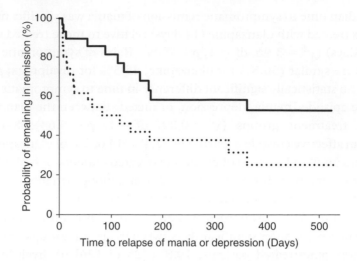

Fig. 5.

Time to symptomatic relapse (mania or depression) of patients previously meeting symptomatic remission criteria. Time to symptomatic relapse was significantly longer ($p = 0.023$,
log-rank test) for the olanzapine combination therapy group ($n = 30$; solid line) than for the
monotherapy group ($n = 38$; dotted line). Median time to relapse was 163 days for combination therapy and 42 days for monotherapy.

manic, mixed, or depressive episode and (2) symptomatic, using the total score on
the YMRS for mania and the HAMD-21 (Hamilton, 1967) for depression. Patients
who met the symptomatic remission criteria (YMRS total score $\leq$ 12 and HAMD-
21 total score $\leq$ 8), in addition to having met the requirements for syndromic remission at the end of the acute phase, were assessed for symptomatic relapse during this
extension phase. Symptomatic relapse to mania was defined as a YMRS total
score $\geq$ 15 after having met the criteria for symptomatic and syndromic remission.
Symptomatic relapse to depression was defined as a HAMD-21 total score $\geq$ 15
after having met the criteria for both symptomatic and syndromic remission. The
primary outcome measure was time to syndromal relapse. Time to symptomatic
relapse of any mood episode, manic, depressive, or mixed, was also assessed.

Of the 99 patients who achieved syndromic remission at the start of the relapse
prevention phase, 68 also met criteria for symptomatic remission. While time to
relapse into a syndromic affective episode did not differ significantly between treatment groups ($\chi^2 = 0.11, p = 0.742$), time to symptomatic relapse was significantly
longer for the olanzapine plus lithium or valproate combination therapy group compared with the monotherapy group ($\chi^2 = 5.19, p = 0.023$) (Figure 5). Median
times to symptomatic relapse were 42 days for the lithium or valproate monotherapy group, and 163 days for the olanzapine plus lithium or valproate combination

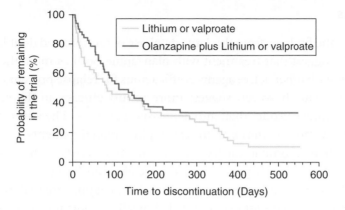

Fig. 6.
Time to discontinuation for any reason among patients with bipolar disorder randomly assigned to double-blind olanzapine in combination with lithium or divalproate or lithium or valproate monotherapy. Time to discontinuation differed significantly between treatment groups (χ^2 = 3.86, df = 1, p = 0.05), with a median length of 111 days for combination therapy and 82 days for monotherapy.

therapy group. Rates of syndromic or symptomatic relapse into either mania or depression did not significantly different between treatment groups (syndromic criteria: monotherapy 31% [15 of 48], combination therapy 29% [15 of 51]; $p > 0.99$; symptomatic criteria: monotherapy 55% [21 of 38], combination therapy 37% [11 of 30]; $p = 0.149$).

Rates of completion during the relapse prevention phase were significantly higher for patients who received combination treatment (31%) relative to monotherapy (10%; $p = 0.014$), and times to discontinuation were significantly longer for the combination treatment group (111 versus 82 days, $\chi^2 = 3.86$, $p = 0.049$) (Figure 6). Reasons for discontinuation were not significantly different between treatment groups. The incidences of treatment-emergent adverse events were similar for the treatment groups, with the exception of insomnia, which occurred more frequently in the monotherapy group (monotherapy 27.1% [13 of 48 patients] versus combination therapy 3.9% [2 of 51 patients]), and weight gain, which was more common with combination therapy (monotherapy 6.3% [3 of 48] versus combination therapy 19.6% [10 of 51]). Mean change in body weight from baseline to endpoint during the relapse prevention phase was greater for combination therapy than for monotherapy (2.0 versus − 1.8 kg), and the incidence of clinically relevant increase in weight was greater for patients receiving combination therapy relative to monotherapy (27% versus 6%). There were no significant differences between treatment groups in the incidence of clinically relevant increases in non-fasting glucose or in non-fasting cholesterol concentrations.

Conclusions

In summary, the findings from this large database of randomized double-blind controlled trials suggest that treatment with olanzapine both as monotherapy and in combination with other active agents is efficacious for relapse prevention in bipolar disorder. The data, however, suggest more robust efficacy in the prevention of relapse into manic episodes than into depressive episodes. The adverse events that were observed most commonly in olanzapine-treated patients at significantly greater rates than in comparator-treated patients were events related to somnolence (somnolence, fatigue, or hypersomnia) and weight gain (weight gain, or increased appetite). Moreover, a larger proportion of olanzapine-treated patients than comparator-treated patients experienced clinically important weight gain.

Taken together with the demonstrated efficacy of olanzapine for treatment of acute mania (Tohen *et al.*, 1999; Tohen *et al.*, 2000), and the efficacy of olanzapine–fluoxetine combination for treatment of acute bipolar depression (Tohen *et al.*, 2003b), the evidence for efficacy in relapse prevention should serve to broaden the armamentum available to clinicians to treat multiple aspects of this condition.

References

Geddes, J.R., Burgess, S., Hawton, K., Jamison, K., & Goodwin, G.M. (2004). Long-term lithium therapy for bipolar disorder: systematic review and meta-analysis of randomized controlled trials. *American Journal of Psychiatry*, 161(2), 217–222.

Hamilton, M. (1967). Development of a rating scale for primary depressive illness. *British Journal of Social and Clinical Psychology*, 6(4), 278–296.

Lin, D., Mok, H., & Yatham, L.N. (2006). Polytherapy in bipolar disorder. *CNS. Drugs*, 20(1), 29–42.

Tohen, M., Bowden, C.L., Calabrese, J.R., Lin, D., Frye, M., Forrester, T.D., Sachs, G.S., Koukopoulos, A., Yatham, L.N., & Grunze, H. (2006a). Factors associated with increased time with subsyndromal symptoms in bipolar patients after remission from a manic or mixed episode. *British Journal of Psychiatry*, in press.

Tohen, M., Calabrese, J.R., Sachs, G.S., Banov, M.D., Detke, H.C., Risser, R., Baker, R.W., Chou, J.C., & Bowden, C.L. (2006b). Randomized, placebo-controlled trial of olanzapine as maintenance therapy in patients with bipolar I disorder responding to acute treatment with olanzapine. *American Journal of Psychiatry*, 163(2), 247–256.

Tohen, M., Chengappa, K.N., Suppes, T., Baker, R.W., Zarate, C.A., Bowden, C.L., Sachs, G.S., Kupfer, D.J., Ghaemi, S.N., Feldman, P.D., Risser, R.C., Evans, A.R., & Calabrese, J.R. (2004). Relapse prevention in bipolar I disorder: 18-month comparison of olanzapine plus mood stabiliser v. mood stabiliser alone. *British Journal of Psychiatry*, 184, 337–345.

Tohen, M., Greil, W., Calabrese, J.R., Sachs, G.S., Yatham, L.N., Oerlinghausen, B.M., Koukopoulos, A., Cassano, G.B., Grunze, H., Licht, R.W., Dell'Osso, L., Evans, A.R., Risser, R., Baker, R.W., Crane, H., Dossenbach, M.R., & Bowden, C.L. (2005). Olanzapine versus lithium in the maintenance treatment of bipolar disorder: a 12-month, randomized, double-blind, controlled clinical trial. *American Journal of Psychiatry*, 162(7), 1281–1290.

Tohen, M., Jacobs, T.G., Grundy, S.L., McElroy, S.L., Banov, M.C., Janicak, P.G., Sanger, T., Risser, R., Zhang, F., Toma, V., Francis, J., Tollefson, G.D., & Breier, A. (2000). Efficacy of olanzapine in acute bipolar mania: a double-blind, placebo-controlled study.

The Olanzipine HGGW Study Group [see comment][erratum appears in *Archives of General Psychiatry* 2002 Jan; 59(1): 91]. *Archives of General Psychiatry*, 57(9), 841–849.

Tohen, M., Ketter, T.A., Zarate, C.A., Suppes, T., Frye, M., Altshuler, L., Zajecka, J., Schuh, L.M., Risser, R.C., Brown, E., & Baker, R.W. (2003a). Olanzapine versus divalproex sodium for the treatment of acute mania and maintenance of remission: a 47-week study. *American Journal of Psychiatry*, 160(7), 1263–1271.

Tohen, M., Sanger, T.M., McElroy, S.L., Tollefson, G.D., Chengappa, K.N., Daniel, D.G., Petty, F., Centorrino, F., Wang, R., Grundy, S.L., Greaney, M.G., Jacobs, T.G., David, S.R., & Toma, V. (1999). Olanzapine versus placebo in the treatment of acute mania. Olanzapine HGEH Study Group. *American Journal of Psychiatry*, 156(5), 702–709.

Tohen, M., Vieta, E., Calabrese, J., Ketter, T.A., Sachs, G., Bowden, C., Mitchell, P.B., Centorrino, F., Risser, R., Baker, R.W., Evans, A.R., Beymer, K., Dube, S., Tollefson, G.D., & Breier, A. (2003b). Efficacy of olanzapine and olanzapine-fluoxetine combination in the treatment of bipolar I depression. *Archives of General Psychiatry*, 60(11), 1079–1088.

Progress in Neurotherapeutics and Neuropsychopharmacology, 2:1, 239–250 © 2007 Cambridge University Press
DOI: 10.1017/S1748232106000176   Printed in the United Kingdom

Can Quality of Life be Improved in Schizophrenia? Results From A Pragmatic, Randomized, Controlled Trial Comparing Olanzapine with First Generation Antipsychotics*

Maurício Silva de Lima

Medical Director, Eli Lilly Brazil; Federal University of Pelotas and Catholic University of Pelotas, Pelotas, Brazil.
Email: limama@lilly.com

Alan Breier

Chief Medical Officer, Eli Lilly, Indianapolis, US. Email: Alan_Breier/AM/LLY@lilly.com

Jair de Jesus Mari

Department of Psychiatry, Federal University of São Paulo and Catholic University of Pelotas, RS, Brazil;
Email: mari@psiquiatria.epm.com.br

Key words: schizophrenia, antipsychotics, quality of life, pragmatic, randomized trial.

Introduction

Although benefits of newer antipsychotics over first generation antipsychotics (FGA) have been reported in a number of randomized-controlled trials (RCTs) and recently summarized in a comprehensive systematic review (Davis *et al.*, 2003), there is still controversy when the higher cost of these newer medications is considered. In general, second generation antipsychotics (SGA) have proved superior efficacy in clinical outcomes, such as general psychopathology, negative symptoms, and adverse events (Lima *et al.*, 2005; Tollefson *et al.*, 1997), but questions remain regarding in what extent these improvements might influence the course of disease and patient's quality of life.

Quality of life measures have been only recently used to assess drug treatments in clinical trials. A bibliographic study has estimated that <5% of all RCTs reported on quality of life. The assessment of quality of life may be impractical within the context

Correspondence should be addressed to: Mauricio Silva de Lima, MD, PhD, Federal University of Pelotas and Catholic University of Pelotas, Pelotas, RS, Brazil; Eli Lilly Brazil, Avenida Morumbi, 8264 – Brooklin, São Paulo, SP, Brazil; Ph: +55 115 532 6790; Email: limama@lilly.com
*Data reported here has been published in the *Journal of Clinical Psychiatry* 2005, 66, 831–838.

of traditional RCTs, when assessment of effects is based on biologically meaningful criteria, and the choice of patients and clinical outcomes is rather arbitrary (Schwartz & Lellouch, 1967). As a result, extrapolating results from these trials to standard clinical conditions is often complicated. Pragmatic trials, an alternative to the traditional RCTs, aim to answer 'real life' clinical questions in 'real life' clinical situations.

We conducted a pragmatic, multicenter RCT comparing olanzapine to FGA, aiming to assess potential differences in terms of symptom change, side-effects and quality of life in patients with schizophrenia. The main findings here reported have been more extensively described elsewhere (Lima *et al.*, 2005).

Methods

Study Design, Sample Characteristics, and Assessments

This is a pragmatic, multicenter, RCT comparing olanzapine with FGAs in patients with DSM-IV (American Psychiatric Association, 1994) schizophrenia and a minimum Brief Psychiatric Rating Scale (BPRS) (extracted from Positive and Negative Symptom Scale, PANSS) score of 24. Patients aged 18–55 years admitted to a psychiatric hospital with an acute exacerbation of their illness were included in this study. The study protocol was approved by the institutional review boards responsible for the individual study sites and by the Federal University of São Paulo ethical committee. Informed consent was obtained from all eligible subjects or from their authorized legal representative.

The study was conducted in three psychiatric hospitals from different cities and regions in Brazil: Anna Rech (Southern Brazil); Salvador (Northeast of Brazil); and Goiânia (Middle West of Brazil).

Patients with serious suicidal risk; physical illness (such as cancer or severe hepatic disease); female patients who were either pregnant or lactating, and those who had received treatment with any SGA in the previous 4 weeks were excluded.

Randomization was performed centrally: after baseline assessment, investigators received sealed numbered coded envelopes, which described the treatment to be given to the patient, from a person who had no contact with the patient's evaluation. This procedure aimed to guarantee adequate allocation concealment.

During training and site initiation, it was emphasized that this was a pragmatic study; it was intended that doctors act as closely as possible to their general practice patterns. In order to allow that, patients and clinicians were not blind to the treatment allocated. An alternative level of blinding was obtained with outcome assessors (psychiatrists and psychologists), who were masked to treatment allocation and had no contact the treating doctors, or the patient's hospital records.

Randomization occurred within a maximum period of 3 days of hospital admission. According to the patient's clinical improvement and/or emergent side-effects doses could be adjusted upward or downward. In case of allocation to the FGA group, psychiatrists also were instructed to choose the drug according to patient's characteristics and his/her own usual clinical practice procedures. Use of concomitant medications was allowed. Prophylactic use of anticholinergic medication was discouraged although not prohibited.

After discharge, patients were followed up for 9 months, at monthly intervals, in the same in-patient facility and under the care of the same doctor. Treatment adherence was assessed by asking patients to bring the medicine boxes for counting the number of pills used in the period. In case the patient did not return for consultation they were contacted to re-schedule the visit. If the patient did not attend at the second recall a trained research worker visited the patient at home.

The main outcomes of the study were results on PANSS (at least 40% of reduction from baseline values in PANSS total score). Clinical Global Impression (CGI), SF-36. Relapse was considered when patients had to be re-hospitalized because of illness-related factors.

Adverse events were recorded at every visit through non-directed, open-ended questioning, spontaneous complaint, and clinical observation. In addition, the Abnormal Involuntary Movement Scale (AIMS) for tardive dyskinesia (Guy, 1976) was used. The AIMS is comprised of 12 items. The first seven items assess specific abnormal movements (face, lips, jaws, tongue, upper extremities, lower extremities, and trunk), scored in a five-point scale (0 for none/normal to 4 severe).

Quality of life was evaluated using the SF-36, a generic health status measure designed to evaluate functioning and well-being in chronic disease; it is used in mental health specialty and general primary care populations (Conley *et al.*, 1998). The SF-36 consists of 36 questions covering eight domains: physical functioning, bodily pain, role limitations due to physical problems, vitality, general health perceptions, role limitations due to emotional problems, mental health, and social function. Each subscale is linearly transformed into a 0 to 100 scale, with higher scores representing better health status and functioning. The SF-36 sub-scales have excellent reliability and good construct validity (Revicki, 1997).

Analysis

Analysis of covariance (ANCOVA) was performed for continuous outcomes. The results are presented as the corrected mean differences between the treatment groups, with their respective 95% confidence intervals (CIs). Dichotomous data, including demographic variables, response rates (defined as at least 40% of reduction in total PANSS baseline scores at end of study), reasons for treatment discontinuation, and treatment-emergent adverse events, were evaluated using Pearson's χ^2 test, with relative risks (RRs) and their respective 95% CIs. Efficacy analysis was based on the intention-to-treat principals, that is, all randomized patients were considered, assuming that dropouts occurred because of lack of efficacy or adverse events. The accepted level of significance was 5%. We entered the site of the study into each of the models to determine whether controlling for this altered our main findings. We also examined whether there were any interactions between site and randomization group.

Results

Patient Characteristics

One hundred ninety seven patients (154 males and 43 females) were randomized to olanzapine or FGA, 104 to olanzapine and 93 to FGAs. Only 1 patient (in the olanzapine group) discontinued treatment because of adverse events; 11 patients (7 in the FGA group) withdrew informed consent and 12 (8 in the olanzapine group) were lost to follow-up for unknown reasons. Overall, the attrition rate during trial was 13.2%, with no statistically significant differences between groups.

Treatment groups did not differ with respect to any patient or illness characteristic. Participants were generally in their mid-30, males, Caucasians, and unmarried. The mean length of illness was about 11 years and age at onset 22 years. The mean baseline scores on the PANSS was 48.3 (SD 12.7), 27.1 (SD 7.5), and 26.1 (SD 7.4), for general psychopathology, positive and negative symptoms respectively (total score 101.5, SD 23.2), indicating this was a population with severe overall psychopathology.

The mean dose of olanzapine was 10.5 (SD 2.5) and the median 10 mg/day. Haloperidol was the most frequently prescribed FGA, used in 74 patients, with a mean dose of 15.8 (SD 23.7) and median 10 mg/day. Chlorpromazine was used in 13 patients in a mean dose of 346.2 mg (SD 150.6) with a median dose of 300 mg/day. Trifluoperazine was used in 1 patient at a dose of 15 mg/day.

During hospitalization, concomitant medication was prescribed for 49.5% of patients on olanzapine, and for 69.4% for those on FGA (Pearson's χ^2 7.4; d.f. 1; $p = 0.006$). This difference favoring olanzapine continued at the end of the follow-up (48.3% versus 65.3%; RR 1.5; 95% CI 1.0–2.1; $p = 0.02$). The most prescribed medications were benzodiazepines for participants taking olanzapine (16.5%) and anticholinergic drugs for those on FGAs (26.3%).

Adherence to prescribed medication was high for both groups at end of trial: 92.1% for olanzapine and 90.7% for the FGA group ($p = 0.79$).

Efficacy Analysis

Results of the PANSS are shown in Figure 1. Both groups showed a substantial improvement in positive symptoms at follow-up, with no differences between groups. Improvement in negative symptoms, general psychopathology, and total score on the PANSS were more pronounced in patients taking olanzapine.

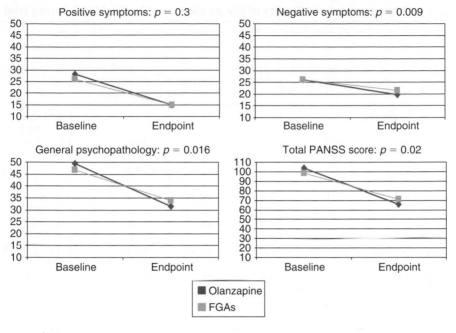

Fig. 1.
Changes in PANSS scores (sub-scales and total score) from baseline.

Clinical Response and Relapse Rates

Clinical response defined as a reduction of at least 40% in the PANSS baseline scores was more prevalent among Olanzapine patients (46% for Olanzapine and 35% for FGAs) but this difference was not statistically significant (χ^2 2.01; d.f. 1; $p = 0.19$). Patients on olanzapine had significantly fewer relapses (re-hospitalization) than those on FGAs (44.1 versus 27.8; $p = 0.02$).

Quality of Life Results

Improvements in quality of life as measured by the SF-36 were observed in both groups over time (Table 1). Patients treated on olanzapine showed superior improvement regarding physical functioning and physical and emotional role limitations compared to those receiving FGAs. Higher scores of borderline statistical significance favoring olanzapine were observed in the domains of general health ($p = 0.05$) and mental health (0.06).

We tested for the effect of site on treatment response and did not find any differences between the three sites in terms of the main outcome measures (SF-36 and PANSS).

Acceptability Results

No patients taking FGAs left the study early because of side-effects; this may be related in part to the naturalistic approach adopted in this trial, allowing clinicians

Table 1.   **Improvements in Quality of Life as Measured by the SF-36 during Trial**

DOMAIN	OLANZAPINE		FGA		MEAN DIFFERENCE (95% CI)[*]
	BASELINE (N = 99)	ENDPOINT (N = 84)	BASELINE (N = 91)	ENDPOINT (N = 72)	LOCF[†]
Physical functioning	65.1	82.3	67.1	73.8	6.6 (1.2, 11.9) p = 0.017
Role physical	34.4	58.1	32.3	40.0	13.7 (3.0, 24.3) p = 0.012
Bodily pain	70.0	86.0	67.6	79.1	6.1 (−1.5, 13.8) p = 0.12
General health	57.1	67.0	59.3	61.1	5.6 (0.0, 11.3) p = 0.05
Vitality	48.6	56.3	44.5	51.0	0.4 (−5.1, 5.9) p = 0.9
Social functioning	48.0	72.2	53.9	67.1	5.4 (−2.3, 13.2) p = 0.17
Role emotional	30.8	58.4	31.8	42.1	12.1 (0.7, 23.5) p = 0.04
Mental health	50.5	64.0	50.9	58.1	5.1 (−0.3, 10.4) p = 0.06

[*] Corrected for baseline values by ANCOVA (positive values favor olanzapine). [†] LOCF: last observation carried forward.

to prescribe lower doses of FGAs and adding other medications, such as anti-cholinergic agents. In the olanzapine group, only one patient dropped out because of side-effects.

At baseline, the mean body mass index (BMI) was significantly higher for patients on olanzapine (25.5 versus 23.4) then for the FGA group. After 9 months, the mean BMI for olanzapine was 28.7 and 25.3 for the FGA group, a difference that was statistically significant (F = 224.3; p < 0.001).

The analysis of the AIMS main components was carried out by grouping rates in global assessment, taking scores 0 (none) not presenting an abnormal movement at all and 1, 2, 3, 4 as presenting some degree of the condition. Patients on olanzapine showed significantly lower scores in all AIMS components: tardive dyskinesia (11.5% versus 38.9%; p < 0.0001); incapacitation (23.0 versus 47.2; p = 0.001); patient awareness (18.4 versus 34.7; p = 0.015); choreoathetosis (0.0 versus 12.5; p = 0.001); dystonia (5.7 versus 20.8; p = 0.004).

Discussion

Principal Findings

In this trial, the use of olanzapine was associated with superior improvements in negative symptomathology and general psychopathology on the PANSS. Patients on olanzapine showed lower rates of extrapyramidal symptoms, whilst the increase in BMI was significantly lower among those taking FGA. Quality of life in patients taking both olanzapine and FGAs substantially improved over time. The significant findings in quality of life favoring olanzapine were related to the physical components of the SF-36 such as physical functioning and physical role limitations.

Methodological

This trial was conducted under novelty conditions of routine psychiatric care in Brazil. Its design incorporated a number of features to increase generalizability to real-world practice. Relatively few restrictions were placed on eligibility, and after randomization, dose adjustments and use of concomitant medications were managed as usual by the psychiatrists. This may partially explain the low dropout rate observed in this study for both groups. These design features provide answers to questions about treatment effectiveness, in this case, how the choice of an antipsychotic affect relevant outcomes, including improvements in negative symptoms and quality of life in real-world practice. Further details on this pragmatic, naturalistic design can be found in a related publication (Lima *et al.*, 2005).

There are very few pragmatic trials in psychiatry although the importance of such studies to provide data for establishing policies (Hotopf *et al.*, 1999) is well recognized. In this trial, the lack of blinding could introduce biases; since it was clear to the patient if he/she was taking a new medication. However, whilst blinding may reduce potential bias, it may cause difficulty with compliance due to adverse effects. Rosenheck *et al.* (2003) used a double-blind design to address similar issues and had a dropout rate higher than 40%. The attrition rate in the current long-term study was low: 13.2%. The advantages of this exceptional treatment compliance rate when analyzing the main outcomes are clear; information on the health status of the majority of patients initially randomized was available for analysis proposes. This also increases the ability to extrapolate current findings.

Efficacy Observations

Patients on olanzapine showed better results in a number of efficacy outcomes as compared to those on FGAs. Results on PANSS indicated that olanzapine has similar efficacy in positive symptoms and clinical response (at least 40% of reduction in PANSS total baseline scores) and superior efficacy in both negative symptoms and general psychopathology. Relapse rates also favored olanzapine as well as CGI scores at visit 11. This superior efficacy profile of olanzapine has been found in other RCTs where it was compared to FGAs (Jakovljevic *et al.*, 1999; Conley *et al.*, 1998; Tollefson *et al.*, 1997; Beasley *et al.*, 1996). Davis, in a systematic review and meta-analysis comparing SGAs with FGAs demonstrated that olanzapine, clozapine, risperidone, and amisulpride have superior efficacy as compared to FGA (Davis *et al.*, 2003).

Olanzapine was associated with marked improvement in three domains of the SF-36 (physical functioning, physical, and emotional role limitations). Data on quality of life has been investigated in another olanzapine trial (Tollefson & Sanger, 1997), but it is difficult to compare the data to the current study. Quality of life data were not fully reported (Tollefson *et al.*, 1997).

Differential improvements in schizophrenia symptoms and relapse rates (hospitalization) observed in subjects on olanzapine can partially explain current findings. Specific effects in cognition and mood, which could also be related to improvements in quality of life, were not assessed in this study. It is also remarkable that even patients taking FGAs were able to improve their scores in the SF-36 over time. Again, the pragmatic approach adopted in this study allowed psychiatrists to treat patients in a way that better resembles their real-world practices, suggesting that treatment outcome in schizophrenia when patients are compliant can be rather positive. In a retrospective analysis of a Health Service Databases, Zhang *et al.* (2004) found that patients with chronic severe psychotic symptoms receiving atypical neuroleptic treatment showed a marked reduction in demand for services, marked improvement on perception of quality of life, and a trend towards reduction in symptom severity over a 3-year period. They suggest these changes could be the result of improved compliance with out-patient services such as follow-up visits and rehabilitative activities.

Other differences between olanzapine and FGAs might exist but were not detected in this trial. Non-statistically significant mean differences in all domains of the SF-36 in patients taking olanzapine were observed; lack of statistical power could contribute to the absence of significance in the remaining domains of the scale.

Acceptability/Side-Effects

The finding of lower rate of dropouts because of side-effects in patients taking olanzapine is not uniform in FGA comparative studies (Mraz *et al.*, 2000; Beasley *et al.*, 1999; Loza *et al.*, 1999). Doses of FGAs and use of concomitant medication can play a major role in controlling serious extrapyramidal effects. We adopted a pragmatic approach allowing psychiatrists to use their routine strategies including use of lower doses of antipsychotic or use of anti-Parkinsonism medications. This may explain why no dropouts because of side-effects were observed among patients taking FGAs.

In this trial olanzapine induced fewer extrapyramidal effects than FGA, an observation also reported in previous studies (Lima *et al.*, 2005; Kinon *et al.*, 2001; Tunis *et al.*, 1999). Absence of extrapyramidal side-effects can impact both acceptability and functional outcomes, including negative symptoms (Tollefson & Sanger, 1997). Along with other factors not directly assessed in this trial these benefits can be related to the higher scores in some components of the SF-36 among patients taking olanzapine.

The use of olanzapine was associated with greater increases in weight and BMI. Further information on laboratory exams were not collected in this study, resulting in lack of relevant data on actual risk of patients taking antipsychotics. Although clinical data suggest that the mean weight gain during olanzapine treatment trended toward a plateau after the initial 39 weeks of treatment (Kinon *et al.*, 2001), the well-known consequences of weight-related problems must be avoided and pro-actively treated. In this study, no preventive actions were taken regarding the need to change eating habits and physical exercise in patients taking olanzapine and other antipsychotics. Although there is still a need for further research to assess the relative medical risk consequent to weight gain with atypical antipsychotics (Lieberman *et al.*, 2003), the significant weight and BMI gains in this trial suggest this issue must be stressed in clinical practice. Recent guidelines have suggested that education on eating habits, practice of simple physical exercises and regular glucose and lipids panel monitoring must be part of the medical prescription of antipsychotics (Expert Group, 2004).

Implications

This pragmatic trial confirmed finding from most trials comparing olanzapine with FGAs. Because of their strong internal validity, traditional blinded trials are still the gold standard for efficacy assessment of medical interventions. However, it is often difficult to recruit subjects to blinded randomized trials and the patients included are often unrepresentative of the clinical problem (Hotopf *et al.*, 1999). If trials are to help in deciding upon which interventions to use, they must be applied to simple and important clinical questions and must be carried out, as far as possible, under usual service condition.

When results from these design alternatives match, one has more confidence in the relevance of the effects of a particular drug in a clinical setting.

The adequate randomization and allocation concealment procedure adopted in this trial avoids a number of biases. On the other hand, its pragmatic approach has the advantage of adding generalizability to the findings.

The choice of primary outcomes was also an essential feature of this trial. Pragmatic trials should compare new treatments using relevant measures. Of these instruments, olanzapine hold better results on psychopathology, relapse rates and quality of life.

Finally, an interesting comparison can be made between the endpoint scores of the SF-36 in patients taking olanzapine in this trial with to those observed in the general population in the USA (Tunis *et al.*, 1999). Scores from this non-direct comparison are similar across two populations, suggesting that patients on olanzapine might achieve health-related quality of life improvements that are clinically relevant. In times of arguments regarding the benefits of newer antipsychotics over old drugs, it is important to distinguish between crude outcomes like time to discontinuation of treatment and more illness specific outcomes, like improvements in cognition and quality of life. Old drugs, when used in low doses, can be associated with good compliance, but it is unlikely that can improve impairments in cognition, social role and overall quality of life. Current evidence supports current beliefs that SGAs like olanzapine may provide benefits in specific areas of functioning of patients suffering from schizophrenia. It is still timely to ask for more long-term, pragmatic, randomized trials, reporting clinically relevant outcomes that could be translated into real life care providers by clinicians, patients, and society.

Acknowledgments

We thank the Principal Investigators in the three participant sites Dr. Elso Barbisan (Clínica Paulo Guedes), Dr. Salomão Rodrigues Filho (PAX Clínica Psiquiátrica), and Dr. Irismar Reis de Oliveira (Federal University of Bahia). Maurício Silva de Lima is a I-D Researcher from the Brazilian Research Council (CNPq). Jair de Jesus Mari is a I-A Researcher from CNPq. Conflict of interests: Dr. De Lima and Dr. Breier are Lilly employees.

References

American Psychiatric Association (1994). Committee on nomenclature and statistics. *Diagnostic and Statistics Manual of Mental Disorders – Fourth Edition*. Washington, DC: American Psychiatric Association.

Beasley Jr., C.M., Sanger, T., Satterlee, W., *et al.* (1996). Olanzapine versus placebo – results of a double-blind, fixed-dose olanzapine trial. *Psychopharmacology*, 124, 159–167.

Beasley Jr., C.M., Dellva, M.A., Tamura, R.N., *et al.* (1999). A randomized, double-blind comparison of the incidence of tardive dyskinesia during long-term treatment with olanzapine or haloperidol. *British Journal of Psychiatry*, 174, 23–30.

Conley, R.R., Tamminga, C.A., Bartko, J.J., *et al.* (1998). Olanzapine compared with chlorpromazine in treatment-resistant schizophrenia. *American Journal of Psychiatry*, 155, 914–920.

Davis, J., Chen, N., & Glick, I.D. (2003). A meta-analysis of the efficacy of second-generation antipsychotics. *Archives of General Psychiatry*, 60, 553–564.

Expert Group (2004). Schizophrenia and Diabetes 2003 Expert Consensus Meeting, Dublin, 3–4 October 2003: Consensus Summary. *British Journal of Psychiatry*, 184 (Suppl. 87), s112.

Guy, W. (1976). Psychopharmacology Research Branch, NIMH. Abnormal Involuntary Scale (AIMS). In: *ECDEU Assessment Manual for Psychopharmacology, revised*. DHEW Publication No. (ADM) 76-338. Rockville, MD: National Institute of Mental Health, pp. 534–537.

Hotopf, M., Churchill, R. & Lewis, G. (1999). Pragmatic randomised controlled trials in psychiatry. *British Journal of Psychiatry*, 175, 217–223.

Jakovljevic, M., Dossenbach, M.R.K., *et al.* (1999). Olanzapine versus fluphenazine in the acute (six-week) treatment of schizophrenia. *Psychiatric Danubina*, 11(1–2), 3–10.

Kinon, B.J., Basson, B.R., Gilmore, J.A., *et al.* (2001). Long-term olanzapine treatment: weight change and weight-related health factors in schizophrenia. *Journal of Clinical Psychiatry*, 62(2), 92–100.

Lieberman, J.A., Tollefson, G., Tohen, M. *et al.* (2003). Comparative efficacy and safety of atypical and conventional antipsychotics drugs in first-episode psychosis: a randomized, double-blind trial of olanzapine versus haloperidol. *American Journal of Psychiatry*, 160, 1396–1404.

Lima, M.S., Mari, J.J., Breier, A., Costa, A.M., Sena, E.P., & Hotopf, M. (2005). Quality of life in schizophrenia: a multicenter, naturalistic, controlled trial comparing olanzapine to first-generation antipsychotics. *Journal of Clinical Psychiatry* 66, 831–838.

Loza, N., El-Dosoky, A.M., Okasha, T.A., et al. (1999). Olanzapine compared to chlorpromazine in acute schizophrenia. *European Neuropsychopharmacology*, 9 (Suppl. 5), S291.

Mraz, K., Gogus, A., Tunca, Z., et al. (2000). Olanzapine versus chlorpromazine in Turkey. Schizophrenia. *Schizophrenia Research*, 41(1), 190.

Revicki, D.A. (1997). Methods of pharmacoeconomic evaluation of psychopharmacologic therapies for patients with schizophrenia. *Journal of Psychiatry and Neuroscience*, 22(4), 256–266.

Rosenheck, R., Perlick, D., Bingham, S., et al. (2003) Effectiveness and cost of olanzapine and haloperidol in the treatment of schizophrenia. A randomized controlled trial. *Journal of American Medical Association*, 290, 2693–2702.

Schwartz, D., & Lellouch J. (1967). Explanatory and pragmatic attitudes in therapeutical trials. *Journal of Chronic Diseases*, 20, 637–648.

Tollefson, G.D., & Sanger, T.M. (1997). Negative symptoms: a path analytic approach to a double-blind, placebo- and haloperidol-controlled clinical trial with Olanzapine. *American Journal of Psychiatry*, 154(4), 466–474.

Tollefson, G.D., Beasley, C.M., Tran, P.V., et al. (1997). Olanzapine versus haloperidol in the treatment of schizophrenia and schizoaffective and schizophreniform disorders: results of an international collaborative trial. *American Journal of Psychiatry*, 154, 457–465.

Tunis, S.L., Croghan, T.W., Heilman, D.K., et al. (1999). Reliability, validity, and application of the medical outcomes study 36-item short-form health survey (SF-36) in schizophrenic patients treated with olanzapine versus haloperidol. *Medical Care*, 37(7), 678–691.

Zhang, P.L., Santos, J.M., Newcomer, J., Pelfrey, B.A., Johnson, M.C., & Erausquin, G.A. (2004). Impact of atypical antipsychotics on quality of life, self-report of symptom severity, and demand of services in chronically psychotic patients. *Schizophrenia Research*, 71, 137–144.

Progress in Neurotherapeutics and Neuropsychopharmacology, 2:1, 251–264 © 2007 Cambridge University Press
DOI: 10.1017/S1748232106000188   Printed in the United Kingdom

Combined Behavioral and Pharmacological Treatment of Opioid-Dependent Adolescents: A Randomized, Controlled Trial

---

Lisa A. Marsch

*National Development and Research Institutes, Department of Psychiatry, St. Luke's-Roosevelt Hospital Center,
New York, NY, USA; Email:marsch@ndri.org*

Key words: opioid dependence, adolescents, buprenorphine, clonidine, clinical trial.

Introduction and Overview

Adolescents are increasingly abusing and becoming dependent on heroin and other opioids. According to the national, school-based Monitoring the Future study (MTF, 2005), the percentage of 8th, 10th and 12th graders in the US who report use of heroin has increased from 0.4% to 0.6% approximately 10–15 years ago to 1–1.6% in recent years. Thirty percent of 12th graders in the US report that heroin is "fairly or very easy to get" (MTF, 2005). This marked increase in the prevalence of use of heroin among adolescents has been attributed, in part, to the increased availability of high-potency, low-cost heroin, which allows for intranasal use (DEA, 2003).

These trends are not specific to heroin use, but rather youth are reporting high rates of recreational use of other opioids as well. A total of 1.8%, 3.2% and 5.5% of 8th, 10th and 12th graders, respectively, report having used OxyContin, and 2.6%, 5.9% and 9.5% of these same age groups report having used Vicodin for recreational purposes in the past year (MTF, 2005). As many as 38% of 12th graders report that narcotics are "fairly or very easy to get" (MTF, 2005). The marked increase in prevalence of non-medical use of prescription opioids among adolescents has been referred to as an emerging epidemic (Sung *et al.*, 2005). Moreover, recreational opioid use has recently been shown to be a new route to heroin abuse and dependence (Siegal *et al.*, 2003).

Illicit opioid use among adolescents has also been shown to be problematic in other countries in addition to the US. For example, according to European School

---

Correspondence should be addressed to: Lisa A. Marsch, PhD, National Development and Research Institutes, 71 W. 23rd Street, 8th Floor, New York, NY 10010, USA; Email: marsch@ndri.org

Survey Project on Alcohol and Drug Use (ESPAD, 2004), conducted with 15- and 16-year-old students in 30 European countries, the percentage of European students who report heroin use is comparable to the current average among US students. Rates of lifetime reported heroin use differed by country and by gender. For female students, the highest rates of lifetime heroin use were in Romania (9%), Latvia (6%), and Croatia (5%), while the highest rates for male students were in Romania (8%), Poland (7%), Latvia (6%), Italy (5%) and Lithuana (5%).

Only a few papers have been published in the last three decades reporting on characteristics of this rapidly growing population of opioid-dependent adolescents (Sung *et al.*, 2005; Clemmey *et al.*, 2004; Gordon, 2002; Hopfer *et al.*, 2000; Crome *et al.*, 1998). Additionally, despite the critical need to identify efficacious treatments for adolescent heroin and opioid abusers, little research has been conducted to evaluate treatment interventions for this population. Although a few small-scale treatment studies were conducted in the 1960s and 1970s with opioid-dependent adolescents (Hopfer *et al.*, 2002), these studies typically did not include control groups or random assignment to treatments, and most studies did not specifically focus on youth under age 18 years.

Purpose of Trial

This report summarizes results from the first randomized, controlled trial to evaluate the relative efficacy of medication-assisted withdrawal with two pharmacotherapies, the partial opioid agonist buprenorphine and the centrally active α_2-adrenergic blocker clonidine, when combined with behavioral treatment of opioid-dependent adolescents (Marsch *et al.*, 2005).

Agents

Buprenorphine

Buprenorphine is a partial mu-agonist whose safety and efficacy as a pain medication has been clearly established in a variety of ages, ranging from infants to adults (Kamal & Khan, 1995; Gitrotra *et al.*, 1993; Maunuksela *et al.*, 1988; Harcus *et al.*, 1980). Additionally, buprenorphine's safety profile and efficacy as a medication for the detoxification of opioid-dependent adults has been clearly demonstrated in the scientific literature (e.g., Fudala *et al.*, 1990; Johnson *et al.*, 1992), and data suggest that it may be similarly useful as a detoxification agent for opioid-dependent adolescents. Buprenorphine has a unique profile of effects which are of considerable clinical utility (Bickel & Amass, 1995). Specifically, as a partial agonist, buprenorphine has been demonstrated to have a ceiling effect on its agonist activity, such that increases in dose will increase the drug's physiological and subjective effects only to a certain level, after which time further increases in dose produce no additional effects (e.g., Walsh *et al.*, 1995). Importantly, by this mechanism, buprenorphine is less likely than full agonists, such methadone, to cause major respiratory depression, the major toxic effect of opioid drugs (Cowan *et al.*, 1977). This property of buprenorphine greatly increases its safety profile and limits its abuse liability as well as the possibility of overdose (Walsh *et al.*, 1994). Another appealing feature of buprenorphine is that its opioid antagonist effects and high affinity for the opioid receptor (Gal, 1989; Lewis, 1985) can dose-dependently block the subjective and, to a lesser extent, physiological effects of exogenously administered opioids (e.g., Walsh *et al.*, 1995). Additionally, due to buprenorphine's high affinity for, and slow dissociation from, the mu-opioid receptor, discontinuation of buprenorphine administration results in markedly reduced withdrawal symptomatology relative to that which typically follows discontinuation of full agonist administration (e.g., Rance & Dickens, 1978; Jasinski *et al.*, 1978).

Clonidine

Clonidine is a centrally active α_2-adrenergic blocker, which has been shown in several studies with opiate-dependent adults to decrease sympathetic nervous hyperactivity during the opioid withdrawal period and thus suppress the acute dysphoric state associated with opiate withdrawal during detoxification procedures (e.g., Cami *et al.*, 1985; Kleber *et al.*, 1985; Gold *et al.*, 1979). Outcomes with transdermal clonidine are generally better than those with oral clonidine, as unlike orally administered clonidine, transdermal delivery assures a constant rate of medication delivery and reduces the incidence and severity of several side-effects of oral clonidine, including drowsiness and a dry mouth (Burris, 1993; Fishbain *et al.*, 1993). Although clonidine has been used with adolescents in the treatment of psychiatric disorders (Dulcan & Martini, 1999; Hunt *et al.*, 1990), no prior studies have systematically examined its efficacy in the opiate detoxification of adolescents who may have a shorter history of opioid abuse and a lower degree of opioid dependence relative to opioid-dependent adults. Although previous studies have shown that buprenorphine is generally a more efficacious detoxification agent compared to clonidine among opioid-dependent adults (O'Connor *et al.*, 1997; Cheskin *et al.*, 1994; Janiri *et al.*, 1994), the relative efficacy of these medications in the detoxification of opioid-dependent adolescents, particularly when combined with intensive behavioral treatment, has not been previously examined.

Clinical Trial

Subjects

Participants were adolescents (ages 13–18 years eligible) who met DSM-IV criteria for opioid dependence. Pregnancy, evidence of an active, significant psychiatric disorder (e.g., psychosis) or significant medical illness (e.g., cardiovascular disease) were exclusionary. To increase generalizability, codependence/abuse of other drugs were not exclusionary. A parent/legal guardian provided informed consent for all participants >18 years of age, and all participants provided assent to participate.

Trial Methods

This trial used a parallel groups, double-blind, double-dummy design. Participants were randomly assigned to either a 28-day medication-assisted withdrawal with buprenorphine or clonidine, with stratification by sex and past-month route of opiate use (injection versus intranasal). This study was conducted at an outpatient research clinic at the University of Vermont (Burlington, VT). All study procedures were approved by the university's institutional review board.

MEDICATION ADMINISTRATION

All participants were required to attend the research clinic daily for medication administration. On intake day, all participants were required to remain at the clinic for a minimum of 3 h after receiving their first medication dose. This observation period allowed for any opiate withdrawal symptoms and agonist effects to be systematically monitored.

Participants in the buprenorphine condition were administered sublingual buprenorphine tablets (Subutex; Reckitt Benckiser Pharmaceuticals; Hull, England) daily under observation. Participants were required to not have used any opioids for 24 h prior to intake and demonstrate observable, mild withdrawal before the first medication dose was administered. Flexible dosing procedures were employed based on a given participant's weight and self-reported opiate use at intake. Specifically, participants <70 kg or who reported 1–3 bags of daily heroin use or the equivalent in other opioids were administered a starting dose of 6 mg of buprenorphine. Participants ⩾70 kg or who reported >3 bags of daily heroin use or the equivalent in other opioids were administered a starting dose of 8 mg of buprenorphine. Doses were then decreased by 2 mg every 7 days. All participants received four tablets daily composed of active buprenorphine and/ or placebo, with all participants in the clonidine condition receiving placebo buprenophine tablets throughout the entire study. All tablets were consumed sublingually (held under the tongue for 5 min).

Participants in the clonidine condition were administered transdermal clonidine patches (Catapres TTS; Boehringer Ingelheim, Ingelheim Germany). On intake day and day 1, a single 0.1 mg clonidine patch was worn by participants in this condition. Additionally, participants in the clonidine condition were given a dose of 0.1 mg of oral clonidine because steady state blood levels are not reached with the patch for 24–48 h (Burris, 1993). A second patch of 0.1 mg was added on day 2 and worn from days 2–6 (for a total dose of 0.2 mg on these days).

An optional third patch could be added on day 4 through day 6 depending on the severity of withdrawal symptoms (for a total dose of 0.3 mg on these days). On day 7, all patches were removed and replaced with a 0.2 mg dose. On day 14, all patches were replaced with a 0.1 mg dose, and on day 21, all patches were replaced with a 0.0 mg placebo patch. Participants in the clonidine group were also provided with the opportunity to consume adjunctive, over-the-counter medications, such as ibuprofen and sleep aids, as needed to help manage symptoms during detoxification. Participants in the buprenorphine condition received placebo clonidine patches throughout the study, which paralleled the timeline of administration of active clonidine patches to those in the clonidine condition.

BEHAVIORAL INTERVENTIONS

All participants received behavioral therapy based on the Community Reinforcement Approach for adolescents (Azrin *et al.*, 1994; 1996) during three 1 h, individual sessions per week by masters-level therapists. Additionally, all participants were offered incentives to reinforce opiate abstinence (Budney & Higgins, 1998). In this process, participants could earn vouchers contingent on the provision of opioid-negative urine samples. The cash equivalent of the vouchers earned were used by staff to buy material reinforcers requested by participants (e.g., ski passes, CDs, gym passes, clothing). As part of their therapy, participants were encouraged to develop new recreational activities and social networks that did not involve drug use. The activities in which patients engaged using the vouchers they earned were used to support these lifestyle changes. Vouchers were also used to reinforce clinic attendance and completion of weekly assessments, as in consistent clinic attendance and in willingness to complete assessments are challenges that are commonly encountered in adolescent substance abuse treatment (Donahue & Azrin, 2001).

NALTREXONE

At the end of this study, participants were offered the opportunity to take the opioid antagonist, naltrexone, to help prevent them from relapsing to opiate use post-detoxification. To be eligible to initiate naltrexone at the end of the 28-day detoxification, all three urine samples that participants provided during the last week of detoxification had to be opiate-negative. If they were not, participants had up to a month to provide three consecutive samples negative for opiates to initiate naltrexone.

Primary Measures

TREATMENT RETENTION

Treatment retention was examined both as the percent of participants who completed the entire detoxification treatment and as time retained in treatment.

OPIATE ABSTINENCE

Opiate abstinence was examined as the percent of scheduled urine samples documented to be opiate-negative during detoxification. Urine specimens were collected at intake, and every Monday, Wednesday and Friday for the duration of the study under the observation of a research staff member. Samples were immediately screened using semi-quantitative urinalysis procedures (MIRA, Syva) for methadone, opiates, propoxyphene, cocaine, benzodiazepines (once weekly) and marijuana (once weekly). If a participant failed to provide a scheduled urine sample, the sample was counted as opiate-positive.

DRUG-RELATED HIV-RISK BEHAVIOR

Drug-related HIV-risk behavior was measured via the drug scale composite score from the HIV-risk behavior scale (HRBS; Darke et al., 1991; 1992) administered once weekly.

Secondary Measures

All secondary measures assessing medication effects were collected at baseline (pre-medication) and 1 h post-dosing daily.

PUPIL CONSTRICTION

Pupil constriction is a physiological indicator of μ-opiate effects, was determined from photographs taken with a Polaroid camera at 2X magnification at 1 ft-c of ambient illumination (pupil radius measured in millimeters).

ADJECTIVE RATING SCALE

Self-reports of drug effects were rated on a modified, computerized version of an adjective rating scale (ARS) (Bickel et al., 1988), standardized measure listing 32 items describing opioid drug effects and withdrawal effects (with scores ranging from 0 to 9, anchored at each end by "not at all" and "severe"). For example, opioid effects included nodding, rush, high, coasting, and itchy skin, and withdrawal effects included irritability, chills/gooseflesh, runny nose and yawning.

VISUAL ANALOG SCALE

On visual analog scale (VAS) the computerized measure (Preston et al., 1988) participants rated the extent to which they experienced six effects (Drug Effect, Drug Liking, Good Effect, Bad Effect, Drug-related High and Sick). The scales were anchored by "not at all" and "severe" (with corresponding scores from 0 to 100).

DIGIT SYMBOL SUBSTITUTION TEST

Digit symbol substitution test (DSST; McLeod et al., 1982) was used to measure psychomotor performance. On this task, the digits 1–9 were displayed continuously at the top of a computer screen, each associated with a 3-step symbol code. One of the 9 digits was randomly displayed on the screen. The participant was to reproduce the correct 3-step symbol code using the numeric keypad. Percent of items correctly matched by participants within 90 s was calculated.

OTHER DRUG USE

We tracked the percent of urinalysis results documented to be negative for cocaine, benzodiazepines and marijuana.

INITIATION OF NALTREXONE

We tracked the percent of participants in each medication condition that successfully initiated naltrexone post-detoxification.

Analysis

Comparisons between groups on baseline characteristics were performed using *t*-tests for continuous measures and chi-square tests for categorical variables. The primary analyses included all participants randomized to treatment groups independent of early dropout, consistent with an intent-to-treat approach to clinical trials (Armitage, 1983). *t*-tests were used to compare groups on the average percent of scheduled urine samples documented to be opiate-negative. A chi-square test was used to compare groups on the percentage of participants retained through the entire detoxification, and time to event analysis, utilizing a log-rank test, was used to compare groups on retention time. Analyses on the HRBS and all secondary outcome measures were confined to data from the time of treatment intake to the end of the first week of the detoxification when retention was still high in both conditions. This procedure allowed for a more direct comparison of outcomes to be obtained before markedly different retention rates across groups were observed. Repeated measures analyses of variance were used in analyzing pre- to post-dosing data during the first week of treatment.

Results

Participant Characteristics

Participant characteristics were equally balanced across treatment conditions. Participants were an average of 17.4 (SD = 0.69) years of age. Sixty-one percent (61%) of participants were female and 98% were Caucasian. Thirty-six percent (36%) reported injection as their route of opioid use, while the remaining 64% reported intranasal use of opioids. Fifty percent (50%) reported heroin as their primary opiate of use at intake, and the remaining 50% reported prescription opioids (primarily OxyContin) as their primary opiate of use at intake.

Retention

Seventy-two percent (72%) of those receiving buprenorphine were retained for the duration of the detoxification compared to 39% of those receiving clonidine.

The time-to-event distributions associated with retention were also statistically significant across groups.

Opiate Abstinence

Participants in the buprenorphine and clonidine groups provided a mean of 64% and 32% opiate-negative urines, respectively during the entire detoxification. When considering results from those retained in treatment only, independent of the larger attrition among those in the clonidine group, 78% and 81% of urine samples were opiate-negative in the buprenorphine and clonidine groups, respectively.

HRBS

Drug-related HIV-risk behavior significantly decreased from treatment intake to the end of the first week, but there was no evidence of differential reduction across groups. Drug-related risk composite scores decreased from 4.93 (SEM = 1.22) to 1.10 (SEM = 1.26) among those in the buprenorphine condition and from 3.99 (SEM = 1.27) to 0.58 (SEM = 1.56) among those in the clonidine condition during the first week.

Pupil Radius

During the first week, pupil radius significantly decreased from pre- to post-dosing among those in the buprenorphine condition but not those in the clonidine condition. Specifically, pupil radius decreased from a mean of 5.87 (SEM = 0.24) to 5.05 (SEM = 0.23) from pre- to post-dosing in the buprenorphine condition, while mean pupil radius was 6.19 (SEM = 0.26) pre-dosing and 6.28 (SEM = 0.25) post-dosing in the clonidine condition.

ARS

The sum of withdrawal scores on the ARS significantly decreased from pre- to post-dosing among participants in both conditions during the first week. Specifically, the sum of withdrawal scores decreased from a pre-dosing mean of 50.88 (SEM = 8.84) to a post-dosing mean of 36.05 (SEM = 7.45) among those in the buprenorphine condition and from a pre-dosing mean of 60.06 (SEM = 9.55) to a post-dosing mean of 41.18 (SEM = 7.99) among those in the clonidine condition. This effect was not treatment group dependent.

The sum of agonist scores on the ARS changed in opposite directions for those in the two conditions from pre- to post-dosing during the first week. The sum of agonist scores significantly increased from a mean of 20.94 (SEM = 2.47) to 26.49 (SEM = 3.48) among those in the buprenorphine condition and significantly decreased from a mean of 23.65 (SEM = 3.90) to 19.45 (SEM = 4.02) among those in the clonidine condition during this time period.

VAS

Participants in the buprenorphine condition reported significant increases on measures of High, Drug Effect, Good and Drug Liking, while participants in the clonidine condition reported no significant changes on these measures from pre- to post-dosing during the first week. Participants in the clonidine condition reported significant increases on the measure of Bad, while participants in the buprenorphine condition reported no change on this measure from pre- to post-dosing during the first week. Participants in both groups reported decreases on the measure of Sick from pre- to post-dosing during the first week, and this effect was not shown to be medication group dependent.

DSST

Percent correct on the DSST task did not differ across groups and did not change from pre- to post-dosing during the first week for participants in either group.

Other Drug Use

Eighty-seven percent (87%) and 85% of urines were cocaine-negative, 90% and 93% were benzodiazepine-negative, and 36% and 29% were marijuana-negative among those in the buprenorphine and clonidine conditions, respectively. None of these results were significantly different across groups.

Initiation of Naltrexone

At the conclusion of the detoxification, 61% of participants who had been in the buprenorphine condition and 5% of participants who had been in the clonidine condition participated in the naltrexone phase of the study.

Unique Aspects of Trial

To our knowledge, this was the first randomized, controlled trial to systematically evaluate combined behavioral and pharmacological treatment for opioid-dependent adolescents. This study was the first in addiction medicine to systematically evaluate how to optimize treatment outcomes for this young and growing cohort of opioid-dependent adolescents. Results of this study underscored how important and effective science-based, early intervention can be in the treatment of opioid-dependent adolescents.

Influence on the Field

Results clearly demonstrated that combining buprenorphine with behavioral interventions is significantly more efficacious in the treatment of opioid-dependent adolescents relative to combining clonidine and behavioral interventions. As a partial mu-opioid agonist medication, buprenorphine functioned to minimize the intensity of withdrawal symptoms and enabled a safe and gradual medication-assisted withdrawal from opiates among adolescents. It promoted much better treatment retention and much higher rates of opioid abstinence among those retained in treatment. It also enabled youth to be well-positioned to initiate treatment with the opiate blocker, naltrexone, post-detoxification. Indeed, two-thirds of participants in the buprenorphine condition initiated treatment with naltrexone as part of the relapse prevention phase of this study at the end of their detoxification, while only 5% of those in the clonidine condition initiated naltrexone treatment. This finding is particularly noteworthy, as prior research has shown that only 10–15% of opioid-dependent adults are generally willing to take naltrexone (Rounsaville, 1995). Our results suggest that adolescent participants who received buprenorphine and behavioral treatment were motivated to maintain the gains they had experienced during detoxification by participating in naltrexone treatment to prevent relapse to opioid use.

Translation to Clinical Practice

Medications are infrequently used as part of treatment for opioid-dependent youth in community-based treatment settings. Given the nature and pharmacological properties of opiate drugs, opioid-dependent individuals will experience an intense withdrawal syndrome if they abruptly discontinue opiate use. Pharmacotherapy has been repeatedly demonstrated to be a critical component of effective treatment for opioid-dependent adults. Results from the present study demonstrated that combined buprenorphine and behavioral treatment is both safe and efficacious in the treatment of opioid-dependent adolescents.

Acknowledgment

This trial was supported by a grant from the National Institute on Drug Abuse and Research Funds from the Department of Psychiatry and the College of Medicine at the University of Vermont awarded to Dr. Marsch.

References

Armitage, P. (1983). Exclusions, losses to follow-up, and withdrawals in clinical trials. In: Shapiro, S.H., & Louis, T.A. (eds.), *Clinical Trials: Issues and Approaches*. New York: Marcel Dekker, pp. 99–113.

Azrin, N.H., Donoue, B., Besalel, V., Kogan, E., & Acierno, R. (1994). Youth drug abuse treatment: a controlled outcome study. *Journal Child Adolescent Drug Abuse*, 3, 1–16.

Azrin, N.H., Acierno, R., Kogan, E.S., Donohue, B., Besalel, V.A., & McMahon, P.T. (1996). Follow-up results of supportive versus behavioral therapy for illicit drug use. *Behavior Research and Therapy*, 34, 41–46.

Bickel, W.K., & Amass, L.A. (1995). Buprenorphine treatment of opioid dependence. A review. *Experimental and Clinical Psychopharmacology*, 3, 477–489.

Bickel, W.K., Stitzer, M.L., Bigelow, G.E., Liebson, I.A., Jasinski, D.R., & Johnson, R.E. (1988). Buprenorphine: dose-related blockade of opioid challenge effects in opioid dependent humans. *Journal of Pharmacology and Experimental Therapeutics*, 247, 47–53.

Budney, A.J., & Higgins, S.T. (1998). *A Community Reinforcement Plus Vouchers Approach: Treating Cocaine Addiction.* Rockville, MD: US Department of Health and Human Services, National Institute on Drug Abuse.

Burris, J.F. (1993). The USA experience with the clonidine transdermal therapeutic system. *Clinical Autonomic Research*, 3, 391–396.

Camí, J., Torees, S., San, L., Sole, A., Guerra, D., & Ugena, B. (1985). Efficacy of clonidine and of methadone in the rapid detoxification of patients dependent on heroin. *Clinical Pharmacology and Therapeutics*, 38, 336–341.

Cheskin, L.J., Fudala, P.J., & Johnson, R.E. (1994). A controlled comparison of buprenorphine and clonidine for acute detoxification from opioids. *Drug Alcohol Dependence*, 36, 115–121.

Clemmey, P., Payne, L., & Fishman, M. (2004). Clinical characteristics and treatment outcomes of adolescent heroin users. *Journal of Psychoactive Drugs*, 36, 85–94.

Cowan, A., Doxey, J.C., & Harry, E.J.R. (1977). The animal pharmacology of buprenorphine: an oripavine analgesic agent. *British Journal of Pharmacology*, 60, 547–554.

Crome, I.B., Christian, J., & Green, C. (1998). Tip of the national iceberg? Profile of adolescent patients prescribed methadone in an innovative community drug service. *Drug/Education Prevention Policy*, 5, 195–197.

Darke, S., Hall, W., Heather, N., Ward, J., & Wodak, A. (1991). The reliability and validity of a scale to measure HIV risk-taking behaviour among intravenous drug users. *AIDS*, 5, 181–185.

Darke, S., Hall, W., Wodak, A., Heather, N., & Ward, J. (1992). Development and validation of a multi-dimensional instrument for assessing outcome of treatment among opiate users: the Opiate Treatment Index. *British Journal of Addiction*, 87, 733–742.

Donahue, D., & Azrin, N. (2001). Family behavior therapy. In: Waldron, H., & Wagner, E. (eds.), *Innovations in Adolescent Substance Abuse Intervention.* Oxford, UK: Elsevier Science Ltd, 206–227.

Drug Enforcement Administration. *Illegal Drug Price and Purity Report.* US Department of Justice. Available online at: http://www.usdoj.gov/dea/pubs/intel/02058/02058.pdf

Dulcan, M.K., & Martini, D.R. (1999). *A Concise Guide to Child and Adolescent Psychiatry.* Washington DC: American Psychiatric Press.

European School Survey Project on Alcohol and Other Drugs (2004). Available online at: www.espad.org

Fishbain, D.A., Rosomoff, H.L., & Cutler, R. (1993). Opiate detoxification protocols: a clinical manual. *Annals of Clinical Psychiatry*, 5, 53–65.

Fudala, P.J., Jaffe, J.H., Dax, E.M., & Johnson, R.E. (1990). Use of buprenorphine in the treatment of opioid addiction. II. Physiological and behavioral effects of daily and alternate-day administration and abrupt withdrawal. *Clinical Pharmacology and Therapeutics*, 47, 525–534.

Gal, T.J. (1989). Naloxone reversal of buprenorphine-induced respiratory suppression. *Clinical Pharmacology and Therapeutics*, 45, 66–71.

Gitrotra, S., Kumar, S., & Rajendran, K.M. (1993). Caudal buprenorphine for postoperative analgesia in children: a comparison with intramuscular buprenorphine. *Acta Anaesthesiologica Scandinavica*, 37, 361–364.

Gold, M.S., Pottash, A.L.C., Sweeney, D.R., & Kleber, H.D. (1979). Clonidine detoxification: a fourteen-day protocol for rapid opiate withdrawal. *NIDA Research Monograph*, 27, 226–232.

Gordon, S.M. (2002). Surprising data on young heroine users. *The Brown University Child and Adolescent Behavior Letter*, 18, 1–3.

Harcus, A.W., Ward, A.E., & Smith, D.W. (1980). The monitored release of buprenorphine: release in the young. *Journal of International Medical Research*, 8, 153–155.

Hopfer, C.J., Mikulich, S.K., & Crowley, T.J. (2000). Heroin use among adolescents in treatment for substance use disorders. *Journal of the American Academy of Child and Adolescent Psychiatry*, 39, 1316–1323.

Hopfer, C.J., Khuri, E., Crowley, T.J., & Hooks, S. (2002). Adolescent heroin use: a review of the descriptive and treatment literature. *Journal of Substance Abuse Treatment*, 23, 231–237.

Hunt, R.D., Capper, L., & O' Connell, P. (1990). Clonidine in child and adolescent psychiatry. *Journal of Child Adolescent Psychopharmacology*, 1, 87–102.

Janiri, L., Mannelli, P., Persico, A.M., Serretti, A., & Tempesta, E. (1994). Opiate detoxification of methadone maintenance patients using leftemine, clonidine and buprenorphine. *Drug Alcohol Dependence*, 36, 139–145.

Jasinski, D.R., Pevnick, J.S., & Griffith, J.D. (1978). Human pharmacology and abuse potential of the analgesic buprenorphine. *Archives of General Psychiatry*, 35, 501–516.

Johnson, R.E., Jaffe, J.H., & Fudala, P.J. (1992). A controlled trial of buprenorphine treatment for opioid dependence. *Journal of American Medical Association*, 267, 2750–2755.

Kamal, R.S., & Khan, F.A. (1995). Caudal analgesia with buprenorphine for post-operative pain relief in children. *Paediatric Anasthesia*, 5, 101–106.

Kleber, H.D., Riordan, C.E., Rounsaville, B., Kosten, T., Charney, D., Gaspari, J., Hogan, I., & O'Connor, C. (1985). Clonidine in outpatient detoxification from methadone maintenance. *Archives of General Psychiatry*, 42, 391–394.

Lewis, J.W. (1985). Buprenorphine. *Drug and Alcohol Dependence*, 14, 363–372.

Marsch, L.A., Bickel, W.K., Badger, G.J., Stothart, M.E., Quesnel, K.J., Stanger, C., & Brooklyn, J. (2005). Comparison of pharmacological treatments for opioid dependent adolescents: a randomized, controlled trial. *Archives of General Psychiatry*, 62, 1157–1164.

Maunuksela, E., Korpela, R., & Olkkola, K.T. (1988). Comparison of buprenorphine with morphine in the treatment of postoperative pain in children. *Anesthesia and Analgesics*, 67, 233–239.

McLeod, D.R., Griffiths, R.R., Bigelow, G.E., & Yingling, J. (1982). An automated version of the digit symbol substitution test (DSST). *Behavior Research Methods and Instrumentation*, 14, 463–466.

Monitoring the Future (2005). Available online at: www.monitoringthefuture.org

O'Connor, P.G., Carroll, K.M., Shi, J.M., Schottenfeld, R.S., Kosten, T.R., & Rounsaville, B.J. (1997). Three methods of opioid detoxification in a primary care setting. A randomized trial. *Annals of Internal Medicine*, 127, 526–530.

Preston, K.L., Bigelow, G.E., & Liebson, I.A. (1988). Buprenorphine and naloxone alone and in combination in opioid-dependent humans. *Psychopharmacology*, 94, 484–490.

Rance, M.J., & Dickens, J.N. (1978). The influence of drug-receptor kinetics on the pharmacological and pharmaco-kinetic profiles of buprenorphine. In: Van Ree, J.M., & Perenius, L. (eds.), *Characteristics and Functions of Opioids*. Amsterdam: Elsevier/North-Holland Biomedical Press, pp. 65–66.

Rounsaville, B.J. (1995). Can psychotherapy rescue naltrexone treatment of opioid addiction? *NIDA Research Monograph*, 150, 37–52.

Siegal, H.A., Carlson, R.G., Kenne, D.R., & Swora, M.G. (2003). Probable relationship between opioid abuse and heroin use. *American Family Physician*, 67, 942–945.

Sung, H.E., Richter, L., Vaughan, R., Johnson, P.B., & Thom, B. (2005). Nonmedical use of prescription opioids among teenagers in the United States: trends and correlates. *Journal of Adolescent Health*, 37, 44–51.

Walsh, S.L., Preston, K.L., Stitzer, M.L., Cone, E.J., & Bigelow, G.E. (1994). Clinical pharmacology of buprenorphine: ceiling effects at high doses. *Clinical Pharmacology and Therapeutics*, 55, 569–580.

Walsh, S.L., Preston, K.L., Bigelow, G.E., & Stitzer, M.L. (1995). Acute administration of buprenorphine in humans: partial agonist and blockade effects. *Journal of Pharmacology and Experimental Therapeutics*, 274, 361–372.

Progress in Neurotherapeutics and Neuropsychopharmacology, 2:1, 265–270 © 2007 Cambridge University Press
DOI: 10.1017/S174823210600019X   Printed in the United Kingdom

Subject Index

Progress in Neurotherapeutics and Neuropsychopharmacology, 2:1, 271–272, © 2007 Cambridge University Press
DOI: 10.1017/S1748232106000206   Printed in the United Kingdom

Author Index